ACKNOWLEDGEMENTS

There are a number of individuals, groups and organisations that we need to thank for the help, advice and support they have given us in the completion of this book.

First, to the Arts and Humanities Research Council (AHRC) (UK) for funding the three-year research project (2015–18) that formed the basis for this book-length study of transnational Moroccan cinema. More specifically, the AHRC funded two post-doctoral research assistants, extended research trips to Morocco and Europe, trips to festivals in Morocco and Europe, as well as the two international conferences (one in Marrakesh December 2016 and one in Edinburgh in October 2019) establishing a vital forum for exchange between filmmakers and researchers from Africa, Europe and North America. The AHRC grant provided the research team with the necessary buyout from their respective home institutions (University of Exeter, UK, and Goucher College, US) in order to complete the writing up of this book. Finally, the AHRC grant promoted transnational talent development by funding a term's residency at the London Film School for two emerging female Moroccan directors. All of the above initiatives have, in different ways, shaped the direction and focus of this co-authored monograph.

We would also like to express our sincere thanks to the following individuals who have helped, supported and informed this book. To the amazing Stefanie Van de Peer, the fourth member of our research team, whose intellectual rigour, knowledge of African and Arab cinema and all-round organisational brilliance we could not have done without. To Gísli Snær Erlingsson,

Director of the London Film School, for his belief in this project as the leader of one of our partner institutions. To our partners at the Africa in Motion Festival (Scotland) for including our panels, workshops and screenings as part of the festival between 2016 and 2018.

A very special thanks to dear friends in Morocco: Hamid Aïdouni, Farida Benlyazid. and Ahmed Boughaba, who all generously shared their contacts, time and knowledge of Moroccan cinema with us. Jamal Bahmad wishes to thank Youssef Ben Moula (Rabat) and Muhmmad Ammouri (Agadir) for their support during his extended research trips in Morocco.

We also wish to thank the following individuals for giving their time to be interviewed, helping secure copies of films and offering their insights into Moroccan cinema from both a national and transnational perspective: Munir Abbar, Peri Abou-Zeid, Fayçal Algandouzi, Nabil Ayouch, Selma Bargach, Hakim Belabbes, Mohamed Amin Benmaraoui, Hassan Benjelloun, Faouzi Bensaïdi, Rémi Bonhomme, Nadir Bouhmouch, Didier Boujard, Tinne Bral, Pablo César, Malika Chaghal, Lamia Chraibi, Meriame Deghedi, Kevin Dwyer, Dalila Ennadre, Ali Essafi, Bouchta Farqzaid, Hicham Falah, Jillali Ferhati, Izza Génini, Ursula Grisham, Abdelillah el Jaouhary, Sofia el Khyari, Abdellatif Labbar, Felipe Lage, Nour-Eddine Lakhmari, Mohamed Lansari, Hicham Lasri, Fatema Loukili, Ahmed el Maanouni, Chiara Marañón, Jawad Mdidech, Younes Megri, Rokhaya Niang, Egil Ødegård, Noureddine Saïl, Viola Shafik, Don Smith, Jamal Souissi, Abdallah Taïa, Zakia Tahiri, Mohammed Abderrahman Tazi, Sonia Terrab, Mohamed Zinedaine and Hédi Zardi.

Thanks also to Moroccan scholar Rachid Naïm, for his gifted translation of specific panels at the conference in Marrakech.

From the Moroccan Cinema Centre in Rabat, we would like to extend our thanks to Sarim Fassi Fihri, Nazik el Hassani, Nadia Janati and Tarik Khalami.

Love and thanks to our families who have supported us throughout this project: Isali, Tom and Clara in Exeter, Robin in Baltimore, and Élodie Martelière-Sadouk, Abdel and Naïm Sadouk, in Rabat.

This book is dedicated to the memory of Jamal's father, Lhcen Ou Youssef Bahmad, who passed away on 27 March 2016, just as the research project behind this book was beginning to take a solid shape. Dad, nothing has been the same since you left us.

Jamal Bahmad, Will Higbee and
Flo Martin, November 2019

MOROCCAN CINEMA UNCUT

Decentred Voices, Transnational Perspectives

Will Higbee, Florence Martin and
Jamal Bahmad

EDINBURGH
University Press

Edinburgh University Press is one of the leading university presses in the UK. We publish academic books and journals in our selected subject areas across the humanities and social sciences, combining cutting-edge scholarship with high editorial and production values to produce academic works of lasting importance. For more information visit our website: edinburghuniversitypress.com

First published in hardback by Edinburgh University Press 2020

Edinburgh University Press Ltd
The Tun – Holyrood Road
12(2f) Jackson's Entry
Edinburgh EH8 8PJ

Typeset in 10/12.5 pt Sabon
by IDSUK (DataConnection) Ltd, and
printed and bound by CPI Group (UK) Ltd, Croydon, CR0 4YY

A CIP record for this book is available from the British Library

ISBN 978 1 4744 7793 2 (hardback)
ISBN 978 1 4744 7794 9 (paperback)
ISBN 978 1 4744 7795 6 (webready PDF)
ISBN 978 1 4744 7796 3 (epub)

MOROCCAN CINEMA UNCUT

CONTENTS

List of Figures and Tables   vii
Acknowledgements   ix

Introduction: Moroccan Cinema: A Story of Transnational
Adaptation   1

PART ONE   PRODUCTION FROM ABOVE: FORMAL NETWORKS

1. Established Sites of Production at Home   15

2. Transnational Crossings   41

PART TWO   PRODUCTION FROM BELOW: EMERGING SITES

3. Alternative and Emerging Networks   95

4. Diverse Voices   123

**PART THREE   DISTRIBUTION NETWORKS: FESTIVALS,
AUDIENCES AND MARKETS**

5. Distribution and Exhibition Networks in Morocco   163

6. International Festivals: An Alternative Transnational Distribution
Network for Moroccan Cinema?   191

7. Sales, Distribution and Digital Disruption: The Unrealised
    Transnational Reach of Moroccan Cinema?   215

    Conclusion: Transnational Moroccan Cinema:
    Of Bumblebees and Butterflies   239

Bibliography   247
Select Filmography   261
Index   271

FIGURES AND TABLES

FIGURES

2.1	*Mimosas* (Laxe, 2015): a Sufi-Western	54
2.2	*Stateless* (Nejjar, 2018)	61
2.3	*Adios Carmen* (Benamraoui, 2013): Bobby playing at the Rif	77
3.1	Opening ceremony of FIDEC 2017, an international film school film festival organised by staff and students at Abdelmalek Essaâdi University, Tetouan	99
3.2	*They Are the Dogs* (Lasri, 2013): a punk road movie at the heart of the Arab Spring	110
3.3	*Amussu* (2019): documentary film as collective activism	120
4.1	*Khadija's Journey* (el Idrissi, 2017)	128
4.2	*The Narrow Frame of Midnight* (Hadid, 2014): a transnational network narrative	133
4.3	*On the Edge* (Kilani, 2011): 'reel bad Maghrebi girls' rebel against patriarchy and the neo-liberal globalisation	145
5.1	FIFM, Marrakesh: Morocco's leading international film festival	167
5.2	The Teatro Español, Tetouan, the central venue for FIDEC	169
5.3	The Colisée Cinema: Marrakesh's last remaining independent cinema that is also used as a screening venue for the FIFM	180
5.4	The Teatro Español: Tetouan's art deco theatre and cinema, home to the FIDEC festival	181
5.5	The Cinémathèque de Tanger during the FNF, March 2018	183

6.1 Masterclass with German–Turkish director Fatih Akin, FIFM, December 2015   195

6.2 Moroccan producer Lamia Chraibi participates in an Arab cinema industry panel at the EFM (Berlin), February 2017   197

C.1 Farida Benlyazid and Nour-Eddine Lakhmari in Edinburgh for the Africa in Motion film festival, October 2018   244

TABLES

2.1 Moroccan co-productions supported by Sanad, in Abu Dhabi, 2010–14   72

2.2 Moroccan projects in progress supported by the Doha Film Institute, 2011–18   74

2.3 Moroccan co-productions awarded grants from the Dubai Film Connection/Enjaaz, 2011–17   78

2.4 Moroccan co-productions: nominations and awards, Dubai International Film Festival, 2006–17   79

INTRODUCTION:
MOROCCAN CINEMA: A STORY OF
TRANSNATIONAL ADAPTATION

The spectacular rise of Moroccan cinema since the late 1990s has seen it ascend to become one of the largest producers of theatrically released features on the African continent – currently surpassed only by South Africa, Egypt and Nigeria.[1] Thanks largely to state-funded initiatives, administered by the CCM (the Moroccan Cinema Centre), Morocco has increased annual cinema production from only a handful of features in the 1960s, 1970s and 1980s to twenty to twenty-five features and fifty to eighty short films since the late 2000s. Morocco is also a thriving and highly lucrative service production hub for inward investment for international feature film and television (TV) production.[2]

Yet this rise in production tells a partial story: more films than ever before are being made, but who sees them in Morocco? And why does this boost in the level of national production so rarely reach an international viewership? With the exception of a handful of critically acclaimed directors such as Faouzi Bensaïdi, Leïla Kilani, Narjiss Nejjar and Nabil Ayouch, whose work is selected for major international festivals and often attracts international co-producers and transnational funding, Moroccan films have largely failed to establish an international presence.

To date, scholars in Morocco, Europe and the US have tended to view Moroccan cinema through a national or a regional lens (within Maghrebi or Arab cinema), without examining its transnational dimension or impact (see, for example: Orlando 2011, Carter 2009 and Brahimi 2005). Although concepts such as the 'transnational' are sometimes discarded as parts of a modish, academic vernacular with little to no currency or relevance in the 'real world' of film practitioners, such notions can usefully inform our understanding of film. The way we categorise individual films, film movements and national cinemas matters enormously, especially for film cultures struggling for visibility in what Mette Hjort memorably described as the small national cinema's 'response to globalization' (Hjort 2003).

The research project that led to this book thus began with a series of questions posed of Moroccan cinema itself, a 'small' cinema in a nation of more than 35 million.[3] How diverse are cinema production models in Morocco? What are the consequences of digital disruption on Moroccan cinema? How has Morocco adapted to the post-cinematic age? What are the barriers at the level of co-production, distribution and exhibition (both commercial and in festivals) that prevent it from making its international breakthrough? Are they due to specific economic, geopolitical, cultural, linguistic, cinematic factors – or a complex combination thereof? What part do education and film training play? With the demise of film theatres in the Kingdom, what kind of audience does Moroccan cinema have at home? What other channels (formal and informal) exist for Moroccan films to reach its audience? Who, indeed, is its audience? What is the dynamic between the national and the transnational within all of this? This book is our attempt to try and resolve some of these questions.

We believe that the recent development of the Moroccan film industry can most meaningfully be understood from a transnational perspective that recognises how film as an industrial art form exists and functions simultaneously within and beyond the framework of the national (through which it is most often identified and organised). The concept of the transnational has, as elsewhere in the humanities, gained considerable influence in film studies over the past two decades (see, for example: Higson 2000, Ezra and Rowden 2006, Ďurovičová and Newman 2009 and Shaw 2016). Higson's initial focus on the triad of production, circulation and reception of transnational cinema has been extended in the 2000s to consider the transnational as a regional phenomenon, often related to funding, co-production and distribution (Nestingen and Elkington 2005 and Steele 2016). It has also been employed in analyses of diasporic, exilic and postcolonial cinema (Marks 2000, Naficy 2001, Higbee 2007 and Enwezor 2007), and of cinema's response and resistance to neo-liberal globalisation and cultural homogenisation more generally 'through, between, and beyond the state' (Galt 2016).[4]

Nevertheless, for all the innovative scholarship that this enthusiastic embrace of the transnational has produced, we must continue to be wary of an over-generalised, imprecise application of the term, especially when questions of power and influence, for instance, are effaced rather than carefully examined (Hjort 2009; Higbee and Lim 2010). While mindful of such concerns, the concept of transnational cinema still seems most apposite to fully understand the complex local, national, regional and international conditions of financing, production, distribution and reception of recent Moroccan cinema. Thinking through Moroccan cinema 'transnationally' requires the film scholar to analyse the interplay between the global and local in a film ecosystem driven by interconnected political, artistic and commercial factors relating to competing production models, the shifting nature of local and global film economies in an age of digital disruption, and the search for an audience, as well as the challenges faced by a small national cinema to define its cinema at home, while announcing its presence abroad.

What, then, are the specific benefits of thinking about Moroccan cinema 'transnationally' rather than in terms of cinema and globalisation, world cinema or, indeed, *cinéma-monde*? For one, the term 'transnational' offers an alternative to the vague term 'globalisation' frequently applied to any and every process or relationship (political, social, cultural or economic) that crosses a national boundary (Bergfelder 2005). In contrast, the transnational is more attuned to the scale, distribution and diversity of such exchanges and their impact locally as well as within and beyond the nation-state. In certain cases, the transnational may even bypass the mechanisms of the nation-state altogether (Hannerz, cited in Bergfelder 2005: 321). Moreover, 'relationships of unevenness and mobility' are implicit in the prefix 'trans-'. The openness of the transnational to 'modalities of geopolitical forms' gives the concept a dynamic force and a greater degree of flexibility than the notion of 'world cinema' (Ďurovičová and Newman 2009). The ability of a transnational approach to accommodate and reflect the complex and shifting movements of film within, across and beyond the national is one of its strongest appeals.

Furthermore, the 'transnational' helps us sharpen our critical analysis of film in this postcolonial, post-cinematic age. Considering the contribution of diasporic and non-diasporic filmmakers to recent Moroccan 'national' cinema through a transnational lens helps reframe perspectives on the ongoing, postcolonial legacies of French and (to a lesser degree) Spanish colonial rule in the Kingdom.

Nevertheless, to view Moroccan cinema in the 2010s as uniquely postcolonial is problematic due to the very socio-political and cultural blind spots the qualifier creates. While the legacy of French colonial rule continues to exert an influence on contemporary Moroccan society, its politics, culture and cinema are not shaped solely by the colonial legacy or by a postcolonial dynamic between the former colonised and coloniser to the extent it was in the 1970s or 1980s, for instance. After independence (1956), the pioneering generation of Moroccan directors (such as Ahmed Bouanani, Jillali Ferhati, Moumen Smihi, Farida Benlyazid, or Mohamed Abderrahman Tazi), often trained in France before coming home to pursue their filmmaking careers. Once back in Morocco, they tended either to shoot state-funded documentaries for the CCM or else focused on documentary and fiction films exploring the nationalist struggle of colonised

Morocco and the Amazigh struggle for independence in the Rif of the 1920s (of which Bouanani's *Memory 14* (1971) remains one of the most powerful examples). In contrast, Moroccan directors born after independence, who did not live through the struggle for liberation from colonial rule, are as likely to direct concerns of inequality and injustice in their films towards the ruling Moroccan elite (the Makhzen) or against the political violence, arbitrary imprisonment, torture and censorship experienced by many Moroccans during the infamous Years of Lead (1960s–1990s) under the reign of Hassan II. Similarly, when looking beyond Morocco today, rather than denouncing the former colonial ruler, post-independence directors are more likely to expose the wider impact of neo-liberal globalisation on contemporary Moroccan society– even if (neo-) colonialism and neo-liberal globalisation often share the same interests and influence.

Undoubtedly, instances of postcolonial influence in Moroccan (and West African) cinema still endure, through the presence of francophone African film festivals and a high proportion of co-productions with France, for example. Nevertheless, Moroccan cinema has, in reality, been 'de-orbiting' from the excessive influence of the former French coloniser for some time now – and not simply thematically or from a linguistic standpoint. It has now reconfigured transnationally, weaving a network of people, languages (no longer 'francophone' in the strict sense of the term) and funding schemes, emanating from multiple centres (for instance, Doha, Amsterdam and Brussels as well as Paris). The polycentric development of a transnational Moroccan cinema that emerges as a consequence of Moroccan cinema's de-orbiting from an exclusive, bilateral relationship with the former coloniser was highlighted at the twentieth edition of the National Festival in 2019 by the two films that garnered the most awards: *The Healer* (Morocco/Italy/Qatar, 2018), a fiction by Mohamed Zineddaine and *We Could Be Heroes* (Denmark/Tunisia/Morocco/Qatar, 2018), a documentary by Hind Bensari. *The Healer* was co-produced by Ouarzazate Films (Morocco), Janaprod (based in Casablanca), Imago Orbis (based in Bologna, Italy), and received funds from the CCM, the Doha Film Institute (DFI) and the Emilia-Romagna Film Commission (a fund granting administration at the level of the Emilia-Romagna region, around Bologna in Northern Italy). The film's narrative, shot in neorealist style, is intensely local, set in the poor section of the phosphate-mining city of Khouribga, and follows the story of M'barka (the healer), a midwife who is also a 'miraculous' healer, her adopted son, Abdou, whom she keeps out of school, and her lover Ch'aayba, a fishmonger and talented pickpocket, plagued with eczema and rejected by everyone. Yet the narrative is also intensely metaphorical according to Zineddaine, and, as such, is imbued with a universal significance:

> M'barka is power, Ch'aayba (a diminutive of Chab) is the people, and Abdou the artist. Power has always opposed the people to artists, to those who seek to understand and know. (Barlet 2019)

Zineddaine's team was Italo-Moroccan for the most part, and the film was shot in Casablanca and in Khouribga. It reaped four awards at the FNF (Moroccan National Film Festival) for best film direction (Mohamed Zineddaine), best actress (Fatima Attif in the role of M'barka), best actor (Mehdi Elarroubi in the role of Ch'aayba) and the jury prize (for the film).

At the same edition of the FNF, the documentary *We Could Be Heroes*, also created outside the orbit of French influence, won the most sought-after prize: le Grand Prix du Jury (having previously been awarded the Hot Docs Canadian International Documentary Festival best documentary prize in May 2018 in Toronto). The film, a transnational co-production, was Bensari's second feature-length documentary: her first, *475: Break the Silence* (2014) had been entirely crowd-funded and became an Internet success, winning critical acclaim internationally. *We Could Be Heroes* was co-produced by Cinétéléfilms (Tunis), Bullitt and the TV channel DR (Netherlands) and with funding from the Doha Institute (Qatar) and the CCM and TV channel 2M (Morocco). The transnational focus of *We Could Be Heroes* is even more prominent than in *The Healer*. Hind Bensari's camera follows Azzedine Nouiri, a Paralympic champion, and his friend Youssef, as they overcome numerous obstacles to qualify for the 2016 Paralympic Games in Rio de Janeiro, Brazil. In Morocco, Azzedine is denied a salary, social care, even the right to train at a sports facility as he prepares to compete as a Paralympian athlete. Even when he returns from Rio with a gold medal, Azzedine is still shunned by many in Moroccan society and denied the basic human rights that should be afforded to him by the state as a disabled citizen. The contrast between the social conditions and marginalisation Azzedine experiences at home in Morocco and his status as a world champion highlights the transnational politics of the film's central message: local issues are shown to be global ones, and human rights are clearly the ultimate prize to be obtained beyond winning the gold medal.

As the above examples demonstrate, if the Franco-Moroccan (postcolonial) axis is still very active in the production and international distribution of Moroccan film, it is now one among many and does not necessarily carry the weight that it did previously. A new set of diverse interactions with different international partners (sometimes operating in tandem and sometimes in opposition to the Franco-Moroccan axis) has opened up new spaces from which to articulate the experience of change in a Moroccan society confronting the challenges of an increasingly globalised world. Moreover, even what we might have traditionally understood as the Franco-Moroccan postcolonial axis is not as straightforward as was once imagined, as the complex and evolving relationship of Moroccan filmmakers who are second- and now third-generation descendants of immigrant parents to both France and Morocco attests. Similarly, the experience and attachment of a group of filmmakers we shall refer to later in this book as the *cinéastes de passage*, who shuttle between France and the Maghreb (while also navigating the pathways of the international festival circuit with their films) is far removed from an understanding of Moroccan cinema constructed exclusively in terms of a Franco-Moroccan axis extending between Paris and Rabat.

To think in terms of transnational Moroccan cinema thus offers the possibility of acknowledging that the former postcolonial dyad is, in fact, one node within a wider global order surfing the waves of capital, networks, experts and technicians, festivals and collaborative ventures. As Flo Martin has already identified in relation to African cinema:

> what now best explains on-screen creation that emanates from North or West Africa for instance is the age of globalism, the diversity of cinematic relationships that are woven transnationally away from France. (Martin 2016: 473)

Once unmoored from the postcolonial francosphere, a de-centred, transnational Moroccan cinema can participate in 'a space of exchange and participation wherever processes of hybridization occur and where it is still possible for cultures to be produced and performed without necessary mediation by the center' (Lionnet and Shih 2005: 5), in what Higbee and Lim (2010) have called 'critical transnationalism'. However, this is not to say that the afterlives of colonialism do not continue to exert an influence on the relationship between the former colonised and coloniser. Yet the latter appears in the subtler, hybrid forms that result from the particular postcolonial negotiations of culture and capital between France and the Maghreb within a larger set of global influences that prevailed at the end of the twentieth century. In this context, our analysis shall, when appropriate, continue to refer to postcolonial theoreticians such as Homi Bhabha, Ella Shohat and Gayatri Spivak when they describe the interstitial locations from which postcolonial creations have arisen, and pose the question of postcolonial audiences that are still germane to what might now be termed a 'post-postcolonial' context (Spivak and Harasym 1990).

The decades that form our main object of study (the 2000s and 2010s) also coincide with the digital 'revolution' that has transformed the way films are produced, distributed and viewed by audiences. The pace and extent of disruption at the level of distribution and exhibition has even led some to bemoan the 'dethronement' or 'death' of cinema. Predictions of the demise of cinema are hardly new and, as David Bordwell has argued, now form an 'established genre of movie journalism' (Bordwell 2016). Moreover, such an absolutist position fails to acknowledge the fact that cinema is one part of a cultural-technological landscape that is constantly evolving:

> Film gave way to television as a 'cultural dominant' a long time ago, in the mid-twentieth century; and television in turn has given way in recent

years to computer- and network-based, and digitally generated, 'new media'. Film itself has not disappeared, of course; but filmmaking has been transformed, over the past two decades, from an analogue process to a heavily digitised one. (Shaviro 2010: 2)

While fully acknowledging the radical transformation that is taking place, scholars such as Shaviro (2010), Hagner et al. (2016) and Denson and Leyda (2016) therefore prefer to theorise in terms of 'post-cinema'. Such discussions tend to focus on medium specificity, realism and the ontology of the image: designating a condition 'in which both the photographic index and the dispositive of cinema are in crisis' (Hagener et al. 2016: 3). Shaviro (2010) has added to this mix the question of post-cinematic *affect*: exploring the structures of feeling that emerge in a (digital) cultural-technological landscape in which cinema's contribution is no longer the dominant medium or aesthetic form and how, in a neo-liberal capitalist system, value is extracted from this affect.

The notion of 'post-cinema' is clearly beneficial to us in the context of our study of transnational Moroccan cinema, in an age when the big screen is rarer in Morocco and small screens multiply to accommodate the lateral distribution (formal and informal) of digital content, first via DVDs and now increasingly through streaming. This, in turn, erodes former vertical hierarchies, where '[n]otions of center and periphery no longer make any sense' (Hagener 2016: 182), as well as radically transforming the time and space of film viewing for audiences: films are now downloadable, to be 'consumed' at any point in time, anywhere.

Although it is tempting to think of post-cinema solely in terms of the rise of the new online majors or FAANG (Facebook, Apple, Amazon, Netflix and Google), the post-cinematic landscape also includes 'digital networks [that] now make marginalised film easily available' (Hagener et al. 2016: 7). Setting aside the question of perspective or unconscious Western bias ('marginalised in relation to which audiences?', we might ask), this reading of the post-cinematic also invites an analysis of how Moroccan (and more broadly African) cinema engages with the possibilities of the new digital cultural-technological landscape to reach audiences both within and beyond the African continent. It encourages us to think of how the post-cinematic may be applied to transnational networks of production, distribution and exhibition that are found beyond the established hubs in Europe and North America.

The age of post-cinema can, moreover, be seen as transnational, in that films are (instantaneously) available on demand across borders and platforms as never before. This final point highlights one of the central tensions in transnational Moroccan cinema's search for its audience: in the dizzying array of films available on the web, how can Moroccan film be distinctly visible? Put differently, which (Moroccan) films are viewed and who views them? Finally, in the current phase of neo-liberal globalisation, the funding and exhibition venues of cinema – in small nation cinemas, especially – are part of transnational, intersecting networks. These range from transnational funding nodes (in Europe and the Gulf especially) to international festivals and markets (most visible in Europe, North America and the Middle East) that cater to a mobile, transnational network of directors, producers, critics and audiences.

Nevertheless – and as we hope shall become apparent in subsequent chapters of this book – to define Moroccan cinema exclusively in terms of 'post-cinema' would elide the more nuanced – indeed divisive – context in which the Moroccan film industry currently functions. Amazigh filmmakers, experimental creatives such as Hicham Lasri and political activist filmmakers such as Nadir Bouhmouch undoubtedly make full use of digital filmmaking technologies to produce work on the margins of the system that is disseminated to local and international audiences. In stark contrast, however, and as is shown by the pessimism concerning the crisis in theatrical exhibition in Morocco and reactionary responses to piracy analysed in Chapter 5, other filmmakers (heavily reliant on support from the CCM and Moroccan TV) remain resolutely wedded to modes of funding, production, distribution and exhibition that do little to adapt to the transforming digital landscape. In this respect, our analysis needs to be attuned to debates and consequences surrounding the uneven process of digital *disruption* (see Iordanova and Cunningham 2012) while also engaging with 'post-cinema' as the conceptual lens through which to view the radical transformation of production, distribution and exhibition in the digital era.

As the above discussion of the post-cinematic digital disruption and the transnational underlines, our methodology in this book must be flexible in order to allow us to fully account for the challenges faced by transnational Moroccan cinema in the age of accelerated global circulation. Hence, instead of focusing exclusively on close readings of films, identifying trends in topics, aesthetics and genre, this study privileges the close (and demanding) examination of the intricate mechanics of funding, development, production, exhibition, distribution, film training and education. In this respect, the current study builds on and updates (in a transnational context) the pioneering work undertaken by Dwyer (2004) and Carter (2009) on Moroccan national production, distribution and exhibition.

Furthermore, the multicultural, multilingual, international dimension and transnational dynamics of such a topic could only be analysed through a transnational collaboration between researchers, filmmakers, industry practitioners, film educators, festival programmers, film critics and policy makers.[5] In keeping with the spirit of the project, this book itself has been co-authored transnationally by three academics,[6] who combine expertise in Maghrebi cinema, Moroccan cinema and diasporic cinema, and who conceived and wrote this volume in a dialogic fashion, accounting for the three distinct voices that are combined in the pages that follow.

The book is structured in three parts. The first takes the long view of Moroccan cinema's established formal spaces of production as they exist within and beyond the nation space. In Chapter 1 we explore Rabat, home to the CCM and the administrative centre of Moroccan cinema; Casablanca and Ouarzazate as different types of production hubs for the Moroccan film industry; and Tangier's development as a cosmopolitan site of cinephile culture and production. We also consider the different modes of international co-production, predominantly with European partners as potential bridging points between national and transnational production. Chapter 2 looks at the more recent 'transnational crossings' that have emerged as an extension of, or in opposition to, these established sites of domestic production. Here, we evaluate the activity of filmmakers from the Moroccan diaspora, their 'rooted transnationalism', their differing attitudes towards and varying proximity to Moroccan culture and cinema. This section highlights the *cinéastes de passage*, an influential group of diasporic filmmakers who are more adept than others at negotiating a position between Morocco and the international film industry. The final section of Chapter 2 considers the growing influence of non-Western co-production networks: on the one hand, the geopolitical alliances forged through collaboration between Morocco and sub-Saharan Africa; on the other, the emerging role of the Gulf States in funding development, training and post-production.

Part Two moves away from these more formal networks to examine alternative forms of production 'from below'. In Chapter 3, the interstitial position occupied by Hicham Lasri – a prolific new Moroccan auteur who functions simultaneously inside and outside of the system – is analysed alongside the work of activist filmmaker Nadir Bouhmouch, who operates entirely outside traditional circuits of national production and distribution. The chapter also considers film education – of crucial importance for the evolution of Moroccan cinema – from the perspective of both the existing film schools and the alternative sites of training born from independent initiatives such as the Sahara Film Lab. Chapter 4 investigates the diverse voices in Moroccan cinema since the late 1990s – in particular Imazighen and women directors – and how these hitherto marginalised filmmakers (thematically, politically, linguistically and culturally) now have a platform in the imagined community of Moroccan cinema. Chapter 4 also expands the concept of Moroccan contestation transnationally as it considers the films of diasporic directors Tala Hadid and Jawad Rhalib.

Finally, Part Three shifts our focus from production to the evolving networks of distribution and exhibition along two axes: domestic and international. Chapter 5 analyses the Moroccan film festivals and their impact, the crisis of exhibition in Morocco (common to many African national cinemas), the informal/illegal distribution networks of DVDs, and the online circulation of films. Chapter 6 focuses on the key role of international festivals as an alternative distribution and exhibition network for Moroccan cinema outside of the Kingdom. Finally, Chapter 7 considers the challenges for Moroccan filmmakers in reaching international audiences through traditional commercial distribution networks, and the opportunities offered by the digital disruption of cinema distribution in the past decade.

Given the transcultural mobility, evolving modes of production and exhibition, and continuing search for transnational audiences of this cinema, the analysis of transnational Moroccan cinema has to be a work in progress. Returning to the image of a de-orbited Moroccan cinematic planet changing course over time across (transnational) space, this volume examines a particular moment in the development of a transnational Moroccan cinema in a process of constant and potentially radical evolution. By way of an example, in the three years that we have been involved in researching and writing this book, the CCM has undergone a significant change of direction under Sarim Fassi Fihri; a militant filmmaker such as Nadir Bouhmouch has moved from street protests and online 'artivism' to participating in the Venice Film Festival; while the Gulf festivals (which had morphed from emerging festivals into international production hubs in the 2000s) betrayed signs of vulnerability at the precise moment when a Marrakesh International Film Festival expanded its team transnationally to return to the international festival calendar in December 2018. As such, describing transnational Moroccan cinema's movements across networks of creation, production, and exhibition across Morocco and the globe is a dynamic endeavour not intended to reach a definitive end. Rather, we have conceived this book as contributing to an ongoing study of a transnational cinema in becoming.

Notes

1. Accurate information regarding levels of feature film production on the African continent is notoriously hard to come by. Not only are reliable data sparse but the definition of what qualifies as 'film' production is not always clear. For example, the Cinema Exhibitors Association of Nigeria (<https://ceanigeria.com/>, accessed 28 January 2020) reported in 2018 there were eighty-seven Nigerian films that gained a theatrical release for that year. In contrast, industry observers of Nigerian cinema often brandish figures of anything between one and two thousand 'Nollywood' films produced per year, a largely unsubstantiated figure that includes the vast majority of low budget-films produced within an informal economy for straight to DVD and online (non-threatrical) release. On this point, see the exchange between industry analyst Stephen Follows and Nigerian cinema expert Nadia Denton in 2015: <https://stephenfollows.com/how-many-films-are-made-around-the-world/> (accessed 28 January 2020). For the purposes of this study, unless explicitly stated, figures realting to film production in Morocco will refer to feature films intended for theatrical or festival release.

2. According to recent figures from the CCM, foreign production companies shot twenty-seven feature films, six short films, nine TV series and fifty-six documentaries in Morocco in 2017 with a total investment of almost 500 million MAD: <http://www.mapexpress.ma/actualite/culture-et-medias/pres-de-500-mdh-investis-par-les-productions-etrangeres-au-maroc-en-2017-ccm/> (accessed 28 January 2020).

3. This description refers to Hjort and Petrie's model for a cinema of 'Small Nations' (2007).

4. For more on the political dimensions of the transnational, see also Hjort (2009), Ezra and Rowden (2006) and Higbee and Lim (2010).

5. Thanks to a substantial research grant from the Arts and Humanities Research Council such a team was assembled and conducted the study over three years (2015–18). In order to paint as large a picture as possible of the challenges and successes of Moroccan cinema today, the research team engaged not only with current scholarship in and out of Morocco, but also, most crucially, with Moroccan scriptwriters, producers, actors, filmmakers and their teams, their critics, as well as the festival directors who organised screenings and members of the CCM. We therefore attended festivals in Morocco (e.g. the National Film Festival in Tangier, the African Film festival in Khouribga, the Women's Film Festival in Salé, the Short Film Festival in Tangier, the International Film School Film Festival in Tetouan) as well as abroad (the Berlinale, the International Film Festival in Tunis). Our analysis is thus informed by interviews and discussions conducted in Morocco, in Berlin, in Paris, and on the web, as well as grounded in international scholarship (we have, collectively, access to five relevant languages) in film studies, cultural studies, postcolonial, and feminist studies. The grant also allowed us to hold two international colloquia: the first one took place in Marrakesh in December 2016, on the margins of its International Film Festival, and the second one in Edinburgh in October 2018 on the margins of the Africa in Motion Film Festival. Each time, we assembled an array of Moroccan film practitioners (directors, producers), critics and academics from Morocco, Europe, Israel and North America. The grant further allowed the creation of a website devoted to Transnational Moroccan Cinema (<http://moroccancinema.exeter.ac.uk/en/>, accessed 28 January 2020). Finally, in partnership with the London Film School, it funded a semester of residency in London for two young Moroccan filmmakers, Mahassine el Hachadi and Saïda Janjague.

6. Professor Will Higbee from the University of Exeter, UK, Professor Florence (Flo) Martin from Goucher College, USA, and Dr Jamal Bahmad, Assistant Professor at Université Mohammed V in Rabat, Morocco. We also gratefully acknowledge the assistance, insight and feedback on certain sections of the book provided by the fourth member of our research team, Dr Stefanie (Stef) Van de Peer.

PART ONE

PRODUCTION FROM ABOVE:
FORMAL NETWORKS

1. ESTABLISHED SITES OF PRODUCTION AT HOME

The story of any cinema resides to a large degree in the history and development of its sites of production. Applying the perspective of critical transnationalism, which 'scrutinizes the tensions and dialogic relationship between national and transnational, rather than simply negating one in favour of the other' (Higbee and Lim 2010: 7–21), this chapter traces the emergence of a transnational Moroccan cinema through its familiar and less known sites of national production from Ouarzazate to Tangier through Rabat and Casablanca. This story is one of evolving sites of film production. Each site explored in this chapter is a *lieu de mémoire* (site of memory), to borrow a phrase of Pierre Nora's (1997), a site full of little known colonial and postcolonial histories and struggles for better films and decent living conditions for the human workers on and off screen. The critical study of this evolution reveals not only the major changes that Moroccan cinema has undergone since independence, but also the economic, cultural and political transformations within the country. The major role played by the different spaces that have produced Moroccan films over the last sixty years has not been well studied. What is more, the material and human dimensions of such spaces are yet to be fully covered by film scholars. Chapter 1 attempts to redress this imbalance somewhat by analysing the colonial beginnings of cinema in Morocco with a focus on institutional spaces created in the 1940s. The Rabat-based Moroccan Cinema Centre (CCM) was established by the French in 1944 and survived Moroccan independence in 1956. The public film body, which acts as both a funder and censor of cinema, has shaped

Morocco's filmmaking history. The second site of Moroccan film production is Ouarzazate. The chapter dwells on this cinema city's international and national histories as a shooting location for famous films from all around the world. In the second part of Chapter 1, we explore the little known history of Tangier as a city that has produced global and Moroccan films since the late nineteenth century. The chapter shows how Tangier's border identity as an international zone in colonial times and a fringe/frontier city in the postcolonial era has marked the character of Moroccan cinema. Finally, Chapter 1 turns its attention to Casablanca, which has emerged as a quintessential production site of Moroccan cinema in the twenty-first century. As Morocco's largest city, and home to 2M, the second public TV channel and a major film co-producer and exhibitor, Casablanca has developed as a key production hub, attracting filmmakers such as Nabil Ayouch, who has established Ali n' Productions as one of Morocco's most powerful media production companies.

RABAT AND THE CCM

It might sound unconventional, perhaps even misplaced today at the height of socio-economic and intellectual globalisation, to say that the story of Moroccan cinema is to a large extent also the story of the Centre Cinématographique Marocain (CCM). However, as the first section of this chapter will explain, this statement is anything but out of place. The chapter's argument concurs with Elizabeth Ezra and Terry Rowden's idea that the national acts as a 'dialogic partner' to the transnational and the regional, that one transcends and presupposes the other rather than the transnational simply replacing the national (Ezra and Rowden 2006: 6). One might still ask the following question: How could the history of a diverse and rich cinema like Morocco's be reduced to that of a bureaucratic office building in Rabat, the country's capital, which is regarded as equally dull? Put differently, how can the evolution of one of Africa's most *transnational* cinemas today be tied to a *national* institution in an ever globalising world? The answer is as complicated and interesting as the relationship between the cinema of Morocco and the CCM, one of the oldest state institutions in the country after the monarchy. Both institutions survived or were created respectively during the colonial period (1912–56) and gained momentum in the postcolonial era. The monarchy and the CCM, which have had an intertwined destiny since the mid-twentieth century, give the novice observer the impression of being archaic and rigid when, in reality, they are adept at changing with the times at their own pace.

While the monarchy predates the colonial era, the CCM was established in 1944 by a royal *dahir* (decree) issued by Sultan Mohammed bin Youssef under the aegis of the French colonial authorities. The French colonial power set up the CCM in 1944 to regulate the production, distribution and exhibition of cinema in Morocco. The institution replaced Le Groupement de l'Industrie Cinématographique (GIC), a public organisation that had been created for the same purpose in 1942 (Carter 2009: 45). This mission was clearly spelled out by Resident General Gabriel Puaux on 3 February 1944:

> It is placed under the authority of a government commissioner named by residential decree on the proposal of the director of the General Service of Information, and charged to take every measure or to insure the execution of those which have been edicted by residential decrees concerning the cinema profession in Morocco, notably those concerning the authorizations to exercise the profession, the organization of cinema businesses, the system of cinema screenings. It encompasses a central service in Rabat, and an administrative inspection in Casablanca, economic capital of Morocco, and principle center of cinema industry activity. (Carter 2009: 45–6)

Another yet undeclared reason behind the creation of the CCM was to counter the growing influence of Egyptian cinema, which was perceived to provide pan-Arab fodder to Moroccan anti-colonial sentiments and nationalism. Egyptian movies, particularly the musicals, were very popular in Morocco during that period and featured stars like Umm Kulthum, Abdel Halim Hafez, Farid al-Atrash, Anwar Wajdi, and Leila Mourad, in lead roles.

On 11 January 1944 the nationalist movement leaders signed the Manifesto for Moroccan Independence. The event sent shock waves through the colonial establishment. It swiftly reacted with measures to counter the nationalists. The CCM was a cultural weapon to be used by the French until independence in 1956. As part of this initiative, the colonial authorities helped set up film studios in Souissi, on the outskirts of Rabat, in 1944. This facilitated the local production of films, which previously had to be shipped to France or Italy for editing and all post-production processes. The forty-two-acre studios consisted of 'several film sets, a development laboratory, an auditorium, a projection room, workshops of all kinds and lodges, a boundless forest; the studios offered French filmmakers wishing to make their films in Morocco all the necessary infrastructure' (Araib 2014). The facility produced numerous fiction and propaganda documentaries to support the French presence in Morocco. Released in either Darija or French versions or both, these largely commercial films included *A Serenade for Meryem* (1946), *The Child of Destiny* (1946), *Yasmina* (1947), *Maarouf, the Cairo Cobbler* (1947) and *The Sand Wedding* (1948). The CCM and the Souissi Studios combined to boost the production of colonial movies and censor films that were seen as rekindling Moroccan national consciousness.

After the proclamation of independence in 1956, most colonial institutions were dismantled and replaced with national ones. The CCM was one of the rare public bodies kept intact. The Souissi Studios also survived and continued to produce films alongside the CCM until 1964 (Zaireg 2016). The CCM has changed little in terms of its role and organisation since its colonial inception. As the country emerged from the long colonial night, it found itself in need of strong national narratives and a common vision for the future. The CCM was tasked as a state agency with the production and circulation of Morocco's postcolonial visual identity. This meant the translation of the abstract idea of Morocco as an *imagined community*, to borrow a concept from Benedict Anderson (1983), into a visible nation that can be seen and pondered collectively on the screen. The country counted various talented Moroccan actors such as Larbi Doghmi and Hassan Skali, who were active during the late colonial era, but it lacked indigenous filmmakers to render the invisible national community visible. In this vein, as Chapter 2 explains in detail, the CCM dispatched young Moroccan students on scholarships to study filmmaking abroad. One of these screen pupils is Mohamed Abderrahman Tazi, who graduated in 1963 from the Institut des hautes études cinématographiques (IDHEC) in Paris. As he recalls his time in France,

> There were five of us and we were a very tightly knit group. My strongest tie was with Ahmed Bouanani, who is a wonderful editor and filmmaker and whose only full-length film, *as-Sarab* [*The Mirage*, 1980], is a very fine film. I was also close to another filmmaker in the group, Majid Rechiche. (Tazi in Dwyer 2004: 83)

Other CCM-funded students attended the Institut national supérieur des arts du spectacle et des techniques de diffusion (INSAS) in Brussels or the National Higher School of Film, Television and Theatre in Łódź in communist Poland, among other film schools.

Upon their return to the country, the graduates worked for the CCM under the directorship of Omar Ghannam, who was among the victims of the failed army coup that killed dozens of dignitaries invited to King Hassan II's birthday celebrations in the royal palace of Skhirat on 10 July 1971. Tazi and his peers travelled up and down the country making documentary and short fiction films for the CCM (Dwyer 2004: 87–9). It was a good opportunity for the future filmmakers to deepen their knowledge of their linguistically and culturally diverse country.[1] They also put to practice the theories and skills they had acquired at the European film schools, and toyed with the idea of making their own films later. The short films focused on topics such as Moroccan traditions, education, healthcare, and infrastructure projects such as Tarik al-Wahda (Unity Road), which was built to connect the Rif region to Fez. Most films had a didactic or touristic nature and contributed to the CCM's mission to create a cohesive Moroccan nation on screen out of the historical, geographical, cultural and social fragments of a new independent nation. The productions were screened in the cinemas in Moroccan cities as well as in remote locations where no film houses were available. The CCM used film caravans to reach out to these communities (Jaïdi 1994: 17).

Even though the young filmmakers working for the CCM were impatient to make their own feature-length films, the national film board refused to create a budget for such films in the peculiar political and economic conjuncture of the immediate post-independence period. Besides being cheaper to produce, the documentary and short fiction films were perceived as the most effective tool to achieve the institution's mission in the nation-building process. Another reason for this situation could be the turbulent political situation, which pitted Hassan II against the socialist opposition and, occasionally, the senior Amazigh officials in the army. Censorship was rampant, and writers, artists and intellectuals were persecuted and fled to exile during the infamous Years of Lead. The CCM policy would continue through the 1960s and 1970s with a few exceptions. In 1968, the country organised its first film festival. The Mediterranean Film Festival took place in Tangier. Interestingly enough and as its name denotes, the first festival organised in postcolonial Morocco was already of a transnational rather than a national nature. The film authorities were thus already thinking of Moroccan cinema as catering to their local, national audience, and beyond to a broader regional and global one. Since then, the CCM has been supporting a variety of international festivals in the Kingdom to promote national cinema and encourage its transnational networks and conversations (see Chapter 5). The CCM realised that they needed some Moroccan feature films to show at the Mediterranean Film Festival in Tangier. They therefore produced Larbi Bennani and Abdelaziz Ramdani's *When the Dates Are Ripe* (1968) and *Life is a Fight* (1968) by Ahmed Mesnaoui and Mohamed Abderrahman Tazi.

Over a dozen feature-length films were produced in the 1970s without the financial involvement of the CCM, although its editing and post-production facilities were open to the filmmakers who sometimes combined their jobs as CCM employees with extramural activities like filmmaking and production. In the absence of state aid for production, the filmmakers resorted to forming collectives to finance their own films. For example, Hamid Bennani, Ahmed Bouanani, Mohamed Abderrahman Tazi and Mohamed Sekkat created the production collective Sigma 3, which produced *Traces* (1970). The film was directed by Hamid Bennani and is widely held as the first breakthrough in Moroccan postcolonial cinema. Sigma 3 broke up after *Traces'* release due to financial problems and disagreements among its members after Benani claimed the success of the collective's first film for himself.[2] Other landmark films made outside the CCM's production circuit in the 1970s, Moroccan cinema's unlikely golden decade, include *One Thousand and One Hands* (1971/1972; winner of FESPACO Yennenga Stallion, 1973) and *Blood Wedding* (1977) by Souheil

Ben-Barka, *Chergui, the Eastern Wind* (1975) by Moumen Smihi, *A Breach in the Wall* (1977) by Jillali Ferhati, *Oh the Days!* (1978) by Ahmed el Maanouni, and *The Mirage* (1979) by Ahmed Bouanani. What these films have in common, in addition to being independent productions, is their small production budgets and reliance on what Fredric Jameson calls 'national allegory' as the dominant mode of postcolonial expression (Jameson 1986: 69). The abstract nature of national allegories allowed the filmmakers to escape censorship at the height of the Years of Lead. In addition, Ferhati, Ben-Barka and Maanouni's films represented a breakthrough for Moroccan cinema in terms of international visibility at Cannes and recognition on the global festivals circuit (*Oh the Days!* in particular travelled very successfully across the world).

In the face of growing demand for state aid for cinema and the risk of filmmakers going underground to produce their works which might potentially be subversive as a result, the Moroccan regime decided to launch a funding system administered by the CCM. In 1980, the state agency invited applications for financial support as part of its newly created Support Fund (*Fonds de soutien à la production cinématographique*). This immediately increased the rate of annual productions from an average of one to two in the 1970s to around seven feature-length films. In all, thirty-five full-length features and thirty shorts were produced as part of this scheme between 1980 and 1987.[3] In the early 1980s, the CCM also launched the most important event in the annual calendar of Moroccan cinema in order to allow film critics and the general public to watch and assess the national productions two years after the creation of the Support Fund. The first edition of National Film Festival was thus held in Rabat in 1982 with the second edition taking place in Casablanca two years later. However, by the CCM's own admission in retrospect, the Support Fund did not meet the institution's high expectations. On its website, the state agency sums up the two main problems with the scheme: first, the automatic and non-selective nature of the Support Fund did not encourage creativity and competitiveness among filmmakers; second, the budgets allocated through the fund were very limited.[4] Film director Souheil Ben-Barka was appointed by royal decree as the CCM director in 1986. He promised to reform the scheme. He immediately overhauled it by making it more selective, on the one hand, and splitting the allocated budget into pre- and post-production grants, on the other. The instalments were paid only if the specific terms of the contract between the CCM and the filmmaker and his producer were met. Finally, Ben-Barka increased the Support Fund budget by introducing tax levies on cinema tickets. These three measures ushered in better quality and more transparency in Moroccan film production. In 1987–99, fifty-eight feature films and thirty-eight shorts were produced as part of this new scheme.

In the 1990s, the CCM continued to be the main engine of change in Moroccan cinema by responding to social change in the country and the increasing influence of globalisation on film industries around the world. On 2–9 December 1995 the fourth edition of the National Film Festival took place in Tangier. The attendees were treated to the usual screening programme of national films made since the previous edition of the festival in Meknes four years earlier. Round tables and press conferences were organised as was usual in Morocco's foremost film festival. But something unusual happened in Tangier, and it deeply changed Moroccan cinema. Young filmmakers from the diaspora were invited to show their short works at the festival. The experience went well, and the CCM promised to accept their applications to its funding scheme although they lived overseas and were dual citizens. As Chapter 2 shows in detail, this policy bore fruit over the next few years with the production of widely acclaimed films like Nabil Ayouch's *Mektoub* (1997) and *Ali Zaoua* (2000), Faouzi Bensaïdi's *A Thousand Months* (2003), Narjiss Nejjar's *Cry No More* (2003), and Yasmine Kassari's *The Sleeping Child* (2004).

In September 2003, Noureddine Saïl was appointed by King Mohammed VI as the new CCM director. The monarch, who ascended to the throne after the death of his father Hassan II in 1999, was working tirelessly to create a new image of Morocco as a dynamic country eager to move beyond its recent past of human rights violations, mass poverty, high illiteracy rates, linguistic and cultural discrimination against its large Amazigh population, and regional disparities. The country was entering a new era of political, economic and social reforms, and the regime relied on national and international media to spread this image. Saïl fitted the bill of a secular intellectual and film professional willing to put his film knowhow and managerial experience at the service of the new monarch. He had been tested and proved himself as the director of 2M, Morocco's second and most liberal public TV channel, from 2000 to 2003. The public intellectual and servant set to work immediately and brought changes to the Support Fund, the lifeblood of Moroccan cinema. He introduced a new funding system based on the *avance sur recettes* (advance on receipts), the French model created by André Malraux in 1959. Saïl also created funds for scriptwriting alongside quality prizes for the films that had benefited from the advance on receipts. The annual number of feature-length films went from five in 2003 to around twenty-five throughout his mandate (2003–14).

Besides his administrative role as the CCM director, Saïl was an ardent advocate of cinema, liberal arts and freedom of speech in Morocco. This endeared him to the liberal segments of Moroccan politics and society. The conservative parties, the Islamist Justice and Development Party (PJD) in particular, marked him as a public enemy. The 2011 street uprisings in Morocco and the MENA region brought the PJD to power in November of that year. It was only a matter of time before Saïl was dethroned. It finally happened in October 2014 when the PJD Minister of Communication Mustapha Khalfi nominated Sarim Fassi Fihri for the job. The Ministry of Communication was the CCM's funding and supervising institution. A government council decision confirmed the change and Saïl has all but disappeared from the public arena ever since. He has disappeared from the institutional world of cinema in Morocco, yet he is still active as the president of the Khouribga African Cinema Festival and the Ouarzazate Film Commission, which promotes Morocco's cinema city as a desirable shooting location for international film and TV productions.

The directorship of Fassi Fihri was embroiled in controversy from the start. He decided to do something the previous CCM boss had resisted: censor or defend the censorship of films seen as going against the grain of conservative definitions of national identity, Islam and moral values. Thus Ridley Scott's biblical epic *Exodus: Gods and Kings* (2014), which had been shot mainly in Ouarzazate, was banned in December 2014 at the risk of tarnishing Morocco's international reputation as a liberal Muslim society and attractive film shooting destination.[5] An edited version of the blockbuster was cleared for national release a few weeks later due to resistance from local and international actors and media (Tartaglione 2015). The next case of censorship occurred less than two years later, when the same Minister of Communication who sacked Saïl in 2014 announced the ban of Nabil Ayouch's *Much Loved* (2015), a drama about sex workers in Morocco's most popular tourist destination, Marrakesh (Alami 2014). The CCM did not resist the act of censorship. The ban was not lifted this time around, and the film has never been released in Morocco. As we will see in Chapter 5, *Much Loved* has however been available in the bootleg DVD market and is one of the most popular Moroccan films in recent years.

While Fassi Fihri has not changed the funding system in line with his production-centred vision for Moroccan cinema like his predecessors, he has focused his attention and promotional activities at international festivals on encouraging more foreign productions in Morocco. In what one might interpret as an influence of his long career as a film producer and the current owner of a large film equipment rental for international and local film crews, he lobbied the government in 2015 to approve a 20 per cent tax rebate for foreign production companies willing to shoot films in the country (Saïl and Lamzouwaq 2017). The idea was first proposed by the CCM in 2011 in the face of competition from South Africa, Israel, Jordan and the United Arab Emirates (UAE), where foreign producers are provided with attractive financial incentives. The aim behind the rebate that Fassi Fihri managed to get approved by the government and both houses of the parliament is to attract more foreign productions to Morocco, a historically famous shooting location in international cinema. Before the introduction of the recent tax rebate, foreign productions benefited from VAT exemption on all purchases of goods and services in the country. Ouarzazate has attracted more than half of these Morocco-shot productions over the last century.

Ouarzazate: The Cinematic City

Ouarzazate, whose name means 'quiet or peaceful place' in Tamazight, is a unique desert town. More international films have been shot here than in any other place in Morocco. The Amazigh-speaking town lying between the High Atlas Mountains and the Sahara is a cinema city par excellence. The mere mention of this natural film studio 200 kilometres southeast of Marrakesh conjures the titles of global films and legendary film directors from David Lean and John Huston to Pier Paolo Pasolini. Since the early twentieth century, international directors and producers have been attracted by the desert location's magical nature, an ethereal light ideal for filming, architectural heritage, friendly and hospitable people, highly qualified technicians, proximity to Europe and low production costs. Housed at the site of an old film studio, Ouarzazate Film Museum bears testimony to almost a century of filmmaking in the southeast desert with its ancient casbahs and palm oases. Since its opening in 2007, the museum has become one of the must-see attractions of the city. Visitors can walk around artefacts, photographic equipment, dresses, statues, and other vestiges from films shot in Ouarzazate ranging from those set in locations from ancient Egypt and Palestine to modern Lebanon, Afghanistan, Iraq, Yemen and Tibet. The success story of Ouarzazate as a shooting location has been helped by the country's political stability and the CCM's streamlined permit system. Headed by the former CCM director Noureddine Saïl, who was reelected as its president in 2016 with fourteen votes against one for Sarim Fassi Fihri (*Aujourd'hui le Maroc* 2016), the Ouarzazate Film Commission secures shooting permits, arranges location shoots and takes care of Moroccan administrative chores to help international film producers focus on their film shoots.[6]

Film studios were built to attract big global production companies to the region. The world's largest film studio by area, Atlas Corporation Studios, which opened in 1983 and sits on twenty hectares out of town on the road to Marrakesh, is one of three major facilities that have attracted big film productions and an increasing number TV shows (*Game of Thrones, Vikings, Homeland, A.D. The Bible Continues, Prison Break, Tut*) from the US, UK, France, India, Japan and China, among others. Cinema is the main provider of jobs in Morocco's poorest region. One hundred thousand locals work as extras and occupy other low-paid technical jobs. Even so, the arrival of film crews is often announced with much fanfare and eagerly awaited, as the Moroccan film *Waiting for Pasolini* (Aoulad-Syad, 2007) shows. Well-known films made in Ouarzazate include *Lawrence of Arabia* (Lean, 1962), *Oedipus Rex* (Pasolini, 1966), *The Man Who Would Be King* (Huston, 1975), *The Message* (Akkad, 1976), *The Last Temptation of Christ* (Scorsese, 1988), *The Sheltering Sky* (Bertolucci, 1990), *Kundun* (Scorsese, 1997), *Legionnaire* (MacDonald, 1998), *Gladia-*

tor (Scott, 2000), *Babel* (González Iñárritu, 2006), and *American Sniper* (Eastwood, 2014). While most producers are from the US and Western Europe, Indian and Chinese film crews are increasingly coming to shoot in Ouarzazate and Morocco. In 2017, the Indian crime action film *Raees*, which stars Shah Rukh Khan, was shot in Morocco. The Chinese mega production *Desert Storm* (2017), starring Jackie Chan, was also filmed in Ouarzazate among other national locations.

Between twenty and fifty foreign feature film and TV productions are filmed in Ouarzazate every year despite infrastructure problems such as the lack of adequate air transportation and healthcare facilities. The scene of the helicopter transporting the wounded Susan Jones (Cate Blanchett) from Ouarzazate to a Casablanca clinic in *Babel* ironically mirrors this reality. On 30 May 2016, *Prison Break* star Dominic Purcell suffered a broken nose and head injury on the set of the Fox drama series. The actor was swiftly flown out of Ouarzazate to Casablanca. Whether they are extras, builders, painters, electricians on film sets, the locals are never airlifted by helicopters to receive medical treatment in more developed parts of Morocco or overseas. Ali Essafi's documentary *Ouarzazate Movie* (2001) unveils the underside of Hollywood's 'door to the desert'. It unearths the dreams, humiliations and precarious life conditions of the little people of film shoots. The 2008 financial crisis and the 2011 uprisings in North Africa made things worse for the local film professionals and extras by triggering a steep decline in the number of film crews coming to shoot in Ouarzazate. The 100,000 film extras and technicians who rely on international film and TV productions for an income were drastically affected. Most were unemployed and had no solution but to wait, hoping film crews would not fail to arrive like Pasolini in *Waiting for Pasolini*. The revenue of Atlas Corporation Studios, for example, declined by 50 per cent between 2008 and 2013 (Jensen and Court 2015). Nicknamed Bin Laden after playing the eponymous Al Qaida leader in a National Geographic documentary partly made in the region, Abdelaziz Bouydnayen sums up the mood of local people during the film economic recession in Ouarzazate: 'The city is poor. There [are] few job opportunities . . . We are all just waiting . . . There are millions of dollars that come into this city, but the city is still poor' (Jensen and Court 2015). Things began to change for the better in 2014 with the return of foreign crews in large numbers. Film productions generated US$120 million with an increase of $23 million from the previous year. Atlas Studios alone saw an increase in film shoots from twelve in 2013 to twenty-two the following year (Jensen and Court 2015).

Despite its significant contribution to the local economy, film shooting activity in the desert region has been criticised for offering little to nothing to enhance Moroccan film culture. With its two film houses closed for years now, Ouarzazate does not have a single cinema theatre despite its reputation as the film capital of Morocco. Another point of contention is that national cinema does not benefit from the well-trained technical crews and talent at the disposal of Hollywood and big international film producers. This is due to national productions being unable to hire these technicians because they prefer working with international film crews, which can afford to pay them more than the national wage average for film technicians. The latter make up 80 per cent of movie staff on every foreign production (Rutherford 2017). This is a key aspect of the friction between national and transnational film production in Morocco. The 20 per cent tax rebates for foreign film productions are likely to heighten this tension. That said, the increasing number of graduates from the local film school, Institut Spécialisé dans les Métiers du Cinéma (ISMC), and the Polydisciplinary Faculty of Ouarzazate (PFO), part of Ibn Zohr University, will perhaps lessen this tension and may even solve the problem by providing Moroccan filmmakers and producers with a growing pool of technical staff. ISMC and PFO students come equipped with academic film knowledge and practical skills learned from interning with international film projects in Ouarzazate.

Tangier: The Artisanal Hub

At the other end of the country to Ouarzazate, a decidedly distinct tradition of filmmaking has emerged in the northern port city of Tangier. The story of Tangier and film goes back to the very beginning of cinema. When they first came to Morocco in 1897, the Lumière brothers stopped in Tangier after shooting *The Moroccan Goat Herder*.[7] Then, Moulay Abdul Aziz IV (r. 1894–1908) invited Gabriel Veyre, a Lumière *opérateur cinématographique* (cameraman–projectionist) to his court. The Sultan was a fan of photography and cinema to the consternation of some of his subjects (Bottomore 2008: 129). It is said that, after he left his court in 1904, Veyre was the first cameraman to have filmed Tangier in colour (Schneider 2008: 81).

The city has since then hosted a number of filmmakers whose careers span the history of Moroccan filmmaking. Its first generation of postcolonial pioneers with clear memories of pre-independence (Moumen Smihi, Farida Benlyazid, Jillali Ferhati) contributed to the beginnings of independent Moroccan cinema in the 1970s–1990s, making Tangier one of the first sites of Moroccan production. The second, post-independence wave is composed of filmmakers born after 1956 who moved to Tangier as adults (Leïla Kilani, Munir Abbar, Oliver Laxe), much like scores of writers and artists before them.[8] Both generations participate in 'the cinema of the north' (*le cinéma du Nord*),[9] one that offers a distinct, 'glocal' view of Moroccan society's attractions and discontents, from a perspective that reflects a thorough knowledge of its traditions and modern tensions, while occupying a critical, multicultural distance.

To understand how cinema has been produced in Tangier, we need to appreciate the idiosyncratic history of the city itself, placing it against the larger history of Morocco's double colonisation by France and Spain. The two nations divided the Moroccan spoils into two zones in 1912: France got the larger and central zone and Spain more or less the Mediterranean coast and what is today the Moroccan Western Sahara.[10] To resolve a dispute between European powers on the African continent, Tangier was given an international status in 1923 so that neither the French nor the Spanish could rule it unilaterally: the demilitarised zone was to be governed by France, Great Britain and Spain jointly. This particular arrangement ensured that European powers enjoyed free circulation in the strait of Gibraltar and prevented all military deployment in neutral Tangier. In 1925, a longer list of signatories (Belgium, France, the Netherlands, Portugal, the United Kingdom, the United States, the USSR and, a bit later, Italy) confirmed the international status of the city and sent their representatives there. A local Moroccan representative, the Mendoub, presided over a legislative assembly (whose twenty-seven members included only nine Moroccans) while the executive power was in the hands of a French governor assisted by two attachés: one British, the other Spanish. Yet after France's defeat in 1940, Franco's troops, with the consent of the Third Reich, occupied the city and the governorate shifted to Spain for five years. The Perla del Norte returned to its international status after World War II until independence in 1956 when it joined the Moroccan Kingdom (although it kept its former legislative and fiscal advantages until 1960). The city had therefore been home to a truly cosmopolitan, multilingual society: in the 1960s, for example, commonly spoken languages included Darija, Tamazight, French, Spanish, Tangerian (an English variant), Haketia (the Tangerine Jewish creole of old Spanish, Darija and Hebrew) and Italian. The multicultural fabric of the city fostered a pluralistic milieu receptive to cinema and movie going from very early on: films were shown from the 1910s in the Teatro de la Zarzuela or the Alcazar, and not just to the expatriate population. At that time, Tangier had an impressive number of movie theatres for a city of 150,000 inhabitants:

> We would go to one of the three movie-theaters that existed in the New City at the time: the Rex, the Paris or the Mauritania. I remember the stars that were in, Bette Davis, Errol Flynn . . . After the war, they built new theaters: the Goya, the Roxy the Alhambra. The Roxy was the first one to show *Gone with the Wind*. Tickets were expensive (25 pesetas) for a four-hour-long screening (*Lo que el viento se llevó, lo que el bosillo le sintió y lo que al culo se dolió/Gone with the Wind*, Gone the money in my pocket, and gone the comfort of my rear). Most films came to us dubbed in Spanish, on occasion in French. (Laredo 2017: 76–7)

At Tangier's Book Fair, on 7 May 2016, Noureddine Saïl, the future head of the CCM and a native of Tangier, described his childhood as a continuous initiation in various film traditions at the Tangerine picture houses, each of them with its own specialty: at the Capitole, American Westerns dubbed in Spanish; at the Alcazar, romance and comedies – including el Pequeño Rosiñol (the Franquist messages of which went over the children's heads); at the Cinéma Vox, Egyptian cinema; at the Mauritania, he saw his first film by Luis Buñuel. However, this golden era of movie-going in Tangier was not to last. The number of theatres declined later under economic and political pressures at home and abroad. The taxation system on theatres changed in the early 1960s in the Rif, driving the cost of tickets up (Carter 2009: 103–4); Hassan II (r. 1961–99) effectively abandoned the impoverished northern province of Morocco, depriving it of much-needed subsidies; and Israel triggered massive *alyas* from 1948 well into the 1960s (Chreiteh 2018: 261) that depleted Tangier of most of its theatre owners (Schneider 2008: 82).

Outside traditional commercial theatres, films were also screened in cheaper venues for targeted audiences. Children who were too young to go to the movies could catch a Laurel and Hardy film for ten centimes in M. Larbi's garage in the working-class district of Emsallah (Berrada and Berrada 2011: 176). Moroccan critic Ahmed Boughaba remembers that, as a child, during the 1960s, free screenings were also held in poor neighbourhoods: people would bring their own chairs or straw mats, and assemble on the terrace of a house, usually, where films were projected on a white wall. At first, these films were part of the communication campaigns by the state (on hygiene, vaccinations, birth control, for instance). Then, food industrial brands started to underwrite the screenings of what became known as 'Lesieur films': Nescafé or Lesieur, for instance, would provide an Egyptian film, a European comedy, a Charlie Chaplin flick, and project their own ads at each reel change. Finally, one could also watch a classic at the Tangier cine-club, founded in 1972 by Noureddine Saïl (Berrada and Berrada 2011: 175–6). In Tangier, as in the rest of the Kingdom – and indeed in the entire Maghreb under French occupation (Corriou 2012), the cine-club fostered a culture of cinephilia through its programmes and discussions after each screening, as well as a political culture. As Ilyas el Omari, the current president of the Tangier-Tetouan-Hoceima region noted in 2017: 'At the cine-club, I learned how film was made and learned that the choices made by the director express a deep socio-political positioning.'[11]

Today, the Cinémathèque de Tanger remains a beacon of independent, foreign and Moroccan cinema viewing in the city. In 2012, it received 636,000 Moroccan dirham (MAD) (US$68,000) from the CCM to digitise its two screening rooms. Although attendance fluctuates, its diverse programming, outreach initiatives with students in underprivileged neighbourhoods, and its partnership with international institutions in Europe and across the Arab world, present a fascinating case study for how Arab film screening/exhibition can both educate and grow transnationally (see Chapter 5).

Tangier's long tradition of film viewing and international cinematic culture provided fertile ground for film production in various ways. First of all, it has been a film location of choice for directors from Europe as well as the United States from the inception of the seventh art. 'Since the 19th century the city has occupied an important place in the imagination of the West and East as an extremely complex, chaotic, dangerous and at the same time alluring and open city', writes Patricia Pisters as she traces the shifting images and values of Tangier in films made by Westerners before and after independence, and the various geopolitical scopes of the nostalgia expressed in them (Pisters 2010: 175–89). The magnetism of the city for the camera has endured from precolonial times until the present. Over the past two decades, Tangier has attracted directors from Europe, who have used the city as the backdrop for a variety of narrative themes. Some have made films about the encounters between tourists and locals such as in the feature-length *Tangerine* (Irene von Alberti, Germany, 2008) and the short film *In/Out* (Olivier Guerpillon, Sweden, 2015). Others have focused on narratives dealing with a postcolonial return to the city, such as *Testament* (Hassan Legzouli, France/Morocco, 2005) and *Far* (André Téchiné, France, 2001). Tangier's location as a port city at the gates of 'Fortress Europe' has also led to a focus on film noir narratives involving criminality and trafficking, including: *El Niño* (Daniel Monzón, Spain, 2014), *The Two Lives of Daniel Shore* (Michael Dreher, Germany, 2009), *Goodbye Morocco* (Nadir Moknèche, France, 2013) and *Changing Times* (Téchiné, France, 2004). Economic migration from both sides of the Mediterranean is visible in a handful of films, such as *Catch the Wind* (Gaël Morel, France, 2017) the story of a French woman relocating to work in a factory in Tangier's free zone. Illegal migration, human trafficking and the desperate plight of the *brûleurs*[12] are foregrounded far more prominently in a larger number of films, including: *Return to Hansala* (Chus Gutiérrez, Spain, 2008), *Hope* (Boris Lojkine, France, 2014), and *Roads* (Sebastian Schipper, Germany, 2019).

Elsewhere, a tradition of European and American action and spy films – international co-productions – shot wholly or partially in the city began with *SOS Mediterranean* (Léo Joannon, France, 1938) and *Mission in Tangier* (André Hunebelle, France, 1949) extending to *Espionage in Tangier* (Greg Tallas, Spain/Italy, 1964) and *The Living Daylights* (John Glen, UK, 1987). More recently, the James Bond series has returned with *Spectre* (Sam Mendes, UK/USA, 2015), while *The Bourne Ultimatum* (Paul Greengrass, Germany/USA, 2007), sees Matt Damon riding on a motorbike at implausible speed through the Kasbah. Finally, Jim Jarmusch's *Only Lovers Left Alive* (UK, Germany/Greece/France, 2013) presents a fantastic vampire rom-com set between Tangier and Detroit that inscribes Tangier on the straits of late capitalism and global culture.

The CCM's end-of-year statement for 2017 lists only one production company in Tangier, Kasbah-Film Tanger,[13] founded in 2006, which operates mostly as a local (co-producer) and fixer of foreign film projects. However, the listing of a single active production company in Tangier fails to reflect the rich history of artisanal cinema production by the *cinéastes du Nord* in Tangier since independence. Their films are shot in Tangier's Darija, and show the distinctive ways in which Moroccans in the north have negotiated their postcolonial identities, given their international cultural history: they operate from a Moroccan–multicultural perspective, always in flux. They were also produced in the context of a total abandon of the region by the Makhzen. In the northern region known as the Rif there is a long tradition among the Amazigh population of fierce resistance to invading powers (the Rif even seceded from the Moroccan Kingdom, after successfully winning against the Spanish coloniser and established the Rif Republic from 1921 to 1927). In 1958, the Rifian sent a list of complaints to Mohammed V in which they remonstrated against their marginalised status and asked to be fully liberated from Spanish occupation in their region (coastal cities Ceuta and Melilla are still Spanish enclaves). The response was repression on a massive scale, intended to punish the Rifian delegation for its audacity: at least 8,000 Rifians were killed, and more, including women and children, were beaten and tortured. Under Hassan II's reign, other demonstrations turned into bloodbaths, notably in 1965 and 1984, and the Makhzen cut off the Rif economically from the rest of the Kingdom for the next four decades. It is against this background that Tangerine filmmakers operated in the post-independence period.

Despite their strong attachment to the city and the region, the *cinéastes du Nord* – like many other Moroccan filmmakers of their generation – are characterised by a cosmopolitanism shaped in part by periods living, working and studying outside Morocco. One of the most influential of the *cinéastes du Nord* is Moumen Smihi. Born in 1945, Smihi studied cinema at the IDHEC (Paris) during the 1960s, 'a sojourn that deeply influenced him as a young postcolonial' (Limbrick 2012: 443). Upon returning to Tangier in the 1970s he founded Imago Film International, to produce his first two *tanjaoui* films: *The East Wind or El Chergui* (1975), the violent wind that blows from the Sahara into Tangier, and *Tales of the Night* (1982).[14] Although he later sought out producers in France to support his films, he used Imago Film International for most of his work.[15] These films, like *A Muslim Childhood* (2005) and *Tanjaoui* (2013), are deeply Tangerine in that they 'articulate questions and problems in a discourse that is distinctively Tangerian, shaking together Arab (both Muslim and non-Muslim) and non-Arab influences, languages and cultural histories' (Limbrick 2012: 453). Even if the viewership of this self-described auteur is an intellectual elite, Smihi is one of the *cinéastes du Nord*, part of the wave of economically marginalised Tangerine auteurs who emerged after independence, whose films tackle patriarchy, the condition of women and the plight of the poor while also valourising a non-Orientalised representation of local traditions.

Another 'young postcolonial', Jillali Ferhati, made his first feature film, *A Breach in the Wall* (1977), in Tangier, where he had moved with his family as a young child. The film, produced by Farida Benlyazid through the short-lived Kamar Films production company, was selected for *Semaine de la Critique* at the Cannes festival in 1978. The narrative follows Ringo, a young, mute public letter-writer, freshly released from prison, who wonders about the streets of the city. Despite such critical recognition at one of the world's leading international festivals, Ferhati struggled to secure funding for subsequent projects. In 1979 he created his own production company, Héraclès, which continues to operate on such limited budgets that, on several occasions, the director has been obliged to contract personal loans in order to complete his films. Even if he now regularly hires an executive producer, Héraclès still co-produces his films, which are shot in Tangier and articulate issues in Tangerine, two qualities he deems essential to his cinema in order to reach his audience through shared intimate connections.[16]

The last 'young postcolonial', Farida Benlyazid was born in 1948 and has filmed both in and out of Tangier. After writing a Tangerine script for Ferhati's *Reed Dolls* (1981) about the sad story of Aïcha, uprooted from the country to Tangier, married, then widowed and abused, she directed her first feature film, *A Door to the Sky* (1988), on the embrace of spiritual Islam by a Franco-Moroccan young woman. A Moroccan–Tunisian co-production (between SAT-PEC, Media SA, Interfilms and the CCM), it was shot in Fes. After *A Door to the Sky*, Benlyazid created her own company, Tingitana (from *Tingis*, the Roman adaptation of the Amazigh name *Tingi* of present-day Tangier) in 1991, through which she produced all her own work up until recently. This allowed her to co-produce, in particular, *La vida perra de Juanita Narboni* (2005), a film shot mostly in Spanish, which traces the history of Tangier's cosmopolitan, multilingual past through the soliloquy of a female protagonist who speaks Tangerine Spanish. As a producer–director–script writer, she operated on such a narrow budget throughout her entire career that she decided a few years ago to never 'manage misery' again: hence, her reliance on Dounia Productions for her most recent series of documentaries today (see Chapter 4). In common with Ferhati, Benlyazid's filmography reflects her deep connection to the northern city and its multicultural negotiations among languages, customs, ethnicities, creeds and traditions. Like most educated Tangerines, she speaks three languages fluently (Darija, French and Spanish) and films in them, even if she privileges Darija to talk to her people.

While dreaming of international critical recognition, this first generation of *cinéastes du Nord*, with modest means, clearly produced films about Morocco and

Tangier for a Moroccan viewership saturated by cinematic imports from Egypt and France in the 1970s–1980s.[17] The Moroccan political and economical context in which they operated during this period (an independent, postcolonial Morocco looked to modernise its economy, while Hassan II's oppressive regime had disregarded the north and its infrastructure) helps to explain the difficulties experienced by Tangerine filmmakers in securing funds and creating their own production companies. In contrast, when their successors such as Leïla Kilani, Munir Abbar and Oliver Laxe started filming in the late 1990s (while Mohammed VI revitalised the north), they often had one foot in Tangier and the other in Europe. As a result, as we shall see in the following section, while they may still have to battle to secure funding for their films, the production model of this next generation of Tangerine filmmakers no longer relies on a purely artisanal approach.

Though she may not be as well known by popular audiences in Morocco, Leïla Kilani is one of the most transnationally visible and critically acclaimed of this new generation of filmmakers based in Tangier. What is also striking is that the majority of this new generation of Tangerine filmmakers are not necessarily native to the city, though they have made a conscious decision to base themselves in Tangier and immerse themselves within the filmmaking networks and cinephile culture that is specific to the city. Though born in Casablanca in 1970, Kilani has divided her time between Paris and Tangier for years, and found production funds on both sides of the Mediterranean to make her films, shot in Tangier or elsewhere.[18] Her first documentary, *Tangier, the Dream of Burners* (2002) was co-produced by Vivement Lundi and French institutions such as TV channel France 3 and INA. However, for her second documentary, a French–Moroccan co-production, *Our Forbidden Places* (2008), Kilani created her own production company in Tangier, Socco Chico Films. Since then, her Tangerine-based company has co-produced *On the Edge* (2010) with Aurora Films and DKB Productions, and *Joint Possession* (still in post-production at the time of writing but due for release in 2020) with DKB Productions and Digital District, two Parisian companies, as well as support from the World Cinema Fund (WCF) (Berlin Festival) and Enjaaz (Dubai Film festival).

Moroccan–German director Munir Abbar, born in 1969 in Germany where he spent his formative years, stopped visiting his Moroccan father's family in Tangier one summer as a teenager. Yet he decided a decade and a half ago to go back to Tangier and now lives a good part of the year there. He has shot two shorts in Tangier, *Paris sur mer* (2007) and *The Target* (2012). Having co-founded a German production company Fifty-Seven in 1999, he set up his Morocco-based production company Fifty-Seven Morocco in 2004, to produce his first short film. However, weary of producing and directing at the same time, he opted to use Kasbah-Film Tanger for his second short film *The Target* (2012). For *Wild Life Instruction Manual*, his first feature film in development at the time of writing,

Abbar will use Rif Film, created in 2002, owned and operated by founding producer Kamal el Kacimi in Marrakesh. Rif Film had produced the Moroccan–German film *24h Marrakech* (2010), an omnibus with six episodes directed by six different young filmmakers from Morocco and Germany,[19] including a contribution by Abbar. As a filmmaker with experience and roots in both Germany and Morocco, Abbar has elected to film in Tangier as the place that most suits a *cinéaste de passage* (see Chapter 2): a place where his combined, fused outsider–insider perspectives are welcome. *Paris sur mer* and *The Target* both explore the theme of contemporary Tangier as a migration hot spot, from the harbour out of which hopeful migrants from sub-Saharan or northern Africa attempt to cross the strait of Gibraltar to reach Europe. *Paris sur mer* was inspired by Abbar's knowledge of migrants who buy Spanish SIM cards for their mobile phones, call their family back in Senegal from the vicinity of Melilla and pretend they have reached Europe. *The Target* plays with viewers' expectations and prejudice as it follows the preparations of a young man who organises his departure from one of the illegal apartments on a terrace of Tangier and tries to master Spanish in order to pass as a Spanish captain. In both films, Abbar clearly looks at Tangier as a liminal space between Africa and Europe.

One other director to have emerged in the past decade and who occupies this interstitial position in relation to Moroccan culture even more strongly (and ambiguously) than Abbar is Oliver Laxe. Born in Galicia, Laxe emigrated with his parents to France as a child, returning to Spain some years later. After an abortive attempt at film school in the UK, Laxe took a trip to Morocco, and ended up making his home in Tangier. Laxe's first feature, the award-winning, micro-budget film-within-a-film, *You All Are Captains* (2010) was mostly shot within the director's adopted city with Tangerine and introduced first-time actor Shakib Ben Omar, who went on to star in Laxe's second feature film *Mimosas* (2016) (discussed in detail in Chapter 2). *You All Are Captains* tells the story of a self-absorbed European filmmaker – played by Laxe himself – whose unconventional methods, employed to work on a film project with socially excluded children in Tangier, meet with resistance from the children themselves. Shot for the most part in black and white, the film fuses documentary with fiction and clearly employs the principles of authorial expressivity and realism that Bordwell sees as central concerns and characteristics of art cinema (Bordwell 2012, 153). Laxe in fact takes this question of authorship even further to critically analyse not only the power dynamics between the filmmaker and the children with whom he is supposedly collaborating, but also the complex cultural politics of a European gaze capturing the Moroccan inhabitants of Tangier – returning us to this concern of Laxe's insider–outsider status in Moroccan film culture and society more generally.

This second generation of filmmakers is clearly changing the landscape of film production in Tangier as they rely on co-productions with outfits outside the city or the country. As an example, Kilani used funding from the Hubert Bals fund[20] and the WCF for her film *On the Edge*, thus taking advantage of her position as a *cinéaste de passage* (see Chapter 2 for a full explanantion of this term) in creative ways to assemble a transnational funding package to produce her film. By resisting or redefining the artisanal production model of the previous generation, Tangerine directors still produce Moroccan auteur cinema, yet are also members of networks linking Morocco and Europe: they are nimble as they experiment with new modes of transnational production often on a small and efficient scale. The stakes are completely different in Casablanca, where production takes another (more commercial) route, and on a much larger scale than in Tangier.

Casablanca: The Industrial and Media Hub

If Tangier is an outpost for artisanal cinema production, Casablanca, Morocco's largest city, has been the focal point of Moroccan cameras since the 1960s. The economic capital of Morocco (where the headquarters of all major companies and a third of Morocco's banking system network are located, and in whose harbour half of Moroccan commerce takes place) 'Casa' is a vibrant city, attracting population from rural areas in search of work in its industrial districts. An hour away from the capital city, Rabat, Casa has been rebellious from colonial times to postcolonial times: the mass demonstrations in 1952 against French occupation were succeeded by the brutally repressed student riots of 1965 (evoked in Bensaïdi's *A Thousand Months*, 2003) under Hassan II, and the 2000 march of women that started a movement towards a reform of the Mudawwana in 2004 (see Chapter 4) under Mohammed VI. As the nation's economic powerhouse and postmodern hub, the home of 2M, one of Morocco's state TV channels, and numerous production companies, the city has remained a magnetic centre for generations of directors. As a location, the city provides a privileged site for capturing on screen the ruthless social inequities of a hugely diverse population amassed in the city and its surrounding slums (10 per cent of Morocco's current 36 million inhabitants live in Casablanca). Latif Lahlou's first postcolonial film, *Spring Sun* (1969), about the struggles of Abdel Hadi, a civil servant of rural origins in Casablanca, largely credited to be among the earliest significant postcolonial Moroccan fiction films (Bahmad 2013a: 80), was entirely produced by the CCM, eager to have a Moroccan production at the following National Festival in Rabat the following year. This initial film marked the first of an ongoing series of productions based in Casablanca that continues to this day with Nour-Eddine Lakhmari's films.

Though undeniably an economic centre of production, Casablanca has also served as a vital creative hub in Moroccan cinema. In 1988, in the footsteps of pioneering directors Hamid Bennani, Ahmed Bouanani, Mohamed

Sekkat and Mohamed Abderrahman Tazi who had created the filmmaking collective Sigma 3 in 1970, five upcoming directors – Hassan Benjelloun, Saâd Chraibi, Mostafa Derkaoui, Abdelkader Lagtaâ, Hakim Noury – founded their own film production collective in the city, Groupement Marocain de Production Cinématographique (Carter 2009: 204–5). Returning from studying film abroad (in Paris or Łódź), these emerging filmmakers were eager to film Moroccan stories, and Casablancan ones, such as Lagtaâ's *A Love In Casablanca* (1992), the story of a teenager torn between two loves in the city. The resourceful collective provided means to overcome the obstacles they encountered making films in a developing country's economy in the 1980s and 1990s: although the CCM had launched a limited film production assistance fund in 1980, followed by an improved version of that fund through a tax system on movie tickets in 1987, producing films was still a steep uphill battle that often led to aborted film projects. Although the collective was short-lived, it had nonetheless imagined an important solution to the disconnectedness of production companies in the landscape of Moroccan cinema that remains a problem to this day – a situation whereby directors typically work in isolation (often doubling up as the producers of their own films), even holding down another day job in order to make ends meet (for example, director Hassan Benjelloun is also a pharmacist).

Recently, however, a double-edged phenomenon has revolutionised film production in Casablanca. First, an influx of Moroccan directors coming 'home' from Europe to Casablanca – such as Nabil Ayouch, Faouzi Bensaïdi, Nour-Eddine Lakhmari, Narjiss Nejjar, Laïla Marrakchi, Selma Bargach, Brahim Chkiri – with their carefully tended transnational connections, have abandoned the problematic model of the isolated producer-director. Second, several production companies have settled in the city, offering their services as both co-producers and executive producers for these Moroccan directors returning from the diaspora, or moving between Europe and the Maghreb. Agora Films, for instance, was created by Bénédicte Bellocq and Souad Lamriki in 1999, and has co-produced Bensaïdi's *A Thousand Months* (2003), *What a Wonderful World* (2006), and *Death for Sale* (2011) as well as Laïla Marrachi's *Rock the Casbah* (2013). Bellocq and Lamriki had both amassed considerable previous experience in production in Morocco and abroad, as co-producers of Moroccan films, and executive producers of foreign films shot in Morocco – most famously, Romanian director Radu Mihâileanu's *The Source* (2011).

Another company, Image Factory, created in 2004, extended its production and executive production to international films in 2007, although it professes to be dedicated primarily to Moroccan cinema. It has produced two Moroccan comedies that were both hits at the box office in Morocco the year of their release: Brahim Chkiri's *Road to Kabul* (2012) and Franco-Moroccan director Ali el Mejboud's *Dallas* (2016). As the name of the company itself would suggest,

Image Factory thus departs entirely from the auteur production model of earlier generations, such as the artisanal Tangerine directors or the Casablancans from the *Groupement*. Rather, the principal aim is to raise capital to make commercially oriented genre films that cater to as wide a Moroccan viewership as possible.

Yet not all production companies are alike: La Prod, founded in 2007 by executive producer Lamia Chraibi (upon her return from Paris where she later created Moon & Deal Films to facilitate transnational productions), is a film/TV production house, connected via international networks abroad. La Prod has co-produced critically acclaimed Moroccan films on difficult subjects: Narjiss Nejjar's *The Rif Lover* (2011) and *Stateless* (2018) on the entrapment of women, Hicham Lasri's *The End* (2011), *The Sea is Behind* (2014) and *Jahiliya* (2017) on the outcasts of Moroccan society. As we shall see in Chapter 2, Chraibi is a producer committed to a model of international co-production that is rarely applied in Moroccan cinema. The producer accompanies the films to international festivals and produces films for TV, ads and clips, diversifying her portfolio. Her films target both domestic and international audiences, though, as Chraibi admits, her feature films that gain critical acclaim at international festivals, such as *Mimosas, Jahiliya* and *Stateless*, tend to be seen as too arty or intellectual at home and thus struggle to find a domestic audience in Morocco.[21]

Athough, as already noted, her model of international co-production remains unusual for Morocco (see Chapter 2), the fact that Chraibi also works for TV is a far more common practice for Moroccan producers and producer/directors located in Casablanca. Another production company, Ali n' Productions works very much in synergy with Moroccan TV. This pairing of formerly unlikely bedfellows results from the evolution of both the media and film production in the changing political landscape of Morocco.

State-owned Moroccan TV has existed in the kingdom since 1962, when the government created its own network, TVM (Moroccan Television), as part of a power structure that included the CCM, and was designed to broadcast the state discourse. If the role of the media elites (the heads of TVM, and later of SNRT and the CCM) is to relay the messages of the King, there has nevertheless been a steady push for liberalisation and democratisation over the years. Under the rule of Mohammed VI this has led to significant reforms in the Moroccan audiovisual sector, such as the creation of HACA (High Authority of Audiovisual Communication) in 2002 – even if such initiatives are often seen as 'camouflaged politics' (Campaiola 2014: 498) in their text or mode of application.[22]

In 2005, the first of these reforms untied the RTM (Radiotélévision Marocaine) from the Ministry of Communication, giving it an independent status under its new name: SNRT (Société Nationale de Radio et de Télévision). The latter comprises seven channels, including 2M. Some channels are more autonomous than others: Al Aoula, for instance, relies on ads for 10–15 per cent of its budget while 2M has depended on ads for 93 per cent of its budget since 2008 (Miller 2017).

The only private channel to exist in Morocco, Africa and MENA for many years, 2M was first created by SOREAD as a Franco-Moroccan pay TV channel in 1989. The channel was nationalised in 1996 yet kept its programmes in French mostly (e.g. broadcasting American series dubbed in French). In 2006, the HACA demanded that 70 per cent of all programming be in Darija, Tamazight or standard Arabic. In response, 2M switched from its elitist, francophone image to one of a TV channel for the people, dubbing all of its imported drama series (Mexican or Turkish) in Darija, and promoting its use of Darija as a fashionable shift in tune with the preferences of a younger Moroccan audiences. A second demand from HACA in 2006 (following an established model in many European nations, most notably France) was that TV channels dedicate 30 per cent of their budget to support national cinema. In response, 2M began allocating broadcasting rights to feature films and producing films for TV with known directors (e.g. Farida Benlyazid, Mohamed Abderrahman Tazi, Jillali Ferhati, Kamal Kamal). Between 2000 and 2010, 2M produced over 130 films for TV, before an editorial shift that saw the channel turn its attention to series rather than TV film. In 2012, however, the new PJD-appointed Minister of Communication opposed the broadcasting of dubbed foreign series – a staple feature of 2M's programming at that time – as 'a danger to Moroccan morals', provoking a protracted crisis in the audiovisual sector that halted the co-productions until Spring 2013.

Predictably enough, the turbulent story of 2M and its forced marriage with cinema since the mid-2000s has had deep repercussions on filmmaking in Morocco. 2M, along with Al Aoula, unlocked access for Moroccan filmmakers to new co-production models and formats; companies that previously produced cinema only for theatrical release, started to diversify their offerings, blur cinema and films made for TV and creatively reimagine and reconfigure different filmic narrative supports. The numbers speak for themselves: 2M co-produces or purchases the broadcasting rights of at least ten features and ten shorts each year (Lange 2013: 60). The impact on production companies is enormous (e.g. forty-five of them worked for 2M in 2010) as the latter start diversifying their offerings to respond to demand for audiovisual content.

One of the most significant production companies in the city in that regard is Ali n' Productions. Created by Nabil Ayouch in 1999, 'the year [he] settled in Morocco', the company was initially intended to provide the Moroccan partner in the co-production of Ayouch's second feature film, *Ali Zaoua, Prince of the Streets* (2000), on the street children of Casablanca. However, following the considerable success of *Ali Zaoua*, Ali n' Productions has diversified into a range of co-production activities: most notably TV fiction projects, and production vehicles to support younger, emerging Moroccan talents. Today the company counts half a dozen subsidiaries, ranging from production hubs to web talent incubators.[23] Over the course of two decades, Ayouch's shape-shifting Ali n' Productions became a major player in TV co-productions (Ali n' Productions, Image Factory and Disconnected won most bids from 2M and SNRT in 2012[24]), while actively stimulating Moroccan film production through its *Film Industry, Made in Morocco* project (2005–10) launched by Nabil Ayouch and Fayçal Laâraïchi[25] to jumpstart the careers of young Moroccan directors. As a result of this initiative, no less than forty-two genre films gave work to Brahim Chkiri, Yassine Fennane, Hicham Lasri, Hicham Ayouch and others. Furthermore, *Film Industry* led to the training of film technicians, and other professional film workers, thus growing a vital skilled film production labour force:

> Although limited in scope (each film had a budget of $160,000 USD and 12–18 days for filming), the project represented a branching out of Moroccan cinema from its auteur tradition to more commercial offerings meant to 'prime the pump for a true film industry modeled on Indian and Egyptian cinemas' . . . Only four films produced by Film Industry were released in theaters, but Ali n' Prod was able to send 5 million MAD in initial profits to SNRT from 'sponsorships, brand partnerships, video on demand services and DVD/VCD sales, while also selling the rights to their catalog to four satellite packages. (Iddins 2017a: 109–10)

Ayouch's company did not stop there, having also produced advertising for an array of companies and agencies. Most recently, it created digital capsules (*Citizens Speak Out*) for the Moroccan think tank *Les Citoyens* (Citizens) founded in 2016, whose function is to reform the education system and protect individual properties in a healthy economy.[26] Then, turning his attention to the Internet and digital film, Ayouch created a talent incubator on the digital platform Jawjab (i.e. 'I fetch' in Arabic). The resulting studio offers space for collaborative work, encourages innovative digital content, and imagines new ways of contributing to the web culture that are Moroccan, African, and not copied and pasted from imported, foreign digital content.[27] Jawjab also supports the Marrokiates project – a series of capsules by Sonia Terrab in the wake of the #MeToo movement (see Chapter 4). Yet is the launching of Jawjab right after 2M had decided to put its programmes online (henceforth accessible to the diaspora) a mere coincidence? Or does it forecast another form of joint venture: that of targeting, beyond a domestic audience, the pan-Arab viewership that has so far eluded Moroccan producers? This pan-Arab audience has been out of reach for Moroccan films for various reasons, such as the issue of language – the frequent (and costly) necessity to dub Moroccan Darija into Syrian or another mainstream Arabic dialect to make it accessible to the Arab viewership.[28]

Casablancan producers have come a long way from the *Groupement* of the 1980s to co-production with 2M and the transnational reach of well-established companies like LaProd and Agora. Although it has definitely given birth to a more varied and commercial film output, it has not reached the scope of Indian or Egyptian cinema, and it has not completely abandoned some auteur characteristics either. Hicham Lasri is a clear example of such an auteur: one who, as we shall see in Chapter 3, maintains a clear identity outside the Ayouch empire in which he participates. The result is an edgier production, films in Darija that can be seen on TV (the productions of Film Industry were broadcast on Al Aoula, after all) and abroad. In many ways, 2M and Al Aoula have provided new energy to production companies targeting a national audience, and, with the evolution of access to web TV, a potential transnational audience.

NOTES

1. Much like the rest of North Africa, Morocco is a mosaic of different languages and cultural communities even though most of the population has Amazigh (Berber) ethnic roots. Arabic and Tamazight are the country's official languages according to the constitution, which also recognises the existence of the minority languages Hassania and Hebrew.

2. In Ali Essafi's documentary *En quête de la septième porte* (*Crossing the Seventh Gate*, 2017), Ahmed Bouanani contests the long-held belief that Hamid Bennani directed *Wechma*. His story is credible because of (1) the nature of film collectives where it is difficult to talk about one director; (2) the consensus around Bouanani's cinematic genius and immense creativity as a filmmaker, poet and novelist (although, officially, he was assistant director for *Wechma*, it is plausible that he did more than his share and ended up almost directing the film himself); (3) the lower quality of Benani's subsequent films.

3. Source: CCM, 'Soutien à la production', n.d. <http://www.ccm.ma/soutien-a-la-production> (accessed 31 January 2020).

4. Ibid.

5. For more on the banning of this film, see Associated Press, '"Exodus" Morocco ban criticized by local politicians, filmmakers', *Hollywood Reporter* (31 December 2014): <https://www.hollywoodreporter.com/news/exodus-morocco-ban-criticized-by-760821> (accessed 31 January 2020).

6. See details from Ouarzazate Film Commission on 'Casting in Morocco': <http://shootinginouarzazate.com/casting-in-morocco.html> (accessed 31 January 2020).

7. They filmed two landmarks of Tangier: the Grand Socco and the Petit Socco (the big market square and the little market square), which are supposed to be in *Le Chevrier marocain*/*The Moroccan Goatherd* (1897).

8. We should also mention Mohamed Ulad-Mohand, a Tangerine who left for France where he established himself as film director and producer (of Moknèche's 2000 feature *The Harem of Madame Osmane*, for instance), and who shot his first short in Tangier: *An American in Tangier* (1993).

9. Flo Martin, interview with Jillali Ferhati, 30 November 2017.

10. For more information on the complex and contested politics of the Western Sahara, see Chapter 3.

11. The roundtable took place as part of the FNF in Tangier on 4 March 2017.

12. The *brûleurs* (burners) are the clandestine migrants from Morocco and sub-Saharan Africa who risk their lives in frail boats to reach the coast of Spain, the southern tip of Europe, and burn their papers prior to leaving, so that they cannot be deported back to their country if they are apprehended at any point in their journey or once they have arrived.

13. See <http://kasbah-films.com/#clients> (accessed 28 January 2020).

14. For his second film, Smihi remembers having obtained funds from the French film and from the Moroccan financial establishment. 'Toute la production et la préparation du film eurent lieu à Paris, où pour la première fois un film marocain et même arabe, obtenait l'Avance sur Recettes du Centre National du Cinéma français. Pour la première fois sûrement un film obtenait le soutien de banques, la SMDC et la BCM à Casablanca' (Smihi, cited in Institut Français 2016: 4).

15. Recently, Imago's website has somewhat diversified its functions (e.g. publishing Smihi's articles; serving as an information centre and discussion forum): <http://www.imagofilm.com/> (accessed 28 January 2020).

16. Interview with Flo Martin, 24 November 2017.

17. Their mode of production is no different from that used bytheir generation of colleagues in the rest of Morocco who also had to create their own production companies – e.g. Hassan Benjelloun's Bentaqerla, Zakia Tahiri's Made in Morocco Films, Daoud Aoulad-Syad's Les Films du Sud.

18. Out of the five films she has directed (which include *Zad Moultaka*, 2003, and *Our Forbidden Places*, 2008), three are completely shot in Tangier: *Tangier, the Dream of Burners* (2002), *On the Edge* (2010), *Joint Possession* (2020).

19. Narjisse Tahiri-Ammor, Danier Gräbner, Munir Abbar, Franz Müller, Mohamed Oumai, Christian Mrazek.

20. Hubert Bals was the founder of the Rotterdam International Festival and of the Hubert Bals Fund: see <https://iffr.com/en/who-we-are> (accessed 17 February 2020).

21. As she said during a round table at Moroccan Cinema Uncut Conference, October 2018, Edinburgh.

22. For instance, the *dahir* that defined the role of HACA (High Authority of Audiovisual Communication) in TV in 2005 to end state monopoly in TV broadcasting (No. 77–03) stipulates that it is 'under the tutelary protection of His Majesty the King' and has, among other functions, that of proposing 'to Our Majesty's choice, personalities to be appointed by Our Majesty in respect of public service or employment they must exercise at the head of government agencies in the audiovisual field' (Lange 2013: 27).

23. Flo Martin's interview with Nabil Ayouch, 17 February 2016; <http://moroccancinema.exeter.ac.uk/en/interview-with-nabil-ayouch-17-february-2016/> (accessed 31 January 2020).

24. See <https://www.agenceecofin.com/audio-visuel/0201-16346-maroc-les-producteurs-de-programme-tv-denoncent-les-appels-d-offres-du-ministere-de-la-communication> (accessed 31 January 2020).

25. Fayçal Laâraïchi is the founding executive of Sigma Technologies, a production company for TV ads, and CEO of SNRT (Société Nationale de Radio Télévision) until this year.
26. See <http://telquel.ma/2016/10/27/les-citoyens-nouveau-think-thank-reunit-gotha-sphere-economique_1520787> (accessed 31 January 2020).
27. See <https://www.therollingnotes.com/2016/09/10/jawjab/> (accessed 31 January 2020).
28. See Will Higbee and Stef Van de Peer's interview with Meriame Deghedi, Distribution and Sales Manager for MAD solutions, Tangier, March 2018.

2. TRANSNATIONAL CROSSINGS

In December 1995, the CCM decided to invite young diasporic filmmakers to the National Film Festival in Tangier. This event opened Moroccan cinema to the inevitable and overall positive winds of globalisation. The technical quality and global reach of Moroccan films were gradually enhanced. The visible improvement in the country's filmmaking was in large part the consequence of the rise of co-production as the dominant mode of making films in and beyond Morocco. As this chapter establishes, Moroccan cinema is a very transnational affair today. Its transnationalism is rooted in the trajectories and networks of filmmakers and producers who cross borders between Morocco, Europe, the Maghreb, the Middle East, Africa and farther afield. No account of Moroccan filmmaking today would be adequate without taking into consideration these global flows of finances, ideologies, media-, ethno- and techno- scapes of film production. The first part of this chapter accounts for the rise and role of European co-production in the story of Moroccan cinema in the new millennium. The second part then argues that this transnationalism is rooted in the realities and politics of cultural relations and financial networks of Moroccan film directors and their producers at home and abroad. Finally, we account for the significant networks of Moroccan film production beyond the Moroccan–European nexus.

THE POLITICS OF INTERNATIONAL CO-PRODUCTION

Speaking at a roundtable on Arab cinema in Rabat in 1995, Noureddine Saïl, at that time director of programming for the French TV channel Canal+ Horizons, made the following observation:

> We have to understand that 95% of African cinema and 80% of Maghrebi cinema is through a French production. Either we feel completely ashamed of this situation and give up cinema production altogether, or we try to include this phenomenon in a way that does not engender a master–slave relationship but a necessary step in the trajectory of artistic creation. (Saïl cited in Carter 2009: 280)

Saïl's comments illustrate how the question of co-production across the African continent has been viewed historically through the charged cultural politics of African filmmakers accepting funding from former European colonial powers. They also reveal a sense of fatalism: African filmmakers needed to reconcile themselves to the fact that European funding was necessary for the continued existence of African cinema. In the two decades that have passed since this intervention, much of this time under Saïl's leadership, the landscape for feature film production has developed considerably. With the assistance of state-induced funding administered by the CCM, Moroccan feature film production has increased exponentially (from three or four to around twenty-five films per year). At the same time, dependence on European funding appears to have decreased; of the twenty-three Moroccan feature films (fiction and documentary) produced in 2017, ten (just under 45 per cent) were international co-productions.[1] Analysing and interpreting existing data on Moroccan international co-production from the late 1990s to the present is complicated, since such co-production activity can be interpreted in a variety of ways, but also because the available information, even from the CCM archive, is partial and, at times contradictory. By way of an example, the CCM's annual report on the Moroccan film industry (*Le Bilan Cinématographique*) contains no complete set of figures for international co-production. As such, this current study can only provide an overview of trends in Moroccan international co-production since the late 1990s, rather than a definitive run of data.[2] Nevertheless, even an overview is important for a better understanding of (transnational) Moroccan cinema today, since the cultural politics, economic and geopolitical benefits, not to mention the logistical challenges associated with co-producing with European partners remain live and contested issues for filmmakers and policy makers in the Moroccan film industry.

In essence, a co-production is 'any type of production which involves more than one party in the production process, through partnership, joint venture or any other means of co-operation' (Neumann and Appelgren 2007: 4). Technically, such co-production activity can have no transnational dimension. In the case of Moroccan cinema, national co-production involving a private production company with support from either the CCM's production fund or via investment from Moroccan TV (or both) continues to be more prevalent than international co-production. However, in the international film business, 'co-production' is generally used to refer to international co-production and tends to be viewed as a strategic priority by many national film councils, serving both diplomatic and screen industry interests (Gregson 2012). Such international co-production can be bilateral or indeed multilateral, with the lead producer working with a number of secondary co-producers, who are required to provide different levels of financial support, expertise and creative input.[3] This results in what Hjort (2009: 13–14) refers to as 'marked' or 'unmarked transnationalism': the extent to which co-production partners are visible on screen in terms of language, talent, cultural input to the narrative and the geographical location of the film itself. In some films such visibility can be almost inconsequential for a producer; in others, how and where a film chooses to locate its narrative and represent a particular culture, people or history can raise the stakes in the cultural politics of co-production.

Formal co-production treaties are seen as beneficial for at least three reasons. First, 'official' international co-production allows producers 'to maximize the value of each national support commitment (e.g. national subsidy support system) and other financing mechanisms in each territory' (Finney 2014: 102). Second, international co-production with the right combination of one or more foreign producers can unlock 'soft money' – in the form of tax rebates, automatic and selective funding from cultural organisations or public funding bodies – from transnational funding schemes such as pan-Arab, pan-African or pan-European initiatives. The key advantage of such schemes is that there is little or no expectation that the money awarded to the production will be recouped, even if the film turns a profit. A minimum of one international co-producer is often required to access funds linked to key international festivals or markets such as the World Cinema Fund – an initiative that emerged from the Berlinale (Berlin international film festival) with support from the European Union (Creative Europe MEDIA), the German Foreign Office and the Goethe Institute. Third, international co-production is seen as desirable by many national film agencies since 'co-production partners help to facilitate better foreign distribution links' (Jones 2016a: 392), bringing these films to a wider audience at international festivals and through theatrical, TV and online distribution in overseas territories. As we shall see later in this section, these perceived benefits of international co-production are not necessarily recognised as of strategic importance by the CCM, nor are they viewed as desirable by all Moroccan filmmakers.

In Morocco, cinematic production involving international partners takes various forms. It can be seen in the function of Morocco as a production service location whereby foreign production companies (American studios, as well as European film and TV producers) shoot in Morocco in order to take advantage of desirable locations, highly trained crew, and a developed studio infrastructure in both Casablanca and Ouarzazate, as well as competitive production fees and tax rebates. At least 200 of these films have been wholly or partially shot in Morocco since the late 1990s – with an average of twenty-three a year since 2014. As we have seen in Chapter 1, such films are heavily promoted by the CCM as a key strand of its production strategy for the Moroccan film industry. They are likely to function as unofficial co-productions, in part to bypass any demands imposed by an official co-production treaty on the minimum level of creative and financial input required from each partner. While such productions undoubtedly bring considerable sums into the Moroccan economy, they are not co-productions in the sense of promoting collaborative, creative exchange. The films offer little meaningful engagement with Moroccan culture, often using the country as an exotic backdrop for Western-centred narratives and protagonists. The desert landscapes of southern Morocco even serve in many of these films as a substitute for other Arab, Middle Eastern and Asian locations (Afghanistan: *Killer Elite*, McKendry 2011; *Iraq: Special Correspondents*, Auburtin, 2009; *Syria: Damascus Cover*, Zelik Berk, 2017) that are considered by Western producers as too volatile to shoot in. When participating in such films, with the foreign production companies maintaining absolute creative and financial control, local Moroccan producers effectively function as location managers, executive line producers or 'fixers', not co-producers.

In contrast to these foreign productions, which tend to function outside of formal co-production agreements, official international co-productions are regulated through treaty-level documents overseen by the CCM. Morocco currently has sixteen co-production treaties: the first signed with France in 1977, the most recent with Portugal in 2017 and the majority created since the late 1990s. These official co-production treaties can effectively be placed into two categories: first, treaties that promote 'geopolitical' co-production with other African nations, where the emphasis is on cooperation and collaboration. The second are international co-productions with predominantly European co-producers. While a number of production initiatives have opened up over the past decade, in particular with Gulf funds such as Doha, these tend to focus on development, post-production and training. Moreover, as outlined later in this chapter, co-production between Morocco and other African and Arab nations is further limited by the fact that that producers from the 'global south' will often find themselves competing for the same regional or international funding.[4]

Though some European co-productions offer possibilities for meaningful cultural exchange, they tend to have a more commercial focus. As a result, issues of cultural influence, control over the production, as well as the perceived impact of Orientalist representations of Moroccan culture and society are generally placed under greater scrutiny in these Western co-productions. The majority of co-productions with Europe take place with countries that have official treaties in place, in order to maximise the financial benefits from state funding mechanisms and tax rebate systems. However, outside of the official treaty system, unofficial co-production and co-financing activity does take place. A prominent example of this is Moroccan–Norwegian director Nour-Eddine Lakhmari and his Norwegian producer Egil Ødegård. While collaborating closely and even receiving some financial aid from the CCM, Ødegård works outside of the official co-production system, since no bilateral treaty currently exists between Morocco and Norway.[5]

Collating information from the various sources relating to international co-production activity in Morocco,[6] we can estimate that from 1998 to 2017 approximately 130 feature-length films have been co-produced under the auspices of official or unofficial international co-productions, a figure that represents approximately 35 per cent of Moroccan feature film production during the same period. This figure excludes both foreign studio feature films shot wholly or partially in Morocco between 1998 and 2017 and the thirty to thirty-five shorts, features and documentaries produced by the CCM in 'cooperation' with sub-Saharan African nations. The level of co-production activity and cooperation in Morocco is higher than in most other African national cinemas (South Africa, which produces roughly the same number of films annually as Morocco, co-produced 30 per cent of its films between 2012 and 2014). It is still, however, lower than in Europe, where, for example, France co-produced 43 per cent of its feature films in 2016.[7]

Compared to the situation in the mid-1990s, where, according to Saïl's estimation, more than three-quarters of all Moroccan co-production activity involved France, the past twenty years have seen an increased diversification of international co-producing partners for Moroccan cinema. This activity is evidence of what was referred to in the introduction of this book as the 'de-orbiting' of transnational Moroccan cinema from an exclusive relationship with France. Nevertheless, if the 'dependence' on France that Saïl bemoaned in 1995 has declined, French producers still remain by far Morocco's most significant co-production partner. The vast majority of the 130 internationally co-produced features between 1998 and 2017 were produced with European partners: France (seventy-nine films) Belgium (twenty-one films), Spain (fifteen films), Italy (ten films) Germany (nine films) with lower rates of co-production activity between Morocco and the UK, Norway, Finland, Switzerland, Portugal and Holland. Given the historical, linguistic, economic and colonial connections between France and Spain, as well as the significant Moroccan diaspora in Belgium, plus the fact that all three countries have active bilateral co-production treaties with Morocco, evidence of higher levels of co-production activity between these nations is hardly surprising.

That the majority of co-production takes place with European partners is also a logical result of the fact that Europe is home to a mature film industry with a well-established tradition of co-production that is heavily subsidised and promoted nationally by individual screen agencies and at a pan-European level by MEDIA programme funding. European co-production activity is further facilitated by the European Convention on Cinematographic Co-production (ECCC), which allows all signatory countries to work together using one treaty rather than a patchwork of bilateral agreements that tend to favour larger territories, and was originally introduced in 1994. The ECCC was modified in 2017 to allow greater flexibility between European signatories to co-produce with partners outside Europe without having to use bilateral co-production treaties (MacNab 2017) – a situation that could potentially benefit Morocco in the future, were they to be invited to join as a non-European signatory to the convention.[8]

In terms of Western co-production partnership outside of Europe (beyond line producing for Hollywood studios) there is virtually no official co-production activity between Morocco and the Americas. Since 1998, there have only been five co-productions in total with North and South America: four co-productions with Canada and one with Argentina. These low numbers are perhaps unsurprising, given the lack of shared language, geographical proximity or levels of migration from Morocco to North and South America compared to Europe. However, this does not mean that an attempt at meaningful cross-cultural exchange between these nations through transnational co-production is impossible. One recent co-production initiative that gives rise for optimism in this regard is the Argentine–Moroccan co-production *The Call of the Desert* (César, 2018).

Although a memorandum of understanding for cinematic collaboration had existed between Argentina and Morocco since 2000, it took almost two decades for the first Moroccan–Argentinian co-production to emerge. Pablo César, an experienced Argentine director with a track record of co-producing in Africa (with projects in Tunisia, Benin, Ivory Coast and Angola) met Souad Lamriki (Moroccan producer and co-founder of Agora films) at an African co-production panel at the Mar de Plata international film festival in 2016 (the only A-list film festival in South America). Significantly, the collaboration between Lamriki and César was, according to the director, forged by a desire to initiate co-production activity between the two nations, rather than to develop a pre-selected project or existing screenplay. The Argentine director thus began searching for a suitable theme for a feature-length drama to co-produce with his Moroccan partner: one that would reflect a genuinely transnational co-production in terms of language, location and cross-cultural exchange.[9]

The resulting film, *The Call of the Desert*, is the first formal Argentine–Moroccan co-production, with the majority of funding for the film's €650,000 budget coming from Argentina's national screen agency (INCA) and the CCM in Morocco.[10] The film tells the story of Omar, a Moroccan émigré living in rural Argentina, who, claiming to have a terminal illness, convinces his wayward grandson, Rahmi, to accompany him on a final trip to his ancestral homeland. Once in Morocco, the pair embark on a journey by road from Omar's home town in southern Morocco to Rabat. In a style consistent with the conventions of the road movie, the journey is one of self-discovery, allowing both Omar and Rahmi, who speaks no Arabic and has never been to Morocco, to (re-)connect with their Moroccan roots. Upon arriving in Rabat, Omar finally reveals to his grandson the true motive for returning to Morocco: he is not dying but rather has decided to appear before the Equity and Reconciliation Commission, testifying publicly about the political violence that forced him to flee from Morocco during the reign of Hassan II.

With its dual focus on a diasporic return narrative and the individual and collective consequences of state repression during the Years of Lead, *The Call of the Desert* draws on two themes that have been relatively prominent in Moroccan cinema since the early 2000s. For his part, the film's director argues that the theme of political violence and reconciliation in *The Call of the Desert* transcends the immediate Moroccan context of the narrative, being equally applicable to the trauma of state-sponsored terror experienced by Argentinians at the hands of the military junta in the 1970s and early 1980s and the subsequent attempts at national reconciliation.[11] Screen time in the film is split between Argentina and Morocco, with a multilingual screenplay delivered in Spanish, Darija and (to a much lesser extent) French. The process of screenwriting for *The Call of the Desert*, reflects this genuine desire for transnational exchange that sparked the original, real-life encounter between producer and director at the Mar del Plata film festival. The screenplay was originally written in Spanish by Jerónimo Toubes (one of the lead actors) and then translated into French, in part so that the screenplay could be considered by the CCM for selective aid, but also to be reviewed by Agora films before retaining the scenes in Spanish and reworking relevant sections of dialogue into Darija.

In aesthetic terms, *The Call of the Desert* uses the journey narrative to incorporate spectacular shots of Moroccan desert and mountains that form the backdrop to Omar and Rami's road-trip across central Morocco. The journey to Rabat is also broken by a brief stay in the ancient coastal city of Essaouira, where Rami encourages his grandfather to participate in a traditional Gnawa music festival. Through the inclusion of such scenes and cinematic vistas it would be easy for *The Call of the Desert* to succumb to the gaze of an exoticised, touristic and ultimately Orientalist depiction of Morocco aimed predominantly at a Western audience. However, for the most part, the director's commitment to a narrative promoting respect through cross-cultural under-standing alongside a transnational collaboration of equals in terms of pro-duction saves this Argentine–Moroccan co-production from falling into such representational traps.

As stated earlier, we could view a co-production such as *The Call of the Desert* optimistically, in the sense that it offers further evidence of an exten-sion of transnational co-production for Moroccan cinema beyond Europe. Significantly, the film was also only the second project directed by a non-Moroccan national to be awarded selective aid from the CCM. Such optimism needs, of course, to be tempered with the reality of the challenges facing the circulation of Moroccan co-productions both at home and abroad. Although completed in 2018, *The Call of the Desert* has yet to make an impact on the international festival network. Nor has the film been granted a theatrical release in either Morocco or Argentina, despite the fact that the conditions of funding from INCA require a commitment to release in a minimum of three domestic theatres. Nevertheless, *The Call of the Desert* offers a different kind of south–south co-production beyond the African continent or MENA region and further evidence of the initiatives within the CCM to expand the offi-cial network of co-production agreements beyond the tradition European and francophone axes that have dominated until now.

In spite of the potential benefits of unlocking foreign funding and distri-bution, engaging with a systematic strategy of international co-production has been prioritised by only a limited number of Moroccan-based production companies, most obviously Agora Films (co-founded by French–Moroccan producer team Bénédicte Bellocq and Souad Lamriki), and La Prod, run by Moroccan producer Lamia Chraibi. Agora films have acted as co-producers for a range of international co-productions: from auteur-led films destined for the international festival network and European art-house cinemas (mostly nota-bly those of Faouzi Bensaïdi) to popular comedies such as *Homeland* (Hamidi, 2013) and *One Man and His Cow* (Hamidi, 2016) that utilise talent on both sides of the camera from the Maghrebi diaspora and have enjoyed success at both the Moroccan and European (mostly French) box office. Although Agora Film's co-production activity is overwhelmingly concentrated on European co-production – mostly France and Belgium but also including Germany, Italy and the Netherlands – they have also explored co-production partnership with South America through *The Call of the Desert*. Alongside this strand of co-production, Agora has gained a well-established reputation as an executive or line producer for international productions shooting in Morocco. These two strands of the company operate to quite different ends. As executive or line producers, Agora will have little or no creative input into the film. And yet, the fact of working extensively with international productions in the capacity of line producers allows a far greater presence and network of contacts across the international film industry, a fact that then benefits their activities (economic and creative) as Moroccan producers working on international co-productions.

The other Moroccan producer with a similar international profile to Agora is Lamia Chraibi. As founder and director of La Prod, Chraibi has established her reputation since the mid-2000s as a Moroccan producer of quality international auteur cinema working on a business model that balances funding from the CCM with expertise and resources from international co-production partners. To build such an international network requires, among other things, a consistent and visible presence beyond Morocco at major international festivals and markets such as Cannes (Marché International du film) and the Berlin (European Film Market, or EFM). While this kind of networking is standard practice for independent producers in most European national cinemas, and despite the fact that the CCM has a national stand at both the EFM and Marché du film each year, very few Moroccan producers have the resources or choose to prioritise attendance at such international markets – making Chraibi, as a Moroccan producer, the exception that proves the rule.[12]

Rather than searching for international co-producers under the auspices of a formal bilateral or multilateral co-production and opening up the possibility of applying for support from the producers' respective national subsidy support systems, most Moroccan producers and directors tend to focus on securing the majority of their budget from selective aid from the CCM and/or Moroccan TV, completing the financial package where necessary with money from private investors within Morocco. The reason for this inward-looking approach is that many Moroccan producers are sceptical of the benefits of international co-production, citing fears of losing creative and financial control to a foreign producer, as well as concerns of increases to the overall production budget. These increases are caused, on the one hand, by the more complex legal and financial structure of co-productions and, on the other, by the obligation to employ crew from the co-producing nation, who, especially in the case of European co-producing partners, are more expensive than those available in Morocco.[13] A lack of experienced producers in Morocco is also a factor: in reality, most Moroccan directors, through necessity, end up producing their own feature films and have little experience or understanding of international co-production practices (Benchenna 2016: 30–31). They are therefore wary of entering into deals with foreign partners and prefer to operate with lower budgets on feature films produced solely in Morocco.

This guarded attitude towards international co-production has arguably been reinforced by the CCM, who, for many years, have chosen not to award selective aid to international co-productions where the films are minority Moroccan co-productions (i.e. in which at least one other country has made a larger investment). The CCM wishes to target its selective aid at majority Moroccan productions. However, given that Morocco tends to act as a minority producer on around a quarter of international co-productions, many transnational projects involving Moroccan producers are excluded, and do not appear to be a priority for the CCM – in the way that tax incentives for 'inward investment features' clearly have been over the last few years. There are some signs, though, that this situation is starting to change: in 2014, Oliver Laxe (originally from Galicia, Spain but resident in Morocco for over a decade) became the first director of non-Moroccan origin to receive selective aid from the CCM for the Spanish–Moroccan–French–Qatari co-production, *Mimosas* (2015). Two years later, awards were also made to the Argentine director Pablo César for the aforementioned Argentine–Moroccan co-production *The Call of the Desert* and French director Olivier Coussemacq for the French–Moroccan co-production *Nomads* (2019).[14] Though all three films received amounts much lower than the average 4–5 million MAD usually awarded to Moroccan productions (between 1 and 1.8 million MAD respectively), this shift arguably signals an opening up to international co-production on the part of the CCM.

Though more could arguably be done to promote international co-production in Morocco, there is also the need to understand the context of production in its national dimension and not simply assume that what works in Europe – where co-productions are heavily subsidised and seen as a key driver of the film business – will work in Morocco. For example, the prevailing logic in European cinema that international partners will allow a film to 'travel better' – attracting a larger, more diverse audience and facilitating distribution in foreign territories – is not necessarily borne out by the experience of all Moroccan co-productions. This interpretation is consistent with Lamia Chraibi's observation that her less commercially oriented co-productions such as *Mimosas* and *Stateless* (Nejjar, 2018) are unable to gain theatrical distribution in Morocco, despite being selected for leading international festivals such as Berlin and Cannes.

While international co-production may increase the chances of a Moroccan film being seen at a broader range of festivals, it will not automatically result in a greater total of admissions for a film. This is because a range of other factors – in particular genre, narrative accessibility and casting – will determine a film's popular appeal at the box office (Bondebjerg and Redvall 2013: 132). In the current market, a Moroccan film's ability to attract a foreign (especially European) co-producer is, paradoxically, likely to have more to do with the film's perceived artistic status than its commercial potential for a popular audience both inside Morocco and abroad. Thus a popular comedy produced solely in Morocco such as *The Rooster* (Toukouna, 2015) with more than 90,000 spectators at the Moroccan box office and no international distribution deal, easily outperformed the combined audiences for Hicham Lasri's Moroccan–French co-production *They Are the Dogs* (2014), which attracted 3,584 spectators in Morocco and barely more than 7,000 spectators on its limited art-house release in France. In contrast, however, the very fact of Lasri's presence in French theatres and international festivals such as Berlin, confirms his status as a transnational auteur, increasing his ability to attract attention and funding from future international (specifically European) co-production partners.

Most recent academic research and industry analysis of international co-production[15] concludes that international co-productions tend to be financially rather than creatively driven. Nevertheless, as Huw David Jones notes, even if most are financially driven, 'the logistics of co-production may still have consequences for the film's cultural identity' (Jones 2016a: 373). Such requirements for the film to fulfil certain criteria set out in the co-production treaty may include: use of a specific language, a defined level of funding or personnel from a specific co-producing nation, or inclusion of scenes shot on location in one or more of the co-producing countries. Here, then, the crucial issue becomes the extent to which the inclusion of such elements has an inherent logic in the narrative world presented on screen, or they are simply a form of cultural compromise. Their presence can be relatively benign, such as the high-octane heist movie *The Crew* (Leclercq, 2015), where the Moroccan coastline is viewed momentarily by the film's central character – the leader of a criminal gang played by Sami Bouajilah – as he flees across the Mediterranean to avoid capture by the French police. With the exception of this final scene, *The Crew* takes place exclusively in and around Paris, leading to the conclusion that the final scene off the coast of Morocco has been included more to satisfy funding requirements rather than foregrounding a connection that is integral to the film's narrative. Elsewhere, the decision to locate action in Morocco has a much clearer influence on the narrative focus, or genre, as is the case with return narratives such as the Franco-Moroccan co-production *Testament* (Legzouli, 2004). The debut feature by Moroccan émigré filmmaker Hassan Legzouli, *Testament* follows a young French taxi driver of Moroccan origin, Nourdine (Roschdy Zem) through Morocco, after a promise made to his dying immigrant father that he would return his body for burial from Nord-Pas-de-Calais to the small village in the Atlas Mountains where he was born. Legzouli uses the conventions of the road movie genre to reveal a journey of discovery and reconnection for Nourdine, whose early hostility to the people, country and culture of his father's birth is gradually replaced by a sense of reconciliation to his ancestral homeland. The narrative structure of *Testament*, its genre and focus on the act of diasporic return, moreover, reflects the dual heritage of its director. Like the co-production itself, Legzouli's creative approach is influenced by the culture, language and society of both France and Morocco.

As the example of *Testament* shows, international co-productions can offer something more than a cynical exercise in maximising the financial value of transnational collaboration – not only in terms of the possibility for all parties in acquiring new knowledge and fresh perspectives from collaborating with experienced creatives from abroad, but also in terms of a genuinely enriching approach to the creative process and transnational shared storytelling. In the Moroccan context, however, such potential benefits are also fraught with complications, compromises and potential controversies surrounding the influence of funding on the politics of representation: which producer (European or African) exerts a greater control over narrative and editorial content? How are African culture, society and history represented? What impact is there from an ideological perspective? Finally, what is the broader worldview of the film itself? The concern for African filmmakers then is of a neocolonial or Eurocentric perspective being imposed on the film (whether consciously or not) by the demands of the Western funder or producer. In some cases, African filmmakers are even asked to modify scripts and ideas in order to appease international funders (Falicov 2010: 7). These situations lead to what Barlet describes as the 'often problematic collaboration with a European producer . . . [which] favors a certain type of film where the emphasis is placed on supposed "artistic quality" as rather than access to market (potentially alienating popular African audiences with films that tend to be seen as too intellectual or too much of a social statement)' (Barlet 1997).

Echoing Barlet's concerns, some Moroccan filmmakers are sceptical of the benefits of European co-production, viewing it as predominantly an option for filmmakers from the Moroccan diaspora who have spent extended periods living and working in Europe. More specifically, they cite concerns with ceding artistic and financial control to a European producer, ultimately feeling that such co-productions often lack a Moroccan sensibility.[16] In contrast, producer Lamia Chraibi, while conscious of the potential dangers of an excessive European influence on content, sees international (and especially European) co-production as central to the development of Moroccan cinema's international reach. For Chraibi, who operates production companies in both Morocco (La Prod) and France (Moon & Deal) international co-production is beneficial since not only does it open up opportunities for access to different strands of transnational funding, but it also allows Moroccan producers to benefit from the experience of their international co-producers. Working in a creative relationship that aspires to a genuine partnership of equals thus permits the European producer to bring a new perspective to the film without the Moroccan producer surrendering to an Orientalist representation of Moroccan culture and society.[17]

The fact that France still is Morocco's most significant international co-production partner is hardly surprising given the two nations' shared colonial history, but it is precisely this (post-)colonial dynamic that can be the source of problems and tensions in terms of the cultural politics of co-production. However, French involvement in these films does not automatically mean that Moroccan producers are secondary or marginal players; nor does it follow that every Moroccan producer looks to the former *métropole* as its central or sole source of funding. Comparing data from the European Audiovisual Observatory with production figures from the CCM suggests that French–Moroccan co-productions represent approximately 25 per cent of annual production in Morocco – hardly a disproportionate or dominant force, and far lower than the figure of 80 per cent cited by Saïl in 1995. Of course, the choice of co-production partner based on nationality alone offers no automatic guarantee of a film's politics. Similarly, the fact that a film is co-produced equitably between France and Morocco does not mean that the resulting work will be free from Euro-centric, Franco-centric or, indeed, conversely 'Morocco-centric' bias. To fully comprehend the nature of collaboration and intercultural exchange at play in these international co-productions requires a detailed analysis of the individual conditions of each (co-)production history, combined with a critical reading of the resulting film itself in order to unpick its ideological positioning and cultural politics. Let's now attempt to do this with a close analysis of a recent international co-production, *Mimosas*.

Mimosas is a Spanish–Moroccan–French–Qatari co-production, shot in 2015, with a budget of €850,000: higher than the average for a Moroccan feature film, though considerably lower than the average budget for an independent European feature. The lead producer was Spanish-based Zeitun Films, led by Felipe Lage, the brother of the film's director Oliver Laxe. Lage had produced Laxe's first film *You All Are Captains* (2010), a low-budget docu-fiction set in Tangier that generated critical attention when screened at the Directors' Fortnight in Cannes 2010, allowing Laxe and Lage exposure at an international festival to pursue funding for *Mimosas*. As is common for an independent, auteur-led co-production, putting together the mosaic of funding for *Mimosas* was extremely challenging and took Lage over four years. The film received funding from a range of sources: Spain (from the national film fund, ICAA), Morocco (from the CCM) France (Rouge Films) with a percentage split of 67 (Spain)–13 (Morocco)–20 (France) between the co-producing nations. *Mimosas* also secured European Union funding for development via the MEDIA programme and from Qatar (via the Doha Film Institute) for post-production, as well as receiving support from several funding schemes at film festivals, including Torino FilmLab (assisting script and production development) and the CPH:Forum in Copenhagen (for helping to develop the film's financial package). Regional funding from Lage and Laxe's native Galicia was awarded very early in development but was first rescinded, due to delays in closing the financing to move into production (principal photography) and then reinstated after a subsequent application.

Figure 2.1   *Mimosas* (Laxe, 2015): a Sufi-Western (Zeitun Films/La Prod)

If Lage used his association with French producers as a way to access European funding schemes, and with Qatar for funding from the Doha Institute, the most important collaboration among producers on the project was arguably between Lage and the film's Moroccan producer, Lamia Chraibi (La Prod). Chraibi's involvement was key for a variety of reasons. First, having previously worked in France in advertising and TV before returning to Morocco to set up as a film producer, Chraibi understood the potential value of international co-production for securing external funding, as well as the need for creating a transnational network of collaborators for such a film with Doha. Second, since *Mimosas* was shot entirely on location in Morocco, Lage needed a reliable co-producer to facilitate the logistics of the shoot. Finally, Chraibi had the connections and professional status as a Moroccan producer to lobby for *Mimosas* to receive internal funding from the CCM to the tune of 1 million MAD (€90,000). Although this was considerably less than the average a Moroccan 'national' production would receive from the CCM at that time (3–4 million MAD) and less than 10 per cent of the total budget, the fact that this was the first international co-production with a foreign director to receive funding from the CCM was a symbolic milestone and a suggestion that the CCM was more open to funding international co-productions with European directors.[18] However, as Chraibi explained, the central argument that convinced the CCM was economic: 'for every dirham they [the CCM] gave me, I promised to find six from funders abroad'.[19]

Despite having a European director at the helm and being a minority Moroccan co-production, *Mimosas* does not follow the pattern established by most European majority co-productions such as *Dunye & Desie* (Nechushtan, Holland/Morocco, 2009), *Hassan's Way* (Araújo and De Nova, Portugal/Spain/Morocco, 2013) or *Love is What We Need* (Marchak, France/Morocco, 2017), which offer a Eurocentric or neo-Orientalist vision of Moroccan society with the narrative focused on the experience of Western protagonists. Oliver Laxe had in fact lived for more than a decade in Morocco before shooting *Mimosas*, integrating himself into the film culture in Tangier, converting to Islam, learning to speak Moroccan Arabic and marrying a Moroccan woman. The film bears the hallmarks of its director's own transnational and intercultural experiences: it is a self-styled 'Sufi-Western' that combines the characteristics of the European art film and the epic with genre cinema (part-Western, part-thriller) with dialogues delivered entirely in Arabic and a screenplay structured around the stations of prayer in Islamic worship – though it concerns Islam far less than spirituality. Though Laxe undoubtedly foregrounds the spectacular natural beauty of the Atlas Mountains, the environment and its people are shot with respect by a director who has an intimate knowledge of these locations, and is sensitive to its people and culture, rather than one who has been helicoptered in to a remote location and uses the landscape as an exotic backdrop for the adventures of its Western protagonists (the standard approach for so many of the Hollywood studio films line-produced in Morocco). Laxe also showed himself to be keenly aware of the delicate politics of intercultural exchange between Morocco and Europe through his collaboration with the British experimental visual artist Ben Rivers on *The Sky Trembles and the Earth is Afraid and The Two Eyes Are Not Brothers* (2015). Rivers' film, a reworking of a Paul Bowles' short story in which the high-handed behaviour of a European professor of linguistics towards the inhabitants of what is probably a remote Moroccan village is met with violence, replaces the university Professor with a filmmaker (played by Laxe himself) and incorporates behind-the-scenes footage of the *Mimosas*' shoot.

In spite of Laxe's integration into Moroccan culture and his sensitivity to the politics of cross-cultural collaboration, a close working relationship between the film's Spanish and Moroccan producers, and of the CCM's effective endorsement of the project (by the award of selective aid), *Mimosas* was seen upon its release as a 'foreign' production by many Moroccan filmmakers and critics, while its art-house credentials meant that, like other Moroccan auteur cinema, it struggled to connect with Moroccan audiences.[20] In contrast with its lukewarm reception in Morocco, *Mimosas* established a presence at major international festivals such as Cannes, Marrakesh, Toronto and Cairo that allowed the film to sell relatively well internationally, securing distribution in France (UFO Distribution), Spain (NUMAX), UK (MUBI), USA (Grasshopper Film), Baltic countries (Must Kasi), Mexico (Mantarraya), Canada (Raven Banner, Middle East and Maghreb (MC Distribution)), Brazil, Greece and the Netherlands (Contact Film).[21] Although such international reach appears to confirm the widely held belief within the industry that co-productions 'travel' better, in terms of impact at the box office, the film in fact attracted a modest 26,657 spectators in cinemas across Europe. This performance placed it in line with similar auteur-led Moroccan majority co-productions such as *On the Edge* (Kilani, 2001: 31,921 spectators), *A Thousand Months* (Bensaïdi, 2003: 23,261 spectators) and *Testament* (25,651 spectators).[22] The key success of the film was, therefore, less its overall performance at the international box office than the transnational visibility that its presence in so many territories and critical success at international festivals brought for both producers (Lage and Chraibi) and director (Laxe) when seeking collaborators and funding for subsequent projects.

Despite the film's international distribution potential and its positive critical reception at international festivals, funders on both sides of the Mediterranean found it hard to conceive *Mimosas* as a 'national' film in the development of which they were willing to invest. Producer Lage suggested that ultimately the film was 'too African for Europe and too European for Africa'.[23] On the one hand, the film was refused funding (automatic and selective aid) from the Centre National de la Cinématographie in France, despite the fact that both producer and director had grown up in France after emigrating from Spain with their parents. On the other hand, with a Spanish director at the helm, *Mimosas* was ineligible for European funding for 'African' or 'Arab' cinema such as the Berlin-based World Cinema Fund. The film even ran into problems with initial funding provided by the Spanish film institute (the ICAA). Despite originally recognising the film as an official Spanish–Moroccan co-production, the ICAA subsequently threatened to withdraw their funding because there were 'not enough Spanish actors' in the film – though Lage suspects this had as much to do with Spanish concerns in funding a film perceived to be 'about Islam'.[24] For Lage, then, while the Spanish–Moroccan co-production worked on a personal level between producers, it was difficult on an institutional level. Lage concluded that the easiest institutional relationship to manage was with the Doha Institute (Qatar) at the point of post-production. A consequence, perhaps, of Doha's relative independence in relation to *Mimosas*: the Qatari institution was removed from the cultural politics of co-production between Morocco and Spain that remain influenced by what Forsdick and Murphy refer to as the complex 'afterlives of empire' (2009: 17).

Even for a transnational film such as *Mimosas* that genuinely engages with European and Moroccan cultural perspectives, the challenges caused by the cultural politics of international co-production remain. Does this mean, however,

that the complexity of co-producing internationally should lead Moroccan directors and producers to eschew such transnational collaboration? In character-
istically direct style, Hicham Lasri provides a simple solution to the problem:
'I have absolutely no problem refusing to work with someone if I don't agree
with them'.[25] Finding the right international co-producing partner is, therefore,
crucial. Just as important, however, if Moroccan cinema is to benefit from the
positive aspects of international co-production, is the need for greater training and
more strategic support for Moroccan producers to establish durable and equitable
partnerships with an international network of co-producers, distributors and sales
agents. This is the case not only in Europe but also across the Arab world and
in the diaspora, where Moroccan cinema has very little visibility and thus little
'value' (cultural or economic) to foreign producers and funding bodies. Targeted
support from the CCM for Moroccan filmmakers, as well as a greater presence at
key internationals and markets, is crucial.

Looking beyond Europe, as Hicham Falah notes, there is also an opportunity
to build on the expanding collaboration between sub-Saharan African cinema
and Morocco and to extend this to greater transnational regional co-production
across the Maghreb, with regional producers looking to Scandinavia as a model
for a cluster of small national cinemas that have built a sustainable network to
work together, drawing on shared cultural experiences in order to multiply the
number but also the diversity of films being produced.[26] A cultural shift, combined
with institutional support, is therefore required if Moroccan cinema is to harness
the potential of international co-production for both its industry and its film culture, and rebalance a film ecosystem in which international 'collaboration' is currently skewed towards Morocco as offering a pool of experienced technicians and
exotic locations to be mined by foreign producers and Hollywood studios with no
concern for bringing genuinely collaborative stories and experiences to the screen.

A group of filmmakers who are central to the type of international co-production that might potentially transform Moroccan cinema are those living
and working in the Moroccan diaspora. It is to a consideration of the 'rooted
transnationalism' of these filmmakers – and the often-ambivalent relationship they must negotiate with those Moroccan filmmakers who remain more
firmly aligned to 'national' modes of production and distribution – that we
will now turn our attention.

The Rooted Transnationalism of Diasporic Moroccan Filmmakers

Many postcolonial Maghrebi filmmakers experience conditions of exile or
temporary displacement (Boughedir 1987: 10) and Moroccan directors are no
exception. From the late 1960s, Moroccan filmmakers have, by necessity, been
displaced for extended periods, living abroad either as émigré artists or studying
at university or film school before returning to Morocco to work in film and TV

production. To cite a few prominent examples: Ahmed el Maanouni studied in Paris and then Brussels in the 1970s before returning to Morocco to shoot *Oh the Days!* (1978); Jillali Ferhati lived in France for ten years, studying literature and sociology, while also performing for some of this period as an actor with the Théâtre International in Paris; Farida Benlyazid graduated from the IDHEC Film School in Paris before producing Ferhati's *A Gap in the Wall* (1978); while the success of Maanouni and Ferhati at Cannes in the late 1970s and early 1980s was facilitated by Izza Génini, a Moroccan–Jewish producer and distributor born in Casablanca who had emigrated to France in the 1950s.[27] Meanwhile, directors Abdelkader Lagtaâ, Mostafa Derkaoui and cinematographer and director Abdelkrim Derkaoui all studied at the Łódź film school in communist Poland during the late 1960s and early 1970s.

Understanding the importance of the diaspora to the development of contemporary Moroccan cinema, as well as the complex and often contested transnational connections engendered by such films, requires a nuanced approach to the diaspora itself. While the CCM's policy of investment in cinema production has seen a rise in feature films directed by home-grown talent, filmmakers from the diaspora – with a range of attachments to and investment in their Moroccan heritage – have also played a key role in the success, diversity and international visibility of Moroccan cinema over the past twenty-five years. The participation of a number of non-resident Moroccans (NRMs) such as Nabil Ayouch, Nour-Eddine Lakhmari and Ismaël Ferroukhi in the fourth National Film Festival in Tangier in 1995 and the subsequent funding of their films by the CCM are commonly cited by scholars, critics and a new generation of filmmakers as a key encounter in the rise of Moroccan cinema in the late 1990s and 2000s.[28] However, in other ways, the success of a select group of filmmakers from the Moroccan diaspora on the international festival circuit merely highlights the divisions (artistic, cultural and economic) between them and their compatriots in Morocco, whose modes of financing, production and projected audience remain very much contained within national boundaries. As in the wider context of Maghrebi cinema, 'diasporic filmmakers are often viewed as being disconnected from the realities of their homeland, incapable of dealing with such realities in their films, and even traitors who sell themselves to the West by making elitist films' (Barlet 1997).[29]

To label all Moroccan filmmakers who live, create and operate to varying degrees outside of Morocco as 'diasporic' is helpful only to a point. While the CCM may have identified an untapped pool of talent from within the Moroccan diaspora by inviting filmmakers such as Lakhmari and Ayouch to the FNF in 1995, there is no homogeneous collective of diasporic Moroccan filmmakers bound by a common worldview or approach to form, theme and style. Individual directors and artists respond in singular ways to the conditions and experience of their own displacement, offering differing and even opposing perspectives on the questions of identity and belonging in relation to the 'host' nation and the Moroccan homeland. Not every film by a 'diasporic' Moroccan filmmaker is obliged to engage directly with his or her status as a member of the diaspora and the extent to which the individual filmmaker (and indeed individual films by the same filmmaker) engage with the diaspora will inevitably vary.[30] Nor should we presume that the presence of a sizeable Moroccan diasporic community in a given country will instantly translate into the emergence of diasporic filmmakers in the 'host' nation.[31] That said, it is possible to trace certain representational trends, thematic concerns and shared approaches to funding and production among these filmmakers.

Among other things, the term 'diaspora' implies the shared experience or collective (post-)memory of displacement, an investment in a common home-land and the notion of return, combined with issues of settlement in the 'host' nation and connectivity to the wider diasporic community. And yet many of the Moroccan filmmakers who have spent time outside Morocco, such Kamal Kamal, Hamid Faridi, Mohamed Asli and Abdelhaï Laraki, have done so for a limited and defined period of time (most often while studying abroad) with a clear intention of returning to Morocco rather than settling permanently abroad. As such, their films do not evoke a strong identification with the shared ethno-consciousness of diaspora. Rather, they speak to the socio-political reali-ties, tastes and concerns of a Moroccan audience. This is not to say, however, that the time spent in the diaspora has not marked or shaped the work of these directors or their collaborations in any way. Director Mohamed Asli, who emigrated to Italy to train and work as a filmmaker, founded a film training centre in Ouarzazate in partnership with Cinecittà studios upon his return to Morocco in the 2000s. His debut feature, the Moroccan–Italian co-production *In Casablanca Angels Don't Fly* (2004), shot with an Italian crew, contains 'genuine echoes of [Italian] neorealism' that emerge from Asli's years working in Italian documentary (Armes 2015: 126).

A second group of filmmakers with an arguably deeper connection to the Moroccan diaspora might best be described as *cinéastes de passage*: filmmak-ers who often hold dual nationality, have a base in both Morocco and Europe (predominantly, though not exclusively, in France and Belgium), and whose presence on either side of the Mediterranean is dictated by the rhythms of production and promotion of their films as well as the political, economic and creative conditions surrounding each new project. Such a group would include (but not be limited to) directors Faouzi Bensaïdi, Narjiss Nejjar, Munir Abbar, Leïla Kilani, Mohcine Besri, Laïla Marrackhi as well as producer Lamia Chraibi. (Nabil Ayouch and Nour-Eddine Lakhmari could also be included in this group though, as argued later in this chapter, their commitment to return-ing to Morocco to establish themselves as filmmakers is slightly different.) The work of these *cinéastes de passage* is not unified by an overarching stylistic approach or set of thematic or political concerns. Consider, for example, the contrast between the depiction (in terms of style, genre and class) of the challenges facing Moroccan (female) youth as a result of the country's exposure to the neo-liberal globalisation in *On the Edge* (Kilani, 2011) and *Marock* (Marakchi, 2005). Nevertheless, the *cinéastes de passage* share a 'rooted transnationalism', creating films with narratives firmly located in Moroccan culture and society (including in their use of language) but employing a breadth of cinematic references, cultural perspectives and political concerns that extend beyond Morocco. Their films tend, moreover, to be auteur-led international co-productions aimed at the world cinema distribution circuit more than the Moroccan domestic market. The international film festival circuit is crucial to such Moroccan *cinéastes de passage* in that it provides visibility for their films to international critics and distributors, who act as the gatekeepers of a 'world cinema' audience of (largely) Western cinephiles in independent film theatres, on DVD and increasingly via niche streaming platforms such as MUBI in the UK and Filmatique in the US.

Prominent recent examples of this rooted transnationalism include Bensaïdi's *Volubilis* (2017) and Narjiss Nejjar's *Stateless*. Born and raised in Meknes, Faouzi Bensaïdi has been based predominantly in Paris since the mid-1990s but has shot all his films to date in Morocco. In each film, Bensaïdi's choice of a specific Moroccan city (Casablanca, Tetouan, Meknes) plays an integral and active role in the project's aesthetic and narrative direction. Narjiss Nejjar, who came to international prominence with her debut feature *Cry No More* (2003), was born in Tangier in 1971 and moved to Paris in the late 1980s to study filmmaking at ESRA, eventually setting up her own production company in Paris (Terre Sud Films) in the 2000s. Like Bensaïdi, she shoots her films in Morocco but lived for an extended period in Paris (moving between France and Morocco) though she is now based in Rabat. Both directors regularly receive selective funding from the CCM as well as investment from European co-producers to finance their films and, where possible, support from 'world' cinema funds from Doha and Berlin. Similarly, while making a point of accompanying their films to compete in the Moroccan National Film Festival in Tangier March 2018, both directors understand the importance of prioritising premieres at A-list international film festivals over the national film festival.[32]

In *Stateless*, a Moroccan–French co-production produced by Lamia Chraibi, Nejjar focuses on a highly localised 'national' narrative of *la marche noire* (the sudden expulsion in 1975 of 45,000 Moroccan families from Algeria to Morocco) to explore the condition of women in contemporary Moroccan society. Hénia, a victim of *la marche noire*, lives in a small village on the Moroccan side of the Algerian–Moroccan border. Trapped in a domineering and loveless marriage with a significantly older Moroccan husband, Hénia struggles to reconcile her sense of belonging and longs to return to Algeria. The social status of women is a well-established theme in Moroccan cinema and Maghrebi filmmaking more generally. The originality of *Stateless* comes from Nejjar's decision to situate this well-worn theme in a liminal, contested border space of geopolitical significance. (The narrative takes place on the border between Algeria and Morocco, a space marked by the expulsion of thousands of families from Algeria to Morocco in 1975 in response to Morocco's annexation of the Spanish-occupied Sahara in the same year.)[33] The fraught and often contradictory nature of existence in such a border space is powerfully evoked through the performances of the lead actors and by the cinematography of French director of photography Stéphane Vallée, who shoots Hénia in close-up and short focus as a motif for her dislocation from the society around her. Narjiss' status as a *cinéaste de passage* arguably permits a point of view that is simultaneously inside and outside of the official 'Moroccan' perspective on this history and contested geopolitical space. In aesthetic terms, however, like many of the films by Moroccan *cinéastes de passage*, *Stateless* employs a stylistic approach (long takes, a focus on feeling and character development as much as plot and action) that is more identifiable with European art-house cinema.

In Bensaïdi's *Volubilis*, a Moroccan–French–Qatari co-production, the film's rooted transnationalism comes less from the exploration of identity politics in a transnational space than it does from a conscious interweaving of Moroccan, Arab and Western cinematic and cultural traditions, styles and intertextual references for dramatic effect. Set in Meknes, the city of Bensaïdi's birth and childhood, *Volubilis* revolves around a recently married, working-class couple, Abdelkader (a security guard in a shopping mall) and Malika (a domestic worker for a wealthy family), who struggle to make ends meet. A chance altercation in the mall with a contemptuous *bourgeois* shopper (unfortunately married to a powerful local government official, played by Bensaïdi), leads to Abdelkader losing his job and suffering a humiliating beating – triggering a spiral of despair that almost destroys his relationship with Malika.

Figure 2.2   *Stateless* (Nejjar, 2018) (La Prod/Moon & Deal Films)

Volubilis is clearly bounded in the socio-political reality of contemporary Morocco – moving between the working-class neighbourhoods and affluent suburbs of Meknes to explore the social pressures facing an 'ordinary' young couple. Nevertheless, this transnational film also draws on elements of American and Egyptian cinema. The *mise en scène* mirrors the suffocating social constraints of the classic Sirkian melodrama from Hollywood of the 1940s and 1950s, while *Volubilis'* final set piece pays homage to the visual and narrative suspense of Hitchcock's *Rear Window* (1954), as Malika watches anxiously while Abdelkader, unaware of the impending danger, searches the rooms of his persecutor's glass-fronted villa. For his part, Bensaïdi has described *Volubilis* as a love story shot in local dialogue and influenced by the tradition of the Egyptian melodrama; hence his careful attention to music and to dramatic structure in the film. This bricolage of intertextual and generic references to other cinemas is common in Bensaïdi's previous films, as is his exploration of the consequences of institutional and personal violence enacted on the individual, though in *Volubilis* the intertextual references also extend to Bensaïdi's own filmography.[34] However, this is not to say that *Volubilis* is an introspective film essay. Unlike some of his earlier films which, as cinematically accomplished as they are, risk becoming exercises in style, Bensaïdi's narrative focus on the young couple as well as references to Egyptian melodrama and song arguably make *Volubilis* his most accessible work to date for a popular Moroccan audience. Equally, the film's range of cinematic references together with its visual and narrative complexities make *Volubilis* an obviously attractive proposition for the international festival circuit and a cinephile 'world cinema' audience – exemplifying once more this notion of 'rooted transnationalism'.

As these recent examples from Bensaïdi and Nejjar demonstrate, the *cinéastes de passage* inhabit multiple positions that are simultaneously anchored in contemporary Moroccan society and between, within and even beyond the film cultures and industries of Morocco and Europe (Higbee 2007: 62). Bensaïdi has spoken of the unique opportunity offered to him as an artist living within and between France and Morocco:

> I'm fortunate to exist between two countries and two cultures. That distance in terms of time and space is always beneficial. This sense of dual-territoriality fits perfectly with the creative act [of cinema]. (Bensaïdi cited in Le Morvan 2017)[35]

Nevertheless, to exist in a state of interstitiality is also to operate and create films in a contested space in relation to Moroccan 'national' cinema. For many Moroccan critics and filmmakers, the fact that these films appear to prioritise funding and audiences from outside Morocco leaves them open to the charge of surrendering to a neo-Orientalist, clichéd view of Morocco and Moroccans that panders to Western stereotypes (Bahmad 2018).

If the work of the *cinéastes de passage* is marked by a combination of a grounding in the space and context of Moroccan culture and society with a more transnational perspective, this is not always the case for those filmmakers born and raised from an early age in the Moroccan diaspora. Neither is it true for those émigré filmmakers who have chosen to settle in Europe, rather than shuttling back and forth between Europe and the Maghreb. Instead, this group of filmmakers has a varying degree of engagement with Morocco and with the myth and reality of return to their ancestral homeland. This is hardly surprising, given that many of these filmmakers are the descendants of Moroccan émigrés who do not consider themselves citizens of Europe rather than immigrants and have a connection to the Moroccan language and culture that is fragmented or partial.

Although this group of diasporic filmmakers presents a range of (sometimes contradictory) approaches to representing and engaging with the Moroccan diaspora, we can identify at least three broad trends in their films. The first draws on return narratives (often road movies) where diasporic characters (typically the descendants of Moroccan immigrants) journey to Morocco in order to reconnect with their Moroccan roots in films that often engender an act of return for the director as much as for the on-screen protagonist. This is exemplified in films such as *Tenja, Beyond Here* (Boucif, 2001), *The Bag of Flour* (Leclere, 2011) and *French Girl* (Bouhati, 2008). Though conventional in terms of its narrative mode and *mise en scène*, Souad el Bouhati's *French Girl* offers an original take on the diasporic return narrative by inverting the traumatic act of displacement and the longing for a perceived homeland. *French Girl* is a French–Moroccan co-production that received 2.5 million MAD from the CCM in selective aid for production. The film tells the story of Sofia, the daughter of Moroccan immigrant parents, who is shown to be content with her life in a provincial town in France until her family decides to return to Morocco, literally dragging her screaming into the car that will transport her to the *bled* (ancestral home). The film then jumps forward ten years. We find Sofia (now played by Hafsia Herzi) living and working on the family farm but still clearly desiring to return to France: her repeated demand that she be allowed to determine her own future (in France) is a source of much tension within the family. At first glance, the preference for a return to France in *French Girl* appears to reflect Bouhati's own background, born in Rabat in 1962 but raised from a very young age in France. It also revisits an established narrative trope in Maghrebi–French filmmaking since the early 1990s, where the prospect of return to a country and culture they hardly know is a non-sequitur.[36] In *French Girl*, while Sofia may struggle to fully master Moroccan Arabic and constantly clash with her mother, she is nonetheless granted a degree of freedom on both the family farm and in the town, where she attends school that appears comparable to what she would experience in France. The decision to repeatedly frame Sofia against the backdrop of the countryside surrounding the farm in

French Girl suggests a profound connection with the family's Moroccan (home-) land that belies her expressed desire to return to France. Ceding to his daughter's repeated demands, the father finally provides Sofia with her passport and, in the film's final scene, we see Sofia working in a modern, multicultural office translating between Arabic and French. However, as she walks down the street after work, the street signs, car registrations and sounds of the city make it clear that she has identified her future as living in Morocco, not France, subverting the established trope of return narratives in Maghrebi–French filmmaking from the 1990s and 2000s (Higbee 2013: 130–53).

Unlike the reconnection with the diasporic homeland found in films such as *Tenja* and *French Girl*, the second approach to diaspora found in films by (second-generation) Moroccan diasporic filmmakers affects a more emphatic disengagement with the Moroccan homeland. The work of Belgian–Moroccan directing duo Adil el Arbi and Bilall Fallah, in particular, exemplifies this trend. In the space of three feature films – *Image* (2014), *Black* (2015) and *Gangsta* (2018) – el Arbi and Fallah have established themselves as one of the most dynamic writer/director partnerships in Belgian cinema, crafting explosive and visually arresting popular narratives that explore the dark and often violent criminal underclass of Belgian–Moroccan youth in the working-class Brussels suburb of Molenbeek. The films explore the problems of violence, racism, social exclusion and media misrepresentation experienced by the disadvantaged (mostly male) youth of Molenbeek and make virtually no attempt to engage with the Moroccan homeland either as a source of cultural inspiration or as a co-producing partner. Outside Belgium, el Arbi and Fallah are clearly looking towards America rather than Morocco to further expand the international reach of their films.[37]

Tellingly, the only time in el Arbi and Fallah's trilogy that the notion of 'return' to Morocco is evoked as a narrative possibility is in their most recent film, *Gangsta*, where the film's youthful protagonists travel to a coastal resort in northern Morocco in the hope of establishing links with Moroccan drug dealers. This sequence is notable for its presentation of Belgian–Moroccan youth in an environment that appears free from the racism, tensions and violence they experience daily in Molenbeek. However, any positive connotations offered by the inclusion of these scenes are undercut by the fact that the gang continue to identify themselves as (Western) tourists, make no attempt to engage with broader Moroccan culture, and see the trip as little more than a brief respite from the drudgery of life in Molenbeek and the opportunity to secure a cheap and reliable supply for drugs to sell in Brussels.

Also raised in Belgium and of Moroccan descent is Nabil Ben Yadir, whose first feature *The Barons* (2009) was a breakthrough success with audiences in Belgium. Like the films of el Arbi and Falah, *The Barons* focuses exclusively on marginalised Moroccan–Belgian youth in a working-class, urban milieu, though with an emphasis firmly on comedy rather than the stylised depictions of crime, social exclusion and violence. Ben Yadir's second feature, a Franco-Belgian co-production, *The March* (2013), extends this concern with the situation of diasporic Moroccan youth in Molenbeek to the struggles faced two decades earlier by Maghrebi–French or beur youth in their political demands for tolerance, recognition and acceptance in France.[38] *The March* adapts the true story of the *Marche pour l'égalité et contre le racisme* – a civil rights protest march from Marseilles to Paris in response to the violence, institutional discrimination and everyday racism experienced by beurs in France. Through its close attention to 'authentic' period reconstruction, an interrogation rather than a celebration of the nation's past, a focus on history 'from below' offering humanistic perspectives that advocate notions such as human justice, *The March* forms part of the trend of new history films found in French cinema of the 2000s (Radner 2015: 290). As such, *The March* seeks to confirm Ben Yadir's credentials as a 'serious' director after the popular success of *The Barons*. *The March* was recognised in Morocco through its selection at the Marrakesh International Film Festival in 2013, but had only a limited theatrical release in the country in 2014.[39] Its inclusion in the official selection for Marrakesh arguably speaks as much to the programming choices of the French co-organisers of the festival at that time (Public System) as it does to a strong desire by the CCM, the Moroccan cinema community or indeed Moroccan audiences to embrace the film.[40] While the inclusion of high-profile Maghrebi–French actors such as Jamel Debbouze and Hafsia Herzi may also have been attractive to the Marrakesh festival, in general actors from the Moroccan diaspora (even *bona fide* stars such as Debbouze) have only limited pull at the Moroccan box office. In the same way, and moving in the opposite direction, the most bankable stars at the Moroccan box office, such as Abdellah Ferkous, make little impression in the European theatrical circuit. (Although, admittedly, it is harder to measure their impact on informal distribution networks – pirated DVDs, streaming – in the Moroccan diaspora or on viewing via satellite and digital streaming platforms.)

As a Belgian filmmaker of Moroccan origin working with high-profile Maghrebi–French actors in a film that charts one of the key moments in the history of the beurs in France, Ben Yadir appears more concerned in *The March* with promoting and exploring a shared history and the creative filmmaking networks of the Maghrebi diaspora in France than in reconnecting with the culture and history of his Moroccan homeland. This focus on lateral connections between members of the Moroccan diaspora in Europe is further emphasised by the fact that *The March* is a Franco-Belgian co-production with no affiliated Moroccan co-producer. Like el Arbi and Falah, Ben Yadir makes no attempt to seek funding from the CCM or to develop his films as international co-productions with Morocco – in part, one assumes, because entering into an official co-production in this way would require such films to comply with conditions surrounding levels of Moroccan investment and crew participation that European producers might see as restrictive or unnecessary.

A third trend that emerges from the cinema of the Moroccan diaspora concerns a more selective group of directors such as Hakim Belabbes, Tala Hadid, Myriam Bakir, Jawad Rahlib and Abdellah Taïa, whose work displays (either through form or content) a keen awareness of their status as diasporic subjects. The films by these directors straddle narrative and documentary modes and are, broadly speaking, auteur-led productions that are politically informed.[41] In these respects, these directors can be seen as 'accented', following Naficy's more general definition of the term:

> situated but universal figures who work in the interstices of social formations and cinematic practices', filmmakers with their origins in the so-called 'global south' who are based in the 'cosmopolitan north' . . . where they exist in a state of tension and dissension with both their original and their current homes. (Naficy 2001: 10)

Any localised focus on the socio-political realities of contemporary Morocco in the films of these directors is, therefore, typically viewed through a broader set of geopolitical reference points and a worldview that reflects the filmmakers' own multi-layered, transnational identity.

The self-reflexive nature of the accented Moroccan filmmakers in relation to their status as diasporic, displaced or transnational subjects produces a different kind of rooted transnationalism from that found in the films of the *cinéastes de passage*. Nowhere is this more apparent than in the films of Hakim Belabbes. Born in Boujad, a small town in central Morocco, Belabbes studied in Rabat and Lyon before moving to Chicago in the late 1980s. An established presence on the international film circuit in Europe, North America and the Arab world, Belabbes returns periodically to Morocco, most recently to work as part of the Sahara Lab, an NGO media and film training initiative based in Western Sahara.[42] In *Boujad: A Nest in the Heat* (1992), he documents a summer visit to the family home – agonising over how to tell his father that he has decided to reside permanently in the US. Belabbes reflects on his reasons for emigrating and the tension that this decision continues to generate. *In Pieces* (2009) offers a deeply personal portrait of the filmmaker's Moroccan extended family, with footage collected over a ten-year period documenting the most intimate, key moments of family life, including the death of his father. The title illustrates the process of fragmentation that structures the film as well as the absence (from home) and displacement (in space and time) of diaspora. A highly intimate and at times poetic film, *In Pieces* oscillates between the personal and the political, for example in the interview with a close family friend, whose powerful testimony surrounding the 'disappearance' of his son highlights the personal cost and unresolved trauma of state political repression for many ordinary Moroccans during the Years of Lead. *In Pieces* is not a return narrative in the mold of *Tenja* or *French Girl*, then, but rather a reflection on the relationship between the diasporic filmmaker and the people and society he has left behind. Belabbes, moreover, uses his diasporic positioning as simultaneously insider and outsider to Moroccan culture, politics and society, to adopt a more critical perspective – even in films that do not ostensibly reflect upon diasporic themes, as his most recent feature *Sweat Rain* (2017) illustrates. *Sweat Rain* won the Grand Prix at the FNF in 2017, and exposes the poverty, deprivation and powerlessness felt by many ordinary Moroccans from the rural areas surrounding Boujad that have been dismissed since the time of the French colonial protectorate as forming part of 'useless Morocco',[43] an image that *Sweat Rain* suggests persists today among Morocco's postcolonial elite. Despite the clear and prominent grounding (artistic, emotional and in terms of funding) to Morocco and Moroccan film culture in his work, Belabbes nonetheless admits to feeling distanced from certain parts of the filmmaking community in Morocco. Maintaining this sense of the insider/outsider status of diasporic filmmakers, Belabbes explains that this divide extends to perceptions around funding:

> There is definitely a gap between the filmmakers who are of the diaspora and those who make their films solely in Morocco . . . People think that if you come from somewhere outside of the country that you have access for more funding and that you are better positioned to make better films.[44]

In fact, as a more experimental, non-fiction filmmaker, Belabbes found it as challenging to access funding for his earlier films in the US, while at the same time being unable to access funding from the CCM (who at this point were only funding fiction films). Instead Belabbes had to rely on money from Moroccan TV, a fact that, in turn, cast doubt for some over the status and positioning of his work in Morocco as 'cinema'.[45]

As the example of Hakim Belabbes illustrates, diasporic directors experience a continual sense of negotiation with the host and homeland, modifying their level of engagement with diasporic themes in their films, depending on the nature and focus of each individual project. The experience of displacement and reconnection with the diasporic homeland not only determines the approach of the filmmaker to a specific film, it can even influence their overall development and trajectory as an artist. This is apparent in the careers of Nour-Eddine Lakhmari and Nabil Ayouch: two of the original group of 'diasporic' filmmakers who were invited by the CCM to screen their short films at the 1995 FNF in Tangier. Lakhmari was born in Safi in 1964 and studied in Oslo, Paris and New York before settling in Norway, where he was a resident for almost thirty years before he settled in Casablanca. While Lakhmari's early short films, such as his comedy *Born Without Skis* (1996), directly explore issues of diasporic identity and integration into the host nation, his feature films (funded with money from Europe and Morocco) are increasingly focused on an examination of inequalities in contemporary Moroccan society, viewed through its largest city, Casablanca. His second feature film, *Casanegra* (2007) became one of the most popular and controversial films in the history of Moroccan cinema, attracting over 500,000 spectators nationally. The original script for *Casanegra* was an émigré narrative about the experiences of two Moroccan youths who travelled to Scandinavia. According to his Norwegian producer Egil Ødegård, it was only after Lakhmari had returned to Morocco in the 2000s to take advantage of the incentives offered by the CCM for NRMs to shoot and develop projects that the film's narrative became focused on Casablanca. This shift in focus, argues Ødegård, was largely shaped by the director's own act of diasporic return. Lakhmari's displaced view of contemporary Moroccan society at the start of the new millennium is incorporated into the film's narrative by reversing the conventional diasporic narrative about the the newly arrived young migrant's experiences in the (European) host nation.[46]

In a similar way, Nabil Ayouch, born and raised in France to a Moroccan Muslim father and a Tunisian Jewish mother, has played out his reconnection to Moroccan culture and society through his varied filmography. Whereas Lakhmari used the act of return to craft his Casablanca trilogy at the centre of Morocco's New Urban Cinema (Bahmad 2013a), Ayouch's 'personal history of difference and disconnect with Morocco has served as major theme and inspiration in his work' (Smolin 2015: 216). In his debut feature, *Mektoub* (1997), Ayouch constructs a police thriller/road movie hybrid that combines the contemporary Moroccan public's ongoing fascination with the political corruption surrounding the real-life Tabit affair with a journey of reconnection and rediscovery for the film's central diasporic protagonist, a Moroccan eye surgeon (Toufik) who has emigrated to America and returns to Tangier for a conference.

Following the commercial and critical success of *Mektoub*, Ayouch has adopted, in the space of eight feature films, multiple directorial strategies as a means of engaging with his own hybrid status within and between the culture, politics and history of France, of Israel and the Maghreb (his father is Moroccan and his mother is a Tunisian Jew). This ranges from the investigation of social taboos and marginalisation in contemporary Moroccan society (*Ali Zaoua*, 2000; *Much Loved*, 2015; *Razzia*, 2017); and the dangers of Islamic fundamentalism (*Horses of God*, 2012); to a documentary about the Israeli–Palestinian conflict (*My Land*, 2011), which also functions as a means of exploring Ayouch's own Muslim–Jewish heritage, and finally *Whatever Lola Wants* (2007), a transnational romantic comedy-musical about an American who relocates to Egypt to further her career as a dancer.

In this respect, Ayouch transitions between almost all the previously outlined positions occupied by filmmakers of the Moroccan diaspora: the 'rooted transnationalism' of the *cinéaste de passage* (*Ali Zaoua*), the more politicised and self-reflexive accented cinema of Belabbes and Hadid (*My Land*), the focus on symbolic narratives of return and reconnection with Moroccan culture, people and traditions (*Mektoub*) as well as films that appear disengaged or uninterested in the diasporic homeland and more concerned with a Western audience (*Whatever Lola Wants*). Film critics and fellow filmmakers in Morocco have criticised Ayouch for what they perceive as his clichéd and even neo-Orientalist vision of Moroccan society.[47] Yet ironically, of all the post-1995 diasporic filmmakers, it is Ayouch who has most enthusiastically embraced the CCM's call to return to Morocco. As discussed in Chapter 1, Ayouch has established not only a permanent base in Morocco, but also (with the help of his father) a veritable media empire via Ali n' Productions that has promoted and nurtured home-grown Moroccan talent in the 2000s, including Hicham Lasri.[48] He is arguably Morocco's highest profile international director, has been selected twice by the CCM to represent Morocco for the best foreign language picture at the Academy Awards and tends to identify himself as a 'Moroccan' (not 'Moroccan–French') director, despite the fact that he was born and raised in France. Nevertheless, the controversy surrounding the effective banning of *Much Loved* in Moroccan theatres, following opposition from the ruling PJD government in Morocco in 2015, forced Ayouch to raise funding for *Razzia* without funding from the CCM (Dale 2015).

As the experiences of even its most famous and successful returning NRM director suggest, the place of diasporic filmmakers in contemporary Moroccan cinema is ambiguous and at times ambivalent. For some, diasporic filmmakers have been vital in contributing to the flourishing of Moroccan cinema since the late 1990s and its transnational reach. For others, they occupy a precarious and contested position: simultaneously inside/outside the space of Moroccan 'national' cinema and incapable of offering an authentic view on Moroccan socio-political realities. As such, their presence exposes divisions between contemporary Moroccan cinema's desire to look inward and reconnect with a popular audience, on the one hand, and the global ambition, on the other, to promote Morocco internationally as a force within world cinema.

Non-Western Production Networks

As the first two sections of this chapter have identified, when we speak of international co-production or the influence of diasporic filmmakers, we tend to think of the relationship between Morocco and Europe, and more specifically

France. However, just as a transnational Moroccan cinema cannot be conceived exclusively along the lines of the French–Moroccan (post-) colonial axis, so we must acknowledge the alternative routes of collaboration, cooperation and co-production that have opened up outside of the West for Moroccan cinema over the past two decades.

If, as noted earlier, the CCM's website provides partial and/or contradictory information on international co-production (especially when Morocco is not a majority producer on a project), it is remarkably silent on co-production with the more recent Arab players beyond the Maghreb: Qatar and the United Emirates. Yet the latter have been actively supporting the production of Arab cinema in MENA for well over a decade, through financial support at their festivals and film incubating programmes, while giving it accrued transnational visibility. This pan-Arab turn in filmmaking is something the old European film establishment (e.g. Cannes) paid attention to: 'Having local producers developing Arab films rather than European ones can become a game changer for the region's cinema going forward', Rémi Bonhomme, Head of Cannes' *Semaine de la Critique*, declared in 2015 (cited in Vivarelli 2015a: 58). But to what extent has it been a game changer for Moroccan productions?

At the turn of the millennium, three international film festivals were created in the Middle East that gradually eclipsed the hitherto sole longstanding Cairo International Film Festival (Wong 2011: 2): DIFF (Dubai International Film Festival), launched in 2004; ADFF (Abu Dhabi Film Festival), from 2007 to 2014, with its Sanad production support system (until 2015); and DTFF (Doha–Tribeca Film Festival), from 2009 to 2012, which gave way to the Doha Film Institute (DFI) and its film support institution Qumra. Hence, after the initial festival effervescence fizzled out, only one of them has survived: Dubai – although its future is somewhat unclear, its 2018 edition having been abruptly cancelled, pointing to the fragility of such initiatives for filmmakers across the Arab world, even when they are backed by the seemingly bottomless funds of oil-rich states (Vivarelli 2018a). The impetus behind their creation is multifaceted. It is economical –the oil money is reinvested in developing cultural global metropolises in the region, and building their museums and cinemas (Wong 2011: 12). It is diplomatic, in its desire to respond to the widely felt need to bridge East and West after 9/11 with Arab cinematic narratives, as explained by Abdulhamid Juma, Chairman of DIFF (Vivarelli 2015b). It is also pan-Arab: here, the promotion of the production, exhibition and distribution of Arab cinema adds a pan-Arab twist to Thomas Elsassaer's notion of a 'post-national' cinema.[49] Finally, it is Gulf-centred – the creation and promotion of the cinema of the Gulf region and the development of its production and film markets (Wong 2011: 140). Rising from an intentional intervention on the part of the political leaders of the region in the discourse that followed 9/11, the three festivals turned into de facto geopolitical cinema institutions that aimed to articulate local (regional, pan-Arab) dynamics into the global network of film festivals and co-productions.

The initial vision of co-production and exhibition in the festivals was transnational and transcultural as it sought to integrate Arab productions into the traditional Western international market venues. Nevertheless, the three festivals, originally packaged as sites for both local and regional film education, promotion and production, *and* partners in exhibition with the (Western) global film establishment (such as Cannes, Arte, Canal+ and the Hollywood studios), have independently renegotiated these relationships with their Western collaborators along the way. The result is an array of MENA co-productions with transnational values at the pre- and post-filmmaking stages: Moroccan directors view these available funds as new opportunities to make or complete a film, and as possible avenues to reach beyond a national or even a regional audience to a global viewership, as we shall see below.

Abu Dhabi Film Festival created its own grant competition to stimulate Arab film production: the Sanad ('support') programme that between 2010 and 2015 disbursed $500,000 annually through grants of $20,000 for development and $50,000 for post-production, for 'narrative' films (fiction) and documentaries, and gave transnational visibility to the supported films, at least on the festival circuit. Sanad helped the development or the production of two to four Moroccan films a year annually between 2010 and 2014 and none in 2015, its last year (see Table 2.1).[50] The films supported and made by eight male and four female directors (some of them first-timers, others quite experienced) do not offer any discernible pattern in terms of budget, theme or genre (four documentaries and eight fictions; eleven features, one short), and respond to the availability of the grant in what Mette Hjort calls 'opportunistic transnationalism' (Hjort 2009: 19–20), rather than a more durable artistic and creative form of transnationalism. Ali al Jabri, former director of Sanad, describes his programme as 'supporting and developing international quality Arab films . . . *Sanad* provides not only funding but valuable industry support at critical stages of production and continues this support during later stages of release and distribution'.[51] Hence the form of transnational collaboration provided in Abu Dhabi is not marked as a transnational team's effort to create, for instance, a distinctive pan-Arab film aesthetics or narrative form. Instead, the collaboration derives from a very intentional endeavour to place Arab films in professional networks (Cannes, Berlin and distributors) as it also aims to put Arab cinema (including Moroccan cinema) on the global map. In that respect, the transnational value of Abu Dhabi's co-productions corresponds to Hjort's 'globalizing transnationalism' in that it 'pursues a global cinemagoer' rather than, strictly, a national one or a regional one (Hjort 2009: 21, 28).

Table 2.1 Moroccan co-productions supported by Sanad, in Abu Dhabi, 2010–14

Year	Working title	Director	Type of funding
2014	The Birds of the Mountains	Aoulad-Syad, Daoud	Documentary – development
	Joint Possession	Kilani, Leila	Narrative feature – development
2013	A Place Under The Sun	Aïtouna, Karim	Documentary – development
2011	Pirates of Salé	Addou, Meriem and Rosa Rogers	Documentary – development
	The Wall	Bensaïdi, Faouzi	Narrative short – development
	99	Lasri, Hicham	Narrative feature – development
2010	On The Edge	Kilani, Leila	Narrative feature – post-production
	My Brother	El Mahouti, Kamal	Narrative feature – post-production
	Death for Sale	Bensaïdi, Faouzi	Narrative feature – post-production
	Zanka Contact	El Iraki, Ismaël El Maoula	Narrative – development
	Playground Stories	Fritah, Brahim	Narrative – development

Note: In 2012, only 6 Sanad grants were given out for post-production (3 narratives and 3 documentaries). Unless "short" is mentioned, all films are feature-length. For more details, see: <http://www.sanadfilmfund.com/en/projects/2015/> (accessed 31 January 2020).

The Doha International Film Festival parted ways with New York-based Tribeca in its fourth edition (2012) and changed the orientation of their global partnership.[52] The ensuing reconfigured DFI created two events alongside its grant programmes: the youth festivals Aiyal and Qumra. The latter was thus named because it is believed to be at the origin of the camera: 'It was used by Arab scientist, astronomer and mathematician Alhazen, whose work in optics laid out the principles of the camera obscura' (Vivarelli 2014). At Doha, it is the name of a film workshop and showcase designed to help and educate filmmakers from Qatar, the MENA region and the rest of the world. While it retained the competitive elements of an international festival, the DFI morphed into a national/transnational film incubator under the helm of Palestinian director Elia Suleiman (Vivarelli 2015b).

Created to accompany and financially support Middle Eastern production, Qumra soon expanded its grants to first- and second-time directors from outside the Middle East, including filmmakers from north Africa and its diaspora (Anonymous (2013). In the fall of 2015, the DFI awarded grants for development, production or post-production to thirty projects[53] from nineteen countries: twenty-four of them hailed from MENA, with a focus on first- and second-time talents (Levine 2016), including four from Morocco (see Table 2.2). More recently, among the thirty-four projects from twenty-eight countries at various stages of development in 2018, two were Moroccan, i.e. less than 15 per cent of their nation's production – and by female directors: Meriem Addou's feature documentary *Suspended Wives* (in development) and Meryem Benm'Barek's feature fiction *Sofia*.[54]

The film projects selected by the DFI in some ways illustrate its first and foremost goal after 9/11: to tell Arab stories, and provide an Arab perspective on Arab characters that is absent from or only partial in Western film. The initial 'corrective' to a Western filmic discourse broadly construed certainly explains the choices in 2011 and 2012, for instance: each film (whether documentary of fiction) comes from Moroccan voices at home (e.g. Jillali Ferhati; ESAV graduates Alaa Eddine Aljem and Hicham Elladdaqi) and gives a voice to subaltern Moroccan characters (such as the long-distance runner Aïcha in Hakim Belabbes's *Aïcha Bonheur*, the daughter of a prostitute in Jillali Ferhati's *Pillow Secrets*, the characters in the old medina of Casablanca in Dalila Ennadre's *Of Walls and Men*). All of the films testify to a high degree of *arabité* ('Arabness') and have an international competitive edge, clearly intent on putting the selections on the map. It is also worth noting that the gender of the grantees might also illustrate some of the organisers' pan-Arab discourse, running against the grain of the Western clichés about Arab culture's treatment of women. Giving as many chances to women directors as to men shows that there is more gender parity in the selection in Doha than there is in Hollywood: in 2012, out of seven directors, three are women; in 2015, out

Table 2.2   Moroccan projects in progress supported by the Doha Film Institute, 2011–18

Year	(Working) title	Director	Type of funding
2018	*Suspended Wives*	Addou, Meriem	Documentary, production
	Sofia	Benm'Barek, Meryem	Narrative, production
2017	*The Unknown Saint*	Aljem, Alaa Eddine	Narrative; production
	Saffron's Land	El Idrissi, Yassine	Narrative; development
	Joint Possession	Kilani, Leïla	Narrative; post-production
	The Healer	Zineddaine, Mohamed	Narrative; post-production
	Sofia	Benm'Barek, Meryem	Narrative; production
	Suspended Wives	Addou, Meriem	Documentary; production
	Ceuta's Gate	Maroufi, Randa	Short experimental; production
2016	*Volubilis*	Bensaïdi, Faouzi	Narrative; post-production
	Zanka Contact	El Iraki, Ismaël El Mouala	Narrative; production
	Joint Possession	Kilani, Leïla	Narrative, production
	Headbang Lullaby	Lasri, Hicham	Narrative; post-production
	Mimosas	Laxe, Oliver	Narrative; post-production
	Stateless	Nejjar, Narjiss	Narrative; post-production
	We Could Be Heroes	Bensari, Hind	Documentary
	House in the Fields	Hadid, Tala	Documentary; post-production
2015	*Pagan Magic*	Boulifa, Fyzal	Narrative; development
	Behind the Doors	Elhababi, Yakout	Documentary, development
	Weight Throwers	Bensari, Hind	Documentary, production
	Behind the Wall	Zoubir, Karima	Short narrative, production
2014	*None*		
2013	*None*		
2012	*Aïcha Bonheur*	Belabbes, Hakim	Feature narrative, production
	The Bastard	Benyamina, Houda	Feature narrative, development
	Pillow Secrets	Ferhati, Jillali	Feature narrative, production
	Salaam Plenty	Kassari, Yasmine	Feature documentary, development
	Walls and People	Ennadre, Dalila	Feature documentary, production
	The Desert Fish	Aljem, Aala Eddine	Short narrative, production
	The Third Hand	Elladdaqi, Hicham	Short narrative, production
2011	*My Brother*	El Mahouti, Kamal	Feature narrative, post-production
	The Maghrebim	Boccara, Ivan	Feature documentary, production

Note: Unless "short" is mentioned, all films are feature-length. For more details, see: http://www.dohafilminstitute.com/financing/projects/grants (accessed 26 February 2020).

of four directors, two are women; in 2016, out of eight, four are women; in 2017, out of seven, four are women; and in 2018 the two filmmakers selected are both women (Table 2.2). These numbers align with those advanced by a study from Northwestern University in Qatar and DFI,[55] which demonstrates that 30 per cent of Arab independent cinema screenwriters and directors are women – a much higher percentage in women's participation than Hollywood's 7 per cent directors and 13 per cent screenwriters (Brown 2016). The kind of transnationalism activated through DFI is goal-oriented rather than content-oriented: it aims at both enhancing the quality of a Moroccan auteur's film product and widening its international viewership, rather than promoting a transnational creative process in terms of aesthetics, photography or ways to convey a narrative on screen – with the possible exception of an overall 'modernising' postcolonial value affect. Dalila Ennadre's polyphonic documentary *Walls and People*, for instance, represents both the long history of Casablanca through the lyrical 'voice' of Anfa (the ancient name of the city) emanating from its walls at night, and the present-day multiple voices of the people in the medina grappling with the injustices of twenty-first-century global economics as well as the stark difference between values promoted at home and everyday realities (e.g. local campaigns and elections, emigration, democracy, the price of tradition).

In Dubai, the strategy of DIFF, according to the aims stated on their official website, was to 'promote creative excellence in Arab cinema' while initiating 'cross-cultural dialogue' through a film competition (the Muhr Awards for Excellence in Arab Cinema) along two criteria: 'Films directed by an Arab, whether residing in the Arab world or abroad', or 'Films reflecting Arab sociocultural issues'.[56] Ten films were nominated in each category (documentary, narrative, short) for three possible awards (a gold, a silver, or a bronze *muhr*, 'foal or stallion').[57]

The festival also featured a parallel competition in scriptwriting for UAE nationals,[58] as part of the UAE's plan to stimulate film culture aggressively in a territory in Dubai that was completely devoid of cinema theatres until the mid-1990s, with the opening of multiplexes offering mostly Hollywood, Bollywood and Egyptian fare (Yunis 2014: 70). The DIFF targets three objectives: a global film festival and competition (with all the Hollywood, Bollywood, European and Arab stars on its red carpet), with a parallel Arab international film competition, and a grant programme, film market and laboratory to promote film production aggressively in the Emirates. As an example, the Arte award and the Dubai Film Connection (DFC) were added in 2008 to enhance pan-Arab film production.[59] DIFF also boasts a strong Dubai Film Market (DFM) for film and TV distribution of Arab film. The DFM has supported over 300 Arab filmmakers and promoted projects that 'otherwise might have remained unseen' since 2007, as it links the local to the global: its team works with Cannes, Arte, Hollywood and others; it also works through DFC and has its own digital acquisition platform for film (and TV) content: Cinetech.

Finally, and most importantly for the purposes of this study, a post-production enhancement programme, Enjaaz ('achievement'), was launched in 2009, to provide, according to the DFF's website, 'vital post-production financial support to film projects led by Arab filmmakers, and production funding to film projects helmed by Gulf filmmakers'.[60] Several Moroccan directors could not have completed their films without an Enjaaz grant. Such was the case for Moroccan–Belgian Mohamed Amin Benamraoui, who received one for the post-production of his first feature fiction *Adios Carmen* in 2013, in the nick of time. The award of Enjaaz for his film presents a unique case study for Dubai's support of a Moroccan production in several ways.

After Benamraoui obtained generous support from the CCM in 2010 (4,600,000 MAD/$480,000) for his first feature film, Belgian producer Geneviève De Bauw (Thank You and Good Night Productions) joined the production team. The shooting started but money was anticipated to be more than tight at the post-production stage. The exact estimate for post-production came very late: 'it was neither very honest nor very professional. We had to see if we could swing it if we accelerated the work pace on the shoot etc . . . And finally, I was told we only had 10,000 euros for the post-production and that I would not be paid.'[61] Belgian editor France Duez put together the forty-minute rough cut that Benamraoui took to Dubai, in order to apply for and receive the Enjaaz fund as well as obtaining help from the Global Film Initiative in the United States (currently the American distributor of *Adios Carmen*). The entire transnational production structure connected the project to companies as well as to individual talent (in Belgium, sound engineer and mixer Alek Goosse ended up co-producing too). The making of the film is thus the result of a collaboration across multiple borders by the creative team (Ivan Oms Blanco, DoP, hails from Cuba; France Duez, editor, from Belgium; protagonist Amar is played by Benjalil Amanallah, a non-professional child actor from the Rif, while Paulina Gálvez, a Chilean–Spanish star, plays Carmen) and the production one (with its Belgian, Moroccan, US and Enjaaz sources of funding). It has a transnational identity (Morocco/Belgium/UAE) of a variegated nature: while the creative and production teams clearly cross-pollinate their nationally and culturally grounded creative solutions to filmmaking problems in both an 'affinitive' and 'milieu-building' collaboration with Spanish, Belgian and Moroccan partners, the UAE's input in the film, given perhaps its nascent cinematic culture at the time, remains invisible on screen, or 'unmarked' – to use Hjort's terminology (2009: 13–14).

Figure 2.3   *Adios Carmen* (Benamraoui, 2013): Bobby playing at the Rif

The narrative of Benamraoui's very first film, is both 'accented' (it is 'simultaneously global and local, and it exists in chaotic semiautonomous pockets in symbiosis with the dominant and other alternative cinemas', Naficy 2001: 19) and firmly rooted in the Rif (the northern region of Morocco) while it also deploys postcolonial questions of global reach. The time frame is the 1970s: Hassan II cuts off the Rif economically from the rest of the Kingdom, triggering massive Rifian emigration, and organises the Green March in 1976 to annex Spanish-occupied Western Sahara;[62] meanwhile, Franco (the Spanish occupier of the Rif until 1956) dies.

The shooting of *Adios Carmen* in the Rif and in Tarifit (the local variant of Tamazight) has serious political implications: the characters, location, language and history are non-Arab (as the Makhzen claims Morocco is) but Amazigh, with edgy identity politics. The Enjaaz post-production grant ($40,000) (and the subsequent 'special mention' awarded at the DIFF) honours not so much an Arab cultural product as a film that highlights the Amazigh component of Moroccan culture and originates in a traditionally marginalised indigenous group in the Kingdom.

Benamraoui is one of eleven Moroccan directors to have received an Enjaaz grant between 2011 and 2017. The total number of grants awarded to Moroccan directors in Dubai via the DFC and Enjaaz is a healthy twenty-six (see Table 2.3). Some of the directors received several awards, like Narjiss Nejjar, who secured funding for three films (*The Rif Lover, A Step Behind the Sun, Stateless*), and Hakim Belabbes for two (*Aïcha Bonheur, Weight of the Shadow*) – Belabbes also regularly reaps awards from the festival (see Table 2.4).

Table 2.3   Moroccan co-productions awarded grants from the Dubai Film Connection/Enjaaz, 2011–17

Year	Working title	Director	Type of funding
From the Dubai Film Connection			
2017	*School of Hope*	El Aboudi, Mohamed	Narrative
	The Unwanted	Boulifa, Anwar	Narrative
	It's Far Away Where I Must Go	Saudi, Karima	Narrative
2016	*Touda*	Aoulad-Syad, Daoud	Narrative
	Stateless	Nejjar, Narjiss	Narrative
	The Treasure	Taïa, Abdellah	Narrative
2015	*Weight Throwers*	Bensari, Hind	Documentary
	Pagan Magic	Boulika, Fyzal	Narrative
	A Step Behind the Sun	Nejjar, Narjiss	Narrative
2014	*None*		
2013	*None*		
2012	*Dance with Outlaws*	El Aboudi, Mohamed	Documentary
	Free Men	Ferroukhi, Ismaël	Narrative
2011	*Death for Sale*	Bensaïdi, Faouzi	Narrative
	The 5th String	Bargach, Selma	Narrative
From Enjaaz			
2017	*Joint Possession*	Kilani, Leila	Narrative
	Urgent	Besri, Mohcine	Narrative
2016	*None*		
2015	*Weight of the Shadow*	Belabbès, Hakim	Documentary
2014	*The Sea is Behind*	Lasri, Hicham	Narrative
2013	*Adios Carmen*	Benamraoui, Mohamed Amin	Narrative
	Sotto Voce	Kamal, Kamal	Narrative
2012	*Aïcha Bonheur*	Belabbès, Hakim	Narrative
	When Home Becomes Hell	Ennadre, Dalila	Documentary
	Salaam Plenty	Kassari, Yasmine	Documentary
	The Rif Lover	Nejjar, Narjiss	Narrative

Note: All films are feature-length. For more details, see: https://dubaifilmfest.com/en/completed-projects.html; https://dubaifilmfest.com/en/page/328/2015.html (accessed 26 February 2020).

Table 2.4 Moroccan co-productions: nominations and awards, Dubai International Film Festival, 2006–17

Year	Title	Director	Nomination/Award
2006	*Why the Sea?*	Belabbes, Hakim	Bronze Muhr, fiction
2007	*Sarah*	Leclere, Kadija	Nomination, short
	The Burned Hearts	El Maanouni, Ahmed	Nomination, cinematography (Pierre Boffety)
2008	*These Hands*	Belabbes, Hakim	Nomination, documentary
	Française	El Bouhati, Souad	Nomination, actress (H. Herzi)
	Casanegra	Lakhmari, Nour-Eddine	2 nominations: actor (A. el Baz), cinematography (L. Coassin)
2009	*The Man Who Sold the World*	Noury, Iman and Swel	Nomination, actor (Said Bey)
	Majid	Abbassi, Nassim	Nomination, fiction
	In Pieces	Belabbes, Hakim	Special mention (documentary)
2010	*Short Life*	Al Fadili, Adil	Nomination, short
	Dès l'aube	Ferhati, Jillali	Golden Muhr, scenario (J. Ferhati)
	Pegasus	Mouftakir, Mohamed	Nomination, cinematography (X. Castron)
2011	*Boiling Dreams*	Belabbes, Hakim	2 Golden Muhrs: scenario (H. Belabbes), cinematography (R. Bauche)
2012	*Defining Love, A Failed Attempt*	Belabbes, Hakim	Nomination, production (L. el Berki)
	Zero	Lakhmari, Nour-Eddine	Nomination, fiction
	My Brother	El Mahouti, Kamal	Golden Muhr, director
2013	*Adios Carmen*	Benamraoui, Mohamed Amin	Special mention (fiction film)
	Pillow Secrets	Ferhati, Jillali	Special mention (fiction film)
	Rock the Casbah	Marrakchi, Laïla	Special mention (actress Raouia); nomination, production (S. Carreras)
	They Are the Dogs	Lasri, Hicham	2 Golden Muhrs, actor (H. Badida); special jury prize, production (N. Ayouch)
2014	*The Narrow Frame of Midnight*	Hadid, Tala	Nomination, fiction
	The Sea is Behind	Lasri, Hicham	Nomination, fiction
2015	*Weight of the Shadow*	Belabbes, Hakim	Nomination, non-fiction
	Starve Your Dog	Lasri, Hicham	Nomination, fiction
2016	None		
2017	None		

Note: Unless "short" is mentioned, all films are feature-length.

In 2015, however, the Emirates NBD (an Emirati bank) partnered with Enjaaz to support the completion of film projects 'in the region', i.e. the Gulf Cooperation Council Countries (UAE, Saudi Arabia, Kuwait, Qatar, Bahrain, Oman).[63] The very notion of 'Arab film' seems to have shifted in Dubai from MENA productions – including one in Tarifit – to productions from the Gulf, and more specifically from UAE's nascent cinema. Moreover, as will become clear below, one perverse side effect of the competition for post-production grants in Doha or Dubai might ultimately stand in the way of Maghrebi co-productions, rather than reinforce Moroccan–Tunisian or Moroccan–Algerian collaborative projects. At this point, it is difficult to predict the future of co-production with the Emirates and Qatar, given the vagaries of regional and global politics and economics that affect the staging of festival local/global dynamics, in the way Bill Nichols theorised them (1994). Yet Dubai has hitherto provided much-needed support and transnational visibility to Moroccan productions – at least until the 2017 edition of the DIFF, which screened Nabil Ayouch's *Razzia* (2018) and Nour-Eddine Lakhmari's *Burnout* (2018). More crucially, perhaps, by offering an alternative hub for funding and co-production initiatives, it has also played a significant role in the 'de-orbiting' of Morocco from the former (French) coloniser's co-production system and Morocco's historical co-production partners. The funding sources were now diversified and included resources clearly outside the *francosphère* (Martin 2016). Finally (beside Saudi Arabia's latest radical changes around cinema going[64] and film production) Jordan might be the next game changer in terms of transnational visibility for first-time Arab directors with its announced International Arab Film Festival, which will welcome solely Arab film entries for competition (and screen films from the rest of the world outside competition) and award an *Awal* prize ('first') to first works, expanding the incubating film programme at the Royal Film Commission in Amman (since 2003) from Jordanian to pan-Arab.

Non-Western Co-production Networks (with North and Sub-Saharan Africa)

African co-productions with Morocco present a very different picture altogether, even if it is, once again, linked to geopolitics rather than commercial ventures. On the official intercontinental level, institutions created after independence (such as the two oldest Afro-Arab international festivals: JCC (Journées Cinématographiques de Carthage) in Tunis in 1966 and FESPACO (Festival panafricain du cinéma et de la télévision de Ouagadougou) in Ouagadougou in 1969; or the two laboratories: the Souissi Studios in Rabat and SATPEC in Gammarth, Tunisia), and treaties signed between nations reflect a national will to co-produce with African neighbours. However, the level at which the CCM seems able to invest money in international co-productions varies from treaty to treaty. For instance, the co-production treaty with the Union du Mahgreb Arabe (UMA) stipulates only that 'a general equilibrium must, as much as possible, be found among the producers',[65] whereas the proportion of each country's production funds can vary between 30 and 70 per cent in the treaty of co-production with France,[66] so that, according to Hicham Falah, the area for co-productions in treaties is quite circumscribed.[67] Another unofficial form of creative co-production takes place routinely in north and sub-Saharan Africa with Morocco, in the form of a circulation of experts and technicians from one country to the next, negotiated among individuals rather than institutions.

The official number of Moroccan co-productions on the CCM's website reveals two significant points. First, that co-productions between Morocco and its neighbouring Maghrebi nations are few and far between. Second, that those between Morocco and sub-Saharan African states happen more regularly and on a larger scale. Why might this be the case? The geopolitical lines (along the politics of the Moroccan state in the continent) seem to privilege a pan-African vision over a pan-Arab one. The data from the Moroccan Film Council[68] indicate that, since the mid-2000s, the CCM has co-produced a range of documentary and narrative shorts with filmmakers in Iran, Angola, Nigeria, Cape Verde, and, across the French-speaking African world, in Algeria, Benin, Burkina Faso, Cameroon, Guinea, Ivory Coast, Mali, Senegal and Tunisia. Here, the CCM focuses on 'lateral' collaborations, mostly with other francophone nations in sub-Saharan West Africa as well as in the Maghreb, in its attempt to reach alternative production hubs away from the former métropole (France). Longstanding cooperation with sub-Saharan African filmmakers – such as Ousmane Sembène, who first came to Rabat to use the CCM's post-production facilities as early as the 1970s – remains a strategic priority for the CCM.[69] According to Malika Hammoucha, external relations manager for the Khouribga African Cinema Festival, the CCM engaged in the co-production of as many as thirty-three African films – shorts, features and documentaries between 2005 and 2015.[70] Stef Van de Peer identifies such initiatives as part of a recent trend for greater pan-African (rather than francophone) collaboration in both African festivals and production practices (2016: 5–6) – hence the creation of five bilateral treaties between Morocco and sub-Saharan West African nations (Senegal, Mali, Niger, Ivory Coast and Benin) since 1984. In each case, these official agreements tend to emphasise the geopolitical focus of international cooperation between both signatory nations, rather than any commercial venture.

They also reflect the history and politics of the Kingdom of Morocco in Africa, and the history of continental initiatives such as the Pan-African Federation of Filmmakers (FEPACI), created in 1969 in Algiers. Its members, mostly from francophone Africa, whose 1970s' vision of an anti-imperialist pan-African cinema has evolved into one that defends the rights of filmmakers to the free expression of diverse cultures throughout Africa, seeks to share scarce resources across borders, and demands the creation of the FPCA (Pan-African Fund for the Cinema and Audiovisual Industry)[71] from the leaders of the African Union. The governmental winds blowing in Morocco are in favour of African collaboration as well. After a thirty-three-year hiatus created by the Sahrawi conflict (the majority of the Organisation of African Unity (the predecessor of the African Union) had voted to recognise the Sahrawi Arab Republic, siding with the Algerian Polisario on the Western Sahara dispute), the Kingdom reintegrated the African Union and Mohammed VI created a Ministry for African Affairs. The King's political will to further strengthen Moroccan economic links to the rest of the continent has had a direct impact on the CCM. In 2017, Sarim Fassi Fihri, bemoaning the absence of co-productions in the preceding two years, announced that the CCM was planning to set up a pan-African film fund supported by Moroccan companies throughout the continent. The aim was to accelerate the rhythm of Moroccan inter-African co-production with the continent, open up new avenues of co-production and reinforce existing Moroccan–African collaboration (Crétois 2017). For Africa can now claim some experience as shown by Hubert Laba Ndao's *Sidewalks of Dakar* (2013).

Sidewalks was co-produced by Senegalese production company Mediatik Communication and the CCM (with the participation of Fonds Sud, CNC, Conseil International de Radios-Télévisions d'expression française du Sud (OIF-CIRTEF), and Visions Sud Est). The film project was also supported by the ACP-Cultures + Programme (2012–17), an initiative implemented by the secretariat of the African, Carribbean and Pacific (ACP) States and funded by the European Development Fund. The aim of the programme was to stimulate transnational collaboration in order to develop viable and sustainable cultural industries and respect cultural diversity in the three regions. To that end, it aimed not only to reinforce film production and distribution in the ACP states, but also to professionalise the sector via international collaborations. The grant (€285,080, or 37 per cent of the total budget of €770,488) allowed Ndao to produce *Sidewalks*, to ensure its post-production on the African continent, to take part in the markets at Cannes and Locarno film festivals, and to distribute it in over a dozen countries in West Africa and Central Africa, while 'the fruits of South–South cooperation, provided the opportunity to turn actors and technicians into professionals' through exchanges of best practices between technicians from various African nations (Senegal, Congo, Mali, Cameroon, Central African Republic, Benin) as well as workshops to train ten non-professional actors.[72] The film presents an intriguing case of Moroccan–Senegalese co-production in that it was entirely shot in Dakar, more precisely in the Plateau district of the capital (the old European quarter made famous on screen in the very first postcolonial fiction film from francophone Africa, *Borom Saret*, by Ousmane Sembène in 1966), an Afropolitan space that encapsulates the multiple layers of society in a postcolonial city in Africa in the 2000s. The film focuses seemingly on a Senegalese local narrative circumscribed in time and space that is emblematic of most postcolonial cities in Africa and elsewhere. The camera thus shows the change in le Plateau's space occupation from a global business district by day into the shady marketplace for various illegal traffics run by squatters at night. The narrative (a love story between Salla and Siriou, two youngsters caught in the crosshairs of the nocturnal drug economy in which they try to survive), editing, art and rapper Didier Awadis's soundtrack definitely target an international audience, as attested by the various nominations and awards the film received on the international film festival circuit.[73] Here, the transnational co-production scheme with the CCM includes both a vital technical collaboration (in particular its post-production done by the CCM) and a shared African postcolonial theme: telling a story about illiterate youngsters trying to make a living in a global, clandestine economy in most cities on the continent.[74]

The CCM's focus on cooperation with sub-Saharan filmmakers rather than those from the Maghreb region (via a multilateral co-production treaty between Morocco and the Arab Maghreb Union) is striking. For example, between 2009 and 2015, the CCM website lists five co-productions with the Maghreb (three with Algeria, two with Tunisia), and twenty with francophone sub-Saharan Africa (two with Benin, four with Burkina Faso, one with Cameroon, six with the Ivory Coast, two with Guinea, two with Mali, three with Senegal). It also lists three co-productions with non-francophone sub-Saharan nations (Angola, Cape Verde and Nigeria).[75]

This dearth of collaborative projects with the Maghreb may result from several factors: Morocco and Algeria still face ongoing political tensions (around the Saharan question). Also, the Arab Maghreb Union, created in 1994, has mostly failed in growing intra-regional trade between Algeria, Morocco, Mauritania, Libya and Tunisia (Chtatou 2017). Or, as Moroccan producer Lamia Chraibi argued during a panel on international co-production at the nineteenth FNF (Tangier, 10 March 2018), the transnational hubs of production may have a perverse side effect, since producers from Africa and the Arab world often find themselves competing for the same regional or international funding from organisations such as Doha or the WCF for development, production or post-production. According to Hicham Falah, the small number of Maghrebi co-productions is mostly due to the financial limitations of Moroccan public funding, institutional barriers in each country and occasional political red lines, in spite of a commonly shared landscape and cultural references off screen, which unite film viewers across the borders (beyond the linguistic hurdles).[76]

Finally, unofficial co-productions between Morocco and other Maghrebi or sub-Saharan nations take the shape of the circulation of experts across borders and arise from individual meetings rather than official agreements. An excellent example of such collaboration is Farida Benlyazid's recurring use of experts in Tunisia and Senegal from her first feature film, *A Door to the Sky* (1988), a Tunisian co-production (before the treaty was signed with UMA) with the Tunisian state institution SATPEC and Tunisian producer Hassen Daldoul, with a Tunisian team (editor Moufida Tlatli and sound engineer Faouzi Thabet, who worked again with Benlyazid on her 1999 film, *Women's Wiles*). Later, Benlyazid's personal connection with Rokhaya Niang, whom she had met at the International Women's Film Festival in Salé led her to cast the Senegalese actress in her film for TV *Family Secrets* (2M, 2009).[77] As a result of this personal and artistic connection with Benlyazid, Niang found further work in Morocco, starring in Kamal Kamal's film *Sotto Voce* (2013). The more informal transnational collaborative networks established over the years by Benlyazid are an important reminder of how much emphasis filmmakers place on trusting individual relationships based on shared artistic values and a solid track record of collaboration, which often lie beyond the official structures of institutional initiatives or formal bilateral agreements.

Indeed, such individual instances of creative collaboration, under the radar of official co-production treaties, so to speak, are nonetheless regular occurrences in Moroccan and Tunisian cinema. Faouzi Thabet has been the sound engineer for numerous Moroccan productions, including Jillali Ferhati's *Make-Believe Horses* (1995), Saâd Chraibi's *Women . . . and Women* (1998), Ahmed el Maanouni's *The Burned Hearts* (2006), Daoud Aoulad-Syad's *Waiting for Pasolini* (2007), Hassan Benjelloun's *Where Are You Going, Moshe?* (2007), and Selma Bargach's *The 5th String* (2011). Algerian director Nadir Moknèche directed *Goodbye Morocco* (2013) with Moroccan director and actor Faouzi Bensaïdi in his cast. More recently, the latter also acted in Sofia Djama's *The Blessed* (Algeria/Belgium/France, 2017) as well as in Moknèche's *Lola Pater* (France/Belgium, 2017), while Hicham Rostom was cast in Selma Bargach's *The 5th String* (2011) and in Nabil Ayouch's *Whatever Lola Wants* (2007), with Tunisian actress Hind Sabri for the latter.

In the end, international Moroccan co-production possibilities with the Maghreb and the rest of the African continent have always existed, whether sanctioned by a co-production treaty or not. The current political climate is encouraging and might lead to the accelerated cooperation that the director of the CCM hopes for. At this point, co-productions outside European hubs are no longer strictly pan-Arab or pan-African, Maghrebi or sub-Saharan, but global in their financial dynamics and the expertise of their teams.

NOTES

1. For statistics on production, see *Le Bilan Cinématogropahique* (2017), available to download from the CCM's website: <http://www.ccm.ma> (accessed 31 January 2020).

2. Available data on co-production from the CCM are partial, relating to a range of international co-productions between 2009 and 2016 but including official international co-production feature films and some short films as well as TV films shot in Morocco by foreign production companies. Data on Moroccan–sub-Saharan African co-production are recorded separately on the CCM's website and the only data available are for 2011, 2012 and 2013. Data from the Lumière database, which include listings of all European–Moroccan co-productions distributed in Europe from 1996 to the present arguably provide a fuller picture, given that most co-production activity is with European producers and it is reasonable to assume that most European–Moroccan co-productions will have received some form of distribution in Europe.

3. For example, under the terms of European Convention on Cinematic Co-production (ECCC), renegotiated in 2017, the minimum contribution rate for each co-producer is now 5 per cent of the overall budget. This means that smaller territories are able to collaborate on bigger projects with producers from the big five of European cinema (France, Italy, UK, Germany and Spain).

4. An argument raised by Moroccan producer Lamia Chraibi during a panel on international co-production at the 19th Festival National du Film, Tangier, 10 March 2018.

5. Will Higbee and Flo Martin, interview with Egil Ødegård, Tangier, March 2018.

6. Figures for this study have been obtained by cross-referencing records from the CCM and other national film agency websites (e.g. the CNC in France) with industry databases such as the European Audiovisual Observatory (EAO) (Lumière) IMDB and CBO cine-chiffres, as well as the information available from individual producers' websites.

7. Source: Centre National du Cinéma et de L'Image Animée (2018), *Bilan 2017 du CNC*: <https://www.cnc.fr/cinema/etudes-et-rapports/bilans/bilan-2017-du-cnc_559489> (accessed 17 February 2020). Other issues of *Bilan* are referred to elsewhere in this text.

8. For more on the international dimension to the ECCC, see MacNab 2017.

9. Pablo César, Skype interview with Will Higbee, 9 August 2019.

10. According to the director, funding was initially split between INCA (51 per cent of funding) and the CCM (49 per cent funding) making Aregntina the majority producer. However, this split was revised to 55 per cent–45 per cent when less money was forthcoming from the CCM than had been hoped and as fluctuations in currency exchange, caused by a sudden weakening of the Argentinian peso meant that more money had to be found from private Argentinian investors to fill the gap (Pablo César, Skype interview with Will Higbee, 9 August 2019).

11. Pablo César, Skype interview with Will Higbee, 9 August 2019.

12. The reasons for this relative absence of Moroccan producers at key international festivals and markets are explored further in Chapter 6.

13. Flo Martin and Will Higbee, interview with Farida Benlyazid and Jillali Ferhati, Tetouan, November 2017.

14. Serge Le Péron was awarded 2.5 million MAD in production aid from the CCM in 2004 for his feature *I Saw Ben Barka Get Killed* (2005), though the film was co-directed with Moroccan director Saïd Smihi.

15. See, for example: Gregson (2012), Finney (2014), Jones (2016a and 2016b).
16. Flo Martin and Will Higbee, interview with Jillali Ferhati, Tetouan, November 2017.
17. Lamia Chraibi, EFM Panel on Arab Cinema, Berlin February 2016.
18. Oliver Laxe, cited in an interview with *Le Film Français*, 2015.
19. Will Higbee interview with Lamia Chraibi, Berlin, 13 February 2017.
20. 'I don't think the problem is the film; I think it's that they [Moroccans] prefer to support local filmmakers' (Will Higbee, Skype interview with Felipe Lage, September 2016).
21. Details obtained from *Mimosas'* international sales agent, Luxbox Films.
22. All figures from the EAO's Lumière database.
23. Will Higbee, Skype interview with Felipe Lage, September 2016.
24. Ibid.
25. Jamal Bahmad interview with Hicham Lasri, Casablanca, September 2017.
26. Will Higbee and Stef Van de Peer, interview with Hicham Falah, Tangier, March 2018.
27. Génini worked as the manager of the Club 70 screening room from 1970 to 1986, building an extensive network of contacts with the (mostly European) producers, distributors and festival directors, who screened films there. Capitalising on her association with Club 70, Génini established herself as an independent producer and distributor, specialising in promoting African and Arab (not to mention Moroccan) cinema before transitioning to a career as a critically acclaimed documentary filmmaker (Izza Génini, interview with Will Higbee and Flo Martin, Edinburgh 28 October 2017).
28. See Carter (2009: 227–29); Bakrim 2017; Adil Semmar, interview with Jamal Bahmad, 2017; Hicham Lasri, interview with Jamal Bahmad, 2017.
29. '. . . les cinéastes de la diaspora seraient déconnectés des réalités de leur pays, inaptes à en traiter, et même des traîtres qui se vendent aux Occidentaux en faisant des films élitistes.'
30. The example of veteran Moroccan director Ahmed el Maanouni serves as a useful example of how the filmmaker's response to his/her place in the diaspora – as well as the conditions and circumstances that led to 'displacement' from Morocco – is entirely personal. The first Moroccan director to achieve sustained international attention with his first two films *Oh the Days!* and *Transes* (1981), el Maanouni has been predominantly based (by choice) in Paris for many years. However, he is an active presence in Moroccan cinema (and was president of the Moroccan Chamber of Film producers in the 2010s), returns to Morocco to make his films and is more concerned with narratives located in Moroccan culture and society than in the diaspora. Indeed, his most recent feature *Fadma* (2016), a popular comedy, consciously orients itself towards a Moroccan, popular audience rather than the cinephile tastes of the international festival circuit.
31. As Arne Saeys' unpublished PhD thesis on ethnic minority filmmaking in the Netherlands explains (Saeys 2017), a handful of Dutch popular comedies focusing on the Moroccan diasporic community have achieved box-office success in the past decade . However, these have been directed by mainstream Dutch filmmakers, not directors of Moroccan origin.

32. *Volubilis* premiered in September 2017 at the Venice film festival, while *Stateless* received its premiere at the Berlinale in February 2018; both in advance of being screened at the FNF in 2018.

33. Approximately 350,000 people were expelled, a number that was intended symbolically to match the number of Moroccans who had apparently entered the Sahara as part of the Green March.

34. In *WWW – What a Wonderful World* (Bensaïdi, 2006) the serial killer muffles the sound of gunshot by systematically opening every single faucet in the lavatory. In *Volubilis*, having ordered Abdelkader's torture, the government official covers the sound in a similar fashion by opening all windows looking out onto the street below. Two friends in *Volubilis* try acting like fundamentalists by putting kohl around their eyes, just as they had in *Death for Sale* (2011). In *Volubilis*, a couple starts a possible love story over the phone, just like in *WWW*.

35. 'C'est une chance d'être entre deux pays, deux cultures. On a toujours besoin d'une distance dans le temps, l'espace. Cette double appartenance convient parfaitement à l'acte créatif.'

36. See *Cheb* (Bouchareb, 1991), *Bye-bye* (Dridi, 1995) and *Bled Number One* (Ameur-Zaïmeche, 2006). In these earlier Maghrebi–French authored films, beur protagonists are depicted as entirely alienated from the culture, language and community of the diasporic homeland (and in the case of *Cheb*, Malika is held against her will by the oppressive patriarchal regime of her extended family in Algeria).

37. In June 2016, el Arbi and Falah were signed up by Hollywood major Paramount to direct *Beverly Hills Cop 4*. They also recently directed two episodes of the US TV drama series *Snowfall*, created by John Singleton, about the impact of crack cocaine on the African–American community in Los Angeles in the early 1980s.

38. The neologism 'beur', derived from Verlan (French back-slang for Arabe), came into common usage in France during the 1980s. It referred to the descendants of North African immigrants who were either French citizens by birth or who had been raised in France from a young age and felt themselves to be as 'French' as they were 'Arab'. For more on the etymology and problematic politics associated with the term 'beur', see Durmelat 1998.

39. According to figures provided by the EAO, *The March* attracted 182,556 spectators in Europe, mostly in France – a respectable if relatively modest performance for a film of this budget and scope. The film was released in Morocco in late 2013, though information for the exact number of entries is not available. CCM records for the Moroccan box-office 2013/14 show that *The March* failed to break into the top thirty most popular Moroccan films, suggesting that the film would have attracted (at most) hundreds rather than thousands of spectators during a very limited theatrical release in Morocco.

40. For more on the politics of film festivals in Morocco, and the Marrakesh International Film Festival in particular, see Part Three.

41. The specific politics of Rhalib and Hadid's work are analysed in Chapter 4, 'Diverse Voices'.

42. The Sahara Lab initiative is analysed in detail in Chapter 3, 'Production from Below'.

43. 'Le Maroc inutile' refers to areas of the country identified by the French colonisers as of little economic value or strategic political or military importance (see: Gershovich 2000: 113). The term has since persisted to describe economically and socially disadvantaged spaces (Hoffmann 2013: 158–77).

44. Hakim Belabbes, interview with Will Higbee, July 2018.

45. 'I would say that for four of my films, the one thing I had access to was the television network in Morocco. I would get whatever I could to make a film, that was supposed to be a "made-for-television" film . . . When *Fragments* landed in the hands of Noureddine Saïl at the CCM, he basically asked me to blow the film up to 35mm, for the film to be shown in Tangier that year . . . first because it was non-fiction, which was not considered filmmaking and second because it needed to be in 35mm to be screened at the festival. I refused to do that because my point was that this film was not even supposed to be a film, it was just stuff that I was shooting. [In the end] the film was shown and I think that that film [*Fragments*] made a difference that year because there were 23 feature films – 21 were fiction films funded by the CCM, the exceptions being *Fragments* and Nabil Ayouch's *My Land*, another documentary. And Fragments ended up winning the prize for best picture that year' (Will Higbee, interview with Hakim Belabbes, July 2018).

46. Will Higbee and Flo Martin, interview with Edil Ødegård, Tangier, March 2018.

47. This assessment of Ayouch's work was offered by a number of Moroccan filmmakers present in discussion with the American TV producer and showrunner Alan Boul at a workshop chaired by Ahmed el Maanouni at the FNF in Tangier, March 2017.

48. For a detailed analysis of Hicham Lasri, see Chapter 4, 'Playing Around the System'.

49. '. . . the film trade and its exchanges of cultural capital have become global, with reputations even in the art cinema and independent sector rapidly expanding across national borders thanks above all to the festival circuits' (18) . . . Signifiers of the regional and the local are often successfully marketed in the global arena, while a more ethnographic impulse and purpose can be detected behind many of the films made in Europe, registering the fact that cinema has become part of culture as a resource for the general good: shared, prepared and feasted upon like food at the dinner table, rather than values only for the uniquely personal vision of the artist-auteur' (19) (Elsaesser 2010).

50. Sanad was part of Abu Dhabi's government-funded Media Zone Authority that shifted its focus by injecting funds into the UAE's film and TV production and job creation. Part of the 2014 $110-million package aimed at turning the UAE into a revenue-generating filming destination: together with Twofour54, the Media Zone Authority offers attractive incentives for anyone to film and produce in the Emirates, including a 30 per cent cash rebate on production spent on site, and free scouting assistance (thus fast becoming a real competitor for Morocco, deemed the safest country to film in – especially since the many filming spots in the Tunisian desert have been deserted since the Arab Spring).

51. See <http://www.sanadfilmfund.com/en/news/2016–02–25-SANAD-Films-Win-Big-at-the-Berlin-International-Film-Festival> (accessed 31 January 2020).

52. After their disastrous co-production of Jean-Jacques Annaud's *Black Gold*, the organisers of the DIFF started to rethink its financing of non-Arab directors, and

to sever Hollywood ties that did not serve a specific strategic purpose (Vivarelli 2015b).

53. Sixteen works of fiction, ten documentaries, four shorts.

54. In 2017–18, the DFI was somewhat affected by Saudi Arabia's air and land embargo against Qatar, which prevented some Arab directors from coming to Doha (for fear of repercussions at home), and, in turn, affected co-production and collaboration, but not for the two Moroccan projects.

55. See *Media Use in the Middle East*, 2016 (2016): <http://www.mideastmedia.org/survey/2016/> (accessed 31 January 2020).

56. See festival website: <https://dubaifilmfest.com/en/news/17/13128/dubai_international_film_festival_goes_competitive.html> (accessed 10 August 2018).

57. The first prize gave $50,000 in cash to the winner. In 2008, the festival added a Muhr AsiaAfrica Awards competition, and multiplied the prizes available in both Arab and AsiaAfrica categories to include best actor, actress, cinematographer, screenplay, composer for films that are 'Gulf premiere[s] and not previously shown on any television channel or streamed via the internet to any public audience'.

58. For the UAE competition: first prize: $13,500.00; second prize: $11,000.00; third prize: $8,200.00.

59. '. . . the Dubai Film Connection . . . introduced a co-production market in the UAE for the first time and 3 out of 15 projects for films from across the Arab world won prizes of $15,000 each and a chance to participate in the 2008 Cannes Producers Network' (Sekler 2008).

60. See <https://dubaifilmfest.com/en/page/158/about_enjaaz.html> (accessed 31 January 2020).

61. Mohamed Amin Benamraoui's interview with Flo Martin, Tangier, 8 May 2016.

62. In 1912, France and Spain agreed to formalise their zones of influence into two protectorates: the Spanish one in the northern part of Morocco (except for Tangier), Ifni, and Western Sahara, then called Sahara Español, and a French one in the rest of the country. The Spanish left the north (not the Sahara region) at independence (except for two cities, Ceuta and Melilla, which are still Spanish territories today). However, Franco was in power in 1956, and many Spanish citizens stayed in the Rif instead of moving to Spain.

63. Even festival nominations seem to concentrate on the Mashreq rather than the Maghreb these days, as do the latest Filmmaker awards. In 2015, the IWC Filmmaker Award is launched: named after the Swiss luxury watchmaker IWC Schaffhausen, it gives $100,000 to the best feature (over seventy-five minutes long) by an Arab director. But there's the rub: he/she has to be a citizen of one of the Gulf Cooperation Council Countries.

64. See <http://www.arabnews.com/node/1270436/saudi-arabia> (accessed 31 January 2020).

65. See article 7 in <http://www.ccm.ma/pdf/uma.pdf> (accessed 31 January 2020).

66. See article 4 in <http://www.ccm.ma/pdf/france.pdf> (accessed 31 January 2020).

67. Interview with Will Hibee and Stef Van de Peer, 15 March 2018.

68. See <http://www.ccm.ma/docs/liste-cooperations-internationales> (accessed 20 May 2018).

69. Will Hibee's interview with Hicham Fallah, Tangier, March 2018.
70. Hammoucha, cited in *Article 19*, 2017.
71. See FESPACI charter: <http://www.fepacisecretariat.org/wp-content/uploads/2016/05/FEPACI-Constitution-(FR).pdf> (accessed 21 May 2018).
72. See ACPCulture+ website: <http://www.acpculturesplus.eu/?q=en/content/dakar-trottoirs-0> (accessed 2 August 2019).
73. *Dakar Trottoirs* won the Grand Prix (Festival des Lacs et Lagunes, Ivory Coast, 2014), while Prudence Maïdou won best actress award at the African Film Festival of Khouribga (Morocco, 2014). It was also screened at the Festival Écrans Noirs (Cameroon, 2013), *FICA* (Burundi, 2014), Namibian Film Festival (Namibia, 2014), Toumai Film Festival (Chad, 2014), Festival du Cinéma Africain d'Apt (Marseille, 2014), Festival International du Film Panafricain de Cannes (France, 2014), Cinémas d'Afrique de Besançon (France, 2014), Vues d'Afrique (Montréal, Canada, 2014) to name a few.
74. See Olivier Barlet's interview of Hubert Laba Ndao (Barlet 2015).
75. These numbers were obtained by consulting two sources: the CCM data (sadly incomplete), and the Euromed report, op. cit. <http://www.ccm.ma/docs/liste-cooperations-internationales.pdf> (accessed 20 May 2018).
76. Hicham Falah interviewed by Will Hibee and Stef Van de Peer, March 2018.
77. Flo Martin's interview with Rokhaya Niang, Dakar, 27 May 2016.

PART TWO

PRODUCTION FROM BELOW: EMERGING SITES

Although the institutionalised spaces of production that we have just seen are central to the making and viewing of film in Morocco, parallel initiatives have developed to allow directors to produce films along distinct models. Of chief importance are the fairly recent film school and training programmes available in the Kingdom, through which young directors in the making are learning their trade. Some of them are national, others transnational, some are officially sanctioned by the state, others are not. The strength of the relationship with the state – with the CCM in particular – and the degree to which projects (whether educational or creative) are approved by the cinema authority vary across the various initiatives developed alongside the central system. The latter take on distinct and variegated forms: they are the alternative network developed by Hicham Lasri, for instance, who has achieved international fame and navigated transnational systems of funding successfully to produce his films; the one created by Nadir Bouhmouch who engages in guerrilla digital film production to make documentaries on themes that extend from the very local to the transnational. These initiatives are also those of Amazigh or of female Moroccan directors who surf the waves of transnational production to create their filmic narratives focused on their marginalised communities, yet always in solidarity with others over the border of their region or nation. It is to these rich diverse voices in cinema that exist side by side with a more officially sanctioned form of filmmaking that we now turn, as we decipher the ways in which the directors and their producers play within and outside the limits of the institutional system in place in Morocco.

3. ALTERNATIVE AND EMERGING NETWORKS

Alongside the institutional networks of production described in Chapters 1 and 2, alternative networks have arisen in the third millennium that have added diversity to the film landscape in Morocco. The creation of film schools and training programmes in various cities throughout the Kingdom has made it possible for budding filmmakers and film technicians to grow their skills locally rather than abroad. These establishments rooted on Moroccan soil offer training in a variety of skills, produce a wide range of practitioners, and have national and transnational dimensions. They rely, for instance, on national and transnational funds, invite experts from the nation and from abroad, and are increasingly part of networks with transnational reach. These systems of film training and production are not the only ones to offer parallel networks of production that are not always under the helm of the CCM: a couple of directors have found their own ways into filmmaking outside the ecosystem of Moroccan cinema, and reinterpreted the transnational in singular ways. Two radically different directors' trajectories will be explored as case studies: those of emerging auteur Hicham Lasri and activist-filmmaker Nadir Bouhmouch.

Film Schools, Education and Training

As the Moroccan audiovisual sector has expanded since the late 1990s, with growth in domestic film and TV production as well as the influx of foreign productions, an increasing need has arisen to provide formalised training for a new generation of Moroccan artists and technicians. Such education and training are achieved primarily through programmes delivered in either film schools or universities or through shorter industry workshops, often delivered in association with film festivals. Demands from within the industry that training be at least partly subsidised by the state via the Moroccan higher education system showed a will to rely no longer merely on a privileged minority of Moroccan filmmakers who are trained abroad or who can afford to study in private film schools (Carter 2009: 200). As a result, the number of institutions offering film training across the private and public sector, including standalone conservatoire style or industry-oriented film schools, as well as professional programmes delivered within the university system, has increased over the past decade. In part this can be seen as a consequence of the greater accessibility and affordability of digital production and post-production facilities, combined with steady economic growth in Morocco since the early 2000s that has led to capital investment from the state for such projects. It also comes, perhaps, from a relative opening up of freedom of expression in audiovisual media in Morocco over the past decade. However, this is not to say that Morocco benefits from an integrated network of film schools. The current structure might best be described as a system containing pockets of good practice in a general network of film training, educational programmes and curricula that is far from coherent and unified. It is, moreover, a system from which the CCM has tended to remain somewhat distanced, in terms of driving policy or training initiatives.

Though more exist across Morocco, the CCM identifies seven institutions that specialise in providing professional training and film education.[1] These seven specialist programmes (or, in some cases the institutions themselves) have all been founded since the early 2000s. One of these institutions, the Institut Supérieur des Métiers de l'Audiovisuel et du Cinéma (ISMAC), is in Rabat, two in Marrakesh (the Ecole Supérieure des Arts Visuels de Marrakech, ESAV, and a film programme taught from the School of Humanities at Cadi Ayyad University), one in Casablanca (in the humanities faculty at Ben M'sik University), two in Ouarzazate (Institut Spécialisé dans le Métiers du Cinéma Ouarzazate (ISMC/OFPPT) and the Faculté Polydisciplinaire de Ouarzazate) and one in Tétouan (a specialist documentary Masters programme based in the School of Humanties at Abdelmalek Essaâdi University). These seven institutions, spread out across Morocco, offer a range of programmes focusing on cinema, TV, visual arts and communication. Some place an emphasis on 'professional' (technical) training, while others provide a more rounded approach to film education that includes film history and theory, as well as practice-based training and research.

This final point is an important one, since it addresses the bigger question of the precise purpose of film education in the contemporary audiovisual landscape of Morocco. Should the primary goal be to train 'industry-ready' technicians equipped with the skill and knowledge to service primarily the Moroccan TV sector or the demands of foreign production companies working out of studios in Ouarzazate – a fact that might explain why four of the seven institutions recognised by the CCM are based in the south of Morocco (either Marrakesh or Ouarzazate)? Or might the need for film programmes that educate their students about the history and theory of the moving image – in the context of both cinema as a global art form and Moroccan cinema as a national cinema – be equally important? Indeed, the need for film schools and universities to promote a greater appreciation of film culture, history and cinephilia has become even more pressing with the demise of local ciné-clubs and the alarming decline in film theatres across Morocco (see Chapter 5). For his part, Jillali Ferhati, celebrated Moroccan director and film tutor at Abdelmalek Essaâdi University, laments the general lack of cinephile culture among Moroccan film students:

> These days, when you ask prospective students to name their three favourite Moroccan films, the majority will name three Moroccan TV films! As for a general cinema culture, most have no idea who directors such as Bergman, Griffith and Fellini actually are.[2]

Viewed from this perspective, film education and training also encompass an appreciation of cinema as a culturally and socio-politically relevant art form, allowing a plurality of authentic Moroccan voices to emerge from the next generation of filmmakers as well as a proficient group of technicians to populate the audiovisual industry. A brief consideration of three of these institutions – ISMAC, ESAV and the filmmaking programme at Abdelmalek Essaâdi University– will give a clearer sense of the varying offer for film students in Morocco as well as the challenges in creating a coherent training and film education network.

Founded by governmental decree in 2012 and opened in 2013, ISMAC is the first public film school in Morocco. Students are admitted on the basis of their *baccalauréat* grades (end of secondary school national exam) and a national entrance exam. There are no tuition fees. The school maintains a clear focus on the technical craft of development (screenwriting), sound, production and post-production and the explicit aim of training a generation of technicians to populate the national film and TV industry in Morocco.[3] Located in Rabat, the ISMAC has a clear proximity to both the administrative centre of the CCM (with whom the ISMAC signed a partnership agreement in 2015) and the Ministry of Communication, which ultimately controls its funding and management. This obviously practical focus on training technicians to work within the national audiovisual sector has two consequences: first, it limits the transnational reach of the ISMAC in terms of forging partnerships and initiatives for training and development outside Morocco. Second, it prioritises technical training, potentially neglecting how a broader understanding of film culture and cinema as a global art form might inform the artistic quality and reach of the work produced by its students.[4] The creation of Morocco's first public film school is, in and of itself, to be celebrated. However, ISMAC's location within the public education system can lead to problems in that it limits the ability of filmmakers without higher academic qualifications (Masters and PhD) to occupy permanent positions at the school.[5] Students have also complained more generally about a lack of access to practical training and equipment across the programme.[6]

Outside the public sector, the most prominent film education institution is the ESAV, a private (fee-paying) film school located in Marrakesh. Founded in 2006 and billed as 'Morocco's first bone fide film school' (Variety 2006), ESAV incorporates training in graphic and digital design with film and TV. ESAV was created and continues to be funded by donations from the Dar Bellarj Foundation (created by Swiss philanthropists Susanna Biedermann and Max Alioth), working in partnership with Cadi Ayyad University (Marrakesh), which donated the land for the film school and accredits the ESAV diplomas. ESAV charges high fees (approximately €6,000 per year in 2018) compared to other institutions in Morocco. Even with the current system of bursaries for applicants at ESAV, the film school is clearly not as accessible to most Moroccan students as ISMAC or other professional programmes running in state universities, where there are low or no tuition fees. Nevertheless, the school's guiding principle (as stated in its promotional literature) is to promote international cultural exchange through arts training, not to generate profit.[7] As such, the outlook of the school is resolutely international. ESAV has an international staff of film tutors, accepts students from across the world and has been run since its inception by Vincent Melilli, who used to work in cinema exhibition in France and as the director of the French Institute in Marrakesh prior to taking up his post at ESAV. Although the nationality of ESAV's principal benefactors and director, as well as its close links to film schools in France (La Fémis and l'École Nationale Supérieure d'Audiovisuel, or ENSAV) and Belgium (INSAS in Brussels), could lead some to presume that the school is essentially a Eurocentric institution, ESAV has fostered a transnational network of partnerships that includes but is not limited to collaboration with Europe. In addition to its partner institution in Toulouse (ESNAV, founded in the 1980s and one of three public film schools in France), ESAV has an international presence as a member of CILECT (the International Association of Film and Television Schools), via the exhibition of its students' work at international film festivals and participates regularly in a variety of transnational training and talent development initiatives involving European, African and Arab film schools, such as Meditalents and Dia-Sud-Med.

Located at the other end of the country, the Abdelmalek Essaâdi University in Tétouan operates somewhere between the nationally focused ISMAC and the internationally facing ESAV. The university has established a strong reputation for teaching a combination of film history, theory and practice since the introduction of its Masters programme in Cinematographic and Audiovisual studies (documentary filmmaking) in 2010. A limited number of students are admitted to the programme, based on a written application and interview. The focus on Moroccan film history and a broader appreciation of global cinema culture is significant in that it addresses a consistent gap in Moroccan training and film education. Hamid Aidouni, director of the film programme at Abdelmalek Essaâdi, suggests that young Moroccan filmmaker's insufficient knowledge of their own cinema culture, politics and history effectively creates a barrier to engaging with and developing the cultural specificity of their own films.[8] Though located within a humanities faculty, the programme at Abdelmalek Essaâdi arguably operates in a way that is closer to a film school than a university film department: students work extensively with Moroccan filmmakers, the programme has established partnerships with the Tangier Cinémathèque, the Chambre des Techniciens et Créateurs de Films and the Association of Moroccan Film Critics, while films by its students have been accepted into major international festivals, including Cannes. Abdelmalek Essaâdi's international reputation is further enhanced by its annual International Film School Festival (FIDEC), organised and hosted by staff and students since 2015, which plays to appreciative local audiences in Tetouan, includes masterclasses with visiting filmmakers, and attracts entries from film students in the Americas, Europe, Africa and the Arab world, as well as a programme that showcases the best work from the Masters in documentary filmmaking at Abdelmalek Essaâdi.[9]

Figure 3.1   Opening ceremony of FIDEC 2017, an international film school film festival organised by staff and students at Abdelmalek Essaâdi University, Tetouan (photo by authors)

Beyond producing technically proficient filmmakers to work across production and post-production in Moroccan cinema and TV, enhancing provision for training and film education is beneficial in relation to what Mette Hjort describes as 'transnational talent development' (Hjort 2018). One obvious example of such transnational talent development is the participation of Moroccan film students in internationally funded training initiatives, often with money from the European Union. Programmes such as Meditalents and Dia-Sud-Med bring film school graduates and emerging filmmakers from various countries and film cultures together to participate in targeted workshops in areas such as script development and writing funding applications.

Meditalents is a transnational talent development initiative, operating for almost a decade on both sides of the Mediterranean. Founded in 2011 by producer Didier Boujard with support from Canal France International, the CNC and the CCM, the scheme initially focused on short film development, expanding in 2013 to include development of feature-length film projects. Each year Meditalents selects eight to twelve projects by emerging filmmakers from across the Mediterranean, inviting them to participate in a series of three week-long writers' residences and then pairing them with experienced international filmmakers, who act as a project mentors. The scheme is also expanding into its first Mediterranean co-production workshops in 2019. By sponsoring and facilitating these initiatives in development and production, as well as hosting industry masterclasses at festivals and film schools, Meditalents aims to promote an intercultural dialogue between filmmakers from Europe and the Arab that functions as a genuine partnership of equals. The CCM (under the direction of Noureddine Saïl) was, in fact, instrumental in establishing the scheme in 2011. A number of Moroccan filmmakers have since benefited from the programme, with various script labs and workshops linked to the scheme being hosted in Ouarzazate and Tangier between 2012 and 2018. However, despite this strong Moroccan presence since the start of the scheme, the intense competition for places means that access to Meditalents is out of reach for most young Moroccan filmmakers, for a variety of reasons. Beyond the more predictable issue of lack of access to funds and resources, Boujard sees limited access to a more diverse film culture and contact with international film professionals and artists as a key barrier to young Moroccan filmmakers being accepted onto the scheme (for this reason, he argues that successful Moroccan candidates for the scheme are filmmakers of Moroccan origin living in the diaspora).[10] As with access to funding for international co-production, discussed in the previous chapter, an imbalance of opportunity emerges between the Moroccan cinéastes de passage and those based predominantly in Morocco.

Beyond technical training, such initiatives also present important networking opportunities for emerging Moroccan filmmakers to forge creative collaboration and target funding cooperation with foreign partners. They can even be seen as fulfilling a geopolitical and/or ethical role: fostering cooperation between filmmakers from Morocco and sub-Saharan Africa (such as in the labs and workshops offered as part of the Agadir International Documentary Film Festival (FIDADOC)), promoting collaboration and intercultural exchange between young filmmakers from across the Mediterranean region and audience building for such cross-cultural cinematic collaboration (Meditalents). Moreover, these activities can, as Hjort (2018) suggests, promote solidarity (rather than playing to a more cynical, politically motivated agenda) based on artistic and cultural values. In this context, a true collaboration of equals can enhance both the production contexts and artistic value of the filmic outputs that emerge from such training initiatives. Evidence of such transnational collaboration can, for example, be found in the ongoing success of the Tetouan International Film School Festival. Organised by staff and students of the Abdelmalek Essaâdi University, in 2017 the third edition of the festival attracted filmmakers from over fifteen different countries and hosted a series of masterclasses with Lebanese and Egyptian filmmakers and French film critics as well as a delegation from the London Film School and the Fresnoy (national studio of contemporary arts, Tourcoing, France). The festival also plays an important role in nurturing local film culture and connecting the university to local film audiences. Free festival screenings are open to a Moroccan public in the Teatro Español (an independent theatre and cinema located in the centre of Tetouan), bridging the gap between specialised film education and a more general cinephilia.

While Moroccan film students and emerging filmmakers are hungry for the opportunity to participate in such training and networking initiatives, nationwide provision is too often ad hoc, with insufficient coordination and support offered by the CCM, who, with the exception of limited workshops organised at their partner institution ISMAC (Rabat), seem happier to allow the film schools and film festivals to take charge of organising such events.[11] A common complaint from young and emerging Moroccan filmmakers (made, for obvious reasons, off the record to the authors of this book) is that they feel marginalised or overlooked by the CCM and at major film festivals in Morocco (such as the FNF) in terms of access to training, industry forums or masterclasses.[12] Evidence of the CCM's somewhat distanced attitude to emerging young Moroccan talent can be found in the selection criteria for the 'writers residency', funded with support from the Marrakesh International Film Festival Foundation, which has taken place annually in Ifrane since 2015. The week-long residency is exclusively open to Moroccan filmmakers developing a screenplay who have (crucially) already received an *avance sur recettes* award for the project. As a result, the residency is designed to benefit more established Moroccan filmmakers, with very few first-time writer/directors and no space for participation from emerging filmmakers or film students.[13]

ALTERNATIVE TRANSNATIONAL TRAINING NETWORKS: SAHARA LAB

While public institutions such as the ISMAC and private film schools like the ESAV may have a more visible presence at an institutional level, the ecology of practice-based film education in Morocco extends beyond film schools and university campuses to include informal, temporary or de facto training networks. The most obvious space for these alternative networks to thrive is under the auspices of the myriad film festivals across Morocco. However, as already mentioned – and with some notable exceptions such as the transnational training initiatives and workshops associated with FIDADOC – this is not happening in a sufficiently coherent or sustainable way under the direction of the CCM. Indeed, given that it controls a large share of public funding for film festivals across Morocco, the CCM could insist on more systematic inclusion of training and industry networking events for young filmmakers as a pre-condition of funding, if they so wished. Too often, these training networks rely on external funding from foreign sources, leaving Moroccan film educators and trainers at the whim of the politics and preferences of external funders, with little ability to build viable training initiatives in the medium or long term. Nevertheless, in the vacuum left by the CCM, other innovative, and potentially transformative, possibilities emerge – albeit in a rather precarious environment with regard to funding.

One of the most interesting recent initiatives as a site of alternative practice-based training comes in the form of the Sahara Lab. It is worth analysing the genesis and aims of the Sahara Lab in detail at this juncture, since it illuminates some of the limitations of the current system for training while offering alternative possibilities for future training and film education policy in Morocco. Created in 2015, the Sahara Lab is a Moroccan educational and media NGO that aims to address the current funding imbalance in Moroccan cinema towards fiction filmmaking by offering training and mentoring to emerging documentary filmmakers and new media artists from the south to 'tell their own stories about Morocco's diverse desert cultures'.[14]

Though the founders of Sahara Lab have not attempted to politicise this filmmaking and training initiative, the fact that the Western Sahara – a vast but sparsely populated desert territory of 266,000 square kilometres straddling Mauritania, Algeria and Morocco – is the site of one of the African continent's longest running conflicts, cannot be ignored. Colonised by the Spaniards in the nineteenth century and occupied by Morrocco since 1975 – or, reclaimed by Moroccans as part of Greater Morocco (al-Maghrib -al -Kabir), depending on the political perspective one adopts – the Western Sahara has been the site of decades of war, exodus, occupation and ongoing conflict 'irresolution' between the Moroccan state (including some ethnic Sahrawis) and native Western Saharans, who demand the right to self-determination:

Both sides agree that the dispute is over a piece of land. Yet abstractly, at the level of 'metaconflict', the dispute stems from mutually exclusive differences in the self perceptions that ground Moroccan and Western Saharan nationalism. It pits Moroccan irredentism against an indigenous desire for independence . . . From the Moroccan national point of view, the Western Sahara conflict presents a double affront: it seeks not only to undo Morocco (again) but also to do so through the validation of boundaries imposed through the original sin of colonialism . . . For Sahrawi nationalists, the conflict is just as much a matter of identity, a democratic claim to their exclusive right to the territory. Their conviction is as much the assertion that they are, first and foremost, Sahrawis – ethnically and nationally. (Zunes and Mundy 2010: xiii)

Whereas the Moroccan state identifies the protests and resistance of native Sahrawis through the Polisario Front as acts of terrorism, native Sahrawis view the Moroccans as an occupying force and point to the fact that nearly half of the indigenous Sahrawi population have been living in refugee camps in Algeria since 1976. Claimed by the state as a Moroccan territory since 1957, the Western Sahara is listed by the United Nations as a 'non-self-governing territory' – which is to say, subject to the process of decolonisation. While the Moroccan government speaks of regional autonomy, the UN considers the Polisario Front to be the legitimate representatives of the Sahrawi people and maintains the Sahrawis' right to self-determination – with reports by international observers of violations of the human rights of those Sahrawis who challenge the Moroccan authorities. Clearly then, in such an entrenched and extended conflict – and regardless of the intentions of the founders and participants of the Sahara Lab – the activities and outputs of this cinematic initiative will inevitably be seen by some on both sides of the conflict as an instance of soft power, inflected by the politics of the Western Sahara.

The Sahara Lab is the brainchild of Moroccan documentary filmmaker Hakim Belabbes, a lecturer in film practice at Columbia College (Chicago). In addition to teaching in the US and developing his own film projects, Belabbes worked for the DFI in 2014, restructuring the foundation's grant programme and its training arm, Qumra. He was also approached in 2015 to advise on the teaching programme at the ISMAC. In part, Belabbes' decision to set up the Sahara Lab emerged from his experience as an advisor to the ISMAC and what he saw as the more limiting possibilities and lack of innovative film education programmes in Morocco.[15] Belabbes elected to develop a new approach to film training in Morocco with the help of Don Smith (Professor in Cinema Art and Science at Columbia College, who had also worked as a producer on Belabbes' films and had extensive experience of working both in Morocco and as a story analyst for the DFI) and Hammadi Gueroum (Professor of Cinema Aesthetics at Hassan II university, Casablanca, and Artistic Director of the Rabat Cinema of Auteurs festival). Belabbes also invited a range of international filmmakers, including Tunisian cinematographer Amine Messadi and Swedish Moroccan post-production supervisor Peter Cohen to mentor participant filmmakers of the Sahara Lab initiative, working alongside film graduates from Columbia, who assisted in the production and post-production phases for the short films. Workshops in 2015 were based in the city of Laayoune, though the resulting short films were shot in a variety of locations across the Western Sahara. The following year, largely for logistical reasons, shooting for the Sahara Lab was limited to the city of Dakhla and its immediate vicinity.

For the inaugural Sahara Lab programme in 2015, Belabbes and his team received forty-five applications, from which fourteen participants were selected; the following year (2016), there were over seventy applications for seventeen places. The programme was innovative in its attempts to extend access to the world of film and image making/training to wider Moroccan–Sahrawi society. Applications were received on the basis of word-of-mouth publicity; some applicants came from outside the Western Sahara but the majority were Moroccan–Sahrawi (though none from the indigenous Sahrawi population who supported self-determination). Prior filmmaking experience or studies were not pre-requisites: 75 per cent of the participants in the two years of the Sahara Lab had never made films before, while only four of the fourteen participants in the initial 2015 cycle were film school students and there was no upper age barrier placed on participants.[16] Two films to emerge from the scheme, *Amchakab* (Maalainine, 2015) – a documentary about a young female Sahrawi journalist who attempts to ride on camelback as her mother once did – and *Shaor* (Mayara, 2016) – a contemplative film that explores the natural environment of the Sahara – were directed by a woman farmer and a calligrapher respectively, neither of whom had any previous filmmaking experience.

From the outset, a key focus in the Sahara Lab programme was on storytelling, ideation and development, with equal time devoted to the development phase and to production and post-production. The emphasis was on learning by doing and, just as importantly, according to Smith, creating a supportive environment where, creatively speaking, students had 'the opportunity to fail'.[17] As a result, although all the films produced by students concentrate on a unified geographical space (the Moroccan-controlled territory of the Western Sahara), they nonetheless display a range of stylistic and narrative approaches: from what might be considered more 'conventional' documentaries, with observational and *vérité* realism, to poetic, non-linear and more abstract forms of storytelling.[18] All films focus on the history, culture and geography of the Sahara. Most tend to foreground the natural environment, landscape and traditional customs of the region rather than the modern urban spaces of the Western Sahara. This is not to say, however, that the films offer a simplistic or clichéd representation of Sahrawi–Hassani culture that panders to an exoti-cised/Western view of the region (even that held by Moroccans from outside the Sahara). For example, the Sahara Lab film *Eid* (Ataalah, 2015) contains images of mint tea and Sahrawi tents but, particularly in its graphic docu-mentation of the ritual slaughter of a goat, is far from the folkloric image of the Sahara imagined in the West. Moreover, the festival of Eid is used in the film to contemplate a personal story of loss for the young female protagonist (the emotional trauma caused by her absent father) rather than an exoticised anthropological documentation of an indigenous religious festival. Nor is it the case that the films of the Sahara Lab retreat entirely from the juxtaposition of tradition and modernity: in *The Tree* (Horma, 2015) as a Sahrawi lumberjack traverses the timeless desert landscape, we see the encroaching activity of an industrialised phosphate mine on the horizon.

The guiding principal for Sahara Lab, as identified by Smith, was to give those who did not necessarily have access to the means of production the opportunity to 'find their voice' as artists and 'tell a Saharan story'.[19] Though, as already noted, the question of exactly what constitutes a 'Saharan' story is complicated by the geopolitical conflict in the Western Sahara; with the debate risking being hijacked by competing ideological and nationalist discourses beyond the control of the filmmakers involved in the Sahara Lab. The decision to focus on the art of storytelling addresses the general consensus across the Moroccan film indus-try (maintained by industry figures outside Morocco) that the areas in need of greater investment include development, pre-production and above all screen-writing. Story is placed at the heart of the process: participants in the Sahara Lab are selected based not on prior qualifications or experience but in relation to the stories that they have to offer. It is also important here to emphasise that such a focus on storytelling does not turn the Sahara Lab into a screenwriters' retreat to finesse narrative screenplays. As with Belabbes' own films, documen-tary was prioritised as much as fiction filmmaking, with a blurring of boundaries between the two. Belabbes, Smith and Gueroum thus dismissed a binary distinc-tion between documentary and fiction, embracing Italian neorealist screenwriter Cesare Zavattini's claim that: 'it is not important to invent a story that looks like reality . . . the most important thing is to tell reality as a story':[20] a bold statement of intent in the context of a film system in Morocco where, until very recently, documentaries were excluded from funding via the CCM's *avance sur recettes*, with documentary funding largely confined to the TV sector. The statement offers further evidence of a revival in documentary filmmaking in Morocco, supported not only by the Sahara Lab and FIDADOC but also by the MA in documentary filmmaking at Abdelmalek Essaâdi University (Kellou 2018).

Given the complex and potentially incendiary geopolitics of the Western Sahara region on a local, national and international scale, the act of giving a voice to young, predominantly Sahrawi filmmakers could, in and of itself, be seen as a political act. Though initially established with promises of financial support from the Ministry of Communication via the CCM, in the end the Sahara Lab only received a small proportion of the promised public funding.[21] In Smith's opinion, neither the CCM nor the Ministry fully understood the creative and educational aims of the Sahara Lab but were keen to offer support for other, more political, reasons:

> My feeling was that the CCM and the Ministry [of Communication] didn't really get it [the Sahara Lab] but what they liked about it was that it seemed to fit with the King's narrative [sic] of the Sahara as self-governing. They agreed to fund the films and then wanted to know where the films could be shown. In a very uncoordinated way they thought: 'There's something positive here for the King.'[22]

The emergence of the Sahara Lab must therefore also be viewed in the broader context of soft power and the cultural policies adopted by the Moroccan state since the constitutional reform in 2011 aimed at offering a greater visibility to the Western Sahara. Most pertinently for Moroccan (and specifically Moroccan-Sahrawi) filmmakers, these include the creation of both a fund to support documentary and feature film production related to the history and environment of the Sahrawi–Hassani culture (co-ordinated by the CCM) and an annual National Film Festival of Sahrawi–Hassani culture held in Laayoune since 2015. As already discussed, given the politics of the region, films depicting the Western Sahara risk almost inevitably becoming embroiled in a heavily politicised debate, while the question of who is funding such films (and why) can leave their creators open to charges of bias and propaganda from either side.

Although initially accepting modest funding from the Ministry of Communication via the CCM, and encouraging participants in the training programme to subsequently apply for funding from the CCM Sahrawi–Hassani fund for later films, the Sahara Lab strives to maintain its creative independence. Its aim appears to be to cater to the potential of a diverse group of Moroccan-Sahrawi filmmakers to tell their own stories, rather than creating politicised films from either side of the debate. In practical terms, Sahara Lab crews experienced problems shooting in Layoune due to the heavy police presence in the city. Such issues of the politics of representation, agency and who has the right to speak for the Sahrawi–Hassani people or represent the region have inevitably emerged in discussion among the participants and even in the films produced by the Sahara Lab. However, as Don Smith notes, any meaningful engagement with the politics of representing the Sahara also extends to a self-examination of the Moroccan-Sahrawi's own attitudes towards who has the 'right to representation' – an issue that is most keenly felt with the inclusion of women filmmakers in the Sahara Lab initiative.[23]

Beyond the obvious points of stepping outside of the established hubs of film production in Morocco (Casablanca, Rabat and Ouarzazate) to allow artists from an under-represented region to tell their own stories, the Sahara Lab has been innovative in its focus on development and storytelling as well as facilitating access for emerging filmmakers, artists and storytellers from non-traditional backgrounds to short film production. Though only in existence since 2015, the impact and legacy have been considerable: short films from the Sahara Lab have been screened in Morocco and internationally, including at the Smithsonian Institution in Washington, DC. Former participants in the programme have also been successful in applying for funding from the CCM's Sahrawi–Hassani film fund – which was previously criticised for supporting work of varying quality and being a source of income for a limited group of local filmmakers, rather than fostering genuinely creative filmmaking.[24] The Sahara Lab programme's emphasis on practice-based instruction (learning by doing) is also significant in a film training culture, such as that of the ISMAC, where, as Belabbes learned from first-hand experience, many Moroccan students are frustrated by the lack of access to equipment and sufficient technical training.[25] In addition to script and story development, Smith sees cinematography and sound design as areas where there is a skill shortage in Moroccan cinema, and where the Sahara Lab might direct its attention in the future.[26] In terms of training, while the Sahara Lab has initially relied on mentors from outside of Morocco, the medium- to long-term goal is to produce a pool of skilled local filmmakers; former participants will themselves become future mentors and tutors on the programme in years to come.

While the Sahara Lab is resolutely local in its focus on the Sahara region – with all the potential political complications that this can generate – it is far from provincial in its outlook on collaboration and educating filmmakers. Though the organisation's official website mentions the possibility of establishing a Sahara Lab Institute in the future, both Belabbes and Smith are wary of falling into a political compromise: that of being funded as a 'government' programme or by accepting funding from corporate sponsorship (most obviously from the economically powerful phosphate mining companies that operate in the region).[27] The independence and mobility of the Sahara Lab, as well as its relative freedom from the complexities that characterise institutional life, are undoubtedly part of its strength. When interviewed, Don Smith discussed the possibility of taking the training programme to another region of Morocco that is under-represented in terms of audiovisual presence in Moroccan film and TV (such as the Rif in Northern Morocco) or even expanding the training and production programme beyond Morocco if the right partners could be found.[28] Through its belief in the value of local stories told by Moroccan Sahrawi filmmakers, its ethical commitment (particularly in foregrounding female voices in the programme) and the success of its films with both national and international audiences, the Sahara Lab appears to confirm Mette Hjort's observation that an ethical 'scaffolding' and a 'collaboration of equals' behind such alternative training networks can lead to a practice of transnational talent development that ultimately enhances the artistic quality of the films being produced (Hjort 2018).

Two directors outside the Sahara Lab also share similar ethical values of solidarity and collaboration, albeit in markedly different contexts: Hicham Lasri and Nadir Bouhmouch. It is to the singular vision, practice and mode of screening of their films that we now turn.

Playing Around the System: Hicham Lasri

Hicham Lasri is not only one of the most talented and prolific Moroccan filmmakers today, but also a peculiar director, scriptwriter, novelist and playwright in several ways. Unlike most of his peers who belong to one category or another of Moroccan cinema depending on their film style, aesthetic choices and modes of production, Lasri is difficult to classify. This ability to defy categorisation is due to the fact that he occupies a liminal position. He is both an insider and an outsider in Moroccan cinema as a regimented system of visual production. This productive liminality is due to Lasri not being, like most filmmakers, markedly either a local or a diasporic filmmaker, nor is he someone who makes films neatly within or outside the funding and censorship ecosystem of Moroccan cinema. A second way in which Lasri's liminal status comes to the fore is through his experimental aesthetics; his films are liminal in not being avowedly experimental but rather formalist essays on a Moroccan society framed as absurd. A third manifestation of Lasri's liminality is embodied by the raw state and texture of his films, which require the viewer to be engaged and finish making the film in one's mind, so to speak. Fourthly, Lasri has recently turned out three web series on different issues occupying Moroccan and global society; the self-produced series have been released on YouTube alongside some of his short and early feature-length films, thus breaking away from traditional distribution networks. Lasri's films are also steeped in local and global popular culture, particularly alternative music and youth subcultures, in a way that renders parts of his films less conventionally cinematic. Last but not least, his movies have a political edge without aiming to be perceived as political cinema; as he explains, 'I'm not a committed filmmaker. I do not do politics' (Lasri, cited in Bougrine 2017a). Lasri and his films sit astride many worlds. As this section will show through film examples, he is an irreverent filmmaker and the *enfant terrible* of Moroccan cinema in the early twenty-first century.

Lasri was born in Casablanca in 1977. He has rarely left or worked outside his birthplace, a sprawling urban conglomeration and Morocco's largest city.

Everyday life in Casablanca and the absurd contradictions of urban society and modern Morocco at large are the main themes of his films. As he puts it:

> in all my films, the absurd occupies a significant part. Our society is so absurd that people do not even see that anymore. This absurdity is permeable. I am from Casablanca; I can't live elsewhere, but by living in one place, we are inhibited and saturated by information; we do not feel anything anymore and have no empathy left. (Lasri, cited in Bougrine 2017a)

Lasri studied law at Hassan II University in Casablanca, but his passion for creative writing and cinema made him pursue a career in fiction and filmmaking. After a series of shorts and TV films, Lasri jumped spectacularly onto the scene with *The End* in 2011. The black and white political thriller puts centre stage marginal characters and their impossible love stories in the urban jungle of Casablanca during the last years of King Hassan II's reign. The King ruled the country with an iron fist from 1961 until his death in 1999. Police violence, forced disappearances and arbitrary trials were rampant (Slyomovics 2005: 48). This created a claustrophobic society, where every aspect of life was dramatically affected by political violence. Lasri grew up in the shadow of Hassan II and his mighty Interior minister, Driss Basri, who prominently features in *The End* as the police commissioner Daoud, nicknamed the System's Pitbull. Basri is also the main character in Lasri's *Starve Your Dog* (2015).

Lasri's personal and cinematic obsession with Hassan II's regime, or rather what it was like growing up in Morocco during his reign, forms the background to most of his films. Even when the 2011 uprisings swept across Morocco and the MENA region and Lasri decided to make a film about the ongoing events, he could not avoid Hassan II and Basri. *They Are the Dogs* (2013) opens in the main square of Casablanca, where a group of young people are shouting slogans against the rising cost of living and calling for political reforms in Morocco. Whilst the youth are protesting and their cheerleader calls for the fall of the regime, a TV crew is seen trying to film a news story about the street protests. While the crew are struggling to find something interesting to say about the daily protests, another figure makes its appearance in the square: a frail man holding his shoes in his hands. The Beckettian character looks out of place in 2011 Casablanca. He catches the attention of the journalists, who try to interview him in vain. He has just been released from a secret prison, where he was interned following the Bread Riots of June 1981 in Casablanca. The former prisoner Majhoul (literally 'unknown' in Arabic) has forgotten his own name after thirty years in jail. His inmate ID is 404, and that is all he remembers. The TV crew accompany him around Casablanca while he searches for his family. They take him to the cemetery where the dead victims of the Bread Riots were buried. He chances upon his own name on a grave, where his family had been told his body lies. The dead–alive 404 finally finds his family, who refuse to accept his return. His wife has married another man and has had children with him. His only son is now married and has a son of his own. On leaving the family house, 404 meets his own grandson who has spent the night in detention at a police station because of his involvement in the ongoing 2011 protests. The shoeless grandson takes to his grandfather, and the film manages to make the connection between the past and present struggles of Moroccans for a better political system. Lasri's punk road movie at the heart of the 'Arab Spring' is shot with a handheld camera. The shaky camera movements and affective charge of every moment of the film translate the urgency of its subject matter (i.e. the 2011 uprisings) and the confusion surrounding Morocco's past, present and future.

The filmmaker has carried the same technical experimentation, especially the innovative in-camera effects and the thematic concern with everyday life under an authoritarian regime, into his next two films in the Dog Trilogy: *Starve Your Dog* (2015) and *Headbang Lullaby* (2017). *The Sea is Behind* (2014) and his most recent feature film, *Jahiliya* (2018), are along the same line of the canine trilogy. Unlike *They Are the Dogs*, which was made on a shoestring budget without the financial involvement of the CCM or any foreign producers, the dog trilogy and the episodic *Jahiliya* are relatively big affairs for a director who has shunned big productions. This is despite the international success of his films, especially *They Are the Dogs* and *Headbang Lullaby*. Unsurprisingly for a filmmaker who does not want to be seen or act

Figure 3.2 *They Are the Dogs* (Lasri, 2013): a punk road movie at the heart of the Arab Spring

as a Global South filmmaker making cliché-saturated films for the Western gaze,[29] Lasri has continued to make sophisticated films centred on unconventional characters in the manner of the 1970s American and German independent cinemas. Lasri stands out in the Moroccan film scene not only thanks to his thematic consistency and filming style, but also because of his innovative production methods. He is more resourceful in looking for funding, unlike most Morocco-based and other filmmakers who rely almost exclusively on CCM funding or money from Moroccan TV.

One needs to go back to the beginnings of Lasri's film career to understand his unique trajectory in the complex world of Moroccan film production. Lasri first emerged on the scene with *The Iron Bone* (2007). The film was commissioned by the Moroccan public TV channel SNRT and produced by Ali n' Productions, the Casablanca-based production company owned by the Moroccan–French director-producer Nabil Ayouch. Lasri has kept a close relationship with Ali n' Productions, the centrepiece in the Ayouch media empire, which has produced many of his films and almost all his work for Moroccan TV. In 2008, he made *TiphinaR* thanks to funding from Ali n' as part of its SNRT-funded Film Industry – Made in Morocco (2005–7), a scheme created to boost film production in the country by training new 'directors, screenwriters, assistant directors and producers, photo directors, lighting designers, stage managers, costume designers, decorators, props, cameramen, editors, and special effect designers' (Ayouch 2009). Thirty films were reportedly produced under this scheme, although only eighteen have been shown on TV (see Chapter 1). The scheme was critical for the emergence of Lasri in a country where young filmmakers find it hard to get established. The CCM funding system has often been criticised for favouring already established filmmakers (Bougrine 2017b).

It usually takes three to five years for Moroccan directors to make a film with funding from the CCM and potentially some international co-producers. Lasri has managed to be an exception by turning out roughly one film every year since 2011.[30] What is more, this high level of productivity has not come at the cost of the quality of his films. Lasri is unique among Moroccan filmmakers (indeed unique among filmmakers worldwide) in the sense that his last four films have been selected in four consecutive years for the Berlinale, one of the world's leading and most prestigious A-list film festivals. This achievement is thanks to his work pace and creativity:

'I think I'm still lazy because I can do more', he opines. 'I think it's the film production scheme in Morocco which is too long. Today, to make a movie according to the CCM standards, it takes 4 years! It's way too long. My pace is much more in sync with society than with the slow film institutions.' (Cited in Boushaba 2017)

Produced by Ali n' Productions, Lasri's third feature film *They Are the Dogs* (2013) illustrates his varied and creative production methods. The film's from-below mode of production was almost unheard of in Morocco. When the so-called Arab Spring events began unravelling in 2011, many filmmakers felt the urge to address what was happening. Many documentaries and fiction films were made about the uprisings, but this was done mostly in countries like Tunisia where regimes were toppled and, with them, the spectre of censorship. In Morocco, the situation was unique. The regime swiftly responded to the protests with some political reforms and temporary salary increases in the public sector. Most filmmakers in the country avoided the hot topic of the 2011 protests, especially because the main funder of film production remains the state agency, CCM. Believing that freedom is always taken and never granted, Lasri decided to tackle the ongoing uprisings.[31] Without applying for filming permission nor funding except for a small budget (100,000 MAD) from Ali n' Productions, he took his camera into the streets of Casablanca and shot *They Are the Dogs* in about a week. The film was an immediate sensation. It won multiple prizes at international film festivals and made Lasri a household name in Moroccan cinema.

Another way in which Lasri has diversified his production methods is by producing his web series, which put him somewhat outside the film production system. In an interview in September 2017, he reveals how web series allow him to react to political, social and cultural questions in Morocco immediately, with more freedom of expression, and in a language that is genre-specific. During the month of Ramadan in June 2016, Lasri surprised everyone by releasing daily episodes of his first YouTube web series, *No Vaseline Fatwa*, after *Iftar*. Episodes were timed to appear online at precisely the time of the day in Ramadan when every Moroccan family is glued to their TV set to watch comedies, sitcoms and soap operas. Lasri, who regularly makes such programmes for TV with Ali n' Productions, made the side-dish web series *No Vaseline Fatwa* with a discourse and language that would be too shocking to show on TV. The self-produced thirty-episode series stars Salah Bensalah, the cowboy-looking tall man who has featured in many of Lasri's films. In the series, he is a Moroccan Jihadi in Afghanistan who threateningly issues fatwas on different subjects with a Kalashnikov in one hand and a Vaseline jelly jar in the other. He uses swear words and sexual language in contrast to religious preachers. Lasri capitalises on the unfamiliarity of his mufti to deconstruct various living contradictions of Moroccan and Muslim societies. The self-production methods, three-person film crew (actor, Lasri as cameraman and director, and an editor), and free online distribution via YouTube allowed Lasri a large margin of freedom of expression during the holy month, when Moroccans devoutly surf the Internet during the long Ramadan nights consulting everything from soccer and religious websites to porn hubs (Albertelli 2016).

Released in late November 2016, the seven-episode and self-produced *Bissara Overdose* focuses on the misogyny and hypocrisy of men in a patriarchal society. The actress Fadoua Taleb does not mince her words on the subject, using every entry from the swearing dictionary of Darija. In the first episode, Fadoua is shocked because her Moroccan boyfriend ditched her by going to Italy and marrying a *gawriya* (European woman),

> who would not know how to make him couscous nor accept to be beaten by him. Here [in Morocco], we beat them [women], we break their teeth, we tear their hair, and then in the end, they wear makeup to hide the scars on their bodies and tell their neighbors: 'It's my husband, he beat me but he would not let anyone else touch me!'

Released in mid-December 2016 and produced by Lasri, the four-episode *Caca-Mind* stars Badia Senhaji, who berates Moroccans for aspects of their everyday behaviour such as throwing trash almost anywhere in the streets, insensibly honking the horns of one's car or jumping the queue. The web series have allowed Lasri both a vast freedom of expression and the capacity to react swiftly and with biting humour to social and political events in Morocco and abroad. Although the mosaic structure of his feature film *Jahiliya* already provides some evidence, it remains to see how this new genre will impact the filmmaker's future movies and career.

Lasri is both an insider and outsider in the Moroccan film world. His prolific output, unconventional film style and production resourcefulness have helped establish him as a significant voice in Moroccan cinema and an international film festival fixture. He started as an insider by working with Ali n' Productions making films for TV. His subsequent films made for the cinema and the web series have revealed him also as an outsider in the sense that he can also produce films with personal, minimal or international funding. He has established himself as a maverick filmmaker whose every film surprises even his most ardent followers. Yet he is the same insider filmmaker who makes popular sitcoms shown on Moroccan TV during Ramadan, one of the most profitable time markets for TV productions in Morocco and the Islamic world (Armbrust 2005: 214).

GUERRILLA FILMMAKING AND POLITICAL ACTIVISM: NADIR BOUHMOUCH

A mere 140 kilometres to the northeast of the Atlas Film Studios in Ouarzazate, where dozens of Hollywood and other international films have been shot over the decades, lies Imiter (also spelled and pronounced as Imider). The inhabitants of this Tamazight-speaking community of seven villages have lived on transhumance and subsistence farming for centuries. Tourists who flock to Ouarzazate, a major destination for international holidaymakers thanks to its film and natural attractions (see Chapter 1), are unlikely to have ever visited or heard of Imiter. Not that they would be encouraged to do so by the Moroccan authorities, for Imiter is the scene of a drama of a different nature from the celluloid mythologies of Ouarzazate. The poor community at the epicentre of 'Useless Morocco' is home to the biggest silver reserves in Africa and seventh in the world. The profitable mine is exploited by the Société Métallurgique d'Imiter (SMI), a subsidiary of the mining group Managem, which is mainly owned by the private holding company Société Nationale d'Investissement (SNI) of the Moroccan royal family. SMI has been operating in Imiter since 1969. On its website, Managem reveals that the mine has an annual output of 300,000 tons of silver-metal with a purity rate of 99.5 per cent.[32]

Although SMI is the main employer in the community, the people of Imiter are not happy about it. In fact, they have been involved in a long struggle against the mining company. The locals decry its overexploitation of the arid region's limited underground water reserves in the processing of the extracted silver, the rising air and water pollution levels caused by the use of toxic chemical products in the processing plant, and SMI's prioritisation of non-locals in job creation. The Moroccan authorities have stood by the mine in this long struggle against the local community. The first face-off between the company and the locals took place in 1986 after the company decided to dig a new well to supply its processing plant with water. The community raised concerns about the well's impact on the underground water reserves. SMI turned a deaf ear to the protests and dug the deep well of discontent. The authorities arrested many protesters and sentenced six of them to one to two years behind bars for taking part in 'a revolutionary rally in order to attack the authorities'.[33] Led by local mine workers and the villagers, the second major confrontation occurred a decade later, after SMI became a private company with SNI as the main shareholder with 80 per cent ownership of its capital. The peaceful sit-in by the side of N10, the national road linking Ouarzazate to Tinghir, lasted for forty-five days before the security forces crushed it, leading to the death of one protester, Lahcen Usbddan, and more absurd jail terms. Demonstrations reoccurred again in 2004 after SMI decided to dig yet another contentious well.

In summer 2011, events took a turn with an impact felt way beyond Morocco. Led by university students and armed with an acute awareness of indigenous rights and similar global struggles, the villagers shut off one of the pipelines supplying the mine processing plant with water after failed attempts to get the authorities to listen to their woes against SMI. On 1 August, they set up a protest camp on Mount Alebban next to the blocked pipeline. Defying the extreme desert weather, they built makeshift huts on the hilltop and set up a school for the village children, who boycotted their local school the following year in order to draw attention to their community's ordeal. The camp also served as a hub for cultural activities such as music, theatre and (significantly fort the purposes of this study) a film festival. The stone huts were adorned with graffiti and slogans, from the protest movement's motto, 'To Exist Is to

Resist', to quotations by Martin Luther King and Mother Teresa. The delicate context of the 2011 uprisings in the MENA region forced the regime to refrain from direct action to break up the camp, which until its lifting by the protesters in late September 2019 was Morocco's longest running sit-in. Instead, the authorities sporadically arrested thirty-three activists and sentenced them to up to four years in jail on flimsy charges (Amnesty International 2015). Meanwhile, the actions of the protesters continued to have a significant impact on SMI: the production output of the mine dropped by 40 per cent in 2012 and 30 per cent the following year due to the water supply cut by the protesters camping on Mount Alebban (Alami 2014). Calling their protest movement 'Amussu Xf Ubrid n 96' (Movement on the Road of 96) in reference to the events of 1996, the activists on Mount Alebban mobilised social media and amateur filmmaking to publicise their protests, especially the weekly peaceful match along N10 and the ensuing *agraw* gathering, an age-old Amazigh form of democratic government, whereby the villagers discuss their struggle and take decisions openly.[34] 'After each meeting held at the foot of the hill', *The New York Times* reported in 2014, 'the villagers walk back home holding up three fingers – one for the Berber language, one for the land and one for mankind – hoping for someone to hear their call' (Alami 2014).

The controversy and environmental impact of the SMI's expropriation of the wealth beneath Imiter's surface is not a typical subject for Moroccan cinema. Despite having been lauded for breaking various taboos over the last twenty years, Moroccan filmmakers have carefully refrained from tackling issues such as the Imiter protests that would be considered too sensitive (politically and economically speaking) by the Makhzen. For example, talking about human rights violations in the present would be a matter of crossing the red lines of permitted freedom of expression. The story of Morocco's 'Years of Lead II' as it takes place in Imiter or the Rif has therefore to wait for several more years (or even decades) before it can be told in Moroccan cinema, and, when it finally arrives, it will be celebrated for its audacity and political commitment. Another notoriously taboo topic is the exploitation of highly profitable mines by corporations owned by the royal family. Such is the case of Imiter, and hence its untold story on the screen. Only a radical filmmaker would dare to film the struggle of a small mining community against the politico-economic Goliath.

In early 2011, Nadir Bouhmouch was a film studies student at San Diego State University in California and had the bright future of any upper-class Moroccan young person ahead of him. However, the 'Arab Spring' dramatically changed his life. The street protests in Morocco led Bouhmouch to return to the country to film and take part in the demonstrations. As his first documentary *My Makhzen and Me* (2012) chronicles, he became close to the youthful February 20 Movement (20FM), the main organising body of the street protests beginning on 20 February 2011. The demonstrations lasted for months demanding political reforms and social equality in the neo-liberal kingdom, but the monarchy reacted swiftly with the King's address on 9 March promising various reforms through a new constitution. The constitution went into effect after a popular referendum on 1 July 2011 approved it with a reported Yes vote of 98.5 per cent. The rate and intensity of 20FM demonstrations decreased until they stopped altogether in 2012 (Shirk 2014). Meanwhile, Bouhmouch and thirty members of 20FM embraced what they call artivism, a combination activism and art, and established the Guerilla Cinema group to continue their resistance to the regime through independent filmmaking and cultural activism (Shirk 2014).

In Morocco and beyond, guerilla filmmaking is a form of political cinema infused with a Third Cinema spirit. It is distinguished by its low-budget films, short shooting schedules in real locations, small crews, improvisation, shooting without filming permits, and non-commercial distribution (Xavier 1997). Bouhmouch has chosen this path since 2011. *My Makhzen and Me* was self-produced by its director and screenwriter. It was made on a minimal budget and released online free of charge. By making his work available for free, Bouhmouch is refusing to implicate himself within the film industry as a commercial enterprise. It allows him an ethical and political freedom from the system/industry. It is a principled stance and a political act. Moreover, the film was notoriously made without the mandatory CCM filming permit. Neither did Bouhmouch apply for a professional card from the CCM to be legally considered a filmmaker. The next documentary films that Bouhmouch made as part of the newly created Guerilla Cinema are even more radical and typical of guerilla filmmaking. They were made collectively with members of the Guerilla Cinema, all former members of 20FM, alternating in directing, producing and scriptwriting the films. The group's first film, *475* (2013), is directed and produced by Bouhmouch. The first black frame informs the audience, 'This is not commercial film'. The next frame states the following in Darija, colloquial Arabic – rather than French or classical Arabic as is customary in Moroccan cinema – 'This film was made outside the law as a form of civil disobedience to demand freedom of speech and art in Morocco, and also to protest the monopoly of film production by the CCM'. Produced by Guerilla Cinema and freely distributed on Vimeo and YouTube, the militant documentary focuses on the Amina el Filali affair to question Moroccan society and law about women's rights and sexual violence. In March 2012, sixteen-year old Amina shocked the country by committing suicide after she was forced to marry her rapist in accordance with Article 475 of the penal code, which allowed rape perpetrators to escape jail terms by marrying their victims. The infamous article was repealed in 2014 following national and international outcry helped by Guerilla Cinema's *475* and Hind Bensari's web documentary *475: Break the Silence* (2013).

The guerilla artivists' next film, *Basta: The Film That Was Never Made* (2013), was shot simultaneously with *475*. *Basta* is co-directed by Younes Belghazi and

Hamza Mahfoudi, both former F20M activists. The thirty-minute documentary questions the state of Moroccan cinema and criticises the CCM's censorship of independent filmmakers. Faithful to the principles of guerrilla filmmaking, Belghazi and Mahfoudi made the film without the state agency's permission and distributed it online free of charge, thus benefitting from the new distribution opportunities offered by the digital revolution (Bahmad 2016: 90–1). The camera became a weapon of resistance to the Makhzen and its sanctioned cinema made through the CCM production circuit. *Basta* documents the problems that the guerrilla team faced as they were making *475* without permission. It also secretly films the offices of CCM staff members, who are not in their offices in daytime when they are supposed to be there to help filmmakers, aid researchers and promote Moroccan cinema. The CCM is revealed as a bureaucratic machine to censor and block the development of independent cinema.

The Guerilla Cinema group is in a dormant state today with its members having moved on to do different things on their own or with other partners. Such is the case of its co-founder, Bouhmouch, who has shifted his attention to the environment and social justice issues in recent years. Since 2015, Bouhmouch has spent extensive periods of time immersed in the Mount Alebban camp. He learned some Tamazight in the process and became one of the spokespeople of the struggle through his journalism and films. The participant observation and transnationalisation of the struggle have allowed him to gain a deep understanding of Imiter's saga as well as that of similar global cases. This experience enriched him as a Marxist militant and filmmaker, who has matured politically and honed his cinematic skills on the ground. He recently finished a documentary called *Amussu* (2019), which he had been making with the Imiter community since October 2016. During that period, he has also helped create the International Imider Environmental Justice Film Festival (IIEJFF). He has also made two short documentaries, *#300kmSouth – Imider has a Speech* (2016) and *Timnadin N Rif* (2017).

#300kmSouth (2016) is a four-minute, short documentary made and released on the occasion of Morocco hosting the 2016 United Nations Climate Change Conference (COP22) in Marrakesh, 7–18 November 2016. For environmental and anti-globalisation activists such as Bouhmouch, the UN summit was evidence of Morocco's greenwashing or the use of climate change rhetoric to mask the neo-liberal expropriation of natural resources and impoverishment of human communities such as Imiter (Bouhmouch 2016). The conference was sponsored by multinational corporations such as Managem and OCP, the Moroccan phosphate company, which is also blamed by activists for environmental damage. Bouhmouch finished *#300kmSouth* a few days ahead of the event. Imiter activists joined other national and international grassroots environment activists in Marrakesh, where they marched and held film screenings to counteract COP22 greenwashing. For example, Imiterians marched next to representatives of Standing Rock, the Native American tribe that has

been fighting against the Dakota Access Pipeline since early 2016. For days, Marrakesh was an arena of transnational resistance against neo-liberal globalisation and its symbols from Coca Cola to Managem, which owns SMI. *#300kmSouth* was a perfect tool to promote the transnational resistance of the activists at COP22 thanks to its short duration, hashtagability, and strong evidence of environmental damage caused by the silver mine just 300 kilometres south of the COP22 summit village in Marrakesh.

First screened in Imiter as part of the first edition of IIEJFF (8–12 November 2016) on Mount Alebban, the documentary is directed by Bouhmouch and produced by the Temporary Cinematographic Committee of the Movement on the Road of 96. The film opens with arid scenes and a young female voice-over telling us that we would be forgiven to think that this is a desert. The narrator emerges as a young girl speaking in Tamazight, who informs us further that her native land is one of plenty. The film shows scenes of green fields and water abundance managed through the *khattarat*, the traditional irrigation system in North Africa. The fields are full of blossoming apricot, almond and olive trees, but this is threatened by human forces, the articulate narrator tells us. As the camera zooms in on dried-up land and dead trees, we are told that Managem is responsible for this environmental disaster due to its depletion and pollution with toxic wastewater of Imiter's underground water reserves. The girl says that her village is just 300 kilometres south of the COP22 village in Marrakesh, but the UN summit will never solve her community's problems because those who are still creating these problems cannot be expected to solve them. The solution is in the hands of her people, who are shown protesting along N10 and holding *agraw* meetings.

Made a few months later, *Timnadin N Rif (Rif Blues)* connects the Imiter struggle with the Rif events that lasted from October 2016 until mid-2017, with the arrest and imprisonment of hundreds of protesters, including the charismatic Nasser Zefzafi, who was sentenced to twenty years in jail on 26 June 2018, six months after the film's online release. The Rif uprising started in the city of Al Hoceima following the tragic death of the fishmonger Mohcine Fikri when he tried to reclaim his swordfish from being confiscated by the police using a rubbish truck. Fikri met his death when the rubbish compactor was switched on by an unidentified party, although activists claim it was done at the supervising police officer's order. Street protesters engulfed Al Hoceima and other towns in the Rif for months. Amazigh and leftist activists showed solidarity with the Rif from the beginning by organising demonstrations all over Morocco. Bouhmouch made his own singular contribution through *Timnadin N Rif*.

The short documentary consists of a filmed poem by one of the Mount Alebban activists. It is addressed to the people of the Rif in solidarity with their struggle against the same oppressive regime. Released at the height of arrests among Rifian activists in summer 2017, *Timnadin N Rif* poetically frames two struggles as one story of resistance to environmental damage and political authoritarianism embodied by the Makhzen. This powerful militant act of intersectionality is not directly stated as in *#300kmSouth*, which is more explicit both visually and discursively. Before the Imiter activist at the centre of *Timnadin*, 'a film in solidarity with our siblings in the Rif', begins to recite his *tamnat* (lyrical poem in Tamazight), we hear the sound of an Arabic radio anchor saying that many Rif protesters have been arrested and sentenced to jail. This happens against the footage of Mount Alebban graffiti on the blocked pipeline and hut walls. As an old pickup makes its way on the dirt road leading up to the hilltop, we hear the voice of the Rif protest leader Nasser Zefzafi explaining why his people have risen against the despotic Makhzen, which has depleted their sea of fish while leaving young people without jobs or a future in a region historically notorious for its high cancer levels since the Rif War in the 1920s when the Spanish colonisers aided by the French army used chemical weapons to suppress the native resistance movement led by Abdelkrim al Khattabi.

Following the online release and popular acclaim of his Imiter short documentaries, Bouhmouch travelled to Tunisia in 2017 at the invitation of War on Want, a UK-based charity active in anti-neoliberal resistance. Produced by the UK organisation, filmed in Tunisia and directed by the Moroccan Bouhmouch, *Paradises of the Earth* (2017) takes Moroccan cinema in barely travelled directions. What state and corporate actors have often failed to do is here achieved by transnational activists, opposed to the same official and capitalist film bodies. The four-part web documentary is a socialist international story that weaves the transnational narratives of oppression and struggle into its form and content. Released weekly from 5 to 26 November 2017, the film accompanies a solidarity caravan of twenty-five activists from North Africa and Latin America on a trip to southern Tunisia, which War on Want sponsored in Spring 2017. The first three episodes focus on the pollution and social despair generated by the phosphate industry in Gabes, Redeyef and Oum Laarayes in Tunisia. The last instalment takes the viewer to Jemna, where the activists speak with and mostly listen to the local farmers who have managed to take back their own lands. *Paradises of the Earth* tries to strike a balance between sad stories of dispossession and happy tales of resistance in neo-liberal Tunisia.

In September 2018, Bouhmouch's documentary project *Amussu* was selected among six projects from around the world to participate in the Final Cut workshop at the Biennale in Venice. The workshop was created to provide a platform that presents films in the production stage in front of an audience of international professionals with the intent of promoting co-production and providing access to international film festivals and markets. Released in the festival circuit in 2019, *Amussu* has been Bouhmouch's international breakthrough. The film documents the struggle of the Imiter community against Managem and climate change. Unlike all the previous films by Bouhmouch, *Amussu* benefited from a post-production grant from the DFI in Qatar, which helped him finish the film and give it international visibility beginning with the Venice Biennale. Its first international appearance was at the Toronto Hot Docs Film Festival in April 2018. Back at home two months later, *Amussu* made the news headlines by winning the first prize at FIDADOC, Morocco's most important documentary film festival. The decision by the organisers of the Movement on the Road of 96 to bring to an end their eight-year protest camp on Mount Alebban in late September 2019 has only increased interest in *Amussu* and the work Bouhmouch has been doing with the Imiter community. The film has been selected at the Journées Cinematographiques de Béjaïa in Algeria, the Rencontres Internationales du Documentaire de Montréal (RIDM) in Canada, and at the International Documentary Film Festival Amsterdam (IDFA) in the Netherlands.

The radical politics and counter-institutional production of Nadir Bouhmouch's films are evidence of his earned reputation as a singular voice in the Moroccan film landscape. His combination of political activism and independent filmmaking have helped him use his camera to record and question his society and its present condition in a way that connects Moroccan film to global radical cinema. This has garnered him growing attention among local and international activists and film scholars.

Figure 3.3 *Amussu* (2019): documentary film as collective activism

NOTES

1. The seven institutions are listed in the 2018 information brochure provided by the CCM to foreign producers considering using Morocco as a production service location. A common estimate (gained from speaking to Moroccan industry professionals) of the number of film schools in the Kingdom is around forty-five. If this number is correct, it would mean that currently there are more film schools than film theatres in Morocco.
2. Jillali Ferhati, interview with Flo Martin and Will Higbee, Tetouan, November 2017.
3. The government decree no. 2.12.109 (15 March 2012) concerning the creation of ISMAC describes the mission of the institute as 'contributing to the development of the nation [Morocco] through training, research and service provision in the fields related to cinema and the audiovisual' ('de contribuer au développement du pays par la formation, la recherche et la prestation de service dans les domaines en relation avec les métiers de l'audiovisuel et du Cinéma et les domaines s'y afférant, et notamment dans les: Métiers de l'image; Métiers du son; Métiers du montage et de la post production; Métiers de l'accompagnement de la réalisation; Métiers de l'accompagnement de la production; Et métiers de la conception écrite').
4. Such concerns were raised by director Hakim Belabbes, who was invited by ISMAC in 2015 to review the teaching programme, in an interview with Chakir Alaoui in *Le360* in 2015: 'J'ai constaté que la formation à l'ISMAC se limite à dispenser un enseignement restreint lié spécifiquement à former un gabarit, un modèle conforme à la discipline. Actuellement, ajoute- t-il, on forme par exemple un spécialiste du son, sans aucune culture générale. Je pense à une réévaluation du système pédagogique en y intégrant un programme global destiné à donner à l'étudiant une connaissance élargie sur le monde qui l'entoure.'
5. Don Smith, Skype interview with Will Higbee, July 2018.
6. Hakim Belabbes, Skype interview with Will Higbee, July 2018.
7. See <https://ledesk.ma/encontinu/au-maroc-les-femmes-ninteressent-pas-les-medias-haca/> (accessed 7 February 2020).
8. Hamid Aidouni, interviewed by Flo Martin and Will Higbee, Tangier, March 2018.
9. Most recently, Abdelmalek Essaâdi has entered into a partnership with the Marseille Film School so that both institutions will have an exchange of students based around intensive collaboration on film projects in both Tetouan and Marseille.
10. Didier Boujard, interview with Will Higbee, 1 December 2018, Tetouan.
11. By way of an example, at the 2018 FNF in Tangier, a session on how to write funding applications for documentary films was organised by Hicham Falah, director of FIDADOC.
12. As part of the Transnational Moroccan Cinema research project, an online questionnaire was sent to students at film schools across Morocco, allowing young Moroccan filmmakers to respond anonymously to a range of questions about film education, training and access for young filmmakers in the Kingdom.
13. For more on the residency scheme and the list of participants, see reports in CCM from *Le Bilan Cinématographique*, 2015, 2016 and 2017.
14. See <http://www.saharalab.org/> (accessed 31 January 2020).
15. Hakim Belabbes, interview with Will Higbee, July 2018.

16. Figures obtained from Hakim Belabbes and Don Smith (interviewed separately by Will Higbee in July 2018).
17. Don Smith, interview with Will Higbee, July 2018.
18. A sample of the Sahara lab films can be viewed at: <http://www.saharalab.org/films/> (accessed 31 January 2020).
19. Don Smith, interview with Will Higbee, July 2018.
20. Zavattini is cited on Sahara Lab's website as a guiding principle for the project: <http://www.saharalab.org/about/> (accessed 31 January 2020).
21. Hakim Belabbes, interview with Will Higbee, July 2018.
22. Don Smith, interview with Will Higbee, July 2018.
23. Ibid.
24. Hakim Belabbes, interview with Will Higbee, July 2018.
25. Ibid.
26. Don Smith, interview with Will Higbee, July 2018.
27. Hakim Belabbes and Don Smith (interviewed separately by Will Higbee in July 2018).
28. Don Smith, interview with Will Higbee, July 2018.
29. 'I hate third world cinema. I hate the idea that because you come from a part of the world, you make a certain a type of cinema' (Lasri cited in Bougrine 2017a).
30. His short films up to 2011 are *Géométrie du remords* (*The Geometry of Remorse* (2002), *Ali J'nah Freestyle* (2004), *Lunati(K)a* (2005) *Jardin des Rides* (*Wrinkles Garden*, 2005), and *Android* (2011). He made the following films for Moroccan TV during the same period: *Le peuple de l'horloge* (*The Clock People*, 2005), *L'os de fer* (*The Iron Bone*, 2007), and *TiphinaR* (2008). The latter is in the Amazigh language, one of Morocco's two official languages since 2011. As a writer, he has published a play *(K)rêve Le Haïtiste, ou, Pétition pour la création d'un hôpital pour les poupéescassées* (2006), two novels *STATIC* (2008) and *Sainte Rita* (2015), and two graphic novels *Vaudou* (2016) and *Fawda* (2017). His web series are *No Vaseline Fatwa* (2016), *Bissara Overdose* (2016), and *Caca-Mind* (2016).
31. Interview with Hicham Lasri by Jamal Bahmad (Casablanca, September 2018).
32. See <http://www.managemgroup.com/mine-dimiter-0> (accessed 8 February 2020).
33. Amussu: Xf Ubrid n 96– Imider (Movement on the Road of 96). 'Our History': <http://imider96.org/about-us/our-history/> (accessed 14 January 2018).
34. Facebook account of the movement: <https://www.facebook.com/Amussu.96Imider>; Twitter: <https://twitter.com/Amussu96ImiDer> (accessed 31 January 2020).

4. DIVERSE VOICES

AMAZIGH CINEMA: THE GLOBAL FLOW OF LOCAL IMAGES

Moroccan cinema has often been defined and studied as the body of films made by Moroccan filmmakers and sponsored and/or licensed by the CCM. This narrow definition has ignored other types of Moroccan cinema, broadly writ, such as regional cinema, TV films and Amazigh cinema. Each one of these production strands is part of Moroccan cinema, but they have yet to receive the adequate attention of film scholars and ultimately be included in a broader definition of Moroccan cinema. Such a move would make Moroccan cinema inclusively Moroccan and broadly transnational and result in new research questions and insights, which would eventually change our current understanding of the cinema of Morocco and the country's mosaic of cultural identities.

Born in the 1990s, cinema in the Amazigh homeland of North Africa has a short yet rich history. Its late arrival on the scene in Morocco and Algeria, which is also home to various Tamazight-speaking communities making up over a third of the population by official estimates, is due to myriad historical, political and technological factors. Imazighen and their language, Tamazight, were systematically suppressed in postcolonial Morocco. Like its counterparts in North Africa, the Moroccan state was determined to Arabise its majority population in line with the ideological constructs of Arab nationalism, which was the dominant political and cultural ideology in the postcolonial Maghreb (Maddy-Weitzman 2012: 110). Tamazight was not part of school curricula and every attempt was made to marginalise its speakers, who made up around 80 per cent of the Moroccan population in the post-independence period. The idea behind Arabisation was that by undermining and virtually annihilating the language, Imazighen would speak Arabic and therefore become Arabs. This linguicide was resisted by the Amazigh civil rights movement, which was born in the late 1960s and grew in influence despite repression and imprisonment during the Years of Lead. With the death of Hassan II in 1999, the political terrain began to change in Morocco with the new King acknowledging the central place of Amazighness in Moroccan history and national life. After his Ajdir speech in October 2001, the state created the Royal Institute for Amazigh Culture (IRCAM) and started introducing the Amazigh language, history and culture into school curricula, public space and mass media. Despite resistance from the vanguard of Arabism in traditional and Islamist parties, Tamazight was made the second official language of the country in the constitutional revision of 2011 in response to the mass street protests in Morocco and North Africa.

Meanwhile, the technological revolution in the late twentieth century opened up a new space for minor cinemas and their cultural resistance to hegemonic ideologies such as Arab-Islamism in Morocco and North Africa. The first films in Tamazight were made in Morocco and Algeria. The political opening in both countries in the 1990s allowed local filmmakers and investors to shoot films in their native language. In Algeria, for example, Abderrahmane Bouguermouh was finally able in 1994 to shoot *The Forgotten Hillside* (1996), an adaptation of the eponymous novel by Mouloud Mammeri, the famous novelist and anthropologist hailed today as the founding father of the Amazigh movement in North Africa. Bouguermouh had to wait and suffer personally and professionally for thirty years before he was allowed to make the film (Bahmad 2013b). In 1995, Belkacem Hadjadj made *Once Upon a Time*. In 1997, Azzedine Meddour finished *Baya's Mountain* despite the high security risks in Algeria during the civil war of the 1990s. Thirteen members of the film crew died after a suspected terrorist attack on the team (Barlet 1997). All three films were well received both locally and internationally (Devaux Yahi 2016: 15–16). They are set in the northeastern region of Kabylia, and deal with the Amazigh population's timeless traditions and resistance to Ottoman and French colonisation.

In Morocco, Amazigh cinema was born simultaneously, albeit with some major differences from Algeria. While 35mm films made by Bouguermouh, Hadjaj and Meddour launched Amazigh cinema across the border, it was video cinema with its state-independent production and distribution networks that solely launched Amazigh filmmaking in Morocco, where it dominated the scene for over a decade before Mohamed Mernich made his 35mm film *Tilila* (2006) and, with financial support from the CCM, *The Upper Village* (2008). Unlike the Algerian state, which provided some support to Amazigh cinema through the Ministry of Culture in the 1990s, Morocco did not offer any financial aid until the late 2000s. This has to do not only with the state's reluctance to support Amazigh cinema and cultural nationalism, but also with the nature of this cinema in Morocco. It was born as a regional cinema in Souss, Morocco's southwest region, more particularly in Agadir, the region's capital. The Souss-based film industry has sometimes been referred to in Morocco as Soussywood. Its first film was long in the making. In 1985, Lahoucine Bizguaren was the director of the theatre group Tifawin in Agadir. However, his dream was to make a film in his native language, Tamazight. The lack of financial support combined with the political volatility and cultural repression of the Lead Years delayed the project. The dream became a reality in 1993 when Bizguaren finished his hugely successful film, *The Golden Woman* (1992). Thus was born Amazigh cinema in Morocco. The four-hour video film was released in VHS format, which was a new technology on the rise at the time due to the electrification of rural Morocco. The VHS format was also convenient for shipping the films to the large Amazigh diaspora in Europe.

The transnational dimension of Amazigh cinema is evident in the very first scene of the very first Amazigh film. *The Golden Woman* opens with the village Muqaddem, the local state employee and spy who also doubles as a postman in rural communities, delivering a letter to Ibba Mamas. The letter is from her son, Idder, who lives in France. The illiterate mother begs the Muqadem to read the letter for her. The reluctant postman opens the envelope and delivers in Tamazight the full message written in classical Arabic. Idder informs his mother that he has sent her a remittance and that he will be visiting the village in the coming summer. He is planning to get married to his cousin, Ijja, which enormously pleases his mother. This opening scene is a significant testimony of Amazigh cinema's transnational roots. Instead of a mere regional local cinema, this category of Moroccan cinema was born in the embrace of the techno-, ethno-, finan- and media-scapes of globalisation that Arjun Appadurai conceptualises in his seminal essay on the disjunctures of the global flow economy (Appadurai 1990: 295–310). Amazigh cinema illustrates the production of identity through these scapes, which provide the infrastructure of cultural globalisation.

Amazigh cinema, especially in its first two decades, is dominated by rural settings and themes. *The Golden Woman* takes place in Idder's native village and catalogues key aspects of Amazigh culture and space, particularly traditional houses and other village spaces from the agora to the mosque. The simplicity of rural life has allowed the films to reconstruct the marginalised Amazigh culture and stage its modern revival through the film medium. In this open space, the filmmakers weave their stories in a simple way that showcases timeless values such as love, loyalty, family, belonging and hard work. The films project these values through simple plots often involving the eternal battle between good and evil. The good is embodied by ancestral values. Evil is often incarnated by malicious characters who either embody traditional evil such as witchcraft and jealousy, or by misguided youth trying hopelessly to undermine traditions because they do not fit their new visions of life born from their exposure to urban living or to mass media.

Cherished by Tamazight speakers both in Morocco and in the diaspora, Amazigh cinema has provided fodder to nostalgia about simple village life and values in a rapidly changing country and world. To domestic audiences, who increasingly live in cities, given the lack of economic opportunities in rural Morocco, this cinema has provided a welcome source of entertainment and a virtual reenactment of community life from the distance of living in Casablanca and other cities. As home to the largest migrant population from the Souss region from colonial times (Adam 1972: 26), Casablanca is a significant market for the production and consumption of Soussywood. Many production companies are based in the city such as the prolific Povisound directed by Lahcen Biyjeddigne. In terms of production volume alone, '28 production companies made 158 films between 1992 and 2008' (Idtnaine 2008). Mohamed Salout (aka Archach Agourram), for example, directed eighteen films between 1993 and 2001.

For the Amazigh diaspora, the circulation of VHS tapes and, much later, VCD, DVD and now online copies of the movies have provided both welcome entertainment and easy access to the homeland and its culture. Cinema strengthened the ethnoscapes of Amazigh identity and allowed immigrants in France, Belgium and further afield to cement their belonging to the imagined community of Imazighen. Even though Soussywood films are made in Tashelhit, the dialect of Tamazight spoken in southwestern Morocco, the films are understandable to broader audiences of Tamazight speakers in Morocco, North Africa and the diaspora. Cinema thus strengthened the common identity of a people long divided by the complex mountainous geography of Morocco, colonialism, postcolonial state repression in the name of an imposed Arabism, and intensive international migration since the 1960s (Bokbot and Faleh 2010: 61). Films were made in Morocco and exported alongside other consumer products such as argan oil and henna to France and other parts of the Amazigh diaspora (Merolla 2005: 50). People bought or borrowed them as a matter of cultural necessity. They have fallen in love with their simple plots and stars.

The emergence of a recognisable Amazigh star system within the films produced since the early 1990s has played a major role in the popularity of Amazigh cinema. One of the first stars of this cinema is Amina Elhilali, who played Ibba Mamas in *The Golden Woman* (1992). She has been known by her character name ever since. Ibba Mamas has starred in other popular films such as *Hope* (2008). Another popular face of Amazigh cinema is Lahoucine Ouberka, who played Dda Hmad Boutfounast in the massively popular film series *Dda Hmad Boutfounast and the 40 Thieves* (1993), which catapulted him to a lead role in the multi-episode *Moker* (Mohamed Salout, 1996) that built on the former film's success. Some of the film stars are also famous singers such as Fatima Tabaamrant, who stars in *Tihiya* (1994) based on her own life. Tabaamrant has built on her success, and became a Moroccan member of parliament from 2011 to 2016. Another iconic star of Soussywood is Larbi Lhdaj, who has defined Amazigh film comedy. He achieved immediate stardom in the mid-2000s thanks to his lead role in the Sasbo film series. The films subvert consensual social values and reframe reality through farce. Sasbo is a young peasant with no education or steady source of income. He revolts against his family and bucolic society through wry humour and eccentric actions by refusing to assume his masculinity. Today, the mere mention of his name draws laughs from his broad fan base in Morocco and abroad. More recent stars have emerged in recent years such as Mbarek Bihmaden and Zahia Tahiri; both are especially known for musicals. It is thanks to such stars that Amazigh cinema has never had an audience problem as has been the case with 'national' cinemas in Morocco and the Maghreb (see Chapter 5).

In addition to popular comedies, Soussywood has produced historical films that are similar in tone and purpose to the Algerian *Baya's Mountain* and *Once Upon a Time*. *Hammu Unamir* (2003), for example, belongs to the consciously committed genre of Amazigh filmic production. The film's plot is a retelling of the Oedipal myth of Hammu Unamir, a young man who fell in love with the celestial beauty Tanirt, and managed to marry her in the end despite all the ordeals he had to go through to find and bring her to earth from the seventh sky, where she escaped after Hammu's mother confronted her about her secret nightly visits to her son (Bounfour 1996: 120).

In the Rif and other parts of Morocco, Amazigh cinema emerged a few years later. In the Rif, the first full video film was directed by Mustapha Chaâbi. *Night Boats* (1997) is dramatic fiction about the perils of clandestine migration to Europe from the Mediterranean shores of Morocco's Rif region. Before making this film, Chaâbi had worked as an assistant cameraman for various Moroccan and international films shot in Morocco, including John Glen's James Bond films in the 1980s. The prolific director has made two dozen films about migration and other social issues in Tamazight and Darija, which have been shown on Moroccan TV and the Qatari TV channel Al Jazeera Documentary. Amazigh cinema in the Rif was catapulted into international fame by Mohamed Amin Benamraoui with his prize-winning *Adios Carmen* (2013). Another notable filmmaker from the Rif is Tarik el Idrissi, who has directed two widely circulated documentary films in Tamazight: *Rif 58/59: Breaking the Silence* (2014) and *Khadija's Journey* (2017). Both films won prizes, at FNF 2015 and 2017 respectively.

Figure 4.1   *Khadija's Journey* (el Idrissi, 2017)

The arrival of new directors in the 2000s ushered in the professional era of Amazigh cinema. The emergence of diasporic filmmakers like Yasmine Kassari and Mohamed Amin Benamraoui revolutionised the erstwhile video cinema. Even though most Amazigh cinema practitioners stuck to video cinema, the new films made in 35mm and increasingly by the digital camera brought diversity to this cinema, enhanced the technical quality of the films, and gave them more international visibility on the festival circuit. Yasmine Kassari's film *The Sleeping Child* (2004) was the first Moroccan film with extensive dialogue in Tamazight. The Moroccan–Belgian production tackles the question of international migration through the eyes of young Amazigh women left behind by their fiancés and husbands in remote parts of Morocco. *The Sleeping Child*'s national (FNF Grand Prix 2005) and international success conquered new territory for Amazigh cinema by making the culture and language of Imazighen known to international festival audiences. The film's European release brought more visibility for Amazigh cinema. In 2007, the CCM selected Mohamed Mernich's *Tillila* (2006) to screen in the official competition at FNF. It was the first Amazigh film to be shown at a film theatre after its premiere at Cinema Rialto in Agadir. Mernich (1951–2012) obtained CCM funding for his second 35mm film *The Upper Village* the following year. The film won Belaid el Akkaf the Original Music prize at FNF 2008. Mohamed Oumouloud Abbazi's *Itto Titrit* (2008) won the Image prize at FNF the same year. The spectacular rise of Amazigh cinema at FNF was confirmed by Kamal Hachkar's *Tinghir-Jerusalem: Echoes of the Mellah* (2012), which won the First Work prize in 2013. Amazigh cinema won FNF's Grand Prix the following year when Benamroaui's *Adios Carmen* (2013) stormed the festival. From the very margins of Moroccan cinema, Amazigh filmmaking was thus consecrated at the high temple of Moroccan cinema twenty years later. It is now accepted as part and parcel of Moroccan cinema and a vehicle for the promotion of cultural diversity, Muslim–Jewish coexistence (*Tinghir-Jerusalem*), and other secular values rooted in Amazigh culture.

More special exhibition venues have emerged to promote Amazigh filmic production in recent years. The first National Festival of Amazigh Film at Ouarzazate was held in 2000. The festival has awarded prizes and lifetime achievement awards to Amazigh filmmakers, who had been categorically ignored by other national film festivals and the state agencies until the mid-2000s. The next major film festival with a bigger international scope and reach was born in Agadir in 2006. Issni N Wourgh, which evokes *Tamghart wurgh / The Golden Woman* (also spelled *Tamghart N Wourgh*), has specialised not only in showing Amazigh films, but also in screening films about Imazighen and other indigenous films from around the world. In addition to Amazigh film festivals in Algeria (e.g. Tizi Ouzou), which have provided a cross-border platform for this North African cinema, Europe and North America have seen the emergence of festivals dedicated to Amazigh films. In Paris, the first International Festival of Amazigh Films took place in 2013. The event is sponsored by Berbère Télévision (BRTV). The Los Angeles Amazigh Film Festival, created by American anthropologist and Amazigh–Jewish cultural activist Helene E. Hagan, has been held since 2007. The New York Forum of Amazigh Film has been held annually since 2015. In Canada, the Montreal International Amazigh Film Festival was born in 2017. These international festivals have promoted the pan-Amazigh dimension of this cinema and brought it into further contact with international filmic production.

Another venue that has opened up for the promotion of Amazigh cinema in Morocco is television. The relationship between national TV and Amazigh cinema began in 2005 when the SNRT and Ali n' Productions produced thirty films in and around the city of Agadir. Two-thirds of the films were in Tamazight, including Hicham Lasri's first feature *TiphinaR* (2008). The Film Industry – Made in Morocco productions were of a higher technical quality than the dominant video films of Amazigh cinema. The films were shown on national TV. In 2010, Tamazight TV was created as part of the state broadcaster SNRT. Not only has this TV channel regularly shown old and new Amazigh films, but has also produced its own films. As a nationwide broadcaster, it has sponsored films in the three main variants of Tamazight spoken in Morocco: Tashelhit, Tamazight and Tarifit. The channel has also been innovative by dubbing these films so that they are shown in the three Tamazight dialects and Darija. It also shows Moroccan films made in Darija and dubbed in Tamazight by the channel or its partners. The TV outlet regularly features Tamazight-dubbed Turkish and other international TV dramas and soap operas. To enhance the reach of Amazigh cinema in Morocco and the diaspora, the channel often shows Amazigh films with subtitles in Arabic and French. The channel has provided a welcome source of revenue for Amazigh filmmakers, who have suffered from the lack of state support (unlike Darija filmmakers, who still represent the majority of CCM-funded cinema) and the prevalence of film piracy. The latter was there from the very beginning of Amazigh cinema. *The Golden Woman* (1992) was pirated before its public release even though the film went on to be a huge success (Idtnaine 2008). The commercial success and revenue from these popular films can sometimes go to the pirates rather than the production companies, which are private investors with small budgets.

Born in the embrace of globalisation and against the odds of the dominant ideological apparatus in Morocco, Amazigh cinema has travelled a long way from its beginnings as a regional video cinema in the 1990s to a visible and transnational branch of Moroccan cinema today. Its popular appeal at home and increasing visibility abroad have made it a strong voice for a long marginalised and ideologically minoritised ethnic majority. The directors and producers of this cinema have responded with an open mind, and with messages of tolerance and secularism rooted in Amazigh civilisation, to the exclusionary logic and aims of Arab nationalism in the postcolonial Maghreb.

TRANSNATIONAL CONTESTATIONS: TALA HADID AND JAWAD RHALIB

As noted in Chapter 2, the significant and growing influence of Moroccan diasporic filmmakers since the mid-1990s has encouraged a greater diversity of political and artistic voices to emerge as part of a transnational Moroccan cinema. The status of these filmmakers as simultaneously insiders and outsiders to Moroccan culture and politics, gives them access to a space of cinematic contestation in which they are often freer than those based in Morocco to critique the establishment and access funding for films addressing sensitive political issues or social taboos (see, for example, the portrayal of homosexuality in Abdellah Taïa's *Salvation Army*, 2013). A detailed analysis of two such filmmakers in this section – Tala Hadid and Jawad Rhalib – illustrates how the worldview of these diasporic filmmakers oscillates between the global/local, insider/outsider dyad, and how the politics of institutional funding impacts on a transnational politics of the image.

Tala Hadid was born in London in 1974 to Moroccan and Iraqi parents. A university-educated visual artist (with an MFA from Columbia University, New York) who works across photography as well as film, Hadid came to the attention of international film festival audiences in the mid-2000s with her short film

Your Dark Hair, Ihsan (2005), which was awarded several prizes, including the Panorama short film award (Berlinale), Cinecolor Kodak Prize and a silver medal in the USA Student Academy Awards. Despite the initial impact of *Your Dark Hair, Ihsan*, it would take Hadid nine years to complete her first feature, *The Narrow Frame of Midnight* (2014). During this time, she was simultaneously working on pre-production for the project that would eventually become her award-winning documentary *House in the Fields* (2017) and a photography exhibition about a New York brothel, *Heterotopias* (2011).

The Narrow Frame of Midnight is a Morocco/UK/US/Qatar/France co-production, which gained a plethora of institutional support from (trans-) national funding bodies such as the CCM, British Film Institute, Doha Film Institute, Sundance Institute, Alwan Foundation for the Arts and Le Fonds Francophone de Production Audiovisuelle du Sud. The film's Moroccan producer was K Films, a service production and international co-production company based in Ouarzazate, led by Khadija Alami, whose credits include: *The Gaze* (Lakhmari, 1998), *Tea or Electricity* (Lemaire, 2010) and *Rebellious Girl* (Rhalib, 2015). The film also attracted US-based Louverture Films as an additional co-producer. Founded by Hollywood actor turned cultural activist Danny Glover, Louverture has established a reputation on the world cinema circuit for producing and promoting the films of emerging auteurs and experimental filmmakers such as Abderrahmane Sissako, Elia Suleiman, Apichatpong Weerasethakul and Lucrecia Martel, and was thus a good fit for Hadid.

A transnational network narrative, moving between Morocco, Turkey, Kurdistan and Iraq in a manner reminiscent of *The Edge of Heaven* (Akin, 2007), *The Narrow Frame of Midnight* revolves around the destinies of three characters whose lives intersect by chance in Morocco. Zacaria, a Moroccan–Iraqi writer living in the UK, has returned to Morocco to track down his brother, who is presumed to have run off to Iraq to become a jihadist. Judith, Zacaria's former French girlfriend, lives in an isolated house in the Moroccan countryside and struggles to come to terms with a previous trauma –probably the loss of a child, though it is never directly stated. Finally, Aicha, a young girl from Timahdite (a small town in the heart of the Middle Atlas) is a victim of human trafficking. After a chance meeting, Zacaria rescues Aicha from her captors and leaves her with Judith, while he continues on to Iraq. The trajectories of these three central protagonists overlap, sometimes in non-linear fashion. Hadid combines these multiple, entwined dramatic arcs with pseudo-documentary interludes. In one scene, a young Kurdish refugee recounts to Zacaria his experiences of crossing from Northern Iraq into Turkey. He is shot as if speaking directly to the camera, rather than as the film's central protagonist. The direct, documentary-style address to the audience then cuts to an altogether more stylised set-up, in which the camera appears to float around the derelict building where the refuges are sheltering while the young man continues to speak of his journey from Iraq to Turkey.

While the narrative of *The Narrow Frame of Midnight* begins in rural Morocco – with the Iraqi–Moroccan origins of Zacaria clearly signalling an autobiographical nod to Hadid's own heritage – the film soon extends its gaze beyond the Middle-Atlas, as Zacaria continues on his improvised journey from Casablanca to Istanbul, Kurdistan and finally Iraq, in search of his lost brother. Such transnational border crossing permits the film to extend its gaze to the broader geopolitical conditions that resulted in the violence and chaos of the Iraq War. Hadid has spoken when interviewed (Rastegar 2017) of how the script was initially conceived after 9/11 and the March 2003 invasion of Iraq. And yet, despite the fixed (situated) nature of the film in both space and time, the film also transcends the confines of specific time and place. Hadid evoked the idea of a 'map drawn in pencil' to describe how the film could constantly be redrawn by the spectator in light of 'the unfolding of the interior life of a film and the unfolding of "History"':

> There is no time [in the film], and yet a very specific time . . . The Baghdad makeshift morgue scene for example, where the main character enters a space of the dead, can just as easily be read as a scene in Syria or Egypt, or elsewhere for that matter, depending on when it is viewed in 'historical time' or 'real' time and depending on what is happening on the political terrain. (Hadid cited in Rastegar 2017)

In a similar way, the presence of Zacaria's French girlfriend Judith, and the strains of the *chanson française* standard 'Mon Amant de Saint-Jean', which resurface in the soundtrack, are reminders of an earlier period of Western colonial expansion that echoes the neo-imperialist ambition of the American allied invasion of Iraq in the early 2000s. Hadid's form of transnational contestation thus comes in the way in which her film subtly exposes the inadequacy of a simplistic, Eurocentric linear history as a means of explaining the origins and geopolitical complexities of the current conflicts affecting the MENA region.

Further endorsing the film's transnational credentials, *The Narrow Frame of Midnight* was shot by Russian cinematographer Alexander Burov. This creative collaboration reflects a conscious move by Hadid towards an Eastern European tradition of filmmaking imbued with 'a concept of time (in cinema) that is very different from our own, that . . . allows you time to interpret and understand, like the reading of a geographic map, on which lines can always be redrawn and are constantly shifting' (Hadid cited in Sammarco 2014). Burov's influence is writ large on the film: windows become frames within frames, the camera smoothly tracks and pans (at times almost floating) through the timeless countryside of the Middle-Atlas and streets of Istanbul and Iraq. The confined interiors and local neighbourhoods of Casablanca and Istanbul are lit in

Figure 4.2 *The Narrow Frame of Midnight* (Hadid, 2014): a transnational network narrative

highly stylised chiaroscuro, while an arresting power and beauty emerges from bombed-out shells of Iraqi cities, where life continues despite the conflict.

Hadid's movement between Europe and the US, the cosmopolitan nature of her artistic trajectory and the clear attachment to both her Moroccan and Iraqi roots in her films, well illustrates Naficy's notion (2001: 10) of the 'situated but universal' accented filmmaker previously outlined in Chapter 2:

> My commitment lies not to a specific identitarian group but to a certain way of approaching and producing the image and cinema. Which means that the borders are open, and solidarity, including cinematographic solidarity, is transnational. (Hadid, cited in Rastegar 2017)

The transnational solidarity referred to here by Hadid transfers from the transcontinental, transcultural network narrative of *The Narrow Frame of Midnight* to the highly localised focus of her second feature-length film, the documentary *House in the Fields*. With this film, Hadid consolidated her production model of maximising a jigsaw of institutional funding with post-production grants from the DFI , production and post-production funding from the International Documentary Film Festival (Amsterdam) and the Venice International Film Festival, as well as maintaining the link to Louverture as an executive producer. This time, however, Hadid established her own (Moroccan-based) production company,

Karios Films, to act as the principle producer, since the sums that were required to raise the budget for a documentary of this nature were much lower than for her fiction feature debut. The notion of contestation in Hadid's cinema thus functions both in relation to the images we see on screen and the decisions she makes in terms of funding and production. Following the critical success of her short films and debut feature, Hadid rejects the conventional industry wisdom of prioritising narrative features, in order to return to a documentary project.

In contrast to the transnational border crossing and stylised aesthetics of *The Narrow Frame of Midnight*, *House in the Fields* is an intimate and understated portrayal of life in an Amazigh village high in the Atlas Mountains, focusing on the family of sixteen-year old Khadija. The documentary is constructed and reveals its subjects through a strong identification with time as well as space. The film is structured by the passing seasons and the geographic boundaries of the remote mountain village, observing the daily routine and rituals of the village that have remained virtually unchanged for centuries. Hadid achieves an intimacy with her subjects made possible by the extended periods that she spent living with the villagers. Though it may appear that Hadid is moving away from the transnationalism of *The Narrow Frame of Midnight*, *House in the Fields* nonetheless brings a broader (transnational) perspective to the concerns of local village life despite the geo-cultural specificity of the film's location. In one central scene, Khadija and her sister Fatima (who is engaged to be married and, as a result, has been forced to leave school) sit beneath the trees and discuss the implications for their future of the newly won equal rights for Moroccan women since the Mudawwana of 2004. This intimate exchange provokes the question of whether traditional life in the village is compatible with the progressive transformation of Moroccan society (itself influenced by a broader wave of neo-liberal globalisation), and the young women's own ambitions for their future (Khadija's professed desire to become a lawyer).

Set against this transnational geopolitical perspective, *House in the Fields* makes visible the inhabitants of rural Morocco, who tend to be invisible, marginalised or romanticised on Moroccan and international screens – even if Hadid's status as a transnational auteur means that her work is more likely to be seen on the international festival circuit than by Moroccan audiences. Like *The Narrow Frame of Midnight*, *House in the Fields* has enjoyed considerable success at a range of high-profile international festivals including Berlin, IDFA (Amsterdam) and Toronto. However, both films also remain connected to the national festival scene in Morocco – *The Narrow Frame of Midnight* was screened at Marrakesh, both films were selected for competition and both won prizes at the FNF in Tangier – even if Hadid remains defined by her insider/outsider status as a member of the Moroccan diaspora by the 'border guards' of Moroccan cinema; a view roundly rejected by critic Mohammed Bakrim (2015).[1]

Like Hadid, Jawad Rhalib is a filmmaker from the diaspora whose work explores Moroccan culture and society from an interconnected, globalised perspective. Born in Morocco in 1965 to Belgian and Moroccan parents, Rhalib studied in Europe and lives in Brussels. To date, Rhalib has directed six feature films (four documentaries and two fictions) as well as one short fiction film and a range of documentaries for TV. There is a striking consistency and coherence to Rhalib's filmography. First, themes, subjects and characters are developed and reappear from one film to the next, even crossing from the realm of documentary to fiction. By way of example, his second fiction feature, *Rebellious Girl* (2015), which charts the attempt of Leila, a young female Moroccan immigrant, to mobilise her fellow agricultural workers against the exploitative practices of their Belgian boss, is clearly influenced both by the subject matter of Rhalib's earlier documentary *El Ejido: The Law of Profit* (2006). The character of Laila in *Rebellous Girl* was similarly inspired by the militant female demonstrators involved in the pro-democracy February 20 Movement (F20M) that Rhalib met in Morocco when filming his documentary *The Turtle's Song: A Moroccan Revolution* (2013).[2] There is the consistent development of social and political themes in Rhalib's filmography: immigration, globalisation, human rights and social justice. These are interpreted from a broadly left-wing/socialist position with an attempt to give a voice to the marginalised or dispossessed (illegal immigrants, exploited workers, political dissidents) whom Rhalib clearly sides with as the 'victims' of neo-liberal globalisation. As such, Rhalib's films are more directly politically engaged than those of Tala Hadid.

While tending to focus on inequalities of power in Moroccan society or the Moroccan diaspora, the subjects of Rhalib's fiction and documentary films always exist within the context of a network of economic, political and social relations in which the local and the global are interconnected. *The Damned of the Sea* (2008) – whose original title in French (*Les Damnés de la Mer*) provides a knowing reference to Franz Fanon's seminal anti-colonial text *Les Damnés de la Terre/The Wretched of the Earth* (1961) – explores the economic exile and poverty of Moroccan fishermen from Essaouira, Safi and Agadir, who have been forced south to Dakhla (Western Sahara), as local fish stocks have been depleted by the over-fishing of European trawlers. *El Ejido. . .* exposes the exploitation and racism experienced by the undocumented African migrants (sub-Saharan as well as Moroccan) who work in the intensive agriculture systems of Almeria, in southern Spain. In both cases, Rhalib makes the link between the seemingly unchecked advances of neo-liberal globalisation (in which profit trumps rights) as he documents the disastrous impact of such practices on ordinary Moroccans and the local ecology. *El Ejido. . .* explodes the myth of Europe as an Eldorado for the African economic migrant. Similarly, *The Damned of the Sea* explores not only the role played by industrialised European trawlers in destroying the livelihood of local Moroccan fishermen but also the complicity of the Moroccan politicians in granting permits for European trawlers to fish in Moroccan waters (Rhalib's documentary does, however, remain silent on the fact that some of these fishing waters were gained by Morocco as part of its annexation of the Western Sahara in the mid-1970s).[3] While Rhalib's sympathy is instinctively with the 'ordinary' people, his films are not Manichean diatribes of victimised workers pitted against evil bosses: in *Rebellious Girl*, for example, we learn that the exploitative tactics being employed by the owner of the farm against his workers result from external economic pressures from the global market – cheaper imported fruit that causes him to cut his costs.

Implicit in Rhalib's films is also a call for transnational solidarity and empathy in the face of exploitation. His films play a part in this attempt at fostering solidarity, in the sense that they are largely intended to raise awareness and engagement among audiences inside and outside Morocco. On-screen moments of engagement and empathy, upon which a real politics of transnational solidarity can emerge, appear fleetingly in Rhalib's films. In *El Ejido. . .*, for example, one of the Spanish farm owners recalls how, as a young economic migrant in France, he experienced similar xenophobic hostility from the local French population to that suffered by the African migrants in Almeria. Nevertheless, in Rhalib's documentaries at least, suspicion, hostility and self-interest appear more prevalent than empathy and solidarity among the subjects he films: the captain of the Swedish trawler in *The Damned of the Sea* is either unconcerned or unaware of the detrimental effect his actions are having on the local fishermen and fish stocks; in *El Ejido. . .*, the sole Moroccan farm owner in Almeria tells Rhalib to stop filming when he asks from behind the camera if she employs undocumented workers on the same exploitative pay rate as the Spanish farmers. Indeed, it is perhaps telling that only in Rhalib's fiction film, the social-realist drama *Rebellious Girl*, can the political ideal of transnational solidarity among the agricultural workers in defense of their collective rights become (an on-screen) 'reality'.

The artistic choices and political positions taken by any director have consequences on funding and access. Hadid and Rhalib's films are no exception. Certain Moroccan directors have the impression that their counterparts in the diaspora have access to significantly higher levels of funding. However, Hadid and Rhalib are not filmmakers who can attract high levels of investment in Europe or the US, since their films do not target an explicitly commercial, mainstream audience. Both directors look to a jigsaw of (limited) institutional funding (development grants from national film councils, targeted support from development and post-production funds linked to festivals, specialist funds for documentary filmmakers) that, more often than not, comes from outside of Morocco. Rhalib has consistently relied on funding from Belgian and Walloon audiovisual funding (such as Centre du Cinéma et de l'Audiovisuel de la Communauté Française de Belgique et des Télédistributeurs Wallons) as well as transnational funds that promote francophone culture (Conseil International de Radios-Télévisions d'expression française du Sud (CIRTEF)) and grants from the Hassan II Foundation, set up to promote cultural projects by Moroccans living abroad. The only two productions by Rhalib to have been co-funded by the CCM are a fictional short (*Boomerang*, 2009) and the Belgian–Moroccan co-production feature *Rebellious Girl*. There are two potential explanations for the CCM's limited involvement in supporting Rhalib's films to date: first, Rhalib's proclivity for documentary, which has been underfunded or largely ignored by the CCM production fund since the 1980s and, second, the political nature of his films. In a slightly different way, Hadid's conscious positioning as an international auteur with a presence on the international festival circuit means that, in the current climate, a company such as Louverture is a more obvious long-term co-production partner than the CCM. The experience of Hadid and Rhalib speaks to the way that accented filmmakers must 'play the game' of institutional funding: promoting their credentials as 'European', 'African' or, indeed, as 'international auteurs', as the politics and award criteria of their desired funder dictate, in order to bring their distinctive artistic and political worldview to the screen.

WOMEN'S CINEMA, TAKE ONE: NEGOTIATING WITH THE ESTABLISHMENT

In the 2000s, much changed for Moroccan women both in the Kingdom and behind the camera. The number of new women directors of fiction and documentary films has risen significantly (Armes 2015: 79 ff.), adding new transnational directors to their Morocco-born predecessors at dizzying speed – whether they be *cinéastes de passage* or more permanently (re)located in Morocco (see Chapter 2). Whereas Farida Benlyazid, Farida Bourquia, Izza Génini, and Fatima Jebli Ouazzani had been the only women to produce feature films in Morocco between 1984 (*The Ember*, Farida Bourquia) and 1999 (*Women's Wiles*, Farida Benlyazid), over twenty women joined their ranks and made dozens of films (short and feature-length fictions and documentaries, animations) between 2000 and 2018, such as: Sana Akroud, Jihane el Bahhar, Myriam Bakir, Selma Bargach, Bouchra Belouad, Meryem Benm'Barek, Khaoula Assebab Ben Omar, Souad el Bouhati, Dalila Ennadre, Samia Charkioui, Izza Génini, Tala Hadid, Yasmine Kassari, Sofia el Khyari, Leïla Kilani, Khadija Saïdi Leclere, Rahma Benhamou el Madani, Malika el Manoug, Laïla Marrakchi, Imane Mesbahi, Narjiss Nejjar, Hinda Oulmouddana, Zakia Tahiri, Sonia Terrab, Kathy Wazana and Karima Zoubir.[4]

The majority of this second generation of women, much like the pioneers or their male counterparts, trained abroad, given the absence of film schools in Morocco until a short time ago (see Chapter 3). Some went to Europe – to Amsterdam (Fatima Jebli Ouazzani), Brussels (Yasmine Kassari, Kadija Leclere) or Paris (e.g. Selma Bargach, Laïla Marrakchi, Narjiss Nejjar); others to the

Middle East – to Cairo (Imane Mesbahi), or to North America – to Montreal (Kathy Wazana) or New York (Tala Hadid). Thanks to the creation of film schools and programmes, some rising directors, however, recently studied film at home: Jihane el Bahhar graduated from the audiovisual department of the Ibn M'sik University in Casablanca before she left to be an intern on various films and productions abroad; Mahassine el Hachadi and Saïda Janjague, for instance, both graduated with a bachelor's degree from ESAV (Marrakesh), although Mahassine el Hachadi complemented her training with a Masters in directing at ESAV-Toulouse, in France. At the round table on women in Moroccan cinema in Edinburgh in 2018, animation filmmaker Sofia el Khyari remarked that, no matter what the obstacles for young women to study cinema, they often graduated from film schools in higher numbers than men these days.[5]

However diverse their individual trajectories and biographies might be, the cinematic interventions and innovations of this wave of women directors are notable for two reasons. First, they have become very savvy in negotiating within and outside the frame of the socio-cultural and political order in Morocco – as well as the film establishment (in particular, 2M and the CCM) – in order to produce their own distinct films. Second, they share thematic and representational strategies as they directly address social taboos in their films,[6] whether in documentaries or in fiction, no longer systematically using coded language and images to film around the socio-political issues of present-day Morocco, with which they are profoundly engaged. This strategy had already been employed by Moroccan women directors outside Morocco – Fatima Jebli Ouazzani being the most significant example, with her film *In My Father's House* (1997) about virginity in Morocco, produced by MM Produkties and NPS TV in Amsterdam, the Netherlands (Hillauer 2005: 353). This change in filmic modes of expression can be read in the wake of a more general frankness in recent Moroccan cinematic work (as demonstrated by Nabil Ayouch's or Nour-Eddine Lakhmari's films). It also indicates a desire on the part of these women directors to denounce injustice in a changed political climate since the *Mudawana*; culminating, as we will show below, with the Moroccan take on the #MeToo movement.

The fast pace at which the number of women increased in film direction and production over two decades is all the more remarkable, given the severe lack of gender parity in their representation at institutions in the audiovisual sector in Morocco. As an example, they still represent only 20 per cent of 'news subjects and sources' of the news according to a report published by HACA in 2017.[7] Most significantly, their complete absence from key positions in film institutions in the Kingdom at the turn of the millennium (Caillé 2016) is only now showing signs of sluggishly receding, while their visibility as film producers and film directors is taking hold. For example, the successful International Women's Film Festival of Salé – the only one of its kind in the entire Maghreb – was created in 2004 and has been held annually in September since 2009. Furthermore, in February 2018, a woman director, Narjiss Nejjar, was appointed head of the CCM Cinémathèque in Rabat, while Khadija Feddi heads the CCM Production Division. Finally, in 2019, the commission that delivers funds to help finance Moroccan film projects (Commission du fonds de soutien à la production cinématographique) is chaired by a woman, script writer Fatema Loukili, and six out of its twelve members are women.[8] It is, however, still too soon to consider these steps as precursors of genuine gender parity in the Moroccan film system (especially given the pressures on the Makhzen from the IMF and other international institutions to provide evidence of democracy in the Kingdom, which sometimes lead the government to engineer superficial political and social reforms).

Meanwhile, women have been very active in the film sector: not only as directors, as we shall see, but also as transnational producers such as Lamia Chraibi (La Prod), Khadija Alami (a member of the Hollywood Academy since 2017), Souad Lamriki (Agora Films) transnational film artist curators such as Yto Barrada, Bouchra Khalili, or Malika Chaghal (see Chapter 5). The visibility of women directors, scriptwriters, editors and producers has also grown at home, as they have garnered prizes at the National Film Festival between the third (1991) and the twentieth (2018) editions,[9] and abroad (Saadia and Oumlil 2016: 46). They have, moreover, complemented critical with commercial success, achieving solid standing at the French box office (Caillé 2016) and the Moroccan box office (see below), as well as on Moroccan TV where they have directed TV fictions and documentaries or contributed to series (see Chapter 1). As an example, the recent series *El Hob* (love) for the documentary programme *Des Histoires et des Hommes* (under the helm of Reda Benjelloun, co-produced by Ali n' Productions and 2M) features ten documentaries exploring the various meanings of love in Morocco today, half of which were directed by women: Zakia Tahiri, Sonia Terrab, Dalila Ennadre, Laïla Marrakchi, Narjiss Nejjar.[10]

The creative energy and growing number of Moroccan women directors since 2000 can be read in the wake of a confluence of factors beyond the digital revolution that now provides easier access to filmmaking. These include personal biographical characteristics – the fact that some of these filmmakers were born of émigré parents in Europe, while others studied in Europe or have been travelling back and forth between Europe and Morocco (Armes 2015) – which often leave these women more open or predisposed to a career in film and the creative industries. The increase in women filmmakers can also be explained by access to training as a greater number of film schools are established in Morocco (see Chapter 3). Significant state reforms relating to both the film and TV industry in Morocco and women's equality more generally have also played a part. For example, audiovisual policies that led to co-productions with 2M (see Chapter 1), the expansion of the CCM's aid to a higher number of fiction films and, since 2012, to documentary filmmaking;[11] and state reforms with deep social ramifications (such as the creation of Instance Equité et Réconciliation and the *Mudawana*, or new Family Code that enshrines the rights of women) have all, in their different ways, created the conditions for more Moroccan women to enter the film and TV industry. Women directors have also been recognised both at home and abroad for their films. The funding schemes and modes of production open to them have changed (see Chapters 1 and 2). So have their ways of imagining and staging narratives, as their films have unfolded over the past two decades.

Theirs is a political cinema: the women directors of the late 1990s–2000s take a feminist stance (about the *Mudawana*, for instance). Speaking at a round-table on women's filmmaking in Moroccan cinema in Edinburgh, October 2018, el Khyari observed,

> Moroccan women filmmakers do not hesitate to talk about women', following in their predecessors' footsteps, as Benlyazid's reaction made clear that day: 'I am a woman, I have a woman's imagination and I speak for myself: I can't see why I would be talking about men!'[12]

For, although the discourse of the latter might have been subsumed, initially, under a nation-building one (Kandiyoti 2004), the early women in Moroccan film have always written scripts and directed narratives centred on women's rights. By way of an example, Benlyazid's very first feature film script – for Jillali Ferhati's film *Reed Dolls* (1981) – denounced individual and legal male abuses and the denial of rights when it came to women, as it explored the fate of Aïcha, an illiterate widow in Tangier's medina from Aïcha's own point of view. Since then, however, the changes in some institutions under the reign of Mohammed VI, coupled with the Makhzen's relative relaxation of freedom of expression since the 1990s[13] (in stark contrast to the Years of Lead's heavy curtailing of it) have prompted women to voice their concerns via film – even when in the crosshairs of the PJD's repeated demand for 'clean art'. The latter was a side effect of the party's ardent battle against economic, political, social and moral corruption.[14]

Women filmmakers have been venturing out with fresh political narratives that look back at Moroccan *her*story (rather than history), and are firmly planted in the contemporary socio-political realities of Morocco. Their films push the limits of socially acceptable women's behaviours that espouse Western models of feminism (Khannous 2013), with protagonists that are 'reel bad Maghrebi girls' (Martin and Caillé 2017), via a unifying *écriture féminine* (Orlando 2015: 125) and production schemes that allow them to become public intellectuals (Iddins 2017b). Pisters (2007) argues for a compelling vision of their filmmaking as the performance of a Deleuzian becoming-woman in which both the director and the female subject remain unfixed and turned towards a future becoming. The latter yields a fecund prism through which to examine women's political cinema in Morocco, no longer looking at the myth of a unified nation as the focus of its discourse and narratives, but rather at perceived 'minorities' – or, more exactly, marginalised groups (Chemlal 2018) – that, paradoxically, constitute the nation 'becoming' in all of its diversity:

> There is no simple return to the unified nation, which never existed in the first place. It is only through a becoming-minoritarian related to the bodies of women and other minority groups [sic.] like the Berbers that the nation can invent itself through the transnational speech acts of modern political cinema. (Pisters 2007: 88)

'Diversity' as a qualifier for their cinema also applies, we would argue, to the genres, formats, techniques and political staging of women as Moroccan subjects against the backdrop of late capitalism used in the 2000s. There is no unified 'becoming-woman' or 'becoming-minoritarian', but an array of 'becomings', depending on the director and her itinerary, the film category (documentary, fiction – comedy, drama, historical), narrative(s), languages and cultures depicted (Tamazight or Darija), against the context of 'globalization' (taken in Beck's sense of both 'transnationality' and 'placelessness'[15]). The latter intersects with women's filmmaking and film narratives rooted in Morocco, with a view to a country – or regions in the country – *en devenir*, an audiovisual projection of 'becoming-Morocco(s)' on screen. Thus, if 'becoming-woman' allows a director to engage with today's issues in Morocco (e.g. migration, poverty, as well as the official unveiling of state violence in recent history, the Mudawana), it also looks towards what lies ahead in Moroccan culture, the cultural 'beyond' of the here-and-now.[16] Consequently, the director develops narratives and film techniques with her eyes on a horizon that extends far beyond an immediate political reaction to a particular event: her project simultaneously holds the past that led to the here-and-now and the dreams of its future, as well as the present condition(s) of the individuals that have been hurt (e.g. political prisoners) or disenfranchised (e.g. the mothers of the prisoners). This rich, layered way of filming is often the result of an outside/insider approach that sutures bird's eye views and close-ups on current Moroccan socio-political issues.

This distinctive approach to filming 'beyond' appears clearly in the films about the infamous Years of Lead, following the Makhzen's response to the testimonies of political prisoners who had been freed by Hassan II near the end of his reign (1999), having survived decades of torture and ill treatment away from the public eye in penitentiaries, police stations and prisons throughout the Kingdom. When Mohammed VI ascended the throne, he came under pressure to respond to revelations about the Years of Lead and created the Instance Équité et Réconciliation, Equity and Reconciliation Commission (IER, 2004–5).

The latter investigated 20,000 cases of disappearances, arbitrary arrests and torture between 1956 and 1999, and attempted to reconcile the victims (including the families of the disappeared) with the state – although it never actually named nor persecuted the perpetrators (unlike, say, the South African Truth and Reconciliation Commission after apartheid), and has been seen in some circles as an instrument to shore up an official narrative about democratisation and human rights.[17] This crucial episode also coincided, after years of activism, with a greater freedom of expression that unmuted the voices of the surviving prisoners freed in the preceding years by Hassan II. The political opponents, who had been silenced sometimes for decades, then started to publish narratives about what had happened to them during their incarceration.[18]

While Morocco was grappling with testimonies of its recent history of extreme state violence, directors engaged with it and released a series of films from the late 1990s.[19] The male directors either filmed or evoked/imagined the prisoners and the *lieux de mémoire* (Nora 1997) of their brutal detention or, as Ferhati did, filmed the impossibility of evoking them. All these films[20] follow the trajectory of the (male) prisoner, the primary victim of state violence, his silence, amnesia (mirrored by the state's amnesia) and by projecting images of his suffering, expose the state's role in its horrific abuse of the people of Morocco.[21]

In contrast, *cinéaste de passage* Leïla Kilani also filmed the Years of Lead, but differently, eliciting stunning authenticity and emotions. Kilani produced *Our Forbidden Places* (2008) with funds from the film establishment both at home and abroad, ranging from the CCM and the Instance Equité et Réconciliation (and the Ministry of Culture, and of Foreign Affairs) in Morocco, to the CNC, Fonds Sud, Fonds Francophone de la Production Audiovisuelle, and Région Ile-de-France in France.

Kilani, who divides her time between Paris and Tangier, brought her own double lens to her documentary *Our Forbidden Places*. Instead of zooming in on the victim and his prison cell, now vacated and empty of meaning, she realised that the Moroccan *lieu de mémoire* was not the prison but the sitting-room at home, where silenced, bewildered families had sat for years, waiting for a hypothetical return. Kilani spent three years with four families in order to achieve intimate portraits of characters desperate to find closure and mourn their (disappeared) loved ones. She described *Our Forbidden Places* as 'a project on the representation of trauma' rather than a denunciation of what had gone on, quoting documentary makers who had faced national traumas such as Claude Lanzmann (Shoah), Rithy Panh and André Van In as her influences. Yet she also wanted to 'keep going back and forth between the public and the private', by opting to focus on an exposé of the vivid marks the political system had left on the families of its victims.[22] In that, Kilani's film stands out in the Moroccan filmic treatment of the Years of Lead, as she records the impossibility of 'reach[ing] genuine truth and reconciliation over the recent past and [doing] justice to the true victims of the Years of Lead, particularly women' (Bouthier 2018: 237). The director films both 'beyond' the emptied site of trauma (the detention centre) in the new memory site of the living room, at home, where tongues come untied; and 'beyond' the state's gesture towards reconciliation into the real-life trajectories of the families concerned. At the same time, Kilani, having intentionally inscribed her filmic treatment of collective traumas and state-sponsored injustice in a global documentary tradition, gives the Moroccan political issue a universal aura beyond the borders of Morocco. This dimension was not lost on the international community, as attested by the prizes garnered by the film at festivals across the world.[23]

This is not the only time Moroccan women directors have engaged with Moroccan and indeed international political issues while testing the establishment (in and outside Morocco) in several ways. They too, much like their male counterparts, have produced documentaries and fiction films around emigration and globalisation, for instance, thereby intervening in the polis and culture of the country, joining their peers as equal players and as 'key cultural activists in a socially engaged transnational cinema that sees the state as one element of a creative ecosystem in which capital, producers, texts, and publics are increasingly mobile', inspiring 'debate about the boundaries of politics and culture' (Iddins 2017b: 505). Yet they also intervene in the global community through their films, in which they explore the underside of illegal migration and the underbelly of global capitalism exploitation in the developing world through carefully drawn portraits of individuals, using a double lens once again. As an example, Leïla Kilani's *Tangier, the Burners' Dream* (2002), follows three distinct 'burners'[24] (a Ghanaian man, a Moroccan man and a Moroccan woman), imaging their dreams, their patience, their dangerous crossing from Tangier, all the way to Portugal where many burners land – or don't. Kilani is careful to remind her viewers that illegal migration multiplied after Spain enacted a law in 1991 as a member of Schengen, requiring visas for Moroccan citizens.

Yasmine Kassari also flips the script of the films on emigration (the dream of emigration by the men at home depicted in Nour-Eddine Lakhmari's *Casanegra*, 2008, for instance), in both her documentary *When Men Weep* (2001) and her fiction *The Sleeping Child* (2004). In the first one, she interviews illegal immigrants now virtually trapped in southern Spain, hostages to the social and economic globalisation that has pushed them away from their families and out of Morocco in the first place, and ashamed of their failure to provide for the folks at home; while in the second, she focuses on the women left behind to fend for themselves in rural Morocco (Martin 2011a: 161–82). In the latter, the double lens focuses on Zeinab and Halima, their faces, their tears, their screams, to then zoom out on the immense, barren landscape against which they appear as tiny, vulnerable, figures. *The Sleeping Child*, co-produced by Belgium (Films de la Drève, RTBF, Francophone Region National Cinema Centre), France (Fonds

Sud, Foreign Affairs Ministry) and Morocco (CCM and 2M), was filmed in Tamazight and Darija, with mostly non-professional actors (except for Rachida Brakni) in the Amazigh Rifian region of Morocco that borders Algeria.

Another spin on classic migration filmic narratives is Souad el Bouhati's *French Girl* (2008), centred on female protagonist Sonia, forced to leave France by her parents who were moving back to Morocco when she was barely a teen, and who pines to return to France (see Chapter 2). Here, the layered way of filming comes through visually, as the individual narrative of sullen, rebellious Sonia stands in stark contrast with paradoxical images of both countries: the grey skyline and confined interiors in France where Sonia and her family used to live, which the protagonist nostalgically remembers as liberating, versus the stunning, vast, open expanse of countryside and vibrant colours of textiles decorating the home in Morocco, which Sonia resents as confining.

Finally, Leïla Kilani zeroes in on the treatment of women in a shrimp-packaging factory in the free zone of Tangier in her first fiction feature, *On the Edge* (2011). Kilani's film is interesting in its funding: to produce her first fiction project, which she started after *Our Forbidden Places*, she applied to a number of funds globally. As a result, her film has three nationalities (France/Morocco/Germany) as she produced it with funds from Morocco (the CCM, Socco Chico Films – her own production company in Tangier), Europe (INA, Aurora Films, DKB, Région Ile-de-France in France, Vander-static in Germany), the United Arab Emirates (Sanad in Abu Dhabi). In this respect, Kilani follows the diasporic transnational model analysed in Chapter 2. In the film, we follow Badia, a young, angry woman employed in the factory and shelling rows of shrimp like her fellow women workers, all clad in white. Yet fiercely aware of the system of exploitation that has ensnared her, she constructs and narrates her own sense of self outside the values and worldview that have given birth to the system that oppresses her. She is one of the incarnations of the 'reel bad Maghrebi girl' protagonist of contemporaneous Maghrebi women's cinema: a rebel who stands up against the injustices of patriarchy and globalisation in her own idiosyncratic way, as she refuses to follow the woman's trajectory of emancipation condoned by the West (Martin and Caillé 2017: 176–7). In that, she mirrors Narjiss Nejjar's 'reel bad girl' protagonists. Whether it be Hala, the furious leader in Tizi, the fictitious village of prostitutes in highly controversial *Cry No More* (2002), defiant Aya who ends up in prison in *The Rif Lover* (2011), or even Hénia, desperate to cross the border and find her mother in Algeria in *Stateless* (2018) (see Chapter 2), her protagonists are all endowed with fierce, creative agency even if their space for action is always relentlessly curtailed by the laws and customs of patriarchy, just like Badia in Kilani's fiction. The 'reel bad Moroccan girl' protagonists deviate from prescribed paths in order to survive through coping mechanisms to deal with several levels of gender,

Figure 4.3   *On the Edge* (Kilani, 2011): 'reel bad Maghrebi girls' rebel against patriarchy and the neo-liberal globalisation

class and economic oppression. Similarly, one could argue that the *cinéastes de passage* also become 'reel bad girls', just like the characters they construct, as they operate through various channels, playing with the establishment in Morocco and elsewhere, and freely navigating between the CCM, the Gulf and European establishments to produce their films (see Chapters 1 and 2).

The construction of empowered female characters in film is not new: it has inspired a number of filmmakers (male and female) from the very beginning of Moroccan cinema, yet women's approaches diverge from those of male directors. The latter have often – though not exclusively[25] – constructed their female characters as symbolic sites for the battle for democratisation and modernity (Chahir 2014), victims of Moroccan or global patriarchal power (e.g. Nabil Ayouch's *Mektoub*, 1997, *Much Loved*, 2015; Nour-Eddine Lakhmari's *Burnout*, 2017; Rachid Larossi's *The Divorcee*, 2018), or strong matriarchs (e.g. Ahmed el Maanouni's *Fadma*, 2016; Hakim Belabbes's *Sweat Rain*, 2016).

Women filmmakers tackle the subject on various modes,[26] especially since 5 February 2004, when the king signed a significantly revised version of the 1958 Family Code: the *Mudawana*.[27] Among other dispositions, the dahir put the age of legal marriage at eighteen (article 19), inscribed a woman's right to enter a monogamous marriage, put limits on polygamy (articles 40–46) and legislated on divorce, repudiation and the obligation to pay alimony (article 45). Although the text of the decree concerns the family rather than women strictly speaking, it did expand the rights of the latter significantly. But how would illiterate women ever be apprised of their rights? Women directors started to make films with a view to publicise and explain the content of the *Mudawana* to the illiterate sections of the population. In this way, the women are aligned with the emergent Moroccan cinema of the 1960s and 1970s, when the CCM produced 'how to' films on topics ranging from hygiene to agrarian reforms, designed to educate the population in film theatres around the country. Several intricate documentaries and fiction films were thus created, among which three stand out as diverse works engaging with the *Mudawana*: Dalila Ennadre's documentary *I Have Something to Tell You . . .* (2005), Zakia Tahiri's comedy *Number One* (2008), and Laïla Marrakchi's *Marock* (2005). All address the 'beyond' of the law, focusing on the way the latter affects – and, in places, really does not affect – women's daily lives, depending on their level of education and financial circumstances.

Dalila Ennadre, born in Morocco, grew up in France and was trained by practice, as a production assistant to various filmmakers in different countries, before she made her first two documentaries in Montréal, *By the Grace of Allah* (1987) and *Idols in the Shadow* (1994) in Montreal (Roy 2015: 79). Ennadre produced *I Have Something to Tell You . . .* with 2M in Morocco, NMO (a Muslim organisation in the Netherlands), the CNC, and TV outfits in France (Images Plus, a Vosges TV station; PROCIREP and ANGOA). This explains its length (sixty minutes), fit for a French and/or Moroccan TV grid: Ennadre wanted to reach a wide audience of women TV viewers. The film opens on a rally, in the slums of Sidi Moumen in Casablanca, organised by the Democratic League of Moroccan Women a year after the *Mudawana* was signed. Women and men have lined up to receive free medical care and are being informed about the content of the law. The free-ranging discussions that ensue reveal a total ignorance of the *Mudawana* as well as a woman-centred view of human rights that starts with the right to work (which women feel they have, but which they feel men do not have . . .). *I Have Something to Tell You . . .* then moves on to a poor hamlet in the countryside where farmwives weave carpets, to Marrakesh where a woman has been repudiated and desperately tries to make ends meet to feed her son and herself by baking cakes that she sells on Jamaa el Fnaa, to a sardine-packing factory by the sea with a women-only workforce (reminiscent of Badia's plant in Kilani's *On the Edge*). The film's explanation of the *Mudawana* in the larger context of women's conditions throughout the country frames the League's attempt to publicise the text of the law in a *mise en abyme* that boldly underscores the amount of implementation work left to do after the law was passed, suggesting that this law is only the beginning of a long overdue process.[28] The soundtrack includes both the official accounts (the radio announcements, the Women's League speakers' explanations) and the candid reactions of the women (talking about their work, men) as well as the narrow space of expression they have – one woman with a beautiful voice starts singing outside the factory by the sea while the workers, on their lunch break, await the arrival of a truck to unload, but a man springs out from behind a tree and threateningly reduces her to silence. Clearly, the road is going to be long for the humble, illiterate women in factories, markets, farms, to be able to stand up for their rights – or, as they say themselves, for their daughters' rights.

Zakia Tahiri, born in Lille, was brought up in Casablanca until she returned to France at age seventeen, trained and lived there for many years. Her outlook is that of an insider/outsider and *Number One* (Morocco, 2008) is the first fiction she directed by herself (not with her husband Ahmed Bouchaala, who co-produced it with funds from the CCM, 2M, SNRT and Film Industry – *Made in Morocco*). Tahiri's *Number One* is a comedy that addresses the new rights of women (here, their rights to sue their husbands for divorce) as much as the backlash that inflamed the social networks caused by the perception of the *Mudawana* as an attack against old-style masculinity (Boutouba 2014). To do so, rather than building a strong female character, she zooms on the male protagonist, and deconstructs his masculinity, or, to be precise, forces him to explore his feminine side.

Spinning a cultural cliché on its head for comic effect, the film's female lead protagonist, Soraya, is seen resorting to women's wiles and magic: she has a spell cast on Aziz, her despotic, self-absorbed husband at home and ruthless, tyrannical, exploitative boss at work. The spell literally works wonders: to his own utter befuddlement, Aziz turns into a caring, compassionate companion and boss, eager to share power equally with his wife and employees – he even dabbles in cooking at home – as he acquires qualities traditionally associated with the maternal. The transformation is so complete and the reversal of roles so hyperbolic, shored up by burlesque situations and dialogues delivered with flair (in particular by theatre and film actor Aziz Saadallah) that the hugely successful film made it to second place (after Ayouch's *Whatever Lola Wants*) at the Moroccan box office in 2008 with 57,635 tickets sold.[29]

The comedy came on the heels of a rom-com, set in a different Casablanca – the bourgeois district of Anfa – in the wake of the *Mudawana*, by transnational director Laïla Marrakchi: *Marock* (2005). Marrakchi grew up in Casablanca before she moved to Paris to study and live, and her film is steeped in autobiographical details. It presents an interesting Moroccan film case study, since the CCM did not grant aid for what ended up being an entirely French-backed production. Yet it fared much better in Morocco than in France, scoring 115,000 at the French box office in 2006 while it came second at the Moroccan box office with 136,889 tickets sold[30] in spite of – or partly thanks to? – the heated debate at the highest political level that accompanied its release. The narrative, ostensibly a teen romance developing in the leafy residential part of Casablanca's wealthy francophone elite, touched a nerve in the post-*Mudawana* times.

It offers a tale of secular love between two seniors in high school – pretty Rita, who self-identifies as Muslim, and handsome Youri, who is Jewish – that pushes the boundaries of legitimate courtship and interfaith unions in a somewhat complicated cultural landscape: one where couples strolling or driving at night are still asked by the police to produce a marriage licence to avoid being arrested on the ground of loose morals, and where the *Mudawana* did not change the law that forbids marriage of a Muslim woman to a man from a different faith, for instance. If Marrakchi turns to 'thorny feminist issues that needed to be re-examined after the revision of Morocco's Family Code in 2004' (Hirchi 2011: 94), she clearly showed the Moroccan millennials' discontent with their society in 'scenes where icons or sexuality and religion are intermingled' (Hirchi 2011: 98), which deeply shocked the Moroccan public, even if the latter is used to seeing similarly shocking scenes aired via satellite dishes at home.

It should be noted, then, that 'becoming-woman/minoritarian' has also meant producing films about marginalised sections of the population, in particular Amazigh and Jewish communities. The directors therefore create Amazigh narratives against the Arab-dominant ideology, although here again, Mohammed VI started to relax some of his father's systematic marginalisation of the Amazigh population in the Kingdom (see section above). Women directors have produced a string of fictions and documentaries, after Narjiss Nejjar's *Cry No More* and Yasmine Kassari's *The Sleeping Child*. 'Accented' filmmaker Tala Hadid's beautifully photographed *House in the Fields* even won an award at the National Film Festival in 2018 (Prix Spécial du Jury – see Chapter 2). These films are in Tamazight, as is Malika el Manoug's rom-com, *Tawnza*.

Finally, 'becoming-woman/minoritarian' in the Moroccan context can be related to producing films on Jews from Morocco (and 'Berber Jews' in particular[31]) and their rooted culture intermingled with Amazigh culture, often from a position of exile. Filming the Jewish heritage in Moroccan culture has been the focus of two Moroccan–Jewish documentarians exiled in France: Izza Génini and Simone Bitton. The former directed *Morocco: Body and Soul*, a series of fifteen documentaries shot between 1987 and 1992 on the different strains of Moroccan musical culture (including the Jewish ones, as well as the Andalusian tradition of the *nûba* shared by Jews and Muslims). Simone Bitton's current film project, *Ziyara*, is a documentary on the traces of the Jews in today's Morocco ('I want to know what Jewish element is left in people's imagination. There will be very few Jews in the film. Most characters will be Moroccan Muslims. I am looking for the Jew in them'[32]). Kathy Wazana, based in Montreal, has also filmed two documentaries on the uprooting of the Moroccan Jews: *For a New Seville* (2012) on the alya that emptied Morocco of its Jewish population from the 1960s,[33] and *They Were Promised the Sea* (2013), an intimate documentary inspired by her family's history, about the separation and exile that ended a history of unity in former Jewish Amazigh villages, with four nationalities (USA/Canada/Morocco/

Israel). In these various documentaries, Moroccan culture is imaged as multiple, diverse and transnational, in various 'becomings' that extend beyond its past and present-day conflicts and its geopolitical borders.

Finally, although women directors have negotiated with the establishment at home and abroad to produce their films– and, as shown above, often successfully so – they have also skirted the establishment altogether in creative ways in order to generate yet other films on a wide array of social, cultural and political issues.

WOMEN'S CINEMA, TAKE TWO: CIRCUMVENTING THE ESTABLISHMENT

Given the new flexibility afforded women directors to produce and show their films, they have been able to skirt around the system and, much like Hicham Lasri (see Chapter 3), to become 'trickster figures' in the African–American sense of the term,[34] thinking and playing both within and outside the box of the CCM. (One could argue that they have been under pressure to do so, given the amount of aid they have received from the CCM, even if things seem to be improving in the very recent past.[35]) They can now tap into transnational sources of funding unavailable to them before the mid-2000s, tweak the format of their films and get funded by private or crowd-funding schemes on the Internet, away from the control of the Moroccan state; they can also produce films for private foundations and museums, their documentaries becoming either artistic statements in video installations or the repositories of cultural archives. The question of their visibility also takes on different directions: once they displace the support of their film production, then they also become able to displace their exhibition space, away from the original movie theatre.

First, after a temporary decrease (see above), the production of documentary films by men and women has grown in Morocco. In part this is due to the creation of the CCM's aid to documentary production and the documentary grids on TV.[36] However, increasingly, Moroccan filmmakers (and especially women filmmakers) are seeking funding outside the established channels, and for a variety of reasons. Some of these reasons have to do with the very subject of the documentary; such as activist filmmaking about the Hirak movement in the Rif region (see Chapter 3) or prostitution (see below). Others come as a result in changes of funding to documentary production in Morocco beyond the CCM. With the difficulty of navigating the bureaucratic maze of official authorisations required to shoot a documentary film in Morocco, the French establishment used to offer a solution in the form of TV production, which has by now grown fairly infrequent (Bouthier 2017). In their quest for ways to narrate the stories of forgotten individuals and the communities that have been culturally overlooked, women filmmakers have resorted to sources of funding outside the official channels on both sides of the Mediterranean, thus securing relative freedom in their filming. These funds can be located abroad or in private foundations in the Kingdom.

When Dalila Ennadre chose to film Fadma, hired by the French army to be a comfort woman for the Tabor soldiers recruited to fight in Indochina, she did not ask for money from the CCM to support *I Loved So Much . . .* (2008), since the CCM did not give aid for documentaries at the time. In any case, given the extremely sensitive nature of the subject matter, Ennadre would have been unlikely to gain public (Moroccan) funding for the project. Although shooting a film about an Amazigh prostitute breaks most cultural, social rules, she nonetheless secured support from the transnational organisation, the Arab Fund for Arts and Culture (AFAC), based in Beyrouth, Lebanon. In her cinematographic portrait, Fadma stands tall, proud of her life, even if she is now reduced to begging, deprived of the pension the other military staff received from the French state. Fadma is shot frontally, at eye level, sometimes at a slightly low angle, to underscore her majesty: 'People think I am just an old Berber beggar, but there is more to me than that: I have seen the world!' When she is filmed with Hadj Ali, her old neighbour who enlisted with her in the army, they share the screen equally, in perfect visual gender equity, as the two veterans of the French army that they are. Fadma talks about lovemaking with ebullient frankness to Dalila Ennadre (whose documentarian trademark is the intimacy she achieves with her subjects, thanks, in part, to her own camerawork and the relationship she nurtures with her subject until 'the camera between [them] disappears'[37]), a directness never seen on Moroccan screens. In the end, the intensely democratic film blurs the lines between author and subject as Fadma reflects on their shared experience of the documentary and thus co-signs the film: 'This adventure was sent to us by God. . . . This is Dalila and this is Fadma, daughter of Salah of the Hassan tribe, Azilal precinct. We met and it was perfect.' The film, which, given its topic, would not be broadcast on Moroccan TV, received serious accolades outside Morocco: it was nominated for a Muhr at the DIFF in 2008 and awarded Best Documentary Award at the African Film Festival in Tarifa, Spain.

Transnational funding can also take on different forms when documentarians blur the lines with videographers creating video installations in art exhibitions. Filmmakers-turned-installation artists use the funds made available to them by contemporary arts institutions (distinct from film institutions) to sponsor works of art and, occasionally, to fund research for an ensuing documentary. Such is the case, most famously, for Ali Essafi whose Halakat nord-africaines installation, sponsored by the 2014 Dakar Biennale, was based on a three-way documentary project around memory and transmission in the Maghreb,[38] and was later shown at the Masnaâ interdisciplinary art festival in Casablanca (Bouthier 2017). Among women filmmakers/creative visual artists, Bouchra Khalili masterfully shows how to navigate between various systems to create audiovisual pieces that blur the lines between art installations and documentaries. Born in Casablanca, she studied film and applied arts at the Ecole Nationale Supérieure d'Arts in Paris-Cergy, and started to experiment with the representation of migration, clandestine and interstitial spaces in her ongoing quest for new narrative forms. One of her most famous installations, *The Mapping Journey Project*, went on display at the Museum of Modern Art (MOMA) in New York City (9 April–19 October 2016).[39] In it, she questions the very act of mapping through the compression of temporal and spatial scales, as the hand that maps out the dangerous journey trembles. Instead of being a form of planning looking towards the future, the act of mapping is retrospective and shows not the straightest route between point A and point B, but the detours and wavering lines of the migrant's long, past zigzagging journey across various borders. 'Between 3:00 and 4:30 minutes is enough time to trace, with just a few pencil lines marking the surface of the map, the hundreds of kilometres traversed by several illegal immigrants in search of precarious employment' (Zabunyan 2009: 74). Her video art (*Straight Stories* I and II, 2006 and 2008, a pun on "strait" and clandestine passages from Tangier, Morocco to Spain, and from Asia to Europe in Istanbul) interrogates the genre of film, visual art, the very act of curating both film and art as her work demonstrates how documentary and video art forms cross-pollinate to propose a new polymorphous narrative possibility beyond both, which has found its place in a museum setting, as it did at MOMA. Fittingly, visionary Khalili also became a co-curator with photographer and videographer Yto Barrada of the Cinémathèque in Tangier (see Chapter 5).

With public funders in Morocco often reticent or unwilling to fund such work, private Moroccan funding by wealthy philanthropists (alongside the kind of transnational funding already outlined) can provide the solution for women documentary filmmakers. By way of an example, pioneering female director Farida Benlyazid now shoots documentaries produced by Dounia Benjelloun-Mezian, sponsored by the latter's mother, Leïla Mezian's eponymous private foundation. Dr Mezian Benjelloun's project is to build a museum to 'put on display the entire Moroccan culture, like the urban heritage of Fes, Meknes, Essaouira, Tangier, Tetouan . . . as well as the Amazigh heritage, a very rich and well known culture abroad, since all international museums have Amazigh objects on display'.[40] Hence Benlyazid's documentaries on the musical and dance traditions of the Imazighen throughout the country (ten twenty-six-minute episodes between 2013 and 2016) and on marriage traditions (two to date, in 2017–18) are designed as audiovisual archives meant to find their place in the future museum in Casablanca. They are curated objects that escape the control of the CCM (except in relation to shooting permits) and of producers (as was Izza Génini's series, *Morocco: Body and Soul*). They are sometimes aired on TV, so as to be shared with a great number of viewers.

Displacing film in its various new formats (short documentary series, art video installations) from the film theatre to the art exhibit space or museum archive not only frees its director from concerns about funding, but also allows her to experiment with format, narrative form and shooting equipment (e.g. Benlyazid's Atlas villages are shot from a drone's perspective, in contrast with her almost private close-ups on the characters filmed, thus furthering the sense of Amazigh space, and placing Amazigh culture squarely on a Moroccan map colonised by an Arab minority for centuries). Another form of even more radical displacement is also within reach on the Internet.

Sonia Terrab grew up in Meknes, then moved to France, studied political science and journalism and started a double career as a francophone author: as a freelance journalist by day and a novelist by night. She wrote two novels that both express the malaise of young rebellious Moroccan female intellectuals torn between Paris and Casablanca, between one culture and the next, in the age of the Arab revolutions (Terrab 2012, 2015). After she decided to return to Morocco (she now resides in Casablanca), she tried her hand at filmmaking and directed *Shakespeare in Casablanca* (2016), her first documentary, as part of the *El Hob* series for *Des Histoires et des Hommes* (see above). The documentary shows the difficulty of talking about love through the staging of Shakespeare's *A Midsummer Night's Dream* in a poor district of Casablanca,[41] as well as how segregated the city really is. After her first foray into film, she joined Nabil Ayouch's sponsored digital platform Jawjab, and its talent incubator JawjabT, through which she produced a series of one-minute 'capsules', Marrokiates (*Moroccan Girls*, 2017–18), in answer to the global #MeToo movement (Martin 2018). In each clip, a woman testifies about her sexuality, or male abuses, or her own musings on sex, or her coming out story, or the way her family reacts to her sexual agency, and so on. Each episode features a different woman (ages vary) who has come forward and speaks freely outside on the street, thus reclaiming the public space for her pronouncements. In order to get interviews, Terrab launched a call on Facebook and was actually surprised by the sheer volume of answers coming from a wide array of young girls and women across the urban class spectrum. The result is a series of candid clips available on Facebook for the widest distribution possible, the political, feminist aim of the project being a sharing of female voices and stories (or titbits of stories) meant to free up female discourse on love and sex.[42] The miniature films, unlike the films of yore that meandered and projected images with symbolic meanings in order to duck censorship, are very direct. In the end, the shifting of cinema viewing and cinema production from a traditional production company and location to a virtual one with an online curating space is radical, as it dodges the control of the state, yet is never clandestine (Nabil Ayouch, as Terrab's producer and the creator of Jawjab, is located in the heart of the establishment). Encouraged by her experience, Terrab is now looking for funding to develop a feature film based on these capsules.

To skirt around the Moroccan establishment therefore does not mean to hide from it, or even to counter it frontally, but, rather, to maintain a transvergent relationship with it: the directors at times converge with it, and help themselves to it (Farida Benlyazid is funded by one of the biggest fortunes in Morocco; Khalili's work is displayed in one of the most prestigious places in the circuit of global art exhibitions; Dalila Ennadre's work is financed by a transnational Arab fund and recognised in Dubai; Terrab takes advantage of Ayouch's structures and establishment connections); and they also diverge from it and avoid its pitfalls (the bureaucratic maze and limiting frames and formats of institutions, such as the CCM). Deftly playing the system – or rather playing around it – has become the trademark of many women directors in Moroccan (trans-)national cinema today.

The paradox of the institution is clear throughout these two chapters on alternative networks and the diverse voices of Moroccan cinema: as directive and immutable as the CCM has seemed, and as central to the audiovisual landscapes as Ayouch's empire and 2M have been to the production of Moroccan film, the role of the Kingdom's audiovisual institutions seems to have been reconfigured by imaginative directors. The latter have subverted their use of the institutions both within the Kingdom and outside its borders, in order to create radical new forms of filmmaking. In that sense, the directors practise a type of transnational Moroccan cinema that is revolutionary in both senses of the term – the political and the astronomical. Theirs is a radically innovative, ground-breaking form of film production as the filmmakers venture out to imagine and support their works in creative ways via transnational jigsaws of themes and funds. At the same time, their cinema, like a planet, also completes a 'revolution' around institutions in Morocco and abroad: it first circumvents them (as the Imazighen or the women have done, for instance) before it returns to them, in a position of force to use them. Once the films are produced, however, who is their audience and where and how does their audience see them? This is the subject of the next section of this book.

NOTES

1. 'Lors de son triomphe, largement mérité à Tanger . . . les douaniers du cinéma ont commencé à chercher dans son passeport pour titrer qu' "un film irakien a gagné à Tanger" . . . qui trahit encore davantage le niveau du débat qu'on cherche à imposer au cinéma marocain: "un jury marocain"; "un film marocain" . . . Exprimer cela à Tanger, la ville cosmopolite est une contradiction absurde . . . Tanger qui, en 1995, accueillit les jeunes cinéastes de la diaspora qui donnèrent un coup d'accélérateur à un cinéma déjà prometteur.'/'During her [Hadid's] well-deserved triumph in Tangier . . . Moroccan cinema's customs officials began looking in her passport to claim that "an Iraqi film won in Tangier" . . . which betrays even more the level of debate that such an attitude seeks to impose on Moroccan

cinema: "a Moroccan jury"; "a Moroccan film" . . . Expressing that in a cosmopolitan city like Tangier is an absurd contradiction . . . Tangier, which in 1995, welcomed young filmmakers from the diaspora who gave a boost to an already promising national cinema' (Bakrim 2015).

2. See online video interviews with Rhalib on the Belgian Cinevox website 2017: <https://www.cinevox.be/fr/insoumise-de-jawad-rhalib-interviews/> (accessed 31 January 2020).

3. For more on the complex politics of the Western Sahara, see the section in Chapter 3 on Sahara Lab.

4. The list is non exhaustive, and in particular does not include video installation artists such as Bouchra Khalili, the co-founder of the *Cinémathèque de Tanger* and an internationally recognised prolific artist with Audiovisual media.

5. 'Women in Moroccan Cinema' round table, 'Morocco in Motion: the Global Reach of Moroccan Cinema' Conference, Edinburgh: 28 October 2018.

6. Orlando sees their films as part of educating their viewers: 'They instruct audiences by focussing on once taboo and controversial topics, form rural poverty and prostitution to divorce and repudiation' (Orlando 2011: 152).

7. For a discussion of the report, see: <https://ledesk.ma/encontinu/au-maroc-les-femmes-ninteressent-pas-les-medias-haca/> (accessed 8 February 2020).

8. Full details of the members of the Commission du fonds de soutien à la production cinématographique can be found at: <https://www.ccm.ma/soutien-a-la-production1> (accessed 31 January 2020).

9. Grand Prix for feature films (Yasmine Kassari for *The Sleeping Child*, in 2005; Leïla Kilani for *On the Edge* in 2012; Tala Hadid for *The Narrow Frame of Midnight* in 2015). Grand Prix for shorts (Samia Charkioui for *Fatma* in 2012). Prix du Cinquantenaire (Leïla Kilani for *Our Forbidden Places*, in 2008). Prix de la Première Oeuvre (Narjiss Nejjar for *Cry No More*, in 2003). Prix du scénario (Farida Benlyazid for her film *A Door to the Sky* in 1991 and for Mohamed Abderrahman Tazi's *Looking for My Wife's Husband*, in 1995 and Fatema Loukili for Saâd Chraïbi's *Femmes et Femmes*, in 1998). Prix de la production (Lamia Chraibi for her production of both Narjiss Nejjar's *Stateless* and Hicham Lasri's *Jahiliya* in 2018). Prix du Montage (Tina Baz for *Le Grand Voyage*, in 2005). Prix des Costumes (Kenza Diouri, for Farida Benlyazid's *Keid Ensa*, 2001).

10. The male directors involved in the series were Hakim Belabbes, Faouzi Bensaïdi, Kamal Hachkar, Jawad Rhalib, and Daoud Aoulad-Syad.

11. In 2015, the CCM also opened a special *avance sur recettes* competition to documentary projects on the Sahrawi culture and history.

12. 'Women in Moroccan Cinema' round table, 'Morocco in Motion: the Global Reach of Moroccan Cinema' Conference, Edinburgh: 28 October 2018.

13. The concept of freedom needs to be understood here as framed in order not to offend the sensitivities of the authorities: the monarchy and the territorial integrity of the Kingdom, Islam, and 'women', and sexuality are definitely off limits, as is, most probably, Saudi Arabia.

14. For concrete examples of how Najib Boulif's notion of 'art propre' played out in the debates about Moroccan culture, see Aït Akdim 2012.

15. In particular, the political and economical aspects of globalisation's transnational traffic that impact the sense of the individual's place and becoming at home: 'New is the self-perception of this transnationality (in the mass media, consumption or tourism); new is the "placelessness" of community, labour and capital; new are the awareness of global ecological dangers and the corresponding arenas of action; new is the inescapable perception of transcultural Others in one's life, with all the contradictory certainties resulting from it; new is the level at which 'global culture industries' circulate' (Beck 2000: 12–13).

16. See the introduction to Bhabha 1994.

17. On the surface, the IER had several levels of paradox, the first one being that, by decree, it was to last nine months (renewable for three extra months) to review cases having occurred over an uncommonly long period (1956–99). Political scientists have seen the IER as a sign of political control both at home and abroad, more than anything else. 'L'un des enjeux qu'elle incarne réside donc dans la distinction du moment présent par rapport au règne précédent. Celle-ci passe par la diffusion de représentations dominantes constitutives de la perception de "la nouvelle ère" et de leur réappropriation par la société. D'où, la lutte de la part des divers protagonistes pour infirmer ou confirmer la mise en récit officielle' (Desrues 2006); 'L'IER souligne en outre – et c'est sans doute là son enjeu et sa difficulté – la capacité du régime à détourner les ressources et les énoncés de la mondialisation à son profit, au-delà du soutien d'alliés fidèles comme la France et les États-Unis. Car l'enjeu de cette commission est bien qu'elle soit une commission "comme si . . .", comme si elle indiquait une transition vers la démocratie, comme si elle allait produire de son propre chef une vérité endossable par les victimes' (Vairel 2004: 193).

18. Quite a few had to do with the secret penitentiary in the desert, Tazmamart. For example, Marzouki's *Tasmamart: Cellule 10*, Casablanca, Tarik Editions, 2000; Mohammed Raïss's *From Skhirat to Tasmamart: Return from the Bottom of Hell*, published as a series in the Moroccan Arabic daily *Al Ittihad Al Ichtiraki* in the late 1990s before it was published as a book in 2000. Aziz Binebine's *Tazmamort* (Denoël, 2009) on his stay at Tazmamart from 1973 to 1991, is perhaps the most eloquent and disturbing autobiographical narrative on the matter.

19. Including Nabil Ayouch's *Mektoub* in 1997; Abdelkader Lagtaâ's *The Casablancans* in 1999; Lahcen Zinoun's *False Step* in 2003.

20. To name a few such films: Ahmed Boulane's *Alia, Rabia and the others* (2000) focuses on a prisoner coming out of jail and the challenges of his return to the changed Morocco he discovers; Kamal Kamal's *Nizar's Spectrum* (2002) also focuses on investigating political assassinations, as does Abdelhaï Laraki's *Mona Saber* (2002), which follows Mona's inquiry into what happened to her father during that period; Hassan Benjelloun's *The Dark Room* (2004), an adaptation of Jaouad Mdidech's autobiographical account is squarely on the male prisoners in the sinister Derb Moulay Chérif in Casablanca, while Saâd Chraïbi's *Jawhara, Prison Girl* (2003) evokes detention through one of its youngest victims; Jillali Ferhati's *Memory in Detention* (2004) broaches the difficulty of breaking the silence around the Years of Lead through the journey of his amnesiac prisoner protagonist.

21. Although they provide a look into 'the country's difficult past' (Gugler 2011: 329), they only offer 'a first timid step toward depicting the Lead Years on screen' according to Orlando (2011: 120).

22. See the press dossier of the film: <http://www.docsurgrandecran.fr/sites/default/files/dp_nos_lieux.pdf> (accessed 31 January 2020).

23. Prix du Cinquantenaire, National Film Festival, Tangier, 2008. First Prize for Documentary, Milano Film Festival, 2009. Prix Micheline Vaillancourt for best documentary, Festival PanAfrica International, Montreal, 2009. Grand Prix du Documentaire, FESPACO, Ouagadougou, 2009.

24. *Un brûleur* (a burner), as indicated in Chapter 1, is an illegal migrant who crosses the Mediterranean for Europe, and is thus named because they burn their ID papers so that, once they have reached the shores of Europe, there is no way to identify their country of origin, back to which the authorities might want to deport them.

25. This shorthand version of male portrayals of women does not do justice to more complex characters such as Faouzi Bensaïdi's in *What a Wonderful World* (2006) and *Volubilis* (2017) or to Jawad Rhalib's *Insoumise* (2016), for instance, which are fully developed at the intersection of gender and class.

26. Even a self-referential one as Karima Zoubir's documentary *Camera/Woman* (2012), about a woman behind the camera, shooting wedding videos.

27. See <http://www.hrea.org/programs/gender-equality-and-womens-empowerment/moudawana/#11> (accessed 31 January 2020).

28. In that, it is reminiscent of Selma Baccar's documentary-essay *Fatma 75* (Tunisia, 1976), which celebrated Bourguiba's 1956 *Code Personnel* and also demonstrated that there was much left to do to obtain women's equal rights in Tunisia.

29. See CCM numbers: <http://www.ccm.ma/inter/phactualite/boxoffice2008> (accessed 31 January 2020).

30. See CCM numbers: <http://www.ccm.ma/inter/phactualite/boxoffice2006> (accessed 31 January 2020).

31. We are using the term 'Berber Jews' because the colonial authorities had thus named the Jews in Amazigh rural areas (in their ideological constructs of identities in Morocco) (Chreiteh 2018: 261).

32. 'Je cherche à savoir ce qui reste de juif dans l'imaginaire des gens. C'est un film où il y aura très peu de juifs. La plupart des personnages seront des musulmans marocains. Je cherche le juif en eux' (quoted in Ameskane 2017: 61).

33. In that, it joins a series of films on the topic in Morocco, such as Kamal Hachkar's *Tinghir-Jerusalem: Echoes of the Mellah* (2012) and Hassan Benjelloun's *Where are you going, Moshe?* (2007), Mohamed Ismaïl's *Farewell Mothers* (2007) or Jérôme Olivar Cohen's *L'Orchestre de Minuit* (2015).

34. We are reminded here of Henry Louis Gates Jr's use of the term as a figure of speech empowering the disenfranchised: the trickster figure in African and African American folklore 'signifies', i.e. talks back to the figure of authority on his own terms and beats him at his own rhetorical game (Gates 1988).

35. A quick look at the CCM's most recent end-of-the-year statements reveals a complex picture that seems to belie the progress of women in Moroccan cinema (6–2.5 per cent) in terms of funding by the state until the last three years: 2013: women's film projects

(9.3 per cent of the total) were awarded 0.4 per cent of the aid budget. 2014: women's film projects (12.5 per cent of the total) were awarded 2.72 per cent of the aid budget. 2015: women's film projects (7 per cent of the total) were awarded 15.47 per cent of the aid budget. 2016: women's film projects (12.5 per cent of the total) were awarded 14.7 per cent of the aid budget. 2017: women's film projects (6.25 per cent of the total) were awarded 6.25 per cent of the aid budget.

36. The co-production schemes of 2M with filmmakers (see Chapter 1) opened up grids for documentaries (usually sixty-two minutes) as well as for TV fiction films. Under the programme *Des Histoires et des hommes*, for instance, 2M and Ali n' Productions launched a monthly series on love (*el hob*) on 27 December 2016, with ten documentaries by confirmed Moroccan filmmakers: five men (Daoud Aoulad-Syad, Faouzi Bensaïdi, Jamal Hachkar, Jawad Rhalib, Hakim Belabbes), and five women (Zakia Tahiri, Dalila Ennadre, Laïla Marrakchi, Narjiss Nejjar, and a newcomer to the camera, Sonia Terrab).

37. Interview with Flo Martin, 25 June 2018.

38. See Ali Essafi's masterclass on *Halaqat*: <https://www.youtube.com/watch?v=v_DzdKenghk> (accessed 31 January 2020).

39. See <https://www.moma.org/calendar/exhibitions/1627?#installation-images> (accessed 31 January 2020).

40. See <http://www.challenge.ma/le-musee-de-la-fondation-docteur-leila-mezian-entame-sa-derniere-ligne-droite-90027/> (accessed 31 January 2020).

41. See <http://moroccancinema.exeter.ac.uk/en/2017/10/shakespeare-in-casablanca-by-sonia-terrab-60-minutes-2016/> (accessed 31 January 2020).

42. The clips can be viewed at: <https://www.facebook.com/jawjabma/videos/940812829402889/> (accessed 31 January 2020).

PART THREE

DISTRIBUTION AND EXHIBITION NETWORKS: FESTIVALS, AUDIENCES AND MARKETS

As Noureddine Saïl reminded an audience of scholars, critics and filmmakers at the Carthage Film Festival (JCC) in November 2010, African and Arab national cinemas cannot begin to address the challenges of distribution and exhibition in the digital age until they reach a level of sustainable output in terms of production. That said, and to paraphrase Tahar Cheriaa, the founder of the JCC, it is also true that, regardless of the number of films produced, whoever controls distribution, controls cinema. This question of who gets to see Moroccan films, where, when and in what conditions is of critical importance at a time when the cinema's national infrastructure is in crisis and, despite the increasing opportunities offered through online distribution, Moroccan cinema remains a marginal presence at most major international festivals and markets.

Having looked in detail in Parts One and Two at established and emerging networks of production of Moroccan cinema both at home and abroad, the third part of this book will thus examine (trans-)national Moroccan cinema from the perspective of distribution and exhibition. Continuing from the initial premise articulated in the introduction to this book that to understand the transnational we must account for the dialogic relationship between the national and the transnational, Part Three will consider the conditions for distribution and exhibition within Morocco and how these are directly related to the challenges for Moroccan cinema in reaching international audiences.

Chapter 5 analyses the largely paradoxical situation, whereby the apparent vitality of a growing number and variety of film festivals across Morocco masks a grave crisis of distribution and exhibition within the Kingdom. The condition of both formal and informal distribution networks is also examined in Chapter 5: first, via a more nuanced attempt to consider piracy as symptomatic of a wider crisis in exhibition in Morocco, rather than the sole cause for the decline in the number or movie theatres across the country; second, through an analysis of the Tangier Cinémathèque (an institution that has near-legendary status among Moroccan cinephiles) and its pivotal role within an emerging alternative pan-Arab exhibition network for art cinema.

In Chapter 6, we turn our attention to the presence of Moroccan cinema in the international festival network – considering how, through a variety of major A-list festivals and more niche or boutique film festivals, an alternative distribution network emerges. In Chapter 7, we explore how this presence at international festivals is also linked to visibility and international film markets and the significance of a presence at such markets to attract the attention of international sales agents and distributors. Finally, we consider how digital disruption is transforming the landscape for transnational distribution and exhibition of Moroccan films. How realistic are the chances for Moroccan cinema to reach previously inaccessible audiences in the brave new world of online distribution, streaming and Video On Demand?

5. DISTRIBUTION AND EXHIBITION NETWORKS IN MOROCCO

FESTIVALS IN THE KINGDOM

'Like an ancient animal, a festival devours films and contributes to their creation', writes Mohammed Bakrim in his piece on film festivals in the Kingdom.[1] Today, Morocco has a wealth of film festivals: in 2017 alone, there were around seventy film festivals held in the Kingdom. Of those, forty-eight were sponsored by the CCM, the remainder sourced other institutional funding, and a couple of alternative festivals carefully eschewed the institutional patronage of cinema altogether. Each festival has its own distinct agenda, identity and scale: this section will look at the role these diverse festivals play in the visibility, politics and production of film in Morocco.

CCM-supported festivals are not all equal and their number varies from year to year:[2] they fall into four distinct funding categories according to their local, national and international dimensions.[3] Their geographical locations are spread out throughout (mostly the urban centres of) the nation, and not just along its Atlantic or Mediterranean shores: as far south as Laayoune and Dakhla, as far north as Tangier, as far east as Oujda; and inland (e.g. Ouarzazate). The film festival map covers a wide territory in order to bring films to their Moroccan audience – a primary goal, which has become even more urgent given the current exhibition crisis in Moroccan cinema.

While film festivals have been sites of outreach to public audiences and a forum for intense debate among critics, academics and filmmakers, they have also stimulated film production since the first Moroccan film festival (the International

Mediterranean Film Festival) held in Tangier in 1968.[4] It took Morocco until 1982 to generate enough films produced by its directors to hold its first National Film Festival (FNF) in Rabat. Since then, the mushrooming of festivals and their different levels of support, far from being haphazard, are the direct consequences of a state cultural policy that promotes a culturally engineered image of the nation along two axes: the domestic, inward-looking one destined for the people of Morocco and the transnational, outward-looking one meant for viewers abroad:

> For the state, cultural production should enhance the image of Morocco as an authentic yet modern, tolerant, and diverse country. In this regard, state cultural policy is marked by both containment – as seen in its engagement with *mūsems* or traditional festivals – and excess, encapsulated in the organization of huge budget festivals. (Graiouid and Belghazi 2013: 262)

Predictably, then, Moroccan film festivals remain very much cultural policy affairs: on the national scale, they promote the national cultural production to Moroccan citizens, but also (and often more expensively so) on the international scale, they make both the country and its production visible locally and transnationally. As an example, the goal of FIFM (Festival International du Film de Marrakesh) was to enable Marrakesh and Morocco 'to gain greater visibility in the international film world, adding to the visibility already achieved as a result of the country's location for foreign films' (Dwyer 2007: 279) – even though the number of Moroccan films at the FIFM declined to zero in competition and just a handful in the sidebar screenings in 2016.[5]

Although the intertwined history of festivals, the state and the Moroccan people since 1982 is no secret, it has taken different routes and received various interpretations. Moulay Driss Jaïdi sees the festivals as reaching out into the urban spaces where picture houses are sorely missing (Jaïdi 2012: 211) to compensate for an ebbing number of commercial screens in the nation. Jamal Bahmad, in his comparative study of the National Film Festival and the Marrakesh International Film Festival, carefully traces how the national and transnational politics in each festival fosters changes in cinema production and cinema reception at the institutional level (Bahmad 2014), a point to which we will return below. Graiouid and Belghazi consider the festivals as by-products of the patron-state's relationship with its artists, who end up serving the political agenda of the Makhzen (Graiouid and Belghazi 2013). A political overview of the festivals in Morocco reveals their diversity not only in geographical terms, but also in foci and funding schemes, as well as in their politically inflected *raison d'être* and effects. A closer examination of a handful of Moroccan festivals will help uncover the logic and dynamics that have animated their discrete creation and recent history.

The history of the FNF shows a festival that has taken a while to become stable temporally and spatially: after a somewhat sporadic regularity, it has been held annually only since 2010. It rotated its editions in various cities (Rabat, Meknes, Marrakesh, Casablanca, Oujda), before it settled in Tangier for its eighth edition in 2005. It has remained there to this day – once again, perhaps, illustrating the Makhzen's opening up to the northern region in the 2000s. It is entirely funded and organised by the CCM, which, recently, also arranged press conferences, meetings, workshops and roundtables on the state of Moroccan cinema with Moroccan directors, actors, producers, screenwriters, critics, film theatre managers and academics as well as international film professionals.[6]

The films in competition, co-produced by the CCM,[7] are screened at the Cinéma Théatre Roxy (refurbished in 2016) or at the Megarama, and then again at Cinéma Rif. In order for the national production to reach the local population, the CCM created an 'Itinerant Cinema' programme in 2007. A film caravan offers concurrent film screenings in various venues: the local jail, the Hasnouna Youth Cultural Center, Princess Lalla Hasna's Muslim Benefactor Association, and Theatre Mohamed el Haddad.

If it does not have the glitz of Marrakesh, the FNF nonetheless attracts mostly people from the industry and the press, Moroccan cinema buffs and academics. The films screened trigger lively debates, with far-reaching political and film production effects, making the festival both a fertile annual cinema encounter and a hot forum for political debates – a healthy reminder of the enduring power of cinema today. It also has been instrumental in developing film production: at the fourth edition of the FNF in 1995, in a 'watershed event' as Bahmad reminds us, the CCM invited a new generation of Moroccan diasporic filmmakers to screen their shorts.[8]

The inclusion of these directors (Nour-Eddine Lakhmari, Nabil Ayouch, Ismaël Ferroukhi, Myriam Bakir) is but one of the ways in which the festival furthered and diversified film production. Its 2011 edition broke multiple new grounds: for the first time, the competition listed and rewarded two documentaries: Nabil Ayouch's *My Land* (two prizes: editing and soundtrack) and Hakim Belabbes's *In Pieces* (Grand Prix). It also featured a record number of Amazigh films (Shafto 2011a). It introduced the 'enfant terrible of Moroccan cinema' Hicham Lasri (see Chapter 3) with his first feature *The End* (which got a Special Award). Here, the FNF played another pivotal role in the ecosystem of Moroccan film production: its official stamp of approval fuelled the production of Amazigh films and documentaries thereafter.[9]

The FNF's political role in film selection has sometimes been lambasted by the press as well as by members of parliament. Two episodes come to mind: the inclusion of Laïla Marrakchi's *Marock* in the 2006 competition when (1) the CCM had not supported its production; and (2) the release of the film in 2005 had already caused debates around its sensitive topics (sexuality, interfaith romance) in the media and in parliament. The FNF's inclusion in 2012 of Kamal Hachkar's debut documentary *Tinghir-Jerusalem: Echoes of the Mellah* (2011) again provoked the ire of some members of the PJD, who viewed it as an (anti-Palestinian) attempt to normalise relations with Israel.[10] The film depicts the nostalgia of the Moroccan Jews who migrated from one eponymous city, south of the High Atlas, to the other in Israel in the 1960s.

Here, the politics at work in the FNF align with those of the Makhzen, seeking to promote the image of Morocco as ethnically diverse, open, modern and democratic. Beyond its national borders, it has also built a few important transnational bridges (again deftly endorsing the state's foreign policy). Thus, at the 2011 edition, the head of CCM, Noureddine Saïl, declared that eleven films would represent Morocco at FESPACO in Ouagadougou, adding 'the current vitality of Moroccan film helps African cinema in general, which has been noticeably declining in recent years' (Shafto 2011a), validating a pan-African vision of film production in harmony with the king's continental politics. The FNF, together with other festivals in Morocco, thus seem to be engaged in a distinct patronage relationship with the Makhzen, which Graiouid and Belghazi describe as rooted in the Arabic tradition of *ar-ri'āya*, 'a form of protection which can be material, symbolic, or both', granted by the Sovereign, in several guises, as evidenced by the film festivals.[11]

The other festival in the CCM's A-list, the FIFM, is supported in large part by a non-profit foundation – an economic model the monarchy has actively sought to foster in the economy of art production since the 1980s.[12] Yet this foundation, far from being independent from the Makhzen, is headed by none other than Mohammed VI's brother, Prince Moulay Rachid, who operated in concert with a French company, Le Public System Cinéma, until 2016. Since its first edition in Marrakesh in 2001, the FIFM has flaunted a red carpet studded with international movie stars, and brought international cinema giants to Morocco (with masterclasses by the likes of Martin Scorsese in 2006, and Abbas Kiarostami in 2006 and 2015). The most expensive festival in the Kingdom – and by some margin – it markets itself as an internationally known rendezvous, promoting the viewing of both international and national films in Morocco (Bahmad 2014). It has also sought to promote the present and future production of Moroccan cinema: it has welcomed Moroccan films in competition and in a sidebar programme, set up a 'Cinécoles' competition for shorts by film students from 2010 to 2015; it has reached out of the rarefied atmosphere of the ex-centred Palais des Congrès where the competition is screened, to Cinéma Colisée in the modern downtown area of Marrakesh, where the films can be seen at a discounted price, and has reached a much wider audience of local passers-by and tourists by screening popular films on the famous Jamaâ el Fna square.[13] Despite such initiatives, the FIFM's avowed impulse to foster the visibility of Moroccan cinema had visibly dwindled in recent years (six Moroccan films were screened in 2014, none in 2016). Its 2017 edition was cancelled, in an apparent move for the foundation and the CCM to recalibrate the event as a transnational exhibition hub, 'de-centred' from a French pole (Higbee 2018). Its seventeenth edition was held in December 2018, headed by a new transnational professional team hailing from international A-list festivals (Berlin, Cannes) assembled in the interim year: its artistic director, Christoph Terhechte (formerly at the helm of the Berlin Festival's avant-garde Forum Section), was joined by Rémi Bonhomme (head of the *Semaine de la Critique* in Cannes), as well as Rasha Salti, film selector at various festivals such as Abu Dhabi and Toronto, while Mélita Toscan du Plantier switched roles from former director of the festival to adviser to His Royal Highness Prince Moulay Rachid, President of the FIFM Foundation (Vivarelli 2018b). New and noteworthy programmes were put in place at the seventeenth edition, which suggests a greater attention to both established and emergent Moroccan filmmakers. The festival team added a Moroccan Panorama section with seven films by Moroccan directors,[14] and one Moroccan production (with Switzerland, under the expert lead of Lamia Chraibi) was one of the fourteen in competition: *Urgent* (Mohcine Besri, 2018). The festival also honoured Moroccan pioneer director Jillali Ferhati with an homage that put him in the transnational limelight, next to the three other honorees: AgnèsVarda, Robin Wright and Martin Scorsese. This meant that two of his films were screened (*Pillow Secrets*, 2013; and his most recent, *Ultime Révolte*, 2018). Also, Moroccan director Tala Hadid was a member of the international jury, another judicious choice of the team to give Morocco a voice in the final prize selection and officially recognise its cinema expertise on an international stage.

Figure 5.1   FIFM, Marrakesh: Morocco's leading international film festival (photo by authors)

Last but far from least, the seventeenth edition of the festival sponsored two talent-incubating workshops titled *Ateliers de l'Atlas* targeting emerging filmmakers from Africa and the Middle East. These workshops, conducted in partnership with Netflix, were open to directors making a first, second or third feature film. Eight projects in development and six films in post-production hailing from nine different countries took part in them. These projects included five from Morocco, three of the latter being led by women filmmakers. The *ateliers*, conceived as incubators, also have a monetary incentive: a professional jury gave a prize for best film in development (€10,000) and another one for best film in post-production (€20,000) (Laili 2018). Although it might be too early to divine the future directions of the FIFM, it has clearly shown a commitment to being a more Morocco-grounded event while keeping its international mission. Its mentoring role for emergent filmmakers from Morocco, Africa and the Middle East signals a dramatic shift from its past modus operandi, with a professionalism that augurs well for the future: in July 2019, a call for projects was launched for a second cohort of emergent directors to participate in the eighteenth-edition *Ateliers de l'Atlas*.

These two festivals (FIFM and FNF) present two different funding schemes: the FNF is largely funded by the CCM, an extension of the Makhzen, whereas FIFM receives funds from the CCM and from Prince Moulay Rachid's Fondation Film International de Marrakech (itself supported by sponsors such as OCP, Maroc Télécom and 2M). The FNF, under the exclusive helm of the CCM, presents Moroccan films to Moroccans and the film world of Morocco, while the FIFM, under the direction of an international team (and the CCM – since the head of the CCM is a vice-president of the foundation) has welcomed films from abroad, and used its platform to network with international players. Despite the purported global outlook of FIFM, regularly attracting internationally respected directors and stars to appear on the red carpet, as well as including a sidebar of films each year focusing on a specific national cinema, the festival has arguably not done enough to focus on the opportunities that such a gathering offers to promote collaboration between Moroccan cinema and the international film industry. Industry panels, workshops and roundtables are sporadic and not well publicised; there is no formal or de facto market at the festival (meaning that the festival tends to be overlooked by foreign distributors and international sales agents) while Moroccan filmmakers have little chance of engaging with the directors and producers visiting the festival from abroad.[15]

In contrast, B- and C-list festivals have a specific focus either around a movie genre (e.g. documentary, animation and amateur cinema) or Moroccan cultural politics, be they national, regional, continental, gender or ethnic. An overall look at the difference in the level of funding (between B- and C-list festivals) indicates priorities often imputable to the politics of their distant patron. The B-list festivals clearly reinforce the Makhzen's view of Morocco's geopolitical status within the region and beyond. Thus, the Documentary Film Festival for the Culture and History of the Hassani Sahrawi Space in Laayoune feeds into the rhetoric of the 'territorial unity' of Greater Morocco. While, at the other end of the Kingdom, the Mediterranean Short Film Festival in Tangier and the International Mediterranean Film Festival in Tetouan emphasise Morocco's place within the shared cultures and traditions of the Mediterranean. The African Film Festival in Khouribga reinforces Mohammed VI (and thus the Makhzen's) vision for the (geopolitical) positioning of Morocco in relation the African continent. Finally, the role of women in a democratic society aiming for gender justice is highlighted in the Women's International Film Festival of Salé. At other times, the difference in funding by the state seems to correlate with the presence of a financially secure association or foundation to cosponsor each cultural event, as the following two case studies will show: Salé's International Women's Film Festival (FIFFS) and the African Film Festival in Khouribga (FCAK).

Figure 5.2   The Teatro Español, Tetouan, the central venue for FIDEC (photo by authors)

The FIFFS, created in 2004 by an NGO, the Bouregreg Association,[16] has been held annually since 2009 in the city across the river from the capital Rabat. The director of the festival, Abdellatif Laassadi, describes FIFFS as a meeting across gender, nations and ages to think together about a cinema that still remains minoritarian in the world today.[17] In contrast to FIFM, it relies – beyond the CCM's support – on the local community funding of its organising structure, the Bouregreg Association, and partners with prominent business and financial foundations (e.g. BCME Bank of Africa, Attijariwafa Bank, Société Générale des Banques, all of them patrons of the arts), media institutions (TV5 Monde), and cultural partners (French Institute in Morocco). The financial montage of the festival also includes the cultural foundation of the OCP and 2M, two cultural donors linked to the Makhzen exercising 'state surrogate forms of cultural patronage' (Graiouid and Belghazi 2013) with FIFFS. In this regard, it is similar to FIFM.

It shows films by and about women in four different screening venues in Salé's working-class districts (antithetical to the embassy rows and bourgeois districts of Rabat, a stone's throw away), and holds its press conferences, meetings and discussions in Rabat. The festival bridges multiple spaces: it crosses the Bou Regreg river from film screenings to film discussions, while simultaneously traversing class borders (as evidenced by its diverse audience), gender (in its film focus) and nation (in its assemblage of a transnational jury, corpus and film practitioners). The competition includes an occasional work on women's issues by a male director – such as Mohammed Hammad's feature film *Withered Green* (2016) in its eleventh edition, in 2017. The jury is composed of women from the northern and southern hemispheres, as well as the Middle East and the Americas. The festival also boasts a focus on a 'hosted cinema' (Turkish cinema in 2017), two sidebar Moroccan programmes (feature films and shorts), a master class by an international, renowned woman filmmaker (Simone Bitton in 2017) and a session titled 'filmmakers in dialogue' (Hicham Lasri and Simone Bitton in 2017). Since 2015, it has connected cinema professionals with less experienced screenwriters, through its 'script writing residence' programme, animated by nationally and internationally acknowledged writers.[18] Democratic in its commitment to inclusiveness, the festival opens common screenings to both guests from out of town and local people in theatres located in Salé's hard-to-reach communities (making their access at night somewhat problematic for the Rabat-based attendees). Here, in opposition to festivals such as the FNF and the FIFM, the focus on serving a local audience is primary rather than secondary.

Our last case study in the CCM-sanctioned festivals is the African Cinema Festival in Khouribga (FCAK). Created in 1977 under the auspices of the National Federation of Cine-Clubs, the Khouribga Cine-Club and the Cherifian Phosphate Office (OCP), the festival celebrated its twentieth edition forty years later, in September 2017. The celebration of this longest held festival in

Morocco led to film critic Ahmed Boughaba's penning of *FCAK: Year Forty*, a 112-page volume to commemorate its history.[19] Clearly pan-African in its orientation, the festival has long fostered links between sub-Saharan, North African and Moroccan film professionals.[20]

Given its location in Khouribga (the dusty phosphate capital of Morocco), it is, unsurprisingly, largely co-sponsored by the OCP foundation, as well as media institutions (2M) and bank cultural foundations (CCME, Banque Populaire). In 2017, it also counted the Regional Council of Béni Mellal-Khénifra and the Office of Detention Centers in Morocco among its institutional partners, for reasons that will become clear below. Its programme was ambitious: a competition of international African feature films screened at the cultural complex; the opening of a Rwandan art exhibit (at the Khouribga Media Library); film debates, and the specialty of the FCAK since its first edition: 'midnight meetings' where films and the state of affairs of African cinema are discussed with directors, critics, producers till the wee hours of the morning. Add to this, four colloquia on immigration and cinema,[21] two of which took place in the local penitentiary house, with a mixed audience of illegal migrant inmates and festival attendees (leading to candid discussions about the cinema and media-fashioned images of sub-Saharan migrants in Morocco). Finally, the festival offered three workshops: scriptwriting, digital editing and camera work at the local ENSA (School for National Applied Sciences). The politics of the festival was to cast as inclusive a net as possible.

This desire to connect with diverse audiences recurs time and again in other festivals (as previously discussed in Chapter 3, the International Film School Festival in Tetouan has become an annual rendezvous for the people of Tetouan and its vicinity). If the CCM-sponsored festivals are more often than not perceived as high-culture events, some other 'rogue' festivals have cropped up, promoting a counter-culture for the people and by the people, and reaching their audiences in other ways. For example, the participation of cinema in the Resistance and Alternative Festival (FRA), a cultural, multi-art, activist festival in Morocco, espouses a radically alternative model to the cultural festivals sanctioned – and at least partly sponsored – by the state: the DIY model.[22] The FRA does not have a competition, but, rather, gathers like-minded artists and artisans. It owes its existence to the 20 February Movement of contestation (inspired in part by the Arab revolutions of 2011), whose first two editions, around the anniversary of the movement, were organised by a variety of associations in Rabat.[23] The Guerrilla Cinema collective participating in it has since then disbanded and diversified its 'artivist' cinema of intervention, as it needed other channels to express its Marxist-inflected message against the structural economic injustice of global capitalism in Morocco and beyond. Having used various sites punctually to screen its agit-prop documentaries (see Chapter 3 for more details on how Road 96, an offshoot of the collective, held the IIEJF in Imider in 2016), it is screening its films, as it has done from the beginning on the web – on YouTube or Vimeo. In so doing, the political, counter-cultural movement is reaching a wider audience across time and space, while also laying bare the limitations of the officially recognised festivals; if only in terms of outreach and accessibility of the festival programme to a cyber community of cinephiles and activists.

As the above analysis illustrates, film festivals in Morocco have been active participants in the promotion and stimulation of film production, thanks to the varying degrees to which they have engaged with state patronage. While able to deftly manoeuvre within the frame of this relationship to reach some audiences, Morocco's festival network has not necessarily provided the catalyst for the wider distribution of films across Morocco. In the face of the apparent failure of Morocco's formal distribution network to allow films to reach an audience, informal distribution (piracy) often emerges as an alternative. It is to this question of media piracy and the crisis of distribution and exhibition in Morocco that we now turn our attention.

Piracy and the Crisis of Moroccan Distribution

Moroccan cinema is in crisis. It is in crisis despite the growing international visibility of Moroccan films and filmmakers on the global festival circuit (see Chapter 6). It is in crisis despite the various film schools that opened their doors in the country since 2000 (see Chapter 3). It is in crisis despite the increasing budgets allocated to film production and exhibition. Moroccan cinema is in crisis because, for all the aforementioned reasons, its exhibition infrastructure, beyond a handful of newly opened multiplexes in larger cities, is crumbling. From an all-time high of 251 cinemas in 1981, there are only twenty-eight active cinemas left today for a population of 36 million. The open cinemas are mostly concentrated in big urban centres, with Casablanca and Rabat topping the list. There have been different accounts of this crisis, but the CCM alongside local filmmakers and journalists are keen to blame piracy as the chief culprit (cf. Dwyer 2004: 26, Sail 2009; Fassi Fihri 2016). Roadside stalls selling pirated DVD films and TV shows are almost everywhere in Moroccan cities and *souks* (markets). One can buy copies of the most recent Hollywood and Bollywood releases, among other entertainment fare on offer, at a low price (4–15 MAD/£0.30–£1.20). YouTube, DailyMotion and special websites dedicated to pirated films abound online. Piracy seems to be everywhere, and according to the official line presented by the CCM and other industry associations, cinema theatres might soon be out of business due to this phenomenon.

However, there is more to film piracy than meets the eye. It is a more complicated phenomenon than mass media and formal film institutions like the CCM would have us believe. Piracy has become part of the life of cinema everywhere.

In fact, it was there at the beginning in the form of informal and pirate duplication ('duping') of films. As Jane Gaines explains,

> After all, copying literally followed the first logic of the new motion picture apparatus itself, which is, 'to produce is to reproduce is to produce'. The companion logic of machine-made culture, ease of dissemination or distribution, is also evidenced in the configuration of French, British, and American variant titles indicating early distribution to international markets. (Gaines 2006: 238)

Piracy was necessary for the internationalisation of the film medium. It allowed films to cross borders rapidly and effectively: 'Stories crossed national boundaries shipped in cans, duplication factories were hooked up to the beginnings of distribution routes, only barely imagined as the global networks they would become' (Gaines 2006: 238). Before the 1909 US court case that enforced copyright in the film industry, piracy was a dominant mode of film production and distribution.

Some film historians have blamed this early heyday of piracy (1895–1909) on the failure of the film establishment to innovate (Musser 1991: 13). This speaks to the situation of the Moroccan and other film industries today. The film establishment in Morocco is slow and heavily bureaucratic by nature in a way that allows piracy to operate as an alternative form of rapid and more audience-friendly film distribution and reception. Piracy also has a second broader meaning beyond the one ascribed to it by the 'legal' film industry voices. For the postcolonial critic Ravi Sundaram (2010: 12), the phenomenon should be seen in the context of a new 'pirate modernity', which has blurred the boundaries between legal media regimes and informality:

> Piracy is that practice of proliferation following the demise of the classic crowd mythic of modernism. Piracy exists in commodified circuits of exchange, only here the same disperses into the many. Dispersal into viral swarms is the basis of pirate proliferation, disappearance into the hidden abodes of circulation is the secret of its success and the distribution of profits in various points of the network. (Sundaram 2010: 137)

Compared to the film establishment, pirated cinema is more in sync with the rapid temporalities of globalisation. It is closer to the consumer and her needs than the formal film industry. As Sundaram puts it, 'media piracy's proximity to the market aligns it to both the speed of the global (particularly in copies of mainstream releases) and also the dispersed multiplicities of vernacular and regional exchange' (Sundaram 2010: 137). This is borne out by the everyday life of media piracy in the Global South, where informality occupies a significant share of the local economy. In Morocco, for example, informal activities account for one-third of GDP and 67 per cent of the labour force (Lamchaouat 2014: 4). Taking the case of Delhi in the post-liberalisation era, Sundaram argues that 'pirate modernities' have multiplied in the wake of 'weaker bourgeois institutions', 'political mobilization by the poor' and the latter's greater access to 'urban technological infrastructure' (Sundaram 2010: 12). As one of these proliferating modernities, piracy gives visibility and agency to poor, subaltern populations. These pirate modernities have 'created radical conditions of possibility for subaltern populations in the city, [and] brought them to the edge of permanent technological visibility' (Sundaram 2010: 13). As the reaction of the Moroccan authorities and CCM shows, this has led to increased anxiety among formal bourgeois film institutions and attempts to control pirate practices and, by extension, the poor populations that predominate in cities in the Global South. Piracy is the tip of the iceberg in the battle for representation and the 'right to the city', to borrow Henri Lefebvre's phrase (Lefebvre 1968).

In *Shadow Economies of Cinema: Mapping Informal Film Distribution* (2012), Ramon Lobato challenges his fellow academics in film, media and cultural studies to shift their critical gaze from the formal film industries to cinema's shadow or informal economies, including pirate networks. It is necessary, he argues, 'to recalibrate our research paradigms in order to better fit the realities of how film is being accessed in a globalised and convergent world' (Lobato 2012: 1). Lobato is correct to argue that this shift of the gaze is necessary if we are to understand the complexity of the rapid changes ushered in by media convergence and digitisation in the film industry. Shifting the gaze away from the CCM and official film discourse in Morocco, one can see Moroccan cinema from a new and fresh perspective. To begin with, a casual walk around bootleg film DVD stalls and online catalogues of pirated movies in Morocco shows some subtle patterns in the world of film piracy. Most films on sale are not Moroccan movies; they are actually international films with a prominence of Hollywood productions. The second field observation is that the Moroccan movies on sale are more often than not popular comedies and TV films rather than CCM-sponsored movies that go by the name of 'Moroccan cinema'. The latter's products are hard to come by and the pirates do not have copies of the films because (1) they are not in demand except from a limited audience of film buffs and researchers, (2) they are difficult to find and reproduce, and (3) the CCM with the help of the police have occasionally confiscated the merchandise of those who sell CCM-sponsored films since the passing of Law 305-05 in 2005 (Bahmad 2016: 94). According to Noureddine Saïl (2009), over two million pirated DVDs are confiscated by the CCM every year. It is noteworthy that even in cases where the pirates get hold of a CCM-sponsored film and distribute it through underground networks shortly after the film's release in the cinemas, this has not prevented it from doing well at the box office. Nour-Eddine

Lakhmari's breakout success, *Casanegra* (2008), attracted a record number of 170,000 filmgoers in Morocco, despite being heavily pirated almost from the day of its theatrical release (*Aujourd'hui le Maroc*, 2009). In fact, as has been observed also in other countries, piracy can help films excel at the box office by acting as a form of publicity (Grassmuck 2014: 88). Piracy should not, therefore, be entirely blamed for the crisis of Moroccan cinema, as CCM officials and the wider filmmaking community are wont to do.

The crisis of Moroccan cinema is deeper and has to do with intrinsic failings in the national film ecosystem as well as with radical changes in the film industry in the age of globalisation and digital disruption. The first problem in the former category has to do with the price of film tickets in the country. With limited purchasing power in the predominantly lower-middle income kingdom, many people find it difficult to spare enough money for leisure activities, from going to the cinema to travel. With cinema tickets costing between 30 and 60 MAD (£2 and £4), filmgoing is beyond the reach of large sections of the population. The second problem has to do with the location of cinemas; they are largely concentrated in big cities and, even there, are found in city centres or out-of-town shopping malls, out of easy reach for the majority of urban populations. The third notable issue concerns the state of cinema theatres; few are in good condition with decent sound and image equipment. Another problem that has been pointed out by cinema owners is the tax system, which they blame for over-taxation and the high ticket prices (Bahmad 2017). Last but not least, among the intrinsic problems for Moroccan cinemas is the lack of security and family-friendly conditions in some cinemas. Some young Moroccans go to the cinema not to watch the movies, but rather to steal kisses and caresses given the legal and social constraints on these universal desires elsewhere in public spaces. Others go to the movies to drink a bottle of strong Moroccan red wine or *Mahia*, the local fig-based spirit inherited from millennia of Jewish presence in Morocco. While this image is being reversed by the multiplex theatres emerging in shopping malls on the edge of some larger Moroccan cities, it is still accurate to claim that the declining number of independent cinemas in Morocco maintain this reputation among the wider public as social spaces of dubious reputation.

Moroccan cinema has been affected by the political economy of globalisation in other ways. In the age of media convergence, modes of film production, distribution and consumption have been affected. While filmmakers have gradually shifted to digital methods of production, consumers have also benefited from new opportunities offered by globalisation from the increasing availability of a wide variety of films to the diversification of the means of consumption. In parallel, cinema theatres have seen their business decline (see the section on film theatres in this chapter). It is no longer necessary to go to the cinema to watch one's favourite movie. Many people prefer to watch movies online or buy cheap pirated copies from the bootleg DVD sellers, who also do home delivery. The increasingly cheaper and better quality TV sets, tablets and smartphones have allowed people to enjoy cinema without using dark film theatres badly in need of renovation. This has not necessarily undermined the collective experience of watching films in designated theatres because people can still watch films at home with their partners, friends and family. This infrastructural revolution has caught Moroccan and other formal film industries off-guard. The CCM and other actors in the film community have not been able to react rapidly enough to the radical changes in film consumption in the age of globalisation. In the absence of affordable and adequate online platforms where Moroccan film lovers could watch local and transnational Moroccan movies, consumers have resorted to piracy to satisfy their viewing needs. Despite the existence of streaming websites such as Icflix and Netflix, the phenomenon of piracy is still thriving, perhaps because subscription-based streaming websites, which are popular in affluent Western countries, are not adequate answers the specific realities and consumer desires of African countries like Morocco. The pay-per-view streaming platforms presuppose the availability of adequate purchasing power among their audience, which is usually not the case in Morocco.

Thanks to its speed, economy, subalternity and consumer proximity, piracy has stepped in to satisfy the film consumption needs of large audiences, who had largely been ignored or forgotten by the CCM and the investors in the newer wave of urban multiplex cinemas constructed in Morocco. Piracy is more adaptable to local specificities such as the resilient informal economy, and has thrived in the shadow of rigid and heavily bureaucratised film structures. The latter is aware of the problem, as both the former and current CCM directors have noted (Saïl 2009; Fassi Fihri 2016). 'One way to beat the pirates at their own game would be to experiment with options that allow fast, easy, and cheap public access to films' (Ponte 2008: 354). There is a need for affordable streaming websites where all Moroccan films are available. This is not only a future possibility with the ongoing digitisation of CCM film archives, but an absolute necessity to save the system from more informal erosion and potential collapse. Another area the CCM and all film actors need to work on is speeding up film distribution channels. They can learn lessons from other African film industries operating in similar contexts and conditons, such as Nigeria, where Nollywood has thrived in the midst of intensive piracy. As Volker Grassmuck notes,

A film industry [Nollywood] that has its roots in piracy must itself expect to fall victim to it. It employs many of the same strategies as the book industry in the nineteenth-century US to deal with the challenge. The main strategy is speed in distribution. New films earn their money in the first few days after release. If not enough copies are available to meet the demand, the pirates fill the gap. (Grassmuck 2014: 88)

It is only through such practical steps that Moroccan cinema can survive and face the challenges of globalisation and a rapidly changing audience base. Piracy is not life-threatening to Moroccan cinema, but rather an alternative form of distribution that has thrived on the lack of smart and concrete measures to upgrade Moroccan cinema's distribution and exhibition infrastructures.

EXHIBITION: THE TROUBLE WITH MOVIE THEATRES

As noted in the previous section of this chapter, the demise of cinemas in Morocco (as in the entire Maghreb and beyond) is an undisputed fact. The precipitous drop in their number from 225 in 1990 to twenty-eight in 2018 has been amply documented, *bilan* after *bilan*, by the CCM, as has the correlated decrease in tickets sold (from 2.5 million in 2010 to 1.6 million in 2017, according to the same source). Over the past two decades or so, the rapid decline in audience numbers and the crumbling of Morocco's exhibition infrastructure has tended to be explained by those within the industry as a drama in four acts with the fifth one waiting to be written. Act I: Moroccan audiences change their mode of film consumption to view films at home thanks to a proliferation of satellite channels (satellite dishes still cover most roof tops), online streaming, including free sites such as Cinémaghrebia, and cheap, pirated DVDs (to varying degrees, as the earlier section in this chapter on piracy suggests). Act II: with audiences choosing alternative modes for viewing film, the film theatres, increasingly empty and turning no profit, start to deteriorate. Their resulting decrepit state further pushes viewers away from poor sound or projection quality and dirty, broken chairs not maintained by exhibitors, given their shrinking customer-base and heavily taxed tickets.[24] Act III: the very perception of some theatres changes to that of dark rooms of ill repute: spaces that, naturally, customers 'with good morals' stay clear from. Act IV: the *coup de grâce* comes in the 2010s when digital filmmaking forces the exhibitors, already bitterly complaining about the state taxation rate on their tickets (20 per cent VAT),[25] to swap their 35mm projectors for brand new digital ones at a high cost (in the millions of MAD), if they want their theatres to survive (Roger 2013).

Yet this tragic version of the demise of Moroccan film theatres fails to capture not only the possibility of a coexistence of diverse film consumption modes,[26] but also the ironic twists and turns of distribution and exhibition in Morocco, as well as how national productions have fared in parts of this screening ecosystem. In many ways, it reflects the evolving relationship between a developing private sector and a state-supported film production, on the one hand, and a Moroccan business in the current phase of global capitalism, on the other.

The problems facing distribution and exhibition in Morocco are, in reality, longstanding – as a quick flashback to the beginning of postcolonial Moroccan cinema and its distribution reminds us. Although there were numerous picture houses at the time, there was no apparent marketing strategy available, nor any apparent desire to promote the productions of a nascent Moroccan cinema, distribution being controlled by external – essentially French – influences.[27] After independence, distributors and exhibitors continued to privilege foreign films, which were practically risk-free and much cheaper than national films: they would be screened in Morocco after they had run abroad (sometimes two years later) and already made their profit, and could therefore be priced very low. In contrast, Moroccan films still needed to recoup their costs in the national market (Dwyer 2007: 22–3). Complicating matters further, exhibitors were sometimes also distributors, which limited the choice in film options (Carter 2009: 305). A much-needed working distribution network for national production was thus sorely lacking in Morocco in the decades following independence from French colonial rule.

Farida Benlyazid remembers that no Moroccan distributor wanted to take on the first film she ever produced, Jillali Ferhati's *A Breach in the Wall* (1978), even after its selection at the *Semaine de la Critique* in Cannes. In Tangier, she pleaded for a screening in town with the manager of the Mauritania (one of the largest theatres in Tangier, which specialised in Bollywood and martial arts movies at the time), promising him viewers. In search of this audience she worked with friends and associates of the film to launch a guerrilla advertising campaign, driving up and down the streets of the city and its suburbs in a truck with a loudspeaker and putting up posters of the film in cafés. The theatre was full on the first day and played there to enthusiastic audiences for the whole week.[28] Years later, and in the same city, Yto Barrada would bemoan a similar lack of distribution diversity.[29] In the distribution–exhibition ecosystem, isolated systems of distribution had to change in order for the theatres to survive, and theatres had to survive in order for national production to survive.[30] However, since they belong to the private sector, the CCM, as a state organisation, had stayed away from cinema distribution and exhibition in movie theatres, except for delivering exhibition permits for films – 'limiting' its intervention in Moroccan cinema film to co-production and promotion in the form of festivals.

From an institutional perspective the CCM's attitude to distribution and exhibition started to change on two levels in the 2010s. First of all there is the question of which films are being shown in which theatres. As Noureddine Saïl, head of the CCM from 2003 to 2014, perceptively remarks,

> Morocco has over 50 screens. When you look at the screen occupation, the American film reigns supreme as it does everywhere else in the world. [However] When you look at the films at the box office, the first 2 or 3 are Moroccan. (Saïl 2017: 14)

According to the most recent data from the CCM, in 2017 there were twenty-eight movie theatres (with a combined total of sixty-one screens) active in Morocco. These theatres were all located in major urban centres, catering to viewers from across the socio-economic spectrum, with a ticket price that can grow fourfold, according to the city and the neighbourhood – the variations can be quite significant: from 13 MAD/$1.37 (the Dawliz in Meknes) to 65 MAD/$6.90 (Imax in Casablanca). Furthermore, in spite of their steep admission price, the Megaramas (Casablanca, Rabat, Fes, Tangier) and the Imax (Casablanca) rank as the top ticket sellers in the country. Megarama, a French holding company that imports and screens more than 50 per cent of the foreign films shown in Moroccan cinemas (Serceau 2017: 225), thus 'occupies' 74 per cent of the film distribution market, a figure that might go up a notch or two, given its continued expansion.[31] Megarama has further secured the exclusive distribution rights to American blockbusters (Serceau 2017: 226), which it releases simultaneously on French and Moroccan territories.[32] Each digitally equipped multiplex holds a varying number of screens[33] and offers a small selection of Moroccan films for a limited release next to its larger selection of foreign films: for example, in 2011, out of 101 films screened, seventy-four were from the US, twenty-four from Europe (six from France), and two from Morocco (Benchenna 2015: 223).

To return to Saïl's point on the US invasion of Moroccan screens, it is, for the most part, the multiplexes that are under occupation, not the other theatres. Furthermore, Megarama's expansion and monopoly over some corners of the foreign market has incongruous side effects. First, their business model is being picked up by other transnational competitors: as an example, Ciné Atlas Holding (a recent offshoot of French producer and distributor Pierre-François Bernet's Chrysalis Films), has renovated the old Colisée Cinema in Rabat and plans to open multiplexes in cities with a population of at least one million (Agadir, Casablanca, Marrakesh, Tetouan, Safi, Salé, Souissi) (Savage 2017). As we shall see, this novel impulse to renovate old theatres is largely due to a recent amendment to the CCM's policy regarding exhibitors. Second, in a paradox noted by both Michel Serceau and Abdelfettah Benchenna, Megarama's hitherto exclusive rights on and screening of foreign blockbusters makes room for the other cinemas to show Moroccan films (Benchenna 2015: 231), helping them endure as neighbourhood theatres showing national productions. As a result, notwithstanding some fluctuations, the viewership for Moroccan cinema is, overall, growing strongly in the first two decades of the twenty-first century.[34] Finally, in an even more intriguing paradoxical twist, far from monopolising the Moroccan imagination, the same foreign blockbusters made highly visible on Megarama screens (e.g. *Shrek*) also provide a canvas base for Moroccan video pirate-artists such as Hamada to create their own Moroccan works of art (Edwards 2015). Hamada juxtaposes the images of the computer-animated fantasy feature with Moroccan hip-hop music and dances, riffing on the recycled *Shrek* and actively resisting its fairy-tale format. This type of hybrid creativity that appropriates a Disney parody is one of the ways in which Moroccan artists make their subaltern voices heard over the din of American productions. Their creations are then reproduced on cheap DVDs and sold for $1 or so. In this instance, the Megaramas have unwittingly stimulated the creation of counter-US hip-hop videos by underground Moroccan artists and actually fed the much decried (yet highly visible) DVD street market.

Second, having pursued a policy of wilful inaction in the sector for decades, the CCM changed tack in the early 1990s and started to intervene directly in both distribution and exhibition. In 1991, the CCM invited Moroccan distributor Najib Benkirane to sit on, first, the jury of the Meknes National Film Festival, where he saw Abdelkader Lagtaâ's *A Love Affair in Casablanca* (1991), and then on the CCM funding commission. The CCM had broken new ground: the state had intervened softly to promote national production with the powerful distributor, and Benkirane was hooked: 'Since then, I've become *the* specialist in distributing Moroccan films, and it probably accounts for 70 per cent of my business' (Dwyer 2004: 24). As a result, the twelve theatres owned by Benkirane started to programme Moroccan films.

Finally, and much more recently, the CCM intervened with exhibitors when it became clear that the old cinemas needed expensive, updated projectors to be able to screen digitally produced films, and that their managers were reluctant to invest in their obsolete equipment. A 2012 decree allowed the CCM to have a financial impact on theatres in three ways: digitisation, modernisation and the creation of new screening rooms, leading to the digitisation of 90 per cent of the theatres by 2015.[35]

Figure 5.3   The Colisée Cinema: Marrakesh's last remaining independent cinema that is also used as a screening venue for the FIFM (photo by authors)

Figure 5.4   The Teatro Español: Tetouan's art deco theatre and cinema, home to the FIDEC festival (photo by authors)

The film distribution and exhibition model in Morocco has come a long way from its 1980s decentralised, local, at times artisanal, *bricolage* to its national (Benkirane's) and neo-liberal, transnational (Megarama) chains of theatres. Thanks to the CCM's soft intervention in distribution, Moroccan filmmakers still have a slim chance of accessing the domestic theatrical market. The state-supported renovation of theatres also promises to deliver films to Moroccan viewers, once they can be lured back out of the comfort of their home and into the theatre to enjoy Moroccan and world cinema. To grow the domestic audience, several approaches have been tried by organisations that think outside the (local and national) box. Among them, the Cinémathèque in Tangier offers an innovative, multi-prong model of exhibition that cultivates a diversity of audiences and blurs the lines between exhibition and distribution through national and transnational networks.

PAN-ARAB TRANSNATIONAL EXHIBITION: CINÉMATHÈQUE DE TANGER

The history of the cinema that became the Cinémathèque in Tangier encapsulates the trials and tribulations of a movie theatre that went through several incarnations through the colonial and postcolonial eras, and offers a rich case study in the alternative solutions found to respond to the challenges of Moroccan film exhibition. The original movie theatre that opened on the Grand Socco in Tangier in 1938 was named the Rex. Located in a liminal area between the walls of the Kasbah (the old city) and the Ville Nouvelle (the European modern city), it showed films from around the world to cater to its local multilingual audience (see section on Tangier in Chapter 1).[36] Sold by its Spanish owners at independence, it was renamed the Rif[37] in 1965, when it specialised in Bollywood movies, sold cheap tickets to a much poorer audience from the medina and the suburbs of Tangier, and, poorly maintained, became seedier by the year.[38] Like many cinemas in Morocco, it finally lost its audience and closed down in 2005. That's when Tangier-born photographer Yto Barrada and visual artist Bouchra Khalili rented it from its owner to create and operate the Cinémathèque de Tanger within its walls.[39] The Rif's original screening room of 600 seats was divided into two rooms: one with 350 seats and the other with seventy-five seats, to allow for flexible film programming. Barrada and Khalili had devised the idea from their knowledge of a Tangerine viewership familiar with a wide array of languages (Arabic, Spanish, French, English), allowing for a programming of several films within the space of a day that would attract one group after another, depending on their language(s).[40] The larger room shows films of a more classical nature while the smaller one is reserved for more experimental film and documentaries. The cultural complex also hosts a library with an archive, and a space devoted to film workshops. The institution also has a patrimonial goal: to build and preserve a physical archive of the Moroccan film heritage open to the general public. Finally, the complex contains a café.[41] The fluid space of the Cinémathèque has been conceived to engage both communities dynamically: to lead café customers to the cinema and to have the film viewers sit down at the café after a screening to discuss the movie with the café patrons.[42]

The Cinémathèque's transnational self-described mission is ambitious and in symbiosis with its Tangerine environment: to screen Moroccan and world cinema to a cosmopolitan audience; to promote Moroccan cinema abroad, while stimulating local production and fostering professional cinema networking[43] – a tall order for a cultural centre in a city of barely one million inhabitants.

The Cinémathèque constantly seeks ways to diversify its cultural activities (photo exhibits, series and conferences) and to give access to film to a diverse audience, in particular, to the young and to those who live in areas far from the city centre. For instance, its present director, Malika Chaghal, has partnered with the Ministry of National Education to create the 'Lycéens au cinéma' programme, which reaches ten public high schools. Volunteering teachers receive *cahiers pédagogiques* (film education material designed by the Cinémathèque) to help them analyse three films (a classic, a genre film and a film from Morocco or the larger Arab world).[44]

A second set of initiatives concern the six- to twelve-year-old population, and is meant to grow an audience in the long term. In the wake of Yto Barrada's *Lanterne magique* programme,[45] Malika Chaghal created *Ma petite Cinémathèque* along the same principle, providing her young viewers with *dossiers pédagogiques*, and post-screening discussions for free. The children have been involved in creative ways as well: Oliver Laxe famously gave his camera to the street children to make his film *You All Are Captains* (2010) during an artist-in-residence programme at the Cinémathèque, pushing the pedagogy of informed film viewing to creative practice (and illustrating the meteoric rise of a Tangier-rooted production to transnational cinema recognition, since the film went on to enjoy critical success in Cannes and was followed by Laxe's *Mimosas*). To afford such programming, the Cinémathèque partnered with a public transportation company to bus the children from the distant neighbourhoods in exchange for its logo on the event.[46] The Cinémathèque has developed several other partnerships with international cultural centres in the city (the Institut Français, Goethe Institut, Instituto Cervantes, American Legation) and abroad in order to access films from the various countries involved, and help with its educational mission.[47] It also has partnered with the CCM in two ways: first, the CCM has sponsored the digitisation of its screens; second, when the CCM comes to Tangier for the National Film Festival, it hosts the second screening of the films that are in competition as well as some off-competition, in the retrospective. These are however, limited instances of collaboration: overall, the Cinémathèque strives to retain its autonomy and operates largely independently of the CCM.

Figure 5.5 The Cinémathèque de Tanger during the FNF, March 2018 (photo by authors)

In order to ensure its continued survival, the decade-old Cinémathèque has adopted a policy of anchoring in a dense network of cultural institutions that have expanded its horizons nationally and transnationally, turning the Tangerine institution into a transnational film culture hub. On the national level, enlarging its programming outreach beyond the region of Tangier and the north, the Cinémathèque has developed relationships nationally with other venues in the Kingdom, so that its programme can rotate from one site to the next.[48] For example, it has forged a partnership with L'Uzine in Casablanca, an alternative arts and cultural foundation, and is essentially responsible for its monthly film programme throughout the year.[49] When it launched its 2018–19 series *Arabiyat* on films made by Arab women about women in the Arab world, the Cinémathèque partnered with the Mediterranean Film Festival team in Tetouan, with Martil's University, L'Uzine, and other exhibitors in the Kingdom. The twelve films will also be shown abroad at the various centres of an Arab Alternative network.

The Cinémathèque has sought to forge similar alliances beyond Morocco. At the very beginning in 2007, realising the numerous challenges an alternative movie theatre faced in Morocco, Barrada and Khalili joined a group of Arab film professionals who faced similar difficulties and shared parallel experiences. Yto Barrada met the Head of Metropolis in Beirut (Lebanon), at ArteEast in New York City in 2007 and they started to collaborate in order to share and make the most of their slim resources.[50] From 2007 to 2009, the group developed into a network that exchanged ideas, expertise and knowledge of resources (e.g. grant-writing, fund-raising) and facilitated the circulation of World and Arab films.[51] Thus, the Cinémathèque became one of the founding members of the Network of Arab Art House Screens (NAAS), which included Metropolis Cinema (Beirut, Lebanon), Al Balad Theater (Amman, Jordan), Yabous Cultural Center (Jerusalem, Palestine), and Dox Box (Damascus, Syria). ArteEast (in New York) then incubated NAAS from 2009 to 2017.[52] NAAS now counts twenty members and affiliates in nine different countries (Algeria, Morocco, Tunisia, Egypt, Sudan, Palestine, Lebanon, Iraq, United Emirates), and organises events transnationally throughout their sites, including a week-long workshop in Tangier (22–8 April 2017) attended by twelve representatives of non-governmental NAAS cinema spaces in MENA. Led by Arab and non-Arab international experts, the workshop focused on fine-tuning projects designed to increase the audience and outreach of the alternative venues. NAAS is funded by transnational grants and donations, ranging from Soros's Open Society Institute or the Michigan Theater Foundation to Ginger Beirut Productions, or the Arab Fund for Arts and Culture.

The significant role taken by the Cinémathèque de Tanger in NAAS points to a transnational dimension of the exhibition space and makes Tangier no longer a 'peripheral city' of the CCM or of Morocco, but rather, a key node within a larger nexus of interconnected Arab centres of alternative (transnational) exhibition spaces. Yto Barrada's original artistic alternative vision for a reenergised, modernised Tangerine cinema and cultural centre has now grown into that of a hub in an Arab cinema system that operates outside mostly the purview of governmental structures, and is slowly and tenaciously making progress in building a faithful following. This now well-known institution has passed its ten-year mark and is still forging its own way in a dynamic interplay of national and transnational networks. As such, it provides a hopeful, alternative solution for Moroccan exhibition, as it bravely nurtures its local, national and transnational viewership.

NOTES

1. 'À l'image d'un animal antique, un festival dévore des films et contribue aussi à leur création' (Bakrim 2010: 37).
2. In July 2018, for instance, the CCM commission pledged support for forty-three festivals for the following year. See <https://www.medias24.com/MAROC/Quoi-de-neuf/184805–22-MDH-en-soutien-aux-festivals-cinematographiques.html> (accessed 29 July 2018).
3. Only two festivals star in category A: the Marrakesh International Film Festival (FIFM, which, in 2016, received 11 million MAD, i.e. $1.16 million from the CCM) and the National Film Festival (FNF), held annually in Tangier since 2005 (which, in 2017 and 2018, received 5.75 million MAD, i.e. $606,950 from the CCM). Seven festivals made it to category B in 2017, and received funds ranging from 1.1 to 2 million MAD ($116,100–211,000). Their foci ran the gamut from the Documentary Film Festival for the Culture and History of the Hassani–Sahrawi Space in Laayoune to specialised international film festivals such as the International Women's Film Festival in Salé (FIFS) and the African Film Festival in Khouribga (FCAK). Seven made it to category C, funded to the tune of 150,000–500,000 MAD ($15,830–52,780), and including such recognised festivals as the international documentary film festival FIDADOC in Agadir. Finally, the remaining CCM-supported festivals, labelled *manifestations cinématographiques* (film events), received 40,000 to 100,000 MAD ($4,220–10,550). They too have foci of various dimensions ranging from the International Film School Short Film Festival in Tetouan to the very local Cap Spartel Film Festival (near Tangier). See CCM, *Le Bilan Cinématographique* 2017: 58–72.
4. 'Le Centre cinématographique marocain . . . produced two national feature films for the occasion. Ahmed Mesnaoui and Mohamed Abderrahman Tazi's *Al-hayat kifah* (*Life Is a Fight*, 1968) and Latif Lahlou's *Shams al-Rabii* (*Spring Sun*, 1969) are widely regarded as the country's first postcolonial features even if Mohamed Ousfour's *Al Ibn al bar* (*The Cursed Son*) had been made between 1956 and 1958. The IMFF signaled the official birth of national cinema and set the bar high for the nascent nation's filmmakers to produce cinematic articulations of a society in transition' (Bahmad 2014: 309).
5. Bruno Barde interviewed by Kaouthar Oudrhiri (Oudrhiri 2016).

6. Roundtables include: 'Where is Moroccan Cinema going?' (2016), 'Winning over Moroccan viewers again: a national issue' (2017), 'The Future of Moroccan Cinema' (2018), as well as panels with international speakers on 'Production and Distribution Funding Applications' (2018).

7. With the notable exception of Laïla Marrakchi's *Marock* (2005), which was funded entirely in France.

8. 'The new *cinéastes* met with their older compatriots, discussions flourished about the state and future of Moroccan cinema, and the CCM promised to cast the net of its funding recipients wider to incorporate the new diasporic filmmakers. Their productions over the years have changed the face of this cinema' (Bahmad 2014: 310).

9. Of course, this was not a first for Amazigh films: *The Sleeping Child* (2004), by Yasmine Kassari, as we have seen in Chapter 4, was already in Tamazight.

10. 'Opponents of the film argued that *Tinghir–Jérusalem, les Echos du Mellah* aimed to contribute to the 'normalization' of the relationship with the state of Israel. A PJD member of parliament (MP) called for the direct involvement of the Ministry of Endowments and Islamic Affairs which, in his opinion, should regulate and veto films produced and screened in Morocco' (Graiouid and Belghazi 2013: 268).

11. '*Ar-ri'āya* is based on the tacit principles of guardianship and oversight, and the relationship between the patron and the client presupposes the dependence of the client on the generosity and goodwill of the patron. The client who benefits from *ar-ri'āya* is offered alternative ways of getting things done without having to put up with the frustrating bureaucratic procedures. In exchange, the *ar-rā'i* (the patron) is shown deference and gratitude' (Graiouid and Belghazi 2013: 265).

12. As examples, the royal holding ONA (North African Omnium) has founded and operated Villas des Arts in both Casablanca and Rabat where modern Moroccan art exhibits are curated; and banks such as the Société Générale Marocaine des Banques, Crédit Agricole du Maroc, Attijariwafa Bank have opened galleries of art in major urban centres.

13. In 2009, for instance, Lawrenson reports an attendance of 3,000 viewers on the square. Lawrenson, Edwards. 'Sands of time'. *Sight and Sound*. 2009, 19, 3: 8.

14. Yassine Marco Marrocu's *Catharsys, or the Afina Tales of the Lost World* (Morocco, 2018), Mohamed Zineddaine's *The Healer* (Morocco, Italy, Qatar, 2018), Hicham Lasri's *Jahiliya* (Morocco, France, 2017), Meryem Benm'Barek's *Sofia* (France, Belgium, Qatar, 2018), Narjiss Nejjar's *Stateless* (Morroco/France/Qatar, 2018), Faouzi Bensaïdi's *Volubilis* (France/Morocco/Qatar, 2017), Hind Bensari's *We Could Be Heroes* (Denmark/Morocco/Tunisia/Qatar, 2018).

15. This point about FIFM's preference for the glitz and glamour of the red carpet over the creation of a forum or market for structured exchange with the international film business was acknowledged in various interviews undertaken for this book with film professionals such as Hakim Belabbes (Skype interview, Will Higbee, July 2018), Don Smith (Skype interview, Will Higbee, July 2018) and Hédi Zardi (Skype interview, Will Higbee, June 2017).

16. The Bouregreg Association was created in 1984 with a view to reduce social inequities and to modernise and promote local education and values of tolerance and

democracy and the city of Salé in the Rabat-Salé urban conglomerate and the region: <http://associationbouregreg.ma/fr/> (accessed 20 July 2018).

17. 'Le fait de réussir à réunir toute une pléiade d'artistes du monde entier, d'intellectuels de tout bord, de cinéphiles de tout âge autour des mêmes tables et de les solliciter à réfléchir ensemble sur les tenants et les aboutissants d'un cinéma qui, qu'on le veuille ou non, reste minoritaire, partout dans le monde, est déjà un vrai exploit et permet d'aller de l'avant dans l'encouragement et le respect de la créativité au féminin' (Abdellatif Laassadi quoted in Bennani 2017: <https://lematin.ma/journal/2017/le-cinema-turc-honore-au-festival-international-du-film-de-femmes-de-sale/278413.html>, accessed 20 July 2018).

18. In 2017: Reza Serkanian from Iran, Danièle Souissa from France (who is based and has been teaching in Morocco – at ESAV and ISMAC, most notably) and Mohamed Arious (1959–2018) from Morocco (who wrote the script for Abdelilah el Jaouhary's award-winning short *Water and Blood* 2014), for instance.

19. Written in Arabic, it is in the process of being translated into French at the time of writing, and an English translation is being planned.

20. At its twentieth edition, according to its press release, it paid tribute to Rwandan cinema, aiming 'to strengthen cooperation links between Moroccan and Rwandan film industry leaders' and 'open up opportunities for discussion between Rwandan filmmakers and their Moroccan counterparts' (Boulifa 2017).

21. The Question of Identity in African cinema; Immigration and Cultural Integration: Mechanisms and Challenges; The Image of the Immigrant in African Cinema; Moroccan law on Migration: The Rights and Duties of the African Immigrant.

22. In their source of crowd-funding and artisanal organisation, the festival joins a few predecessors in Morocco, such as L'Boulevard in Casablanca (before the state started sponsoring it) and Hardzazat Hardcore Fest, a counter-cultural, anti-capitalist festival (first edition 2005): <https://www.youtube.com/watch?v=5bvBB5ArdAM&feature=share> (accessed 20 July 2018).

23. 'The first edition of the festival was organized in Rabat from 17 to 20 February, precisely one year after the onset of a new social movement in Morocco on 20 February 2011. The activities took place in different locations such as the headquarters of the Moroccan Labor Union (UMT) and the Moroccan Association of Human Rights (AMDH), high schools, universities and public spaces. . . . The second edition was held between 15 and 20 February 2013 in different venues of Rabat. Within the same spirit as the first edition, the second one was characterized by the support and cooperation of a large number of active citizens, artists, activists, social groups and movements such as the Students Union for the Change of the Education System (UECSE), Guerilla Cinema, Vegetarians in Morocco as well as others.'

24 See blog on the organisation of the third edition of the FRA: <http://www.buala.org/en/da-fala/festival-de-resistance-et-dalternatives-maroc> (accessed 20 July 2018).

25. See Hassan Belkady's complaint in Roudaby 2014.

26. Noureddine Saïl makes the point that in France, the high volume of streaming does not threaten movie-going (Saïl, 'JCC 2010: Allocation d'ouverture', in Caillé and Martin 2012: 18–19).

27. See Férid Boughedir, *Caméra Arabe* (Tunisia, 1987).

28. '... aucun distributeur marocain n'en a voulu. J'ai alors supplié l'exploitant du cinéma Mauritania à Tanger de le projeter. Je lui ai promis, juré qu'il aurait des spectateurs. Je suis allée avec des copines coller des affiches dans les cafés en ville et dans la médina. Nous nous sommes débrouillées, à bord d'une camionnette avec haut-parleur, pour sillonner les rues de la ville et de sa banlieue et faire l'annonce du film. Finalement, nous avons réussi à remplir la salle et le film y est resté une semaine. L'exploitant m'avoua qu'il avait fait une meilleure recette qu'avec *Les Dents de la mer* qui était le film qui avait le mieux marché cette saison-là' (Benlyazid 2012: 41).

29. 'With the three local distributors (and all the films that don't have one) we had to build a new distribution network to get the movies we wanted to screen and self-produce the advertising material to go with them' (Yto Barrada, quoted in Berrada and Berrada 2011: 34).

30. 'Without a national production, there is no strong market, and without movie theaters, there is no national production' (Saïl 2017: 10).

31. It is right now building two theatres: one in Agadir and one in Rabat.

32. 'Rappelons au passage que l'enjeu majeur pour ce groupe est de pouvoir contrôler la circulation dans les salles de cinéma au Maroc des grosses productions américaines et de pouvoir les programmer dans ses multiplexes en même temps que leur sortie en salles en Europe' (226) (Benchenna 2015).

33. Fourteen in Casablanca, nine in Marrakesh, eight in Tangier, three in Fes; Rabat's Megarama is predicted to have eleven screens and Agadir's twelve.

34. According to the various CCM *Bilans*:

	US (%)	Morocco (%)
2017	49.90	30.47
2016	65	18
2015	50	23
2014	47	24
2013	44	24
2012	51	28

35. 'Le décret 2.12.325 du 17/08/2012 a décidé d'attribuer un soutien financier aux salles de cinéma pour leur numérisation, leur modernisation et pour la création de nouvelles salles. Depuis 2013, le passage des salles au numérique est donc soutenu par l'État et en 2015 90% du parc de salles est numérisé': <http://www.ccm.ma/soutien-aux-salles-de-cinema> (accessed 23 July 2018).

36. 'At the Rex we watched American films dubbed in Spanish. And Egyptian films, musical comedies with Leila Mourad, Farid el Atrache, Smahan. They were close to us, but the American films fascinated us far more' (Ahmed Akdi, quoted in *Album Cinémathèque de Tanger*, 2011: 110).

37. It was thus renamed in honour of the Imazighen (formerly referred to as Berbers by outsiders) of the northern region of the Rif, who rose against the Spanish occupier

and the Moroccan Sultan (Yusef) in 1921, seceded from the Kingdom and created the Republic of the Rif that lasted from 1921 to 1926.

38. 'I arrived in Tangier in 1974. But I'd never come to this cinema . . . too dangerous, I'd been to the Mabrouk, the Roxy, the Mauritania, they were quite something, fine cinemas, like actual theaters, where you could go with your family, your husband, people respected you. Here people didn't respect each other, a woman could hear a man proffering insults, dirty words, and so you weren't respected if anyone saw you coming out of this cinema. It was risky too: the audience sometimes threw bottles at the screen' (Fatna Algali, quoted in *Album Cinémathèque de Tanger*, 2011: 129).

39. It took them two years to get the old movie theatre completely renovated by the firm of French architect Jean-Marc Lalo, paid for by donations (the seats in the refurbished Rif bear the names of Agnès B, Pierre Bergé, among others).

40. Yto Barrada and Bouchra Khalili interviewed by Phillipe Ruoy in <https://www .franceculture.fr/emissions/sur-les-docks-14-15/champ-libre-24-tanger-du-cinema-la-cinematheque> (accessed 23 July 2018).

41. This 'alternative' café is where, among other Tangerine characters, Shakib Ben Omar, the actor of the eponymous protagonist in Oliver Laxe's *Mimosas*, 2016, works.

42. Mohamed Ansari, interviewed by Flo Martin, 15 March 2018.

43. 'La Cinémathèque de Tanger est une association à but non lucratif créée en 2006 et a pour mission de promouvoir le cinéma mondial au Maroc et le cinéma marocain dans le monde, créer une collection de films documentaires, de films et de vidéos d'artistes et de cinéma expérimental, de proposer des actions pédagogiques et de créer une plateforme de dialogue et de rencontre pour les professionnels du cinéma': <https://www.cinemathequedetanger.com/la-cinematheque/partenaires/> (accessed 7 February 2020).

44. In 2015, for instance, the three films were: *Eyes without a Face* (Georges Franju, France, 1960), *Timbuktu* (Abderrahmane Sissoko, France/Mauritania, 2014) and *A Thousand Months* (Faouzi Bensaïdi, Morocco, 2015).

45. When the complex first opened, Yto Barrada partnered with the Swiss Association *La Lanterne magique* in order to launch the initial film series programme to educate the children to film viewing.

46. Mohamed Ansari, ibid.

47. For example, ACRIF – Association des Cinémas de Recherche d'Île-de-France Research Cinema (Association of the Ile-de-France region); NAAS (see below).

48. It also hosts its own distribution company (Société Cinématographique Nord Africaine).

49. Malika Chaghal interviewed by Flo Martin, 15 March 2018.

50. Ibid.

51. 'Some common needs included facilitating the circulation of films, sharing pack-aged film programs, building a network for distributing Arab films, and subtitling. To overcome the isolation that each screen faced, they banded together to create NAAS, a structure to share knowledge and expertise as well as tools for development and fundraising.' See NAAS website: <https://www.naasnetwork.org/content/history> (accessed 7 February 2020).

52. The network grew and it changed its name 'from Network of Arab Art house Screens to Network of Arab Alternative Screens, or "شـــبكة الشاشـــات العربيـــة المســـتقلة" to "شـــبكة الشاشـــات العربيـــة البديلـــة", and it was officially registered as a non-profit organization in Beirut, Lebanon' (ibid.).

6. INTERNATIONAL FESTIVALS: AN ALTERNATIVE TRANSNATIONAL DISTRIBUTION NETWORK FOR MOROCCAN CINEMA?

As noted at the start of the previous chapter, the CCM invests a considerable sum of money in support of dozens of film festivals across Morocco. As well as the potential economic and cultural benefits that such events can have at a local level, Morocco's festival ecosystem offers an alternative distribution network for filmmakers who aspire to reach as wide a (national) audience as possible with their films – at a time when traditional exhibition channels are in crisis and film theatres have all but disappeared from large parts of the country. However, to focus solely on the national reach of the festival circuit is to overlook the fact that 'the film festival has always been the site where the inherently transnational character of cinematic art reveals itself most glaringly' (Iordanova 2016: xiii).

THE TRANSNATIONAL FESTIVAL NETWORK

According to industry analyst Stephen Follows, as recently as 2013 there were approximately 3,000 film festivals active globally.[1] This international festival circuit is, of course, far from uniform: encompassing festivals of different scale, reach, duration, focus and with varying levels of transnational connectivity (from the niche, two-day festival organised by volunteers on a shoestring budget to the multi-million-dollar behemoth that is an A-list international film festival). To speak of a homogeneous festival 'circuit' is, therefore, to employ a 'volatile and contingent term' (Loist 2016: 49), given the range of festivals taking place across the world. Likewise, contrary to their presumed status as often the oldest and most important festivals in the world, not every audience member or filmmaker is solely focused on A-list European festivals such as Venice, Cannes, Berlin or the newer international festivals that have come to prominence such as Toronto and Busan.[2]

Rejecting this notion of the circuit, Loist proposes that we think instead in terms of the 'network'(Loist 2016: 50) as a means of emphasising the transnational and interconnected nature of many of these film festivals, as well as the audiences and industry professionals who attend them. Extending Loist's notion of the network one step further, what arguably emerges is an interconnected festival ecosystem that more closely resembles an evolving, rhizomatic network rather than a rigid circuit. Viewing the film festival ecosystem in this way is also to acknowledge that multiple mappings of the 'network' will exist simultaneously. How the festival network is perceived and navigated will depend on the position occupied by the individual filmmaker, company, organisation or institution in relation to both individual festivals, clusters of festivals (for example niche festivals on African or Arab cinema) and the larger festival network itself. It will also be determined by the value that stakeholders assign to the characteristics and focus of specific festivals.

Viewed in this way, analysis of the data compiled by the CCM on the participation of Moroccan cinema at film festivals outside the Kingdom from 2011 to 2017[3] offers insight into what might currently constitute a 'transnational festival network' from a Moroccan perspective. Morocco is an African film culture with a relatively high level of production – fourth in terms of the number of feature films produced annually behind South Africa and Egypt, with Nigeria way ahead of all others – but often perceived by Moroccan industry professionals as struggling to establish visibility internationally.[4] CCM data on the participation of Moroccan films in the official selection of foreign film festivals between 2013 and 2017 suggests that this perception is not entirely just. Between 2013 and 2017 Moroccan films were selected for competition in a total of 294 film festivals and appeared as out-of-competition films in 259 festivals across the globe (in North America, South America, East Asia, the Gulf States, Africa and Europe). There is a strong Moroccan presence across a number of European festivals (in countries such as Italy, Spain, Belgium and Germany) with France, perhaps unsurprisingly given the cultural, historical and linguistic links between the two countries, hosting by far the largest number of Moroccan films at the greatest number of festivals. However, Moroccan cinema is also visible at African festivals (including the most prestigious: FESPACO and JCC), consistent with the geopolitical strategies for cooperation between Morocco and in particular sub-Saharan Africa outlined in Chapter 2. In a similar way, certain inroads have been made into South American festivals – most notably in Argentina, which also reflects the attempts within the past decade to establish closer production links between the two countries. A strong visibility for Moroccan films at MENA festivals is hardly unexpected. However, another noticeable development in the 2000s has been the presence of Moroccan films at a range of festivals created in North America post- 9/11 that focus on a broader engagement with Arab cinema and culture. (Both these trends are discussed in more detail later in this chapter.)

The CCM, working in collaboration with Moroccan embassies and consulates also intervenes to promote Moroccan cinema globally by offering financial and logistic support to cycles or special programmes of films promoting Moroccan cinema in individual cities.[5] International festivals have acknowledged Morocco's diverse film culture and cinematic heritage post-independence with retrospectives in (among others): Bulgaria (Sofia-Manar Festival 2014), Cameroon (*Ecrans noirs* festival, Yaoundé, 2014), Argentina (LatinArab festival, Buenos Aires, 2014), France (IMA, 2014; Fameck Arab Film Festival, 2016), Colombia (Cinema and Human Rights Festival, Bogota, 2015), Sweden (Malmo Arab Film Festival, 2016), Germany (Berlinale, 2016) and Egypt (Luxor African Film Festival, 2017). Moroccan films will thus variously be identified as 'African', 'Arab' or even 'World' cinema depending on the context and editorial focus of the festival that they play in.

On the surface, the CCM data present a compelling argument for the transnational reach of Moroccan cinema via an international festival network. However, further analysis reveals a more complicated picture. For example, if we consider the Moroccan presence at French festivals in 2013, we find that, while there were 101 screenings of Moroccan films (features, shorts and documentaries) at twenty-seven festivals, not all of these films were new to the festival network. Some, such as *Transes* (el Maanouni, 1981), *The Mirage* (Bouanani, 1979) and *Looking for My Wife's Husband* (Mohamed Abderrahman Tazi, 1993) were part of 'homage' or retrospectives of Moroccan cinema screened out of competition; others were selected for their relevance to the particular theme of the festival (e.g. human rights, immigration). More significant, however, is the fact that this total of 101 screenings comprises only forty-one individual films.

A clear pattern emerges from the CCM data, repeated across years and in different countries, whereby certain festival-friendly films are picked up and play repeatedly across multiple festivals, while the majority of Moroccan films produced in any one year gain little or no international exposure. By way of an example: following its premier as part of the prestigious ACID Programme at Cannes,[6] Hicham Lasri's *They Are the Dogs* (2013), an alternative, punk-auteur exploration of social tensions in contemporary Morocco, screened at six different French festivals and ten international festivals in total between May and December 2013. Nabil Ayouch's *Horses of God* (2013), which also premiered at Cannes in the even more prestigious Director's Fortnight sidebar, went on to be selected for twenty festivals in 2013. And this momentum is not reserved solely for feature films: after winning the Grand Prix du Court Métrage at the National Festival in Tangier in 2013, Munir Abbar's short film, *The Target* (2012) – a stylised exploration of media hysteria surrounding the Islamic terrorist 'threat' – was selected for Cannes, six French festivals and nine international festivals in total. All three films, in their distinctive ways, display originality, intelligence and visual sophistication, the hallmarks of a transnational auteur cinema attractive to international festival programmers and audiences. Moreover, in Ayouch's case, *Horses of God* offered a representation of Islamic fundamentalism in Morocco that was seen by many Moroccan critics and filmmakers as offering a neo-Orientalist perspective, more accessible to Western audiences.[7]

The advantages for such films that are selected and 'break out' at A-list festivals like Cannes are obvious. Official selection for these larger, more prestigious festivals means that these films are seen by a range of programmers, who are themselves present at the A-list festivals searching for films to include in their own festivals. This includes programmers from niche festivals (such as Fameck Arab Film Festival) as well as representatives from international 'Festivals of Festivals' (such as the London Film Festival). What is more, the domino effect for a successful film can extend to a presence at a range of festivals across a number of years. For example, after its initial success in 2013, Lasri's *They Are the Dogs* was selected for a further eighteen international festivals in 2014 and four in 2015. While many of these screenings were at more niche festivals (such as those targeted at Arab, African or Mediterannean cinema), they also included a presence at more high-profile festivals such as FESPACO, the Malmo Arab Film Festival and the Toronto International Film Festival. In this respect, the international festival network acts for a limited number of Moroccan filmmakers as an alternative distribution network: 'a discrete *exhibition* outlet [that is] symptomatic of the *lack* of formal and robust distribution opportunities for many films by Africans, both in and beyond the continent' (Dovey 2015: 3, original emphasis). According to Hédi Zardi, sales agent for the Spanish–Moroccan–French–Qatari co-production *Mimosas*, revenue from screening fees generated by the dozens of appearances at international festivals in the first twelve to eighteen months was almost equivalent to the initial minimum guarantees (MGs) paid for the film by international distributors during the same period.[8] While not discounting the potential value of festival screening fees to Moroccan producers, we should be wary of suggesting that such revenue can act as a substitute for commercial theatrical distribution. Not all festivals have to pay screening fees. Those that do are more likely to be niche festivals that can only afford to pay modest fees for their films – typically running in the hundreds rather than thousands of dollars per screening

(Wong 2011: 144). The true value of this international festival network to most African filmmakers has, therefore, more to do with building contacts and engaging festival audiences, than with raising a significant revenue stream from screening fees.

Moroccan cinema's presence at such a diverse selection of international festivals reminds us that individual festivals have different and quite specific aims (political, cultural, socio-economic). These can range from building creative professional networks, engaging cinema audiences, promoting individual cities or regions for tourism purposes, to establishing transnational solidarity for political activism and forging a sense of collective community or identity for minority groups. (Some of these broader functions of the film festival are explored in the next section of this chapter on niche festivals.) However, as the earlier example of Lasri's *They Are the Dogs* illustrates, international A-list film festivals such as Cannes, Berlin, Venice and Toronto remain central to the construction of cinema knowledge as well as the behind-the-scene mechanics of finance, distribution and exhibition.

Figure 6.1   Masterclass with German–Turkish director Fatih Akin, FIFM, December 2015 (photo by authors)

EUROPE: A-LIST FESTIVALS, MARKETS AND FILM FUNDS

Although the contemporary festival network is truly international, film festivals first emerged in Europe, and the continent continues to host some of the most prestigious and well-established festivals: Cannes, Venice, Berlin, Locarno and Rotterdam. Morocco's geographical proximity to Europe should, in theory, offer an advantage – in reality, however, many Moroccan filmmakers find themselves envious spectators, located firmly on the outside of this A-list festival network. From a historical perspective, De Valck (2007) identifies three phases to the development of major international festivals: from a focus on promoting national cinemas from the 1930s to the late 1960s, to an emphasis on programming and curation driven as much by socio-political as artistic concerns, and finally the current phase from the early 1990s with an 'age of festival directors', described by Dovey as 'an era of growing professionalization, institutionalization and internationalization' (Dovey 2015: 39). Progressively since the mid-2000s, then, A-list festivals have emerged as 'intermediaries and increasingly active players in all aspects of the film industry' (Loist 2016: 51), operating alongside film markets or de facto markets (that bring together producers, distributors, sales agents, funders and national film agencies) as well as developing initiatives related to training and funding for all stages of development, production and distribution.

The significance and power of the major international festivals for Moroccan filmmakers therefore rest on the festivals' potential to bring their films to the attention of both wider audiences *and* the international film industry, where building a network of personal contacts and locating funding can be crucial for advancing subsequent projects. Major festivals/markets such as the Berlinale (EFM), and Cannes (Marché International du Film) offer precisely this space to deal with international producers and national funders (essential for unlocking territory specific funds for international co-production) as well as sales agents (who will handle international sales of a given film) and distributors (who have the specialist knowledge to help a film reach an audience in their local territories and may even offer a minimum guarantee or pre-sale that the producer can incorporate into the production budget). Although European and North American companies inevitably have a commanding presence at such festivals, other regions are also represented. For example, the Arab Cinema Centre (organised by pan-Arab distributor and sales agents MAD Solutions) are an active presence at the EFM in Berlin and the Marché at Cannes, as well as other key international film festivals and markets across the year. Large international festivals attract many players within the international film business because they represent valuable sites for networking, training, masterclasses and industry forums.

Figure 6.2   Moroccan producer Lamia Chraibi participates in an Arab cinema industry panel at the EFM (Berlin), February 2017 (photo by authors)

Major international festivals (especially European festivals) also play an increasingly important role in providing funding, grant schemes and mentoring for development (co-production and post-production for cinemas of the so-called Global South). Key international festival funds in this respect include the World Cinema Fund (WCF) (Berlinale), the MAFF Market Forum (the Malmo Arab Film Festival), Hubert Bals Fund (Rotterdam International Film Festival), while other funds, such as the CNC's Aide aux cinémas du monde (formerly the Fonds Sud) are visible at Cannes. Unlike Gulf funding from the DFI (see Chapter 2), these European funds require some form of co-production or collaboration with the country where the related festival is based.

While such funds can only support a proportion of the overall budget, even for a modest feature film, their real benefit is twofold: first, in supporting projects at crucial stages of development and post-production; second in prestige, associated support (in the form of experienced international co-producers), and access to mentoring schemes that such awards attract. An award from the WCF, for instance, can be seen as an endorsement of the overall quality of a given project that will encourage other funders to invest, and can assist with sales to international distributors. Finally, awards from such funding schemes also help 'southern' filmmakers to 'gain access to the inner track of the film festival circuit' (Falicov 2016: 210), and raise their profile and chances of securing transnational grants and funding for future projects. For example, Leïla Kilani was awarded funding from both the Hubert Bals Fund (IFFR) for Script and Development in 2008 and a $40,000 grant from the WCF in 2011 for her feature *On the Edge*. The film went on to enjoy considerable success in the international festival network: premiering at the Directors' Fortnight in Cannes and playing at dozens of festivals over the next three years. The success and transnational visibility of *On the Edge* was undoubtedly a factor that led to Kilani's securing a further grant from the WCF for her latest feature film, *Indivision* (Morocco/France/Qatar/UAE), which was still in post-production in 2019.

The benefits to a filmmaker of becoming a grantee of a scheme such as the WCF are obvious. Nevertheless, the fact that such funds require the involvement of European co-producers, combined with perceived preferences for the types of films that are supported by these funds – auteur-led productions, realist narratives reflecting the 'logic of European humanitarian agenda' (Diawara 2010: 87) – has led to accusations of paternalism, Eurocentrism and neocolonialism on the part of funders (Barlet 2000: 267). Concerns persist over exactly whose perspective of the world such 'world cinema' festival funds may promote, with 'southern' filmmakers potentially adapting their projects in ways that appear favourable to the funder (Falicov 2010: 7). Nevertheless, as Wong reminds us, the reality of such funding is rarely so clear-cut: 'if left with the unregulated global capitalist market and even national support, many of these films would not even be made'(Wong 2011: 157).

For its part, the CCM recognises the economic importance of such festivals to the future of Moroccan cinema and, indeed, to attracting foreign film production to Morocco. It maintains a regular presence at the two largest international festivals and film markets in Berlin (EFM) and Cannes (Marché International du Film), as well as activity at key Arab film festivals such as the Malmo Arab Film Festival (Sweden) and a festival focused on international film but located in the Arab world, such as the Dubai International Film Festival (until its haitus in 2018).[9] Nevertheless, the CCM's central aim – increasingly so under the leadership of Sarim Fassi Fihri – has been to promote Morocco as a service location for foreign productions – especially those from Hollywood – at these international festivals and film markets, rather than the work of Moroccan filmmakers themselves. Hicham Lasri appeared in the sidebar official selections at the Berlinale for the five consecutive years (2014–18), an unprecedented achievement for *any* director in the history of the Berlinale. Yet such artistic success has barely been celebrated on the official Moroccan stand at the EFM, where promotion of the recently introduced tax rebate for foreign producers has taken precedence over the promotion of Moroccan films screening at the festival. It may seem therefore that the CCM has more interest in luring foreign productions to the country than supporting Moroccan filmmakers at international film festivals. There is also a danger of focusing predominantly or even exclusively on international markets outside Africa. For example, although a market has existed at FESPACO for a number of years it remains largely ignored by producers, distributors and sales agents outside West Africa. In the pan-African context, the recent success of the DISCOP markets and co-production forum (analysed later in this chapter) represents a significant but currently unrealised opportunity for Moroccan cinema. The potential opportunities for Moroccan cinema to collaborate with festivals and markets in Africa and the Middle East appears, therefore, to remain overshadowed by the lure of (uncertain and highly competitive) investment from Europe.

In terms of a Moroccan directorial presence at the major international film festivals in the West, a similar pattern to that noted earlier about the general circulation of Moroccan films and filmmakers in international film networks can be observed. Participation in A-list festivals such as Cannes, Berlin and Venice in the last fifteen years has been limited to a very select group of filmmakers – Hicham Lasri (Berlin, Cannes, Toronto International Film Festival (TIFF)), Nabil Ayouch (Cannes, TIFF), Narjiss Nejjar (Cannes, Berlin), Faouzi Bensaïdi (Cannes, Venice, TIFF and Berlin), Leïla Kilani (Cannes), Laïla Marrakchi (Cannes, TIFF), Hakim Belabbes (Rotterdam International Film Festival, IFFR), Tala Hadid (Cannes, Berlin), Abdellah Taia (IFFR), Meryem Benm'Barek (Cannes) and, in her role as producer, Lamai Chraibi (Cannes, TIFF, Berlin). Beyond these major European festivals, Moroccan cinema performs well at FESPACO, JCC and Dubai, though, once again, a similar roster of directorial talent and films that appears repeatedly in the official selection of these festivals.

Moroccan filmmakers have enjoyed even less success in accessing the (admittedly highly competitive) development, production and post-production funds from European festivals. Only two Moroccan filmmakers – Leïla Kilani and Daoud Aoulad-Syad – have been awarded funding from the Hubert Bals Fund since its inception in 1988 until 2019, while grants from the WCF have been limited to two films by Leïla Kilani (again) and two films by Faouzi Bensaïdi. Elsewhere in Europe, awards to Moroccan films from the MAFF Market Forum – aimed at funding Arab–Nordic co-productions – are disappointingly low. More success has come in Venice, where Kilani (in 2017) and, most recently Nadir Bouhmouch (in 2018) have been selected for the festival's Final Cut initiative, a production bridge workshop, aimed at providing post-production support to films from Africa and the Arab world. Though not a funding initiative in the way of the WCF or Hubert Bals, Final Cut is undoubtedly beneficial in terms of the access and guidance that it provides at the post-production stage for African and Arab filmmakers, and a further example of the networking, mentoring and training opportunities offered by the European festival network to a select number of Moroccan filmmakers.

That such a select group of Moroccan filmmakers break into these major festivals and successfully access funding should not come as a surprise: these are, after all, some of the world's leading film festivals that receive thousands of entries each year from filmmakers across the globe with space to select only a few hundred films.[10] Morocco is, moreover, not alone in perceiving itself to be under-represented at such festivals: similar debates resurface annually in the UK, for example, when the official selection for Cannes is announced and the limited presence of British filmmakers at the world's leading film festival is bemoaned.[11] Applications for prestigious festival funds are, similarly, highly competitive. Since its launch in 2004, the WCF has awarded production and distribution funding to a total of 196 projects selected from 3,448 submissions from Africa, Latin America, the Middle East, Central and Southeast Asia and the Caucasus.[12] Moreover, as already noted, only four of these 196 awards from the WCF have been given to Moroccan films (by two directors: Kilani and Bensaïdi).

Arguably what is more pertinent about the 'elite' of Moroccan cinema being selected for these A-list festivals is that, with the exception of Hicham Lasri, all of these filmmakers are *cinéastes de passage*, as discussed in Chapter 2. This phenomenon further illustrates the ability of the *cinéastes de passage* to move relatively freely between Morocco and Europe: their existing network of international collaborators, the repeated visibility of their films at these major international festivals, and their presence at key international film markets, are all factors that facilitate their integration into networks and forums of transnational production, funding, distribution and exhibition. This confirms Dovey's claim that an 'African diaspora language' is what most distinguishes the filmmakers who tend to be featured in large international film festivals from those who have access only to local audiences and markets' (Dovey 2015: 7). The key question, then, remains how those Moroccan filmmakers who are largely excluded from this international film network and could benefit from access to it (which is not necessarily the case for every Moroccan filmmaker) can best be supported by the CCM and learn from the experience of the Moroccan *cinéastes de passage*.

Nevertheless, access, participation and even critical success at such European festivals is no guarantee of distribution for Moroccan films, either at home or abroad. Speaking at a conference linked to the Africa in Motion film festvial in Edinburgh in October 2018, producer Lamia Chraibi lamented the fact that, despite being selected for prestigious international festivals and even winning awards, a film such as *Stateless*, directed by acclaimed Moroccan filmmaker Narjiss Nejjar and produced by Chraibi, was unable to secure either an international release or a domestic theatrical release in Morocco. Another of her films, the Spanish–Moroccan–French–Qatari co-production *Mimosas*, secured a modest international distribution (thanks to the work of international sales agency Luxbox) but failed to achieve theatrical distribution in Morocco, where, according to Chraibi, the film was deemed by distributors too arty and 'difficult' for Moroccan audiences.[13]

While the Moroccan *cinéastes de passage* may prioritise a presence at European festivals and their associated markets, given their focus on an international co-production model to finance their films, not all Moroccan filmmakers see this as an achievable, or even desirable aim. Indeed, an exclusive focus on the status of European A-list festivals can lead to what Dovey, citing Nornes, describes as a '*short* circuit' in the festival network resulting from 'indifference to' and 'ignorance of' those alternative festivals deemed of little industry importance that do not place a European worldview centre stage (Dovey 2015: 39). For many Moroccan filmmakers, then, international festivals beyond Europe, as well as festivals within Europe that focus specifically on Arab, African, Mediterranean or francophone cinema, are more likely to be identified as key nodes in any transnational Moroccan festival network than the seemingly unreachable A-list roster of Cannes, Venice and Berlin. Similarly, the historical, political and cultural significance of pan-African festivals such as JCC and FESPACO could lead Moroccan filmmakers to view them as the more desirable location for their films to engage with transnational and postcolonial audiences. With this alternative perspective on the transnational Moroccan festival network in mind, let us now turn our attention to key festivals beyond Europe, and finally to the significance of niche or boutique festivals across the European continent to the transnational distribution of Moroccan cinema.

International Festivals beyond Europe: The Gulf and Africa

A number of international festivals screening Moroccan films exist as well as the major European festivals, engaging with diverse audiences that include film critics, local or national media, academics and a local public. They roughly fall into three regional categories: (1) the most recently created Arab international festivals in the Gulf that address international film professionals and media, and a Middle Eastern viewership; (2) the African–Arab festivals on the African continent that are designed for African local audiences and international professionals and media; (3) the niche festivals that pepper the Mediterranean, European and American landscapes and attract a steady flow of local and diasporic audiences, as well as media and film critics (as do the other two sets of festivals).

As discussed in Chapter 2, the international film festivals in the Gulf (Doha, Dubai, Abu Dhabi, and more recently Amman) were created in the 2000s as an Arab response to 9/11 and its aftershocks on the global stage: the Gulf needed to produce its own narratives and offer its informed takes on Arab cultures on screen. Responding to a separate geopolitical agenda, they were also intended to provide training opportunities to inexperienced filmmakers in the Gulf, and included a host of sidebar programmes and a market. They gave Moroccan cinema visibility and contributed to its exhibition in A-list festivals such as DIFF (Dubai), which worked with Cannes and European and American film professionals to help develop an international Arab platform of filmmaking and exhibition (see Figures 2.1–2.3, Chapter 2). Hicham Lasri's first part of his 'trilogy of the dog', *They Are the Dogs*, premiered in competition at the DIFF, and was awarded two prizes at the 2013 twentieth edition (a Golden Muhr for his fetish actor Hassan Ben Badida, and a special Jury prize for production by Nabil Ayouch). The film was then screened in the section at Cannes and was in competition at the Hamburg Film Festival in 2014. The film then circulated from the Gulf to an A-list European festival (Cannes), and to European and then US niche festivals, becoming part of three intersecting networks.

However, the closing down of two festivals in the Gulf in recent years (Abu Dhabi in 2014 and Doha–Tribeca in 2012) underlines their vulnerability, given how much these relatively new international film festivals are designed to provide global visibility rather than building a cinematic culture or legacy. They rely heavily and problematically on the cultural and economic politics of each nation's leadership. Beyond the Gulf area, the picture of Middle Eastern festivals is blurry at the time of writing: civil war has postponed the next edition of the Damascus International Film Festival for years; the Cairo IFF has resumed after a hiatus following the Arab Spring; the IFF in Beirut is still holding strong. We are clearly at a time of transition, and Moroccan cinema (which has not been in competition in the 2016 and 2017 editions of the DIFF) has less visibility in the Gulf for a variety of reasons (outlined in Chapter 2). Although it is too early to predict whether this is a hiatus or a lasting trend, it does look like the era of the Gulf festivals as international festivals with an emphasis on MENA productions is over, to be replaced by other initiatives focused on Middle Eastern, indeed specifically Gulf, film production.

In contrast, the deeply rooted postcolonial African continental film festivals offer a more stable if more modest picture and have contributed to the visibility and exhibition of Moroccan films in a markedly different fashion over the decades. Since their creation, the international film festivals in Africa, like the A-list European festivals (see the earlier section of this chapter), have followed a progression in scope and organisation, developing various initiatives in the margin of film exhibition. Although their main focus remains giving visibility to Arab and African cinema, their discourse and practices have changed from their 1960s Marxist-inflected vision of African and Arab cinemas to a 2010s conception of a viable pan-Arab and pan-African film production and distribution in a larger neo-liberal economic context.

The year 1966 was momentous for African and Arab cultures and cinemas: the World Festival of Negro Arts – with a significant film component – opened in Dakar, Senegal; Ousmane Sembène released *Black Girl*, the first postcolonial Senegalese – indeed sub-Saharan – feature film; the international Arab–African film festival *Les Journées Cinématographiques de Carthage* (JCC, the Tunis International Film Festival), still the oldest international film festival running outside Europe, held its first edition in Tunis. Thus 1966 launched '"African Cinema" as a self-consciously defined concept *on* the continent' (Dovey 2015: 95), and, one might add, *for* the continental (African) viewers in the first row, and global viewers in the back seats.

An initiative funded by the Ministry of Culture (Bourguiba saw the development of the audiovisual sector as a priority in the building of the nation[14]), the JCC was the brainchild of Tunisian critic and intellectual Tahar Cheriaa and the two major film associations of independent Tunisia.[15] Its aim was to foster the sharing, visibility, and production of third cinema by Arab and African filmmakers, and to promote the distinct languages, politics and aesthetics of their postcolonial cinemas, as they resisted the 'fatal domination' of the first world in film production and distribution (Chériaa 1978: 34). The latter was in some ways reminiscent of the goal of the early twentieth-century European film festivals.[16] The successful inaugural edition attracted filmmakers and representatives of thirty-one different countries, including ten from the African and Arab world (nine of which were francophone),[17] and inspired two subsequent festivals: one in sub-Saharan Africa and one in the Middle East.

On the heels of the JCC's second edition, Aminata Salembéré's group of cinephiles created the 'African Cinema Week' in Ouagadougou, Upper Volta (Burkina Faso since 1984) in February 1969, which became FESPACO (Ouagadougou's Pan-African Cinema and Television Festival) in 1972, and recurred every other February, ever since. (The second one, the pan-Arab Damascus International Film Festival, was founded in 1979 in Syria, and also alternated with the JCC, until 2011.[18]) Since 1972, FESPACO has been consistently funded by the Burkinabe government – even through its tumultuous history of *coups d'état* in the 1970s–1980s – and by the (French and) European North: the Cultural and Technical Cooperation Agency (ACTT), the European Economic Community and UNESCO; as well as, starting in 1987, Cuba and the USSR. Shunning red carpet glitz, the festival opens in the Stade du 4 Août[19] with music, dance, and other entertainment, and attracts a large public (with cheap tickets at the screening of the competition downtown, and free screenings and discussions facilitated by film critics provided by an itinerant cinema in outlying neighbourhoods). Likewise, the JCC has always opened its doors to the general public with discounted tickets in several venues. In 2017, the screenings took place in ten different theatres in Tunis and six in the suburbs, and in two detention centres, the prison for men and the prison for women, where filmmakers and their teams debated with the inmates.[20]

Together, the JCC in Tunis and FESPACO in Ouagadougou became not only a yearly African rendezvous for directors and their public, but also a forum for filmmakers, critics and professionals, with an international competition reserved for Arab and African films and an exhibition of films from all over the world. The overall purpose of both festivals stayed true to their original manifesto-like declarations, although the strategies deployed to reach their initial goals changed over the years.[21] The JCC subscribed to a double political vision of cinema as pan-Arab and pan-African – hence the birth of the Fédération Panafricaine des Cinéastes, FEPACI, at its 1970 edition. Working with FESPACO and the 1969 Pan-African Cultural Festival in Algiers, it configured 'new circuits of dissemination and circulation linked not just to the new pan-African rhetoric, but also to the solidarity and revolutionary demands of what was still known as the Third World' (Elena 2014: 5). From the start, then, both African festivals developed as self-designated hubs in three intersecting networks for film distribution: Francophone, pan-African and pan-Arab. Founded at the dawn of independence, they responded to common needs (exhibiting African films to African viewers, imaging the cultures of a pre-colonial past and women[22] through cinema), and were supported by their respective governments, even if the politics of the latter sometimes clashed with the politics of the festival organisers. For, over the decades of strong regimes in MENA and sub-Saharan Africa, the political discourse framing the festivals started to also include coded resistance at home, even as, paradoxically, the directors and film professionals were becoming increasingly dependent on 'state surrogate forms of cultural patronage' (see Chapter 5) nationally (e.g. the Ministry of Culture in Tunis, the state in Burkina Faso, the CCM in Rabat) and transnationally (FEPACI has long benefited from technical and financial support from France).

Nonetheless, both festivals are responsible for laying out the basis of canon formation for Arab and African cinemas, as the new films (pan-Arab and pan-African) were introduced and auteurs' careers launched in Tunis and Ouagadougou.[23] The prizes awarded at either festival have triggered articles and interviews in the national and continental (as well as European) media, and greater visibility for each award-winning film and its director transnationally. During the 2010s, Morocco has featured prominently among the prize-winning films. Over the six JCC editions since 2010, five Moroccan features have received a Golden, Silver, or Bronze Tanit, and one short a Golden Tanit.[24] Over the four editions of the FESPACO, three Moroccan features won Yennenga Stallions, and two shorts were awarded Golden Foals.[25] Out of twenty-three Golden Stallions awarded, four were given to Moroccan directors for their films over the years: Souheil Ben-Barka, for *A Thousand and One Hands* in 1973; Nabil Ayouch for *Ali Zaoua*, in 2001; Mohamed Mouftakir for *Pegasus* in 2011; Hicham Ayouch for *Fevers* in 2015. Morocco has been and remains the primary winner of first prizes at FESPACO. The laureates in several categories include the usual *cinéastes de passage* Hicham Ayouch, Faouzi Bensaïdi or filmmakers such as Hicham Lasri – based in Morocco but with access to European co-production and transnational development funds linked to international festivals. FESPACO awarded the first prize not to Sissoko's *Timbuktu* (2014) but to *Fevers*[26] (however, given the timing of the festival, the film had already had its international festival career[27]). Both festivals, in contrast to the major European festivals, significantly also include Moroccan filmmakers who operate from Morocco with Moroccan production companies, like Abdelilah el Jaouhary, Daoud Aoulad-Syad, Mohamed Mouftakir and Saïd Khallaf.

Directors also have access to several programmes that the festival organisers have developed over the years.[28] In 2017, the JCC boasted four sidebar programmes alongside the competition, Panorama section and homage to directors. Of particular interest, the Takmil ('finishing') programme,[29] launched in 2014, supports African and Arab film projects post-production: there, directors and their producers are invited to pitch their film to the jury for one of the seven available most promising film grants. Out of the 2017 selection (four fictions and four documentaries), one hailed from Morocco: Mohcine Besri's fiction *Laaziza*, about the repudiation of a pregnant woman and her son. A second programme, the Producers Network, helps African or Arab film projects at the development stage. Out of this year's fourteen projects, four are from sub-Saharan Africa, and ten from MENA, including one from Morocco: *The Comedy* by Saïd Khallaf, the director of critically acclaimed *A Mile in My Shoes* (2014) who divides his time between Morocco and Canada. Finally, a series of five conferences were also organised on topics including the SouthMed WiA project, co-funded by the European Union under the regional MedFilm programme (its transnational patron)[30] as well as a series of panels, much like the panels at the Moroccan FNF, around the fate of cinema.

In spite of the added value of such initiatives, and although the JCC has given visibility to Arab and African films – including Moroccan ones – it has not been able to propel their exhibition to other major international festivals (especially the European A-list festivals). Nevertheless, as we shall see, it has been successful at promoting the visibility (and exhibition) of JCC-featured films in niche festivals across Europe and North America, and at bringing together key players in Arab and African cinema:

> Film festivals, in the end, offer a place for people who share similar interests, be they artistic, business, or something hybrid. The filmmakers meet other filmmakers to discuss their craft; depending on which stage their projects are at, they (or their people) meet investors to finance the next project, or to finish the present project. . . . The festival organizers' job is

to bring the right kinds of people and the right kinds of films and build structures that enable a fruitful exchange among all these people with different interests. (Wong 2011: 127–8)

Just as the focus and direction of festivals are influenced by the institutions and funding organisations, so their development is also determined by the programmers and directors who led them. Both FESPACO and the JCC's programmes have thus evolved depending on who has been at the helm of the festival (and the country): in 1983, it created the African International Film and TV Market (MICA) alongside the screenings, and revamped it in 2009 to partner festivals with film production agencies, communication agencies and NGOs[31] as well as TV broadcasters – albeit with a hitherto modest reach. In 2007, a documentary section was added to the competition. In 2009, with Nigerian production hitting record highs in the 1990s, FESPACO, whose organisers had traditionally looked down on Nollywood videos, added a sidebar to the festival called 'TV/Video Films' (Dovey 2015: 104). Unlike JCC, FESPACO includes no training session in its programme. One of its main goals is to preserve and promote African film heritage through the African Film Library of Ouagadougou. The festival works very much with Moroccan film circles: its 2017 jury was presided over by Noureddine Saïl,[32] while its twenty-fourth edition in 2015 counted Lahcen Zinoun among its members. This Moroccan–Burkinabe festival connection further mirrors the geopolitical strategy of co-productions in Africa (see Chapter 2). Finally, much like the JCC, it continues to contribute to the traffic of ideas and films between practitioners and thinkers of cinema throughout the continent. For example, the 2017 edition of the JCC invited Moroccan director Hassan Benjelloun, Senegalese critic Baba Diop and Senegalese director Mama Keïta onto its juries.

By the 1990s, these two established festivals were no longer alone on the continent: a plethora of international festivals had gained traction in Africa (e.g. the Durban International Film Festival, and the Zanzibar International Film Festival), as part of the global liberalism order, fuelled in part by 'Africapitalism', based on the involvement of the private sector in the cultural arena, and heavily dependent on the involvement and investment of the global African diaspora (Dovey 2015: 144). The pan-African dimension of such festivals also features prominently in the newest online festival model, such as the Online South African Film Festival held in September 2013 (which seems to privilege the Southern African over the North African region).[33] The model of the latter presents a creative strategy in answer to Chériaa's old desires (in Chériaa 1978) to (1) share pan-African, pan-Arab films with professionals and a large audience, and (2) find distribution networks that are alternatives to the 'fatal domination' of first world cinemas.

One such (pan-)African initiative is DISCOP. Originally created in the early 1990s to explore the opportunites for production and distribution in the nations of the former Soviet Republic, DISCOP has shifted its focus in the past decade to established and rapidly emerging markets in sub-Saharan Africa, Northern Africa and the Middle East. The organisation aims to facilitate and co-ordinate the sustainable production and distribution of audiovisual content (not only film but also TV and gaming) across Africa and the Middle East, with the aim of bringing African stories to Africa.[34] This service is delivered through a series of targeted business-to-business markets held across the African content throughout the year, currently: Johannesburg, Abidjan and Cairo. While the emphasis is on closing deals – servicing buyers and assisting international companies in selling digital content by African companies to African audiences – DISCOP markets create a space for networking, co-production forums and events to educate and inform African content creators around funding, licensing and distribution, like initiatives such as the Africa Hub at the Berlinale. In addition to the presence of these physical markets across Africa, DISCOP also provides an online portal (DISCOP-CLUB) where buyers can view and access (African) films, TV and gaming titles currently on offer, rather than waiting for one of the three markets a year. As Lara Utian-Preston notes, this balance between the frequency of the physical markets and accessing content online is crucial, since:

> a market is hinged on buyers . . . at times the markets are in danger of turning into producer forums with no buyers. In order to make it viable, you need the buyers to be present.[35]

There are, of course, a number of obstacles that complicate Moroccan participation with DISCOP: as with an event such as the Berlinale Africa Hub, the focus is currently weighted far more to co-production with and content from sub-Saharan African nations. Language is also another potential barrier, with English being used far more than French at DISCOP. However, given Moroccan cinema's long tradition of cooperation with sub-Saharan (francophone) national cinemas, it is disheartening to see that in 2019, only one Moroccan film, the thriller *Tears of Satan* (el Jebbari, 2015) is currently promoted via the online DISCOP-CLUB portal. It might be worth exploring such virtual venues to increase the continental, transnational visibility and viewership of Moroccan film, even if it suppresses the physical encounter between film directors, their critics and their audiences that energises the participants of established pan-African festivals such as the JCC and FESPACO.

The African festivals have not been the launching pads of international careers in the way that A-list festivals have. However, among the JCC and FESPACO attendees, attentive niche festival organisers come and select films for their own programmes, ensuring that African and Arab cinemas are seen outside the continent. It is to these smaller festivals that we now turn to end this chapter.

Niche Festivals in Europe and Northern America

The final group of festivals identified at the start of this section are niche festivals that specialise in particular thematic or regional cinemas, among which Arab, Maghrebi and Mediterranean foci feature prominently as likely avenues for Moroccan films to be screened. In Europe and in Northern America, there are dozens of them: they respond to the demands or the availability of a cosmopolitan audience composed in large parts by the Arab diaspora (hence the longstanding success of the Arab Film Festival in Dearborn, Michigan, in the United States, the Arab World Festival of Montreal in Canada, or the *Panorama des Cinémas du Maghreb* in Saint-Denis, in France), but not exclusively so, especially since 9/11.

In the United States, these festivals have spread on the West Coast (the Arab Film Festival in San Francisco and the San Diego Arab Film Festival in California), in the Midwest (the Arab Film Festival at the Arab American National Museum of Dearborn and Ann Arbor in Michigan), and on the East Coast (the Arabian Sights, a stand-alone part of the Washington DC Film Fest, the Arab Cinema Week and the New York Forum of Amazigh Film in New York City). In Canada, they can be spotted in Quebec (the Arab World Festival of Montreal has a prominent film section), Alberta (the Calgary Arab Nights Film Festival), Ontario (the Toronto Arab Film Festival) and soon British Columbia (Vancouver).[36] In Europe they cover a vast territory (e.g. Netherlands, Germany, Belgium, Luxembourg, France, the United Kingdom, Spain).[37] Organisers of these festivals often depend on donors and/or public funds to send their organisers/directors to the JCC, Moroccan FNF, FESPACO and others to see the films, meet the directors and their teams and secure invitations and screening rights, before they can invite the films and often at least a couple of directors to come and meet their public.

In this way, the Arab Film Festival of Fameck/Val de Fensch, founded in 1989, was born from the partnership of two regional organisations (Fédération des Oeuvres Laïques/Federation of Secular Charities, and League de l'Enseignement/Educators League). The festival is mainly financed by the region of Alsace-Lorraine and receives funding from the municipalities hosting the annual festival (the Val de Fensch Conurbation, the city of Fameck), as well as regional boards such as DRAC (Direction Régionale des Affaires Culturelles: the Regional Board of Cultural Affairs) and ACSE (Agence Nationale pour la Cohésion Sociale et l'Égalité des Chances/National Agency for Social Cohesion and Equity). Clearly, the festival has a socio-cultural agenda beyond its exhibition function as is clear from its spread across the towns of the area, with seventeen different screening venues, each of them connected to a local cultural or social association. Each screening is accompanied by a discussion or an ancillary activity with the audience, the latter composed of the Moroccan or Maghrebi diaspora and Alsatians outside the diaspora. For instance, the directors have partnered with the Association des Marocains de Forbach (AMF, the Association of Moroccans of Forbach), who are interested in joining the festival in order to show films to which its members could not have access. The festival directors, Clarisse Bernt and Rudy Dillenschneider, then asked the AMF to frame the screening with an activity that would situate it within Moroccan culture (e.g. a meal, a musical event), so as to dialogically share both the film and the culture that produced it. The aim of the festival is socio-cultural and didactic: Fameck gives visibility to Arab film production in context, and engages the audience actively[38] in learning about Maghrebi culture. It highlights cultural diversity and idiosyncrasies (in stark and welcome contrast with the French Republic's official policy of cultural erasure to facilitate integration). In their quiet ways, and perhaps because they operate at the regional or departmental level, niche festivals like Fameck resist the cultural policies of the state with remarkable success. At the same time, Fameck also acts as a distribution relay at the regional level: the screening venues are more often than not film theatres. In that, it shares the goal of the Panorama des Cinémas du Maghreb in suburban St Denis, outside of Paris, dedicated to screening the diverse films of the Maghrebi region and 'that otherwise would not be seen in the hope that they will find proper distribution, because despite France's substantial Maghrebin population, this cinema remains under-distributed there as well as abroad' (Shafto 2011a). In both cases, however, the festivals also address and hope to engage a diasporic audience. At L'Écran, the film theatre where the festival films of the Panorama are screened, the audience is a mix of viewers: the residents of St Denis, a working-class area that has been home to Maghrebi immigrants and their French descendants since the 1960s; students from the nearby university; and a smaller number from the capital – a mix of cinephiles and those whose interest is more in the culture and politics of the Maghreb region. The festival also functions as a rendezvous for the Moroccan and Maghrebi diaspora in the Parisian region (as was the Arab Film Festival at the Institut du Monde Arabe, downtown Paris).

In both cases, the niche festivals fill several functions at once: they cater to an audience eager to receive images from the country of origin or of one's ancestry; they celebrate a culture and project images from that culture unfiltered by the host culture and discourse; they make visible the cinema of the Maghreb, and therefore of Morocco. As a result, the film viewing experience becomes a communal coming together of audience and film in which the film calls for an active response on the part of the viewers: at the 2014 edition of the Arabian Sights Festival in Washington DC, for instance, women's ululations and comments in three languages greeted *Rock the Casbah* (for which Marrakchi received the festival's Commendation Award).

The niche festivals often work together: Fameck partners with Cinéalma, the annual Carros Mediterranean Film Festival, on the French Riviera. Both sets of organisers (Clarisse Bernt and Rudy Dillenschneider for Fameck, and Moroccan native Brahim Naitijja for Cinéalma who has created the festival and built an impressive Moroccan film address book over the years[39]) scout the films in Morocco and Cannes, and agree on a couple of films for which they can share the costs associated with the transportation of films and invited directors, for instance. Furthermore, distributors in Europe use niche festivals as launching pads for their selected films. For example Tinne Bral of Imagine distribution (see case study in the next chapter) estimates that screening a film at the Flanders International Film Festival in Ghent can result in hundreds of entries as well as generating previous press publicity for the film.[40]

As such, each niche festival constitutes a node in an increasingly interconnected network of festivals, which then intersects with a widening network of distribution. The dynamics of such film circulation rely on the targeting of the diaspora as prime audience, and on the will of these passionate, tireless festival organisers to educate the non-diasporic audience to Moroccan (and other) cinema.

NOTES

1. See <https://stephenfollows.com/many-film-festivals-are-in-the-world/> (accessed 31 January 2020).
2. The term A-list tends to refer to the FIAPF (International Federation of Film Producers Associations) accreditation of international film festivals. However, the FIAPF ranking is not consistent, nor is it accepted by all international film festivals. For the purposes of this section, we understand an 'A-list' festival to represent a major international festival with a competition and significant industry activity linked to the film programme, such as a market or de facto market or series of activities and fora for film industry professionals.
3. See <http://www.ccm.ma/statistiques-manifetsations-cinematographique> (accessed 31 January 2020).
4. Interview with Hicham Falah, conducted by Will Higbee and Stef Van de Peer, Tangier, March 2017.
5. Between 2013 and 2017, cycles of Moroccan film have been held in Australia, Belgium, Bulgaria, Colombia, Egypt, Germany, Holland, India, Ivory Coast, Mali, Poland, Spain, Tunisia and Ukraine.
6. Since 1993, the Association for the Distribution of Independent Cinema (ACID) has screened a programme of nine feature films (fiction and documentary) at the Cannes film festival, chosen from among hundreds of works from all around the world. The principal aim of the programme is to give visibility at the world's most prestigious film festivals to directors whose work is scarcely distributed, in order to facilitate a subsequent theatrical release.
7. A discussion in this context around *Horses of God*, that took place at the National Film Festival in Tangier (March 2017) between American TV showrunner and producer, Alan Boul, and the Moroccan filmmakers who were present makes this point abundantly clear.
8. Will Higbee, interview with Hédi Zardi, Skype, July 2017. A minimum guarantee or MG is an advance payment on a film for the right to license a territory or territories.

The MG is payable to the producer once the film is completed and delivered to the distributor.

9. The future of the Dubai International Film Festival is currently in flux. The festival was 'rested' in 2018, and returned in 2019, planning to recur every other year from then on.

10. This same point about the intensely competitive nature of selection for the major international festivals was made by Rémi Bonhomme, Programme Manager of the Semaine de la Critique at Cannes, when asked to explain the absence of Moroccan directors from the sidebar over the past decade (interview with Rémi Bonhomme by Flo Martin and Jamal Bahmad, Tangier, March 2018).

11. See, for example, Screen International's response to the 2018 selection for Cannes from a British perspective: <https://www.screendaily.com/features/industry-reacts-to-sparse-showing-for-uk-films-at-cannes/5128468.article> (accessed 31 January 2020).

12. See <https://www.berlinale.de/en/world-cinema-fund/news/news.html> (accessed 8 February 2020).

13. Chraibi was speaking on a Moroccan industry panel at the Morocco in Motion international conference, orghanised by the Transnational Moroccan Cinema research project and linked to the Africa in Motion film festival, Edinburgh, 27 October 2018.

14. See Martin 2011b: 271–83.

15. The Fédération Tunisienne des Ciné-Clubs, FTCC (Tunisian Federation of Cine-Clubs), founded in 1950, headed by Cheriaa, and the Fédération Tunisienne des Cinéastes Amateurs, FTCA (Tunisian Federation of Amateur Filmmakers), founded in 1962.

16. Cindy Hing-Yuk Wong describes these as 'one mechanism to address imbalances, creating a space for smaller and alternative productions and audiences' (2011: 31).

17. 'In the end, 31 countries answered the call: ten from the Arab and African countries (Ivory Coast, Guinea, Senegal, Zaïre, Lebanon, Algeria, Morocco, Libya, Kuwait, Tunisia) and 21 from the rest of the world. The programme consisted of 29 features and 22 short films' (Estrada 2014: 320).

18. Although the Damascus festival was cancelled then, and the civil war is still raging on, the General Cinema Authority in Syria announced in 2017 that it would resume in November 2018: <https://english.alarabiya.net/en/life-style/entertainment/2018/06/02/Searching-for-the-Mideast-s-Hollywood-Where-is-the-Arab-film-industry-heading-.html> (accessed 31 January 2020); but it has not done so.

19. Named after the date (4 August 1984) when the country was named Burkina Faso (country of honest people), in a portmanteau of the nation's two main languages (Mossi and Mande) (Dovey 2015: 99).

20. A particularly moving encounter happened between the female inmates and Selma Baccar who showed her film *El Jaïda* (about women imprisoned in a *dar joued*, a special correction house for disobedient wives and daughters that existed before independence and still exists in Egypt . . . The prisoners engaged in a lively discussion with the actors and director, showing how film could free self-expression, even in a detention centre.

21. As examples, the JCC sought, under the helm of Tahar Cheriaa to 'testify to a specific idea of cinema' as a 'tool that must work for the collective struggle in . . . the Third World' and 'support a cinema that shows clear visions of sociological realities' in 1976. The determination to produce a cinema culturally and politically consonant with Arab and African postcolonial realities, actively resisting the oppression of neocolonial powers, was so acute that the JCC jury awarded no Golden Tanit (Tanit is the name of the prize at the JCC, and derives from the name of a Carthaginian Goddess – Anath in the Middle East) in 1968, arguing that no film in the competition had contributed to the struggles of the Third World or to illustrate its dignity (and no Bronze Tanit in 1966, 1974 or 1982, for similar reasons) (Javier H. Estrada, in Iordanova and Van de Peer 2014: 322–5).

22. 'JCC's Tanit d'Or celebrates pre-colonial, pre-Islamic Tunisia through the Phoenician mother goddess, and FESPACO's Étalon de Yennenga may be a "stallion" (*étalon*) of gold, but it references the horse of a female heroine – Princess Yennenga, the mother of the Mossi nation (Burkina's largest ethnic group)' (Dovey 2015: 96).

23. African Festivals' career boosts, however, differ from the ones outlined by Wong, thereby critics and audiences at the Western A-list festivals promote films from outside the West as different, original, and then boost the career of the film and its author by relaying it to other festivals and, hopefully, various networks of distribution (including art house theatres and museums) (Wong 2011: Chapter 3).

24. 2010: Daoud Aoulad-Syad, *The Mosk* (Bronze Tanit)

2012: Faouzi Bensaïdi, *Death for Sale* (Silver Tanit)
Adil Al Fadili, *Short Life* (Golden Tanit for shorts)
2014: Hicham Lasri, *They Are the Dogs* (Silver Tanit)
2015: Mohamed Mouftakir, *The Blindmen's Orchestra* (Golden Tanit)
Jury prize awarded to Nabil Ayouch, *Much Loved*
2017: Faouzi Bensaïdi, *Volubilis* (Bronze Tanit)

25. 2011: Mohamed Mouftakir, *Pegasus* (Golden Yennenga Stallion)
2015: Hicham Ayouch, *Fevers* (Golden Yennenga Stallion)
Abdelillah el Jaouhary, *Water and Blood* (Golden Foal)
2017: Saïd Khallaf, *A Mile in My Shoes* (Bronze Yennenga Stallion)
Violaine Maryam Blanche, *Hyménée* (Golden Foal)

26. See <https://provincedelequateur.blogspot.com/2015/03/fievres-au-fespaco-letalon-dor-attribue.html> (accessed 31 January 2020).

27. *Fevers* had obtained a development grant in Doha in 2011, competed at the International Film Festival in Marrakesh in 2013 (where it won best acting performance for Slimane Dazi and Didier Michon), and was awarded an impressive international list of awards in Abu Dhabi, Egypt, Poland, Spain, Switzerland, Tanzania, Tunisia.

28. At the JCC, each festival director added his or her innovative projects to the sidebar of the competition in an attempt to refine or boost its auteurs' careers. Mohamed Attia turned it into a summit for influential film professionals (directors, producers, distributors) from the north and the south with a view to building sustainable partnerships. He added a Project Workshop in 1992 to help Arab and African screenwriters work on their screenplays as well as a market, the International Market of Audio-visual

Products, in 1994. Mohamed Mediouni added the Screens of the Future programme, a space for young artists from all over the world (not only Arab or African) to exchange and incubate ideas, in the 2012 edition (following the Tunisian Revolution).

29. Takmil is funded by jigsaw of International Organization of the Francophonie (OIF), International Media Support (IMS), the French CNC, the Tunisian National Cinema and Image Center (CNCI), Silverway Media, Image and Sound Production and Creative Agency. And HAKKA Distribution awards a grant for the promotion and distribution of an African or Arab film.

30. The European project is designed 'to promote and support gender equality in the audiovisual sector, contributing to sustainable development and cultural diversity, in seven Southern Mediterranean countries: Algeria, Egypt, Jordan, Lebanon, Morocco, Palestine, Tunisia' (*Carthage Pro*, Tunis: Carthage Film Festival, 2017: 109).

31. See <https://www.fespaco.bf/en/about-fespaco/institutional-informations/233-mica> (accessed 10 August 2018).

32. Saïl has an enviable Moroccan and African pedigree: he is now the President of the African Film Foundation of Khouribga in Morocco, Chairman of Ouarzazate Film Commission and Coordinator of the African Cinematographic Community.

33. 'The arrival, in 2013, of a completely new kind of festival, related to a form of regional African filmmaking – the first Online South African Film Festival – joins other recently created online festivals around the world in unsettling festivals' typical relationship to publics situated in one discrete time and place. Initiated by the VOD platform AfricaFilms.tv, presided over by veteran South African filmmaker Ramadan Suleman, and curated by Lesedi Moche (also director of the Encounters Documentary Film Festival in South Africa), the first Online South African Film Festival ran from 18 July to 22 September 2013, and offered viewers the chance to rent or buy 150 rarely accessible South African films and television series' (ibid: 178).

34. For details of DISCOP activities, see: <https://www.discop.com> (accessed 31 January 2020).

35. Lara Utian-Preston was speaking as part of a DISCOP panel at the Africa Hub, Berlinale Film Festival, 10 February 2019.

36. See: <https://arabfilminstitute.org/festival>; <http://sandiegoaff.org/>; <http://arabamericanmuseum.org/aff18>; <http://www.filmfestdc.org/arabiansights>/; <https://www.eventbrite.com/e/arab-cinema-week-in-new-york-tickets-39078361431#>; <http://www.lpac.nyc/berber-film-festival-2017-7fd9; <https://www.quebecoriginal.com/en/listing/events/festivals-and-special-events/arab-world-festival-montreal-19397492; <https://calgaryarabartssociety.ca/23-content-news-announcements/content-news/78-arab-nights-film-festival-celebrating-fifth-year>; <http://www.arabfilm.ca/> (accessed 31 January 2020).

37. See <http://www.arabfilm-institute.org/resources/arab-film-festivals/> (accessed 31 January 2020).

38. Clarisse Bernt and Rudy Dillenschneider interviewed by Will Hibee and Flo Martin, 3 December 2016, Marrakesh.

39. Brahim Naitijja interviewed by Flo Martin, Will Hibee, and Jamal Bahmad, March 2018.

40. Tinne Bral interviewed by Will Hibee and Flo Martin, 5 December 2016.

7. SALES, DISTRIBUTION AND DIGITAL DISRUPTION: THE UNREALISED TRANSNATIONAL REACH OF MOROCCAN CINEMA?

SALES AND DISTRIBUTION OUTSIDE MOROCCO

International distribution essentially involves selling the rights to a film for a variety of platforms, over differing periods of time and to different territories. From a cultural perspective, the aim of this activity is to reach as large an audience as possible. From a commercial perspective, the goal is to maximise the revenue generated by the film. Depending on the outlook of a film and its filmmaker/the rights holder, these two aims might be compatible: a director such as Nabil Ayouch is as concerned with generating revenue from his films as he is garnering awards and audiences. For others, the commercial imperative and the desire for a genuine engagement with an audience appear mutually exclusive: until his debut documentary feature, *Amussu* (2019), activist filmmaker Nadir Bouhmouch chose to make his films available online for free via Vimeo and YouTube, in order that the political message contained in his work could reach as wide an audience as possible both in Morocco and abroad.

National or international distribution is generally regarded as the stage in the value chain that holds the highest risk – the point at which a film, whether blockbuster or art house, is most openly exposed to the forces of the market, the whims of the film going public and even unforeseen circumstances beyond the distributor's control that can influence success or failure at the box office. However, as many filmmakers know to their cost and continued frustration, this claim needs to be nuanced: not all films automatically benefit from equal access to distribution networks, or the opportunities to compete for exhibition space to reach their audience. Historically, film distribution has therefore adopted a gatekeeping role within the industry; not only selecting and determining which films are marketed and distributed but even which films are made (Finney 2014: 69). Distribution plays a key role in shaping the availability of a range of films to audiences, which in turn heavily influences our understanding and the historicisation of a given film culture, national or regional cinema. JCC founder Tahar Cheriaa understood well this reality for African and Arab cinema, leading him to formulate the aphorism: 'whoever controls distribution, controls cinema'.[1]

African and Arab cinema has long battled with the combined effects of (state) censorship and the disproportionate influence of foreign distributors on the home film market, often compounded by a lack of experienced local distributors. This has led to a situation where, as Elisabeth Lequeret observed in the early 2000s, many African films are absent from screens at home but available to audiences at international film festivals or via specialist world cinema distributors (Lequeret 2001: 82–3). While not necessarily disputed by academics and industry insiders, the reasons for this absence of African films from African screens has been nuanced by, among others, Barlet (2007) and Diawara (2010). The imbalance identified by Lequeret is, therefore, really concerned with a specific type of film; namely, the auteur-led production, popular with festival audiences. A discussion of the 'crisis' of distribution for African cinema in these terms largely ignores a range of popular African films that have been forced to find (legal and illegal) alternative outlets to theatrical exhibition: at first video, DVD and TV and now, increasingly, online. In fact, as research conducted by DISCOP shows, Africa is now arguably the fastest growing audiovisual market in the world, with a rapidly expanding population and a significant youth audience, who consume a huge amount of content digitally and are hungry for local content that can provide 'African stories for African audiences'.[2]

Our analysis in Chapter 4 of Amazigh cinema provides an example of precisely how this duality between auteur-led production and popular cinema manifests itself in the distribution of Moroccan cinema. On the one hand, Amazigh cinema exists as a strand of Moroccan popular cinema that reaches its audience through a range of distribution channels (TV, DVD and increasingly online) rather than relying on the Kingdom's declining theatrical infrastructure. On the other hand, such films as *The Sleeping Child* and *Adios Carmen*, although critically acclaimed in Morocco, obtain a far greater visibility (and attract the majority of their audiences) by virtue of their success by being promoted as 'Moroccan cinema' at national and international festivals.

Traditionally, co-production has been seen as the most direct means to access a foreign territory, since an international co-producer is expected to open up contacts in his/her domestic market to secure a distribution deal or pre-sale as part of the package to finance the film. As Benchenna notes, co-production plays a determining role in the commercial circulation of

Maghrebi films in France: in a study of films produced between 2000 and 2013, the average audience for a film from the Maghreb co-produced with France was 65,000, compared to 3,500 for a film produced solely in Tunisia, Algeria or Morocco – leading to the conclusion that French distribution companies privilege films co-produced with France (Benchenna 2016: 33). For this reason, in the 1980s and early 1990s (prior to the CCM's injection of national funding into production), international co-production was seen as desirable for the handful of Moroccan films produced annually (Carter 2009: 215). However, since the mid-1990s, this situation has changed somewhat and principally for two reasons: first, as discussed in Chapter 1, many Moroccan filmmakers are sceptical of the added value brought by co-production and are, instead, content to budget their production accordingly with internal funding from the CCM, Moroccan TV and private investors. Second, especially within the last decade, the landscape for international distribution and sales has changed so rapidly that international pre-sales for independent or auteur-led productions are, generally speaking, far more difficult to secure.[3]

Indeed, even when Moroccan filmmakers do engage in international co-production, there is no guarantee that this will unlock access to substantial audiences in the co-producing territory, given how little space there is for independent cinema at a box office in an international market dominated by US blockbusters or occasionally local, big budget productions attempting to compete with Hollywood. For example, between 2000 and 2013, thirty-three co-productions were produced involving France and Morocco,[4] though only twenty of these were distributed commercially in France (Benchenna 2016: 33). Neither can Moroccan producers rely on the diasporic audience as a justification for commercial international distribution in a given territory, since the impact of such an audience – on commercial/theatrical distribution at least – is regarded by distributors as minimal and fragmented.

Outside France (Morocco's main co-production partner), Moroccan films seem to fare even worse. Despite making the top ten in 2016 at the Moroccan box office, Ahmed Boulane's Moroccan–Spanish co-production *The Island* (2015) attracted less than 100 spectators in Spain,[5] suggesting an extremely limited festival run rather than a co-ordinated theatrical release on the Iberian Peninsula. A comedy about the international incident caused by the Moroccan 'occupation' of a small Spanish island at the tip of North Africa in July 2002, co-written by Boulane and Spanish screenwriter Carlos Domenguez, *The Island* is told very much from a Moroccan perspective and stars Abdellah Ferkous (a hugely popular actor at the Moroccan box office but virtually unknown in Spain). The film therefore appears designed to cater for a domestic and diasporic Moroccan audience rather than a Spanish one, with little appeal to international distributors.

As the example of *The Island* illustrates, commercial distribution in a foreign territory is by no means a given for every Moroccan co-production.[6] Rather, a conventional international distribution strategy needs to target specific overseas territories where it is considered that a film will play well with local audiences. It also means understanding which platforms are the most lucrative for a given film in a given territory. Although theatrical release has historically been seen (especially in Europe) as the key driver of film exhibition, in parts of the Arab world, TV rights are arguably more lucrative.[7]

As noted in Chapter 6, international and niche film festivals play a vital role as an alternative distribution network for a select number of Moroccan films and filmmakers. For many films from the Maghreb, selection for an international festival is the only way to reach a foreign audience (Benchanna 2016: 32). Yet the major international festivals offer very few Moroccan films the opportunity to be seen and even purchased by foreign distributors. Festivals with markets, or de facto markets such as Cannes, Berlin, Malmo, Locarno and (until recently), Dubai are therefore key sites for Moroccan filmmakers aspiring to bridge the gap and secure deals for international distribution.

Commercial international distribution of independent cinema has effectively been controlled since the 1990s by sales agents, who, acting as the representatives of the producer or financier, sell the film rights to a given territory and are, in many ways, the power brokers of international markets (Peranson 2009: 29–32). Although the arrival of the new digital majors (such as Netflix and Amazon) is changing this situation, the power and influence of the sales agent in the international film business are still considerable. Sales agents work with distributors, who effectively function as the intermediary between a producer and the exhibitor. Distributors use their knowledge of a given territory to exploit a film's theatrical and ancillary rights (DVD, pay TV, free-TV, screening fees from festivals, educational licensing and airline screenings) for an agreed period. The distributor acquires a combination of these rights from the sales agent either in the form of a sale agreed upon after the film's completion, or as a pre-sale or minimum guarantee (MGs).[8] Sales agents rely on the distributors' expertise in their local territories (knowledge and networks) in order to maximise the reach of the film to foreign audiences.

Any Moroccan producer or director looking to secure an international distribution deal needs a presence for their film in at least one of these key international festivals, as well as a sales agent who can act on their behalf to promote the film at the associated markets. Argentinian filmmaker Pablo César, director of the Argentine–Moroccan co-production *The Call of the Desert* (discussed in detail in Chapter 2) goes further, arguing that sales agents are necessary, even to secure entry for films into the most prestigious international film festivals.[9] Since 2009, MAD Solutions, a pan-Arab sales and distribution company with offices in Cairo and UAE, has emerged as an important representative for Arab films at major markets and festivals. MAD Solutions currently acts as a sales agent for around 140 Arab films, a mixture of features, documentaries and shorts.[10] MAD Solutions has also been responsible for co-ordinating the Arab Cinema Centre (ACC), an entirely separate organisation with partners and affiliates from across the world of Arab cinema, including: the Jordanian Film Commission, Arab Film and Media Centre, LatinArab Co-production Forum, Malmo Arab Film Festival and the JCC. The aim of the ACC is to promote the Arab film industry (consolidating its presence in existing markets for Arab film and creating visibility in new territories) and to enhance its global presence by connecting it to local, regional and international festivals, markets and audiences.[11] At the time of writing (August 2019), neither the CCM nor any other Moroccan organisations are affiliated to the ACC. The latter appears more focused on the Middle East than the Maghreb – a reflection of the extremely limited commercial potential for many Moroccan films across the MENA region.[12] However, a MAD Solutions executive was invited by the CCM at an industry panel on distribution held as part of the 2018 National Film Festival in Tangier, hopefully the prelude to a closer alignment with the ACC as a logical strategic step for the CCM in its aims to support the promotion of Moroccan film on the international stage. Beyond initiatives emerging from the MENA region, the most powerful sales agents are based in Europe. France in particular has a large concentration of sales companies: a mix of international mini-majors such as Studio Canal (involved across the value chain in production, acquisition, distribution and sales) and smaller independents such as Luxbox, a Paris-based international sales company, who acted as sales agents for the Spanish–Moroccan–Qatari co-production *Mimosas*. In the opinion of Hédi Zardi, CEO of Sales and Acquisitions at Luxbox, Moroccan filmmakers should be able to develop and exploit relationships with French sales agents given the strong cultural, linguistic and economic ties between the French and Moroccan film industries.[13] Nevertheless, the extremely limited number of Moroccan films gaining international distribution suggests that the majority of Moroccan filmmakers are unable to do so. The reasons for this are complex, ranging from the difficulty for many individual Moroccan filmmakers to fund expensive (speculative) trips to such international festivals and markets as well as problems with travel visas and a general lack of contacts in the international film business beyond Morocco. In this respect, as part of its remit to sustain the commercial viability of the national production abroad, the CCM could play an even more significant role in cultivating both the domestic distribution network and at the same time promoting a transnational network of contacts for Moroccan filmmakers at international festivals and markets. Such targeted support could even extend to a greater focus on English-language training for Moroccan producers and directors, given that English, much more than French, is the common language of film festivals and markets.

The overriding question, of course, is whether sales agents and distributors perceive Moroccan film to have a value (artistic or economic) for international audiences. Many of the international festivals – whose criteria for selecting Moroccan films may range from the purely artistic (cinematic quality) to the cultural or geopolitical – cater to captive audiences willing to take risks and discover new films from across the world as part of the festival experience. Sales companies, by contrast, even if driven by a genuine passion for cinema, must respond to the economic imperatives of the market and the question of how to recuperate their costs for distributing and marketing a film.[14] Sales agents therefore tend to promote Moroccan films with sufficient commercial appeal for international audiences, potentially returning us to the vexed question of European influence on the kind of African and Arab films that can gain access to international festivals, production funds and distribution. This position is further complicated by the fact that international festival programmers, sales agents and distributors often have little sense of Moroccan cinema as a 'brand' on the world cinema circuit.[15] Even European art-house distributors who have previously distributed Moroccan titles, may be unaware of the range and level of Moroccan production, tending to view Tunisian cinema as the leading cinema of the Maghreb.[16]

The CCM undoubtedly has a role to play in enhancing the visibility of Moroccan cinema to international sales agents, distributors and festival programmers. However, as Hédi Zardi suggests, there is a limit to what they can achieve:

> Basically the [Moroccan] films that have international potential find a way to meet the international sales agent that they need with or without the state. They don't need the CCM for this – sales agents can identify the good projects. For me, the most important aspect of the CCM is production. Their promotion [of Moroccan cinema] is not very efficient, as a national film organization has to treat all its films equally. It's very political but not efficient from the point of view of promoting the best films.[17]

An inherent tension exists: national film councils must, in theory, be seen to promote all their national filmmakers, whereas sales agents and distributors are interested in an auteurist strategy; promoting individual talent and films that they feel will attract an audience in a specific territory.[18] For a foreign distributor, to remain fixated on promoting one national cinema would be commercial suicide: 'as a distributor you cannot specialize – otherwise that is your death!'[19]

The considerable difficulties facing Moroccan filmmakers in establishing international visibility for their films are compounded by the fact that, generally speaking, Moroccan distributors are either unwilling or unable to distribute abroad the films they handle domestically (Carter 2009: 215) and the fact that there are, effectively, no Moroccan sales agents. In the opinion of Moroccan director Nour-Eddine Lakhmari, this lack of transational reach is compounded by the lack of a viable domestic market in Morocco from which most producers and directors can launch their films internationally.[20] This situation is due to the fact that the Moroccan films that tend to perform well with local audiences at the Moroccan box office are, precisely, the kind of popular genre films (comedies and dramas) that do not travel well. Moroccan distributors thus have little or no interest in promoting the kind of Moroccan films (auteur-led productions and international co-productions) that are most likely to be selected for the international festival circuit. As a result, many Moroccan directors – who often already juggle the roles of producer and director for their project – are further tasked with attempting to secure distribution deals for their own film outside of Morocco. Out of necessity, the filmmaker ends up assuming a role for which they are not best suited; with the most likely outcome being little or no overseas distribution.[21]

In the context of European distribution, these observations tend to be backed up by the available data from the European Audiovisual Observatory (EAO). According to the EAO, 110 Moroccan films (either 100 per cent Moroccan, majority or minority produced) have been released in across Europe since 1996.[22] Most of these films attract modest audiences (only thirty films recorded European audiences of over 20,000 spectators) and tend to have narrow releases in niche film festivals and on a small number of prints in selected theatres and cities. Of these 110 films, an even more select group (eleven) have secured more than 100,000 entries. Only one film, *Indigènes* (Bouchareb, 2006), has attracted over one million spectators, and this was a film in which Morocco had a minor co-producing role, and where Morocco was most visibly represented via the diasporic presence of actor/co-producer Jamel Debbouze, a French star of Moroccan immigrant origin.

In this environment, it is, once again, the *cinéastes de passage* such as Ayouch, Bensaïdi and Nejjar, alongside producers such as Chraibi, who, due to their participation in the international festivals and the potential for their films to connect with international audiences, are best placed to work with sales agents to broker distribution deals for their films (Benchanna 2016: 32). Though, as already noted in Chapter 6 in the case of Nejjar's most recent film, *Stateless*, even these links and selection for an international A-list festival could not guarantee distribution. Nabil Ayouch is in the unparalleled position for a Moroccan director of having five films in the top twenty Moroccan productions/co-productions distributed in Europe: *Much Loved* (309,439 spectators), *Razzia* (185,477), *Ali Zaoua: Prince of the Streets* (156,262), *Horses of God* (52,509) and *Whatever Lola Wants* (52,093).[23] Ayouch has also established himself as a powerful producer in Morocco who is well connected to the international film market and A-list festivals such as Cannes, TIFF, IFFR and Dubai. However, even with privileged access to international distributors, films by the *cinéastes de passage* still face considerable challenges, finding their audience in a highly competitive independent world cinema market; as the Benelux distribution of Nabil Ayouch's *Much Loved* (2015) illustrates.[24]

Selling Moroccan Cinema to a European Audience – *Much Loved*

Much Loved was Ayouch's seventh feature film and continued the director's exploration of often-controversial social issues in Morocco – here, organised female prostitution in Marrakesh. Ayouch's work has always received a mixed reception in Morocco – with detractors suggesting that he offers a neo-Orientalist representation of contemporary socio-political realities. In contrast, his films have been consistently well received by international festival and European/US art-house audiences since the breakout success (in Morocco and abroad) of his second feature, *Ali Zaoua*. An earnest portrayal of controversial subject matter, *Much Loved* places the experiences of the usually marginalised female sex workers front and centre in its narrative. The result – a 'difficult' but 'worthwhile' film from a critically acclaimed French–Moroccan director shot in a direct, realist style – generated interest from Western festival programmers and independent distributors alike. The film premiered at Cannes as part of the Directors' Fortnight sidebar, where it was well received by critics and audiences. Shortly afterwards, it gained notoriety in Morocco, where it was banned by the conservative Islamist government, officially due to the perceived immorality of the film's depiction of the sex industry in Marrakesh.[25] Controversy built around the decision to ban the film from Moroccan theatres, with prominent members of Morocco's filmmaking community, such as Jillali Ferhati and Nour-Eddine Lakhmari, defending Ayouch's right to freedom of expression. Ayouch's supporters also objected to the fact that the censors, in banning the film, appeared to be responding more directly to the salacious outtakes from *Much Loved* that had been leaked online than judging the seriousness with which the film treated its subject matter. The film's lead actress was then physically attacked in public and fled to France. On an institutional level, *Much Loved* was also one of the first major controversies for the newly appointed head of the CCM, Sarim Fassi Fihri; bringing into focus the conservative Islamist PJD party's promotion of 'clean art' – an attempt to censor artistic freedom and the representation of social taboos in Moroccan cinema.[26]

Following the interest generated by its success at Cannes, *Much Loved* was picked up for distribution in nine European territories, including in Belgium and Holland, where the distributor was Imagine Film. Founded in Belgium in 2002 by Tinne Bral and Christian Thomas, who had previously worked together as festival directors and programmers, Imagine has built a reputation for distributing varied and distinctive high-quality independent cinema from across the world.[27] As Bral explained, an independent distributor like Imagine must feel '*un coup de coeur*': passionately connected to the films they distribute. Bral described her visceral response to *Much Loved* at the buyer's screening she attended in Cannes thus: 'My belly ached, I thought it was so harsh . . . My first reaction was: "Gosh, will we find an audience?" It wasn't an easy sell.'[28] Despite these initial reservations, Bral's belief in the power of the film to connect with Benelux art-house audiences led Imagine to secure the rights to *Much Loved* after Cannes. Working with a select catalogue of (six to eight) films each year, the individuality and vision of each director is paramount to the team at Imagine, who focus on the artistic quality and diversity of their films, rather than on their particular country or region. As a distributor, then, Bral was not so much interested in *Much Loved* as a 'Moroccan' film but rather as an auteur-led production dealing with a hard-hitting subject matter in a powerful way.[29]

For *Much Loved*'s initial release in Belgium and Holland, Bral employed Imagine's tried and tested strategy of rolling out a small tour of selected screenings for the film. Working with the cooperation of *Much Loved*'s international sales agent, the tour included, wherever possible, a post-screening discussion with members of cast and crew, designed to generate interest and encourage local exhibitors to book the film. Imagine also worked closely with the Dutch and Belgian press to secure reviews and feature articles on the film, again to build awareness among exhibitors and art-house audiences. Interest among Dutch exhibitors was greatly enhanced by the film's selection for the Rotterdam International Film Festival (IFFR).[30] *Much Loved* was screened at the IFFR eight months after Cannes, and included a promotional appearance by Ayouch. Afterwards, eight exhibitors wanted to screen the film in their cinemas. The positive response generated by the IFFR reflects both the symbiosis between festivals and the market, and the importance of festivals in promoting independent world cinema. It further highlights the time it takes for an independent film such as *Much Loved* to build its reputation and gain the necessary visibility on the festival circuit for the film to secure international distribution.

The promotion of *Much Loved* was affected by external factors to which Imagine were forced to react and adapt their distribution strategy. First, the ISIS terrorist attacks in France in November 2015 meant Bral had to postpone the film's opening in Brussels (the key driver for theatrical exhibition in Belgium) where, as a precaution following the attacks, film theatres were shut for a week. Second, the controversy that had surfaced around the banning of *Much Loved* in Morocco and the attack on the film's lead actress, Loubna Abidar, led to extensive coverage in the French press, including an interview in *Le Monde*. Though deeply sorry about the personal distress that the personal attacks had caused Abidar, Bral acknowledged that the greater visibility accorded to the film as a result of the media interest surrounding

Much Loved's reception in Morocco led to Belgian viewers' greater awareness of the film at the source of this controversy and their desire to see it: 'people discovered a completely different film from the one that was portrayed in Morocco'.[31] The broader impact of often unrelated events (and the subject matter of *Much Loved*) as they affect perceptions of the wider 'Islamic' or 'Arab' population and the appetite for a European audience to view a film cannot, therefore, be discounted. While the notoriety of Abidar's treatment in Morocco following the release of *Much Loved* ultimately had a positive effect on engaging Belgian audiences for Imagine, in Germany the film's release coincided with highly charged press coverage around alleged sexual assaults by 'Muslim' immigrants against local women in the Christmas markets in Cologne. The negative press and hostile environment generated by these events were identified by *Much Loved*'s German distributor as one of the principal reasons why the film failed to attract audiences in Germany in similar numbers to Belgium.[32]

According to the European Audiovisual Observatory's Lumière database, between 2015 and 2017 *Much Loved* was distributed in nine territories: Belgium, Switzerland, Germany, France, Italy, Luxembourg, Netherlands, Portugal and Austria. Imagine was responsible for distribution in a third of these European territories. Theatrical audiences in Europe since 2015 for *Much Loved* totalled 313,387. The largest single territory by a considerable margin was, unsurprisingly, France, where the film was handled by independent specialist Pyramid Distribution: the national distribution started on 113 copies (twenty-one in Paris alone) and rose to a maximum of 273 copies by the fifth week in cinemas, where it attracted over 250,000 spectators (almost 80 per cent of the total number of spectators in Europe).[33] Though attracting fewer spectators than in France, *Much Loved* nonetheless performed extremely well in Belgium and Holland, relative to the size of audience and number of art-house theatres – supporting the claim made elsewhere in this book that, while France remains an important partner and market for Moroccan cinema, it is certainly not the *only* market in the contemporary audiovisual landscape. The film started in Belgium on eight prints in French-speaking Wallonia and was then released in Flanders. Despite the temporary shut-down of cinemas in Brussels, it attracted 12,000 spectators in Belgium and 7,000 in Holland, with a more modest 400 entries in Luxembourg (the smallest Benelux market). As a rule of thumb, Bral explains that films in Belgium are deemed successful if they achieve 5 per cent of the French box office – a target achieved by Imagine with *Much Loved*.

In common with most independent continental European distributors – and despite the disruption that has been brought to the sector as a result of online platforms – theatrical release is still seen as the key driver for independent 'world cinema' releases such as *Much Loved*. In order to gain access to local film theatres and not alienate themselves from national exhibitors, independent European distributors such as Imagine must respect the tightly

controlled windowing system that privileges theatrical release on the continent.[34] The distributor will then hope to exploit the ancillary rights (DVD,
pay TV, terrestrial TV, VOD[35]) that follow. As Bral explains, the business
model operated by Imagine for any release is that theatrical should cover the
P&A costs,[36] while the MG, paid by the distributor for acquisition of territorial rights for the film, should be covered by DVD, TV and sales to VOD.
Revenue from screenings at festivals is also part of Imagine's business model.
Bral estimates that screenings of Imagine's catalogue at Mooov, a world cinema festival held annually in Turnhout in Belgium, can bring in as many as
2,000 spectators. However, even for a relatively successful release such as
Much Loved, securing ancillary rights in addition to theatrical is by no means
a given: by December 2016, *Much Loved* had still not secured TV rights for
Benelux. Ultimately, the example of *Much Loved* reminds us of the considerable challenges faced by distributors at home and abroad in trying to bring
independent world cinema to an audience. Furthermore, it emphasises the
extent to which the success (or failure) of a film can be determined by external conditions, even if a tried and tested plan for distribution and marketing
is in place. Against such a challenging and uncertain backdrop – and with
only limited or no access to sales agents and international film markets – it is
hardly surprising that Moroccan cinema has traditionally struggled to gain
a foothold in the international market. Should the emerging forms of digital
distribution offer a greater cause for optimism for Moroccan filmmakers?

BRAVE NEW WORLD, OR THE SAME OLD PROBLEMS? MOROCCAN CINEMA,
ONLINE INTERNATIONAL DISTRIBUTION AND DIGITAL DISRUPTION

It is hardly controversial to note that the landscape and conditions for international cinema distribution have experienced radical disruption over the past
decade. Cinema's so-called 'digital revolution' is now a reality for the film industry and even to speak solely in terms of 'film' belies the multiple approaches to
producing and consuming 'audiovisual content'. Many of the former disruptors
(such as Netflix and Amazon) are established as the new incumbents, wielding
considerable power not only in relation to distribution but also, increasingly, in
production. However, the shift to digital is not playing out equally in each territory or national cinema. Nor can we simplistically apply a neocolonial logic
that interprets the (underdeveloped) Global South as consistently lagging behind
the (developed) Global North in terms of adoption and innovation of digital
technologies. Africa is a content-hungry continent: while the traditional theatrical exhibition networks and infrastructure are, in many parts of the continent,
either in crisis or non-existent, distributors and aggregators devise new ways,
formal and informal, to distribute audiovisual content (films, TV series, and
new formats online) to audiences outside of theatres via DVD and increasingly

streaming to smartphones and other digital devices.[37] In contrast, at the level of exhibition at least, such innovation in Europe (especially in its biggest market, France) remains restricted by a dogged adherence (led largely by the established exhibitors who have the most to gain from maintaining the status quo) to a windowing system, where theatrical exhibition is privileged above all else and, if a film is distributed in cinema theatres, it must wait at least twelve months before it can become available on Subscription Video on Demand (SVOD) platforms.

As we have seen in the discussion of the digitisation of exhibition and piracy in the previous chapter, Moroccan cinema is navigating its own path through such changes. As in all other national cinemas, the response to digital disruption is determined by a combination of economic, institutional and cultural factors, influenced by local conditions and consumer habits and practices as much as they are by global developments in technology and the increasing dominance of the new transnational digital majors. While established theatrical distributors and exhibitors – who, of course, have the most to lose in the current phase of disruption – decry a period of crisis and instability, others see an opportunity to break free from established (Western) hegemonies that have dominated the global production and circulation of cinema for so long:

> The opportunity is there for good content and a sufficient number of more openly accessible video platforms now exist to distribute that content. The . . . next generation filmmakers . . . don't necessarily need Hollywood or [its] distributor[s]. (Cunningham and Silver 2013: 5)

At the level of the informal or illegal circulation of films – what Lobato (2012) describes as 'distribution from below' – such disruption already exists in Morocco for producers, distributors and consumers. Alternative modes of circulation and consumption of Moroccan films (both popular and cinephile) through DVD piracy are well established (see Chapter 5), as is file sharing and online streaming via sites such as Cinémaghrebia. Similarly, a growing number of Amazigh filmmakers (see Chapter 4), activist filmmakers such as Nadir Bouhmouch and even established Moroccan directors such as Hicham Lasri (see Chapter 3), employ the digital technology available to them to distribute their work inside, outside and at the interstices of the system to online audiences in Morocco and abroad.

What of the opportunities opening up for Moroccan filmmakers in the context of formal international distribution in the digital age? As noted in the previous section, theatrical exhibition remains the dominant mode of 'formal' international distribution for a small group of Moroccan films; either via commercial distribution in selected cinemas or, more commonly, through participation in international festivals. Even with a limited release, theatrical distribution has a symbolic value and prestige that can convince TV or VOD platforms to purchase the rights for a given film.[38] And with sales of DVD/Blu-Ray in rapid decline globally, online distribution would seem to offer the best opportunity for ancillary distribution after commercial theatrical distribution or a festival run.

While the VOD market is beginning to open up in Morocco – with Netflix establishing a regional office in Casablanca in April 2018 (Benabid 2018) – for Moroccan producers looking to export their films to foreign platforms, the evolving market is unpredictable. A plethora of VOD platforms[39] are emerging, ranging from the new digital majors with tens of millions of subscribers worldwide to niche and boutique platforms, which may count subscribers in the thousands. Online distribution appears as the saviour of independent cinema, providing a long-tail global audience for even the most niche art-house films or world cinema titles. However with VOD platforms highly protective of their audience data, and largely secretive around details of financial deals with filmmakers, it is extremely difficult for independent directors and producers to accurately assess the potential value of their films in the global market.

As with theatrical distribution, the Arab market remains difficult for Moroccan films to access. Currently TV (generally dominated by popular Egyptian films) continues to be the more popular method of viewing films legally in the Arab world, and is therefore still a more lucrative proposition than VOD.[40] Many of the major SVOD platforms in the Arab world (Amazon, Netflix and Starz Play) are more focused on American TV and films. For a time, Icflix, a Middle East and North African streaming platform, founded in 2013 and modelling itself as the Netflix of the Arab world, appeared to offer significant opportunities for Moroccan cinema to break into the pan-Arab VOD market. Following the signing of formal agreements between the CCM and Icflix at the Marrakesh international film festival in 2015, it was announced that Icflix would be the main backer for Nour-Eddine Lakhmari's fourth feature film, *Burnout* (2017) – in the first of what was hoped would be a run of productions financed by the VOD platform. By 2018 such optimism appeared misplaced. According to Lakhmari's Norwegian producer, Egil Ødegård, Icflix had failed to deliver the promised level of funding for *Burnout*, closing their offices in Casablanca with little possibility of investing further Moroccan production.[41] Another problem for Moroccan cinema on Icflix comes from the platform's focus on popular films (Jazzwood, Bollywood and Hollywood) for its (mostly Arabic) subscribers across MENA and the diaspora. This leaves room for only very few Moroccan films deemed to have such popular appeal – comedies such as *The Transporters* (Naciri, 2015) or Youssef Britel's biopic of the Moroccan artist Chaïbia Talal, *Chaïbia* (2015) – with virtually no space for Moroccan films that might be described as auteur-led or desirable to world cinema audiences.

Other barriers for Moroccan films in the Arab market of both the wider MENA region and the Arab diaspora include: (1) language differences and the cost of subtitling (from Darija, Amazigh and even French into Arabic) which must be paid by the distributor;[42] (2) the issue of the type of content provided for the target audience of a given platform; and (3) online distributors' perception of Moroccan cinema. On the final point, Peri Abou-Zeid, CEO of the niche VOD platform MoviePigs (founded in 2015), notes that what she sees as the more 'open' representations of sex, nudity and violence found in Moroccan films are not appropriate for her core subscriber base of diasporic Arab families in the US and Canada. Interestingly, then, Abou-Zeid's view of Moroccan cinema has effectively been shaped by the films she sees at international festivals and markets such as *Much Loved*, *On the Edge* and *Jahiliya* (Lasri, 2018). Such films are likely to be more challenging for an Arab audience in terms of their treatment of socio-political themes than those films produced for a domestic audience in Morocco. This perception of Moroccan cinema, combined with the issues of language and the fact that diasporic Moroccans would make up only a very small part of subscribers in North America, means that MoviePigs had (at the time interviews were conducted with the company in 2018) yet to purchase a Moroccan film for its catalogue.[43] Indeed, we might even see this lack of visibility for Moroccan films as symptomatic of the way that Maghrebi cinema is largely ignored by many distributors focusing on pan-Arab markets (including the diaspora) in favour of cinema from the Mashreq. In Abou-Zeid's opinion, in order to break through to wider audiences on specialist or niche VOD platforms, Moroccan films need to attract Western rather than Arab audiences – and focus on the potential transnational appeal of issues or themes within each narrative, rather than promoting the film's specific national or cultural identity.[44]

In the context of the European or North American markets, VOD has the potential for Moroccan cinema to bridge the gap between the relatively healthy presence of Moroccan films at a range of international festivals and the general lack of commercial distribution for Moroccan cinema internationally. If Moroccan films are picked up by the bigger VOD platforms, the issue becomes one of visibility to audiences in what is an already crowded market. For his part, international sales agent Hédi Zardi is highly sceptical that platforms such as Netflix and Amazon have sufficient interest to purchase and curate Moroccan films appropriately at the current time.[45] A quick search on Netflix in the US in September 2018 would seem to confirm this assessment, as only Ayouch's *Much Loved* appears on the platform. The navigation and user interface on the larger VOD platforms such as Netflix and Amazon is, moreover, driven by a consumer approach, designed by an algorithm ('if you have liked X, then we recommend Y'), instead of classification by national cinemas. In any case, as already noted, the preference of aggregators, distributors and sales agents across the value chain is for individual auteurs rather than national cimemas. The result for Netflix, then, is a largely Western-focused catalogue that, despite the company's global reach remains, in many ways, stunningly insular.

The experience of the Spanish–Moroccan–French–Qatari co-production *Mimosas*, working with UK streaming platform MUBI, confirms a similar focus on individual auteurs rather than an entire national cinema, though offers more optimism for the visibility of Moroccan cinema to an online cinephile audience than that via Netflix in the US. Launched in the UK in 2007, MUBI began with a similar business model to most film SVOD platforms, with a library of aggregated content offered to consumers on a subscription basis. Struggling to convert and retain subscribers, MUBI replaced this with a more innovative model of a curated programme of thirty films available at any one time, with one film replaced every day – a model that saw the company rise to 100,000 subscribers in more than 200 territories by 2017 (Pham 2017). It expanded this model in 2016 to include theatrical distribution for a select number of films (around six per territory). This means that for most films, MUBI only needs to require the online rights for a short thirty-day window (either as closed-revenue shares or set licence fee deals), though for the select number of titles that they choose to distribute theatrically, MUBI enters into longer-term deal for all rights (digital and theatrical) in a specific territory for seven to ten years.[46] According to Bobby Allen, Head of Content at MUBI, the selection of titles for theatrical release has a dual function in that: 'it helps build the value of the film on ancillary media, and the reputation of the filmmaker' (Allen in Pham 2017). This focus on developing the reputation of the filmmaker is significant, since it identifies MUBI as a platform that promotes and programmes in relation to auteurs, rather than genres or national cinemas. With its curated model of thirty films available at any one time and a new title being added/removed each day, MUBI functions very much like an online festival, with its programmers acting as gatekeepers for an audience of cinephile subscribers, unlike the more general audience (which may, of course, include cinephiles) found on Netflix. In the context of Moroccan cinema, a platform such as MUBI would be most beneficial to those filmmakers engaged with the world cinema circuit, international co-productions and the international festival circuit, whose films more naturally tend towards auteur-led productions: essentially, the *cinéastes de passages*. However, MUBI's model of selecting only around thirty films per month, in a catalogue that includes new released but also 'classics' and undiscovered gems from world cinema, means that even those Moroccan films with the visibility that comes from a successful international festival run will struggle to find a window on the platform.

According to Chiara Marañón, Director of Programming at MUBI, over the past three years only a small number of Moroccan films have been considered for screening on MUBI, based on their visbility at international festivals attended by MUBI programmers. These include: *Sofia* (France/Qatar/Belgium/Morocco, Benm'Barek, 2018), which won the screenplay award in the Un Certain Regard section at Cannes in 2019, *House in the Fields* (Morocco/Qatar, Hadid, 2017) the multi-award wining documentary discussed in Chapter 2 and *About Some Meaningless Events* (Morocco, Derkaoui, 1974) a film censored by the Moroccan authorities during the Years of Lead that was restored and screened at the Berlinale in 2019.[47] To date (August 2019), the only Moroccan film that has been screened on MUBI is the Spanish–Moroccan–French–Qatari co-production *Mimosas*, directed by Oliver Laxe (a Spanish filmmaker based in Morocco) and co-produced by Lamia Chraibi (La Prod/Moon & Deal Films). *Mimosas'* success on the international festival circuit, its strong art-house credentials and the singular artistic vision of Laxe made the film a natural fit for MUBI and its cinephile subscriber base. Indeed, even before *Mimosas*, MUBI programmers have been tracking the success of Laxe and had already screened his debut feature *You All Are Captains* (2010), which, although a Spanish production, makes extensive use of Tangier as a location, and of its inhabitants. Although conscious of the fact that a film such as *Mimosas* would be 'difficult' to sell to UK audiences, MUBI's belief in Laxe as an emerging auteur and original directorial voice was such that the company commited to threatrical distribution of *Mimosas* in the UK – thus entering into an all-rights deal for the film in the UK for up to ten years. Following a UK premiere at the Institute of Contemporary Arts in London (including a Q&A with the director) the film received a limited theatrical release in the UK (fifteen screens) in the autumn of 2017, mostly through the independent/art-house chain Picturehouse. Here, it featured as part of the exhibitors 'discover Tuesdays' strand, whereby a lesser known film is presented to curious cinephile audiences. Again, the emphasis with this marketing initiative was placed on curation; on audiences trusting in the exhibitors and distributors (Picturehouse and MUBI) as gatekeepers to quality cinema that would otherwise remain hidden beyond the festival circuit. Though the film, perhaps unsurprisingly, made only modest returns at the UK box office, *Mimosas* did perform well in its thirty-day run on the MUBI platform in 2018 and subsequent re-run as part of the 'Cannes Takeover' in the run-up to the festival the following year, attracting over 2,500 views.[48] Moreover, the fact that MUBI had agreed to an all-rights deal beyond a thirty-day screening window online for *Mimosas* means that the distributor was committed to promoting and enhancing the success of the film in the long term. This included building ancillary markets for film beyond the theatrical release, most significantly through transactional video on demand (TVOD) sales on Apple's iTunes site, where it has been one of MUBI's top performing TVOD titles, and through the film's availablity on MUBI's Amazon channel. Putting to one side the debate as to whether or not *Mimosas* can be seen as a truly 'Moroccan' film (see Chapter 2), what the example of the film's distribution in the UK shows is the how the potential for independent art-house films to reach their audience is best served by a firm commitment from the (online) distributor in curating and promoting the film (and its associated talent) rather than simply leaving *Mimosas* to flounder in a sea of titles that form part of a larger online catalogue, such as that found on Netflix.

One likely strategy for Moroccan filmmakers could, therefore, be to place their films with niche VOD platforms, in the same way that niche festivals offer alternative exhibition and distribution potentials (see Chapter 6). But the VOD market for niche platforms is still not sufficiently developed for either Moroccan filmmakers, or the CCM working on their behalf, to easily and efficiently target such companies, many of whom are still trying to determine who and where their audiences are, and what their preferences are.[49] Moreover, like the A-list festivals and international sales agents discussed in the previous section, such VOD platforms (as with our previous example of *Mimosas'* success with MUBI) are far more likely to be searching for individual films or directors rather than looking to promote a specific national cinema or region. In this context, visibility to programmers and buyers at international festivals and markets is once again crucial – and a presence that is entirely lacking for most Moroccan films.

One such niche distributor attending these festivals looking for hidden gems from world cinema is the North American company Filmatique. Founded in November 2016, Filmatique is driven by a desire to promote outstanding films from 'emerging markets' that have tended to be well received at international festivals but then failed to gain commercial distribution. Filmatique adopts a curatorial role similar to that of a film festival, selecting films, including essays by academics and critics to introduce them, and organising parts of their catalogue thematically (such as a recent special on Arab cinema that included one Moroccan film (*The Miscreants*, Besri, Switzerland/Morocco, 2011), or its January 2019 'In Transit' series on migrants that included Saïd Hamich's *Return to Bollene*, France/Morocco, 2017). As co-founder of Filmatique, Ursula Grisham explains, although they spend much time identifying desired titles at international film festivals such as Berlin and IFFR, sales agents still act as gatekeepers to the North American VOD market for these films.[50] Certain films, such as those at Cannes, will simply be out of reach for Filmatique both in terms of their market value and the fact that producers and sales agents want to sell these films to larger VOD platforms with a greater audience reach and visibility in the market.[51] Like MoviePigs, Filmatique is limited to online distribution in North America, in part because the European market (the other key territory for their potential audience) is so fragmented. In Europe, the costs to the online distributor increase considerably since each country is effectively its own territory, requiring a separate licensing deal and a different set of subtitles, for a potentially small number of subscribers.[52] Formal online distribution for niche VOD platforms is therefore immediately more restricted than informal distribution (or even international festival distribution) due to the need to negotiate rights, often on a territory by territory basis and the availability of films via sales agents.

Despite the optimism and opportunities surrounding cinema's digital 'revolution' around the hope it would open up independent cinema to a long-tail of online audiences across the globe, the problems faced by Moroccan filmmakers in relation to foreign distribution have remained largely unchanged. First, there is the question of the visibility of Moroccan films and filmmakers in a way that would equate Moroccan cinema to a marketable (or even recognisable) 'brand' for foreign audiences. Second, most Moroccan filmmakers lack the necessary contacts with international sales agents and local distributors to complete the deals that would give their films international exposure. Finally, Moroccan producers and directors may not have a thorough understanding of the complex ways in which the international (VOD) market functions and the true value of their films within this market. The most viable option for Moroccan filmmakers would seem to be targeting niche VOD platforms through either regional distributors or sales agents. Niche platforms such as Filmatique and MoviePigs focus on strategic curation, a desire to engage audiences with quality films and a more intimate relationship with their subscriber base, much like international film festivals. In this respect, niche platforms are much better placed to promote and support certain Moroccan films to reach a transnational cinephile audience. As Grisham notes: 'There is a void in the market and people want to see these films . . . companies are beginning to understand that it is better to have these films with platforms such as ours, as at least people are seeing these films and talking about them'.[53]

The trade-off for such potential visibility on specialist platforms for Moroccan filmmakers, however, is their limited reach, in comparison to that of the larger SVOD platforms. Moreover, whichever VOD platform they sell to, the reality of the current market is such that Moroccan filmmakers will be selling their films for digital dimes rather than analogue dollars. Nevertheless, alliances with niche online distributors such as MoviePigs and Filmatique, as well as more substantial players such as MUBI, could become even more valuable in the future. As the sector matures, so there is the potential for greater collaboration and cohesion between a network of specialist VOD platforms (both in terms of subscription, advertising-generated and transactional modes of consumption of these films) as well as the growing incursions of festivals into the VOD arena.[54] Such a development could offer a viable alternative in the future for Moroccan filmmakers to the (largely inaccessible) digital behemoths such as Amazon and Netflix. The danger for the promotion of a truly diverse transnational Moroccan cinema, however, comes in the fact that these VOD platforms would, in all likelihood, want to promote the kind of auteur-led films that gain traction at international festivals: not the popular Moroccan cinema consumed by domestic audiences and viewers in the Moroccan diaspora. With currently little commercial value outside of the Kingdom, popular Moroccan cinema seems destined to circulate within informal distribution networks – which is not to say that its audiences will be any less significant. Digital disruption appears, then, to reinforce rather than bridge the schism between popular domestic productions and the world cinema festival films of the *cinéastes de passage* in contemporary Moroccan cinema.

NOTES

1. 'Qui tient la distribution, tient le cinéma'. Chériaa cited in el Yamani et al. (1991: 75).
2. DISCOP presentation, Africa Hub, Berlinale, 10 February 2019.
3. 'Pre-sales in today's market is very tricky; having a domestic distributor on board is helpful but when you can't guarantee them something wide it makes pre-sales more difficult' (Tannaz Anisi, President of 13 Films, cited in Arnon 2016).
4. Figures on the number of Franco-Moroccan co-productions obtained by searching and collating information for 'producing or co-producing country' on the European Audiovisual Observatory database (Lumière): <http://www.lumiere.obs.coe.int>.
5. See <http://lumiere.obs.coe.int/web/film_info/?id=72519> (accessed 31 October 2019).
6. Although, as we see below, the ascendancy in the last decade of digital aggregators such as Netflix are potentially transforming the landscape in this respect.
7. Meriame Deghedi, Distribution and Sales Manager, MAD Solutions, interviewed by Will Higbee and Stef Van de Peer Tangier, National Film Festival, March 2018.
8. A minimum guarantee or MG is an advance payment on a film for the right to license a territory or territories. The MG is payable to the producer once the film is completed and delivered to the distributor. Pre-sales have traditionally been an important part of the financial jigsaw for international independent film production, since they serve as the basis upon which a bank or financiers will make a loan to a producer to (part-) finance a film's production.
9. Pablo César, Skype interview with Will Higbee, 9 August 2019.
10. Meriame Deghedi, Distribution and Sales Manager, MAD Solutions, interviewed by Will Higbee and Stef Van de Peer Tangier, National Film Festival, March 2018.
11. For more on the activities, aims and partners involved in the Arab Cinema Centre, see: <http://acc.film/> (accessed 31 January 2020).
12. Hédi Zardi, international sales agent with Luxbox, described the distribution of *Mimosas* in the MENA region as a 'symbolic' gesture rather than a commercial strategy (Hédi Zardi, Skype interview with Will Higbee, July 2017). Similarly, Lebanese distributor Zenia Sfier observes that there is no real market for Maghreb films in the Lebanon. Marrakchi's *Rock the Casbah* was an exception to this rule due to the 'palette' of Arab actors in the film who had box-office draw and also due to the fact that, as a French co-production, the film was also accessible for a UniFrance grant (see Caillé 2016: 181).
13. 'There is a huge difference between a lot of festivals where you have a very targeted audience, and a distributor who will put up the money to release a film, recuperate this money and perhaps to make some money to live . . . Liking a film and promoting a film is not the same thing as taking a risk to release a film. The distributor must buy the film, create material to promote it, secure press reviews and send the

film into different theatres. You have distribution costs and you have to recuperate them' (Hédi Zardi, Skype interview with Will Higbee, July 2017).

14. Hédi Zardi, Skype interview with Will Higbee, July 2017.

15. Hicham Felah, interview with Will Higbee and Stef Van de Peer, Tangier, National Film Festvial, March 2018.

16. Interview with members of Europa Distribution (association for independent European distributors) by Will Higbee, Marrakesh, December 2016.

17. Hédi Zardi, Skype interview with Will Higbee, July 2017.

18. As Hédi Zardi put it when discussing the national identity of a co-production such as *Mimosas*: 'For me it's *Mimosas* – I don't care about identity' (Hédi Zardi, Skype interview with Will Higbee, July 2017).

19. Interview with members of Europa Distribution (association for independent European distributors) by Will Higbee, Marrakesh, December 2016.

20. Lakhmari was speaking on a Moroccan industry panel at the Morocco in Motion international conference, organised by the Transnational Moroccan Cinema research project and linked to the Africa in Motion film festival, Edinburgh, 27 October 2018.

21. This was the case for Ahmed Boulane with the earlier example of *La Isla*, who dealt with sales for the film through his production company Boulane O'Bryne Production, according to the *Hollywood Reporter*'s review of the film's premiere at the 2015 Marrakesh International Film Festival (Defore 2015).

22. Figures obtained by collating information for a search with Morocco as 'producing or co-producing country', on the European Audiovisual Observatory database (Lumière): <http://www.lumiere.obs.coe.int> (accessed 31 October 2019).

23. Figures obtained by collating information for a search with 'Nabil Ayouch' as 'director', on the European Audiovisual Observatory database (Lumière): <http://www.lumiere.obs.coe.int> (accessed 31 October 2019).

24. Unless otherwise stated, all information, quotes and data for the distribution of *Much Loved* in Benelux is taken from an interview conducted by Flo Martin and Will Higbee with Tinne Bral (Imagine Distribution) at the Marrakesh International Film Festival, December 2016.

25. As much as the simple depiction of prostitution – which has appeared before in other Moroccan films – it was, arguably, the depiction of sex workers with the Saudi male Nomenklatura in Marrakesh that posed potential economic and political problems for Morocco in terms of its relations with Saudi Arabia. This is most probably why the film was banned by the Moroccan Minister of Communication over the head of CCM director, Sarim Fassi Fihri.

26. In fact, this attempt by more conservative factions in Moroccan society to censor Moroccan cinema had already started before the PJD's electoral victory in November 2011. Laïla Marrakchi faced similar accusations to Ayouch with the release of *Marock* in 2005.

27. Films distributed by Imagine include: *Beyond Gibraltar, Lady Chatterley, 4 months, 3 weeks and 2 days, The Wrestler, Uncle Boonmee, Antichrist, Elena, Monsieur Lazhar and Taxi Teheran.*

28. Tinne Bral interviewed by Flo Martin and Will Higbee, Marrakesh International Film Festival, December 2016.

29. *Much Loved* was, in fact, the first 'Moroccan' film – directed by a Moroccan and set in Morocco – distributed by Imagine, though one of the first films distributed the company has been *Beyond Gibraltar* (2001) by Mourad Boucif, a Moroccan director who has lived in Belgium since childhood.

30. The IFFR, which takes place each year in January, is a highly prestigious international film festival with a strong reputation for promoting world cinema.

31. Tinne Bral interviewed by Flo Martin and Will Higbee, Marrakesh International Film Festival, December 2016.

32. Will Higbee, interview with representative from Arsenal Distribution, Marrakesh, December 2016.

33. Figures for the French box office for *Much Loved* taken from data provided by CBO-ciné chiffres.

34. Whilst under increasing pressure, the windows system and privileging of theatrical release still holds sway in Continental European distribution, rather than experimenting with more innovative forms of multi-platform 'day-and-date' release that have been successfully implemented by art house distributors in the UK such as Curzon-Artificial Eye (see Wiseman 2015).

35. During the 1990s and 2000s, DVD represented one of the most lucrative parts of the market for European distributors. This has rapidly been replaced by VOD and OTT services, to the point where the DVD format is in terminal decline. However, in general, sales (and thus the value of rights) for VOD and OTT services are less lucrative than DVD sales were.

36. P&A refers to 'prints and advertising': the costs related to producing the subtitled prints and the advertising for the release of the film. These costs must be met by the distributor.

37. Nollywood was one of the first cinemas to embrace digital production and distribution in ways that have transformed not only Nigerian cinema but also production and distribution practices in many popular African cinemas for local and diasporic audiences (the rise of iRoko as the self-styled 'Netflix of Africa' for example).

38. Meriame Deghedi, Distribution and Sales Manager, MAD Solutions, interviewed by Will Higbee and Stef Van de Peer, Tangier, National Film Festival, March 2018.

39. Formal online distribution in the form of video on demand (VOD), can further be divided into 'subscription video on demand' (SVOD) and 'transactional video on demand' (TVOD). In the former (SVOD) the importance is to build up a recognisable brand or service from the particular platform and to offer an extensive catalogue of films for the subscriber. The latter (TVOD) essentially works on a pay-per-view model, attracting viewers to specific films.

40. 'Selling to TV is more important than to VOD – they pay more. There are an increasing number of VOD platforms but in the Arab world but people still watch a lot of TV more than in Europe.' Meriame Deghedi, Distribution and Sales Manager, MAD Solutions, interviewed by Will Higbee and Stef Van de Peer Tangier, National Film Festival, March 2018. Peri Abou-Zeid, CEO of MoviePigs, an online platform catering for diasporic viewers of Arabic cinema in North America, also suggested that she saw her platform's competition coming as much from other specialist satellite

TV channels as she did from other SVOD platforms. Peri Abou-Zeid interviewed by Will Higbee and Stef Van de Peer, Berlin, February 2018.

41. In terms of international distribution, this left Ødegård in a difficult position: part of the deal with Icflix included exclusive distribution rights via the company's SVOD platform to many international territories – limiting the producer's ability to maximise revenue from alternative distributors (Flo Martin and Will Higbee, interview with Egil Ødegård, National Film Festival, Tangier, March 2018).

42. 'When you create Arabic subtitles you automatically limit or reduce the boundaries of the language. When we had, for example, two Moroccan films, *The Miscreants* or *A Mile in My Shoes* that we offered to pay TV from the UAE and Egypt, at first they were not seduced by the offer. But when we told them that we would provide subtitles, they said 'OK, let's try!''' (Meriame Deghedi, Distribution and Sales Manager, MAD Solutions, interviewed by Will Higbee and Stef Van de Peer Tangier, National Film Festival, March 2018).

43. 'Moroccan films tend to be a lot more open than the rest of the region which offer more conservative films . . . We haven't picked up any Moroccan films for VOD . . . right now we're focused on the North American market, even though part of our library is available in Europe. We primarily serve the Arab diaspora in North America and the majority of those do not speak French except for the ones in Montreal, Canada. That's a very small group of French speakers that possibly come from that part of the world. The majority would be Palestinians, Egyptians, Lebanese and even other parts of the world like Saudis that would watch Egyptian films in the Middle East but they would never watch Moroccan, Tunisian or even Algerian film. So, looking at it from North Africa, that is one thing that I was always very sceptical of. Is there a market within the Arab diaspora for this particular kind of film, or not?'' (Peri Abou-Zeid interviewed by Will Higbee and Stef Van de Peer, European Film Market, Berlin, February 2018).

44. 'The film would actually do well when the context that it fits in is not necessarily that it's Arab, it's not that it's North African. It's nothing like that: it's the issue base. And that's why *Apatride* (Nejjar, 2018) [screened at the Berlin festival that Abou-Zeid attended] was actually interesting to me, because I thought "it's a woman at the core of it, it's an issue, technically about a refugee or people that were pushed out of their countries or homes". So that to me would be relevant' (Peri Abou-Zeid interviewed by Will Higbee and Stef Van de Peer, European Film Market, Berlin, February 2018).

45. 'There's little or no place for a film such as *Mimosas* on Netflix: how do you find it?' (Hédi Zardi interview with Will Higbee, Skype, June 2017).

46. Chiara Marañón (Director of Programming at MUBI), Skype interview with Will Higbee, 26 July 2019.

47. Ibid.

48. All figures provided by Chiara Marañón (Director of Programming at MUBI), interviewed on Skype by Will Higbee, 26 July 2019.

49. Peri Abou-Zeid, interviewed by Will Higbee and Stef Van de Peer, European Film Market, Berlin, February 2018.

50. Ursula Grisham interviewed by Will Higbee and Stef Van de Peer, interview with European Film Market, Berlin, February 2018.

51. Ibid.
52. 'I can't just say that I'm going to open it up in Europe, no. This means that I will have to have subtitles in German, French and so on. The cost will quadruple or even be ten times greater because every single country is a territory on its own.' Peri Abou-Zeid, interviewed by Will Higbee and Stef Van de Peer, European Film Market, Berlin, February 2018.
53. Ursula Grisham interviewed by Will Higbee and Stef Van de Peer, European Film Market, Berlin, February 2018. Peri Abou-Zeid, interviewed by Will Higbee and Stef Van de Peer, European Film Market, Berlin, February 2018.
54. Recent innovations by IFFR to provide not only online access to current editions of the festival but also access via TVOD to the festival's back catalogue provide one indication of how this area might develop in the future.

CONCLUSION: TRANSNATIONAL MOROCCAN CINEMA: OF BUMBLEBEES AND BUTTERFLIES

When asked in the early 2000s to describe the current state of film production in Morocco, veteran director Mohamed Abderrahman Tazi gave the following reply:

> A bumblebee weighs 40 milligrams, the surface of its wings is 2.2 square centimeters, the wings are inclined at an angle of 30 degrees . . . according to the laws of aeronautics, it's impossible for that insect to fly . . . But bumblebees fly just the same! That's just the way it is for our cinema: there's no infrastructure, minimal financial aid, no public, no encouragement – there's nothing! So, we can't make films, but, just the same, we make films! (Tazi cited in Dwyer 2004: 103)

Tazi's playful analogy masks a serious point: the paradox of Moroccan cinema is that films have been made despite (not because of) the conditions of production and circulation, and despite the obstacles put in place by the political climate in the Kingdom. Since the late 1990s, even in the face of such challenging conditions for filmmakers at all stages of the value chain, a growing range of Moroccan films aimed at local, national and international audiences have been produced. Because of targeted institutional support from the CCM under the leadership of Noureddine Saïl between 2003 and 2014, Moroccan cinema has come to be seen as a model of production for other African and Arab nations, even if the autonomy of the CCM has been complicated recently by increased interference from the ruling conservative PJD party. Today, Moroccan cinema, so long the poor relation of Algerian and Tunisian cinema in terms of prestige, levels of production and international reach, has emerged as arguably the Maghreb's most important national cinema.

The success of CCM-led initiatives such as encouraging (with both gestures and access to funding) the 'return' of diasporic Moroccan filmmakers in the mid-1990s has had a tangible effect: an 'electric shock' that has jolted Moroccan cinema back to life.[1] One such diasporic director, Nabil Ayouch, has become the most visible and commercially successful Moroccan director internationally, while simultaneously transforming the audiovisual landscape in Morocco with the success of Ali n' Productions. Although only a handful of Moroccan filmmakers like Ayouch are able to gain a foothold in the A-list international festivals, the number of Moroccan films on the festival circuit (both major and niche festivals) is, nonetheless, respectable. Similarly, as with selection for A-list festivals, limited success in accessing funding from organisations such as the World Cinema Fund reflects as much the highly competitive nature of such prestigious funds and festivals as it does the 'failure' of Moroccan filmmakers to break ground in these areas.

Within Morocco, a greater diversity of voices and perspectives are emerging than ever before. Some filmmakers are seizing the opportunities offered them to reach new audiences with highly localised content. Amazigh cinema connects transnationally to the Moroccan diaspora through online streaming. Others, in a direct challenge to the Makhzen, choose to bypass traditional systems of production and distribution and the traditional red lines of Moroccan cinema (the Royal family, homosexuality, Moroccan women, the Western Sahara), disseminating highly politicised films that are viewed by youthful, activist and dissident audiences online in both Morocco and abroad.

Yet in common with many African cinemas, Moroccan cinema's success conceals a considerable vulnerability within the film ecosystem, linked to a weakened exhibition sector that is in crisis (and not only due to piracy), as well as limited opportunities for filmmakers to distribute their work both at home and abroad. If the transnational presence of Moroccan cinema at international festivals of all classes is respectable, the ability for a wider base of Moroccan filmmakers to access the same festival network is severely limited (and yet this is arguably their primary means of engaging with transnational audiences and the international film industry). Only a small elite of those filmmakers based abroad (the *cinéastes de passage*) have the requisite knowledge and connection to a transnational network of producers, funders and sales agents to engage in international co-production and commercial distribution. Even filmmakers, such as Ayouch, Nejjar and Bensaïdi, who are connected to such networks, are by no means guaranteed easy and open access to sizeable international audiences. Collaboration between the CCM and sub-Saharan African cinemas, as well as the growing importance of the Gulf States as a source of funding for development and post-production, offer clear instances of Moroccan cinema de-orbiting from the European francosphere. Nevertheless, France remains the principal foreign co-producer and distributor of Moroccan films and Moroccan filmmakers wishing to access the French market must also navigate the often sensitive cultural politics of production and distribution with the former coloniser.

In the more localised context of the Kingdom, other challenges currently exist that obstruct the way of emerging or first-time filmmakers. Most obviously, these concern the varying quality of and access to film education and training, as well as bureaucratic requirements from the system (CCM), such as the prerequisites to obtaining the all-important industry/professional cards. Many young Moroccan filmmakers (including recent graduates from film schools and universities) resent a system they see as designed to marginalise their talent and frustrate their artistic and commercial ambition. At the level of training, there is a particular need for more investment in script development, production and distribution, not simply promoting director-producers who are reliant on funding from the CCM and Moroccan TV. At the level of production, many filmmakers are content to remain focused on internal networks and sources for funding and collaboration. Others are keen to (re-)gain international visibility but are sceptical of the possibilities open to Moroccan filmmakers who are not located within the diaspora and thus not directly connected to the international industry, markets, festivals and audiences.

There is even an argument from some in the Moroccan film industry that this heavy reliance on state-induced funding for national production can actually be counter-productive, insomuch as it discourages transnational collaboration, resulting in a national cinema that, in many cases, is too provincial.[2] The resulting lack of its presence at international markets has led to difficulties in building a national 'brand' or identity for Moroccan cinema on the international festival circuit, in the way that Iranian, Korean or Argentinian cinema has done over the past twenty years.[3] The danger is that, as Moroccan cinema completes its transition to the new digital landscape, the same divisions and interests between an elite group of art-house directors, who are feted in Europe, and the majority of Moroccan filmmakers, who feel effectively locked out of such systems and networks, will simply widen further.

Clearly, then, ever since 1956, the CCM has been an active promoter – albeit at different speeds over the postcolonial decades– of Moroccan film production. Yet at present, given the shifting landscape of transnational production and distribution, it is not as proactive in its promotion of Moroccan productions on the international stage as it is at home. On the other hand, it is quite aggressive in its promotion of foreign production facilities in Morocco; hence the CCM's visibility in A-list festivals tends to advertise Morocco's decors and tax breaks for filmmakers from abroad rather than Moroccan productions screening at the festival. Paradoxically, as instrumental as the CCM has been in the recent takeoff of

Moroccan film production, its role now appears somewhat ambiguous: it seems to be catering to the domestic promotion of Moroccan cinema, while perhaps (unintentionally) hindering its transnational reach (other than as a production location for Western studios). As an example, it has supported refurbishing and modernising film theatres in the Kingdom, in a vital initiative to save some of the screening venues in the digital age, and work in favour of the viability of Moroccan cinema. This focus on reconnecting with a domestic audience is, of course, crucial. However, it should not exclude courting a transnational one, beyond that of international festivals. Here, the CCM seems to still be privileging the audience of an imagined national community, identified at the dawn of independence, when it facilitated the production of 'national' images and narratives destined for a national audience, in the era of postcolonial nation building. But in these post-postcolonial times, it might be marching behind its own shadow. In fact, as we have shown in the preceding chapters, the issue of reaching a transnational viewership is one of the most pressing matters for Moroccan cinema today – as it is, indeed, the globe over, for 'small national' cinemas (with transnational reach), in the age of 'post-cinema'.[4] The Moroccan film audience is layered and complex. At home, some popular genre Moroccan films (in particular comedies) score highly at the Moroccan box office. Abroad, only a handful of transnational Moroccan films are visible outside the festival and the even narrower art-house circuits. Paradoxically, the age of multiple screens has made so many films simultaneously visible to viewers that it has condemned many of them to invisibility in the international context. It is extremely difficult for individual films (or groups of films like Moroccan cinema) to stand out in the tsunami of digital productions available for consumption. This is in large part also linked to the new modes of film viewing that have appeared: the latter have turned into a consumption habit and a 'fragmentation of demand'[5] that no longer espouse the old cinephilic ritual of going out and communing with fellow spectators in a dark room.[6] The sheer volume and speed of film screenings have, according to Ahmed el Maanouni (2013: 42), 'created an all-streaming environment that has inundated our imagination' and transformed the very act of viewing and the postures of the spectator towards film as spectacle and viewing as enacting the power to view on demand. A new audience is born, one that is no longer restricted to the programmes of the neighbourhood movie theatre, but is in the driver's seat to select among long lists of film options. The same phenomenon occurs outside the Kingdom, of course, where the all-streaming environment is even more jammed with major streaming services in which Moroccan cinema barely, if ever, appears.[7] The festival programmers, on the one hand, and niche VOD platforms or online streaming services such as MUBI in the UK and Filmatique in the US, on the other, play an increasingly influential role as gatekeepers and curators of world cinema able to make Moroccan films visible to international audiences online, and affording them a greater prominence in the festival exhibition space.

As far as Moroccan cinema is concerned, then, the question that lingers in the wake of the movie theatre crisis and streaming availability in Morocco and elsewhere no longer is 'where is it?' but 'whose is it?' We know that the old-fashioned cinephile public, whose very identity is crucial for the circulation and distribution of Moroccan cinema, has dwindled. Indeed, this cinephile public has been lost to some degree to a Moroccan viewing public, accustomed to consuming all manner of audiovisual content across a range of platforms and digital devices. In other words, to riff on Gayatri Spivak's famous line (about who speaks and listens in postcolonial times): 'Who should make films?' is less crucial than 'Who will view them?'[8] Who, apart from the usual suspects: critics, academics, students of Moroccan transnational cinema, members of the Moroccan diaspora in Europe and North America? Finding a way to break free from these silos is probably the most acutely difficult challenge facing the directors and their producers in Morocco today. And for the CCM, such a pursuit would require a shift from a strict postcolonial focus on supporting film production in Morocco to devoting resources to a transnational communication strategy in the international markets of film. It would therefore correspond to a next stage in its dialectic development: after its colonial, then postcolonial stage, it would now espouse the post-postcolonial phase of Moroccan cinema, i.e. an age of transnational (as opposed to strictly national) production and film circulation that takes place simultaneously within and beyond Morocco.

Finally, this particular analysis of transnational Moroccan cinema provides a case study in the production of a transnational cinema rooted in the 'national' – Morocco – and casts light on its diverse voices, institutions, and means of production that might be useful to consider in the analysis of African and world cinemas. It highlights the need for (an often lacking) balance and exchange among diasporic African filmmakers and their compatriots in the national space. It shows that a policy of state-subsidised production to promote a national African cinema can only partially succeed when equal weight is not given to the circulation of these films at home and abroad. It underlines the importance of the transnational festival network as an alternative distribution circuit and space for potentially transformative international collaboration and co-production. It suggests that African auteurs could learn from the enthusiastic embrace of digital technologies by Moroccan cinema's entrepreneurial producers and distributors in providing localised 'content' for local audiences. Finally, it showcases the creativity its directors and producers deploy today to assemble intricate financial jigsaws transnationally to fund their films, light years away from the shoestring budget financial montages of the Moroccan film pioneers. In that, and in the way it has managed to achieve some transnational reach, it offers a possible blueprint for the study of other small national/ transnational cinemas in transition – for Moroccan cinema is still shaping and reshaping itself.

The analysis of transnational Moroccan cinema, of Tazi's modest bumblebee, against the fast-changing backdrop of the digital, post-cinema, post-postcolonial, neo-liberal age of transnational cinema, can thus have a welcome butterfly effect. One such example of a small initial encounter leading to a much bigger impact for Moroccan cinema is Ahmed el Maanouni's *Transes* (1981), a masterful documentary portrait of contemporary Morocco viewed through the prism of the 1970s Moroccan Rolling Stones, Nass el Ghiwane. Produced by a Moroccan diasporic distributor (Izza Génini) *Transes* gathered an international audience and cult status as arguably Morocco's first truly transnational film. In the early hours of one morning in the mid-1980s, Martin Scorsese came across the film on a local New York cable channel. The Italian–American director was, by his own admission, transfixed by the power of the music, the strength of the images and the editing in el Maanouni's film. His chance encounter with the Moroccan music documentary left a lasting impression on Scorsese: two decades later, he selected *Transes* as the inaugural film to be restored and distributed as part of his World Cinema Foundation's 'world cinema project'.[9] As the example of *Transes* shows, there is potential for Moroccan cinema to reach a global network of cinephiles in the digital age.

The challenge for the extraordinarily rich cinema of contemporary Morocco is to forge new creative connections, find various new audiences (popular and art-house) at home and abroad, and facilitate the emergence of new cinematic perspectives in a transformative, transnational space of film production, distribution and exhibition.

Figure C.1   Farida Benlyazid and Nour-Eddine Lakhmari in Edinburgh for the Africa in Motion film festival, October 2018 (photo by authors)

Notes

1 Hicham Lasri, interviewed by Jamal Bahmad, Casablanca, September 2017.

2. Ahmed el Maanouni, interviewed by Flo Martin and Will Higbee in Edinburgh, October 2017.

3. This very point was made in interviews with Lamia Chraibi, interviewed by Will Higbee in Berlin, 13 February 2016 and Hicham Fallah, interviewed by Will Higbee and Stef Van de Peer in Tangier, 15 March 2018.

4. The notion of post-cinema here refers to Malte Hagener's definition (Hagener 2016).

5. 'The digital revolution, however, is not "heading in a single direction", a point made by Mike Gubbins in his excellent Cine Regio report, *The Digital Revolution*. Gubbins points out that the fragmentation of demand, rather than shifting taste, is actually the immediate threat, and that this fragmented demand has exacerbated divisions of geography, culture, language, etc. Production levels are out of kilter with demand on current platforms, making it difficult to construct sustainable businesses and leading to much wasted talent' (Mike Gubbin, cited by Finney 2014).

6. In art house cinemas and mainstream cinemas, if films don't make a significant impact on the first weekend at the box office, they are withdrawn, thus not giving time for the audience to meet its film.

7. For example, Nabil Ayouch's *Much Loved* is the only Moroccan production in 2018 to be offered on Netflix in the USA.

8. '"Who should speak?" is less crucial than '"Who will listen?"' (Spivak and Harasym 1990: 59).

9. A fully restored print of the film was screened at the Cannes film festival in 2007 and then distributed internationally on DVD and Blu-Ray.

BIBLIOGRAPHY

Adam, André (1972), 'Les Berbères à Casablanca', *Revue des mondes musulmans et de la Méditerranée*, Vol. 12, No. 1, 23–44.

Aït Akdim, Youssef (2012), 'Maroc: L'art et la manière forte', *Jeune Afrique*, 28 June: <http://www.jeuneafrique.com/140890/culture/maroc-l-art-et-la-mani-re-forte/> (accessed 12 July 2018).

Alami, Aida (2014), 'Morocco defends ban of "much loved"; Attack on actor is called unrelated', *New York Times*, 3 January: <https://www.nytimes.com/2015/06/04/movies/morocco-defends-ban-of-much-loved-attack-on-actor-is-called-unrelated.html> (accessed 2 January 2019).

Albertelli, Mathieu (2016), 'Ce que recherchent les Marocains sur Google pendant le Ramadan', *Al HuffPost Maghreb*, 17 June, <http://www.huffpostmaghreb.com/2016/06/17/ramadan-google_n_10524732.html> (accessed 2 January 2019).

Armbrust, Walter (2005), '10 synchronizing watches: the state, the consumer, and sacred time in Ramadan television', in Birgit Meyer and Annelies Moors, eds, *Religion, Media, and the Public Sphere*. Bloomington, IN: Indiana University Press, 207–26.

Ameskane, Mohamed (2017), 'Simone Bitton: la femme à la caméra . . .', *Challenge*, 6–12 October, 60–1.

Amnesty International (2015), *Shadow of Impunity: Torture in Morocco and Western Sahara*.

Anderson, Benedict (1983), *Imagined Communities: Reflections on the Origin and Spread of Nationalism*, London: Verso.

Anonymous (2013),'Global Village', *Variety*, 14–20 May, 54–5.

Appadurai, Arjun (1990), 'Disjuncture and difference in the global cultural economy', *Theory, Culture & Society*, Vol. 7, Nos 2–3, 295–310.

Araib, Ahmed (2014), 'L'aventure Souissi', *L'opinion*, 27 December: <http://www.lopinion.ma/def.asp?codelangue=23&id_info=42949&date_ar=2015-1-1> (accessed 2 January 2019).

Armes, Roy (2005), *Postcolonial Images: Studies in North African Film*. Bloomington, IN: Indiana University Press.

Armes, Roy (2015), *New Voices in Arab Cinema*. Bloomington: Indiana University Press.

Arnon, Ben (2016), 'Producing Feature Films for the pre-sales market', *HuffPost*, 11 August: <https://www.huffingtonpost.com/ben-arnon/producing-feature-films-f_b_12855630.html> (accessed 8 February 2020).

Association Marocaine des Critiques de Cinéma, eds (2013), *Le Cinéma marocain: Enjeu de l'industrie, enjeu de la création*, issue of *Revue marocaine des recherches cinématographiques*. Tangier: No. 1, November.

Ayouch, Nabil (2009), 'The Film Industry– Made in Morocco', *Africiné*. 19 September: <http://www.africine.org/?menu=fichedist&no=4792> (accessed 2 January 2019).

Bahmad, Jamal (2013a), 'Casablanca Unbound: The New Urban Cinema in Morocco', *Francosphères*, Vol. 2, No. 1, 73–85.

Bahmad, Jamal (2013b), 'Abderrahmane Bouguermouh (1936–2013): between cinema and state in Algeria'. Paris: L'Harmattan, *Africultures*, 6 February: <http://africultures.com/abderrahmane-bouguermouh-1936-2013-between-cinema-and-state-in-algeria-11289/> (accessed 20 July 2018).

Bahmad, Jamal (2014), 'Between Tangier and Marrakech: A Short History of Moroccan Cinema through its Festivals', in Dina Iordanova and Stefanie Van de Peer, eds, *Film Festival Yearbook 6: Film Festivals and), the Middle East*. St Andrews, St Andrews Film Studies.

Bahmad, Jamal (2016), 'The good pirates: Moroccan cinema in the age of digital reproduction', in Malte Hagener, Vinzenze Hediger and Alena Strohmeier, eds, *The State of Post-Cinema*. London: Palgrave Macmillan, 89–98.

Bahmad, Jamal (2017), 'Roundtable Report: Chamber of Moroccan Film Producers (Tangier, 4 March)', Transnational Moroccan Cinema Blog, 5 May: <http://moroccancinema.exeter.ac.uk/en/2017/05/roundtable-report-chamber-of-moroccan-film-producers-tangier-4-march-2017/> (accessed 7 February 2020).

Bahmad, Jamal (2018), 'Morocco Re-orientalised: the postcolonial exotic and the politics of identity in transnational Moroccan cinema', unpublished draft conference paper, Rabat.

Bakrim, Mohammed (2010), *Impressions itinérantes: Chroniques cinématographiques* (self-published).

Bakrim, Mohammed (2015), 'Un thé à Tanger avec Tala Hadid: "Le film est une carte qu'on lit"', *Assaiss: cinéma et citoyenneté*, 12 March: <http://assaiss-tifaouine.blogspot.com/2015/03/un-a-tanger-avec-tala-hadid.html?m=1> (accessed 17 February 2020).

Bakrim, Mohammed (2017), *Abdelkader Lagtaâ, cinéaste de la modernité, ou Comment exister par le cinéma*. Rabat: Éditions Kalimate.

Barlet, Olivier (1997), 'Entretien d'Olivier Barlet avec Azzedine Meddour', *Africultures*, 31 December: <http://africultures.com/entretien-dolivier-barlet- avec-azzedine-meddour-263/> (accessed on January 2, 2019).

Barlet, Olivier (2000), *African Cinema: Decolonizing the Gaze*. London: Zed Books.

Barlet, Olivier (2007), 'Cinema: an audience but no market, translated by Sameena Black. Paris: L'Harmattan. *Africultures*, no. 5851, 22 February: <http://africultures. com/cinema-an-audience-but-no-market-5851/> (accessed 13 February 2019).

Barlet, Olivier (2015), 'Une jeunesse en marge'. Paris: L'Harmattan, *Africultures*, 27 July: <http://africultures.com/une-jeunesse-urbaine-en-marge-13094/?utm_source =newsletter&utm_medium=email&utm_campaign=448> (accessed 28 January 2019).

Barlet, Olivier (2019), 'Mohamed Zineddaine : « des faisceaux de lumière sur des questions que je me pose. » Entretien avec Olivier Barlet à propos de La Guérisseuse', Africultures, 2 July: <http://africultures.com/mohamed-zineddaine-des-faisceaux-de-lumiere-sur-des-questions-que-je-me-pose-14712/> (accessed 15 September 2019).

Berrada, Omar Yto Berrada, eds (2011), *Album Cinémathèque de Tanger*. Tanger: Librairie des Colonnes, 2011.

Beck, Ulrich (2000), *What is Globalization?* Trans. Patrick Camiller. Cambridge: Polity.

Benabid, Mohamed (2018), 'Le Maroc fait saliver Netflix', *L'Économiste*, 27 March: <https://leconomiste.com/article/1025913-le-maroc-fait-saliver-netflix> (accessed 5 January 2019).

Benchenna, Abdelfettah (2016), 'Les films maghrébins dans les salles en France', in Abdelfettah Benchenna, Patricia Caille and Nolwenn Mingant, eds, *La Circulation des films: Afrique du Nord et Moyen-Orient*. Paris: L'Harmattan, *Africultures*, Nos 101–2: 26–53.

Bennani, Ouafa (2017), 'Le Cinéma turc honoré au Festival international du film de femmes de Salé', *Le Matin*, 20 September.

Benchenna, Abdelfettah (2015), 'L'exploitation des films au Maroc à l'ère des multiplexes Mégarama: la double domination?' in Patricia Caillé, ed., *La Circulation des films en Afrique du Nord et au Moyen-Orient*. Paris: L'Harmattan, *Africultures*, Nos 101–2.

Benlyazid, Farida (2012), 'Réception des cinémas du Maghreb au Maghreb', in Patricia Caillé and Florence Martin, eds, *Les Cinémas du Maghreb et leurs publics*. Paris: L'Harmattan, *Africultures*, Nos 89–90.

Bergfelder, Tim (2005), 'National, transnational, or supranational cinema? Rethinking European film studies', *Media Culture and Society*, Vol. 27, No. 3, 315–31.

Berrada, Omar and Yto Berrada, eds (2011), *Album Cinémathèque de Tanger*. Tanger: Librairie des Colonnes.

Bhabha, Homi (1994), *The Location of Culture*. London and New York: Routledge.

Binebine, Aziz (2009), *Tazmamort*. Paris: Denoël.

Bokbot, Mohamed and Ali Faleh (2010), 'Un siècle d'émigration marocaine vers la France: aperçu historique', *Papeles de Geografía*, 51–2.

Bondebjerg, Ib and Eva Novrup Redvall (2013), 'Transnational Scandinavia? Scandinavian film culture in a European and global context', in Manuel Palacio and Jörg Türschmann (eds), *Transnational Cinema in Europe*, Vienna: Universität Wien, 127–46.

Bordwell, David (2012). *Poetics of Cinema*. London/New York: Routledge.

Bordwell, David (2016), 'It's all over, until next time', Observations on Film Art (Blog), <http://www.davidbordwell.net/blog/2016/09/18/its-all-over-until-the-next-time/> (accessed 20 July 2019).

Bottomore, Stephen (2008), 'The sultan and the cinematograph', *Early Popular Visual Culture*, Vol. 6, No. 2, 121–44.

Boughedir, Férid (1987), 'Malédictions des cinémas arabes', in Mouny Berrah, Jacques Lévy and Claude-Michel Cluny, eds, *Les Cinémas Arabes*, *CinémAction* No. 43, 10–15.

Bougrine, Jihane (2017a), 'Avant-première mondiale de *Headbang Lullaby*: dans la tête "dure" de Hicham Lasri', *Les Inspirations Éco*, 25 February: <http://www.leseco.ma/les-cahiers-des-eco/weekend/55089-avant-premiere-mondiale-de-headbang-lullaby-dans-la-tete-dur-de-hicham-lasri.html> (accessed 2 January 2019).

Bougrine, Jihane (2017b), 'Cinéma marocain: Ça tourne...pas rond!', *Les Inspirations Éco*, 28 January: <http://www.leseco.ma/les-cahiers-des-eco/weekend/54111-cinema-marocain-ca-tourne-pas-rond.html> (accessed 2 January 2019).

Bouhmouch, Nadir (2016), 'Morocco: green for the rich, grey for the poor', OpenDemocracy, 21 November: <https://www.opendemocracy.net/north-africa-west-asia/nadir-bouhmouch/morocco-green-for-rich-grey-for-poor> (accessed 11 July 2018).

Boulifa, Chaimae (2017), 'Khouribga celebrates Rwandan cinema for African Film Festival's 20th anniversary', *Morocco World News*, 9 September: <https://www.moroccoworldnews.com/2017/09/228190/khouribga-celebrates-rwandan-cinema-african-film-festivals-20th-anniversary/> (accessed 20 July 2018).

Bounfour, Abdellah (1996), 'Hemmu u Namir ou l'oedipe berbère', Etudes et documents berbères 15: 119–41.

Boushaba, Amine (2017), 'Hicham Lasri, l'artiste explorateur', *L'Economiste*, 8 January: <https://www.leconomiste.com/article/1006988-hicham-lasri-l-artiste-explorateur> (accessed 8 February 2020).

Bouthier, Marie-Pierre (2017), 'Des créateurs et des curateurs aux frontières des arts visuels et du cinéma documentaire. Maroc – Tunisie (2011–2016)', *Revue des mondes musulmans et de la Méditerranée* (RMMM), 142, December: <https://journals.openedition.org/remmm/10092#ftn11> (accessed 6 July 2018).

Bouthier, Marie-Pierre (2018), 'Documentary cinema and memory of political violence in post-authoritarian Morocco and Tunisia (2009–2015)', *Journal of North African Studies*, Vol. 23, Nos 1–2, 225–45.

Boutouba, Jimia (2014), 'The Moudawana syndrome: gender trouble in contemporary Morocco', *Research in African Literatures*, Vol. 45, No. 1, Spring: 24–38.

Brahimi, Denise (2005), *50 ans de cinéma maghrébin*. Paris: Minerve.

Brown, Colin (2016), 'The pink pussyhats of Arab Cinema, Editorial', *Arab Cinema Magazine*, Vol. 5, No. 3: <http://mad-solutions.com/ac-magazine-issue-5.pdf> (accessed 2 January 2019).

Caillé, Patricia (2010), 'Le Maroc, l'Algérie et la Tunisie des réalisatrices ou la construction du Maghreb dans un contexte postcolonial', in Pierre-Noël Denieuil, ed. *Socio-anthropologie de l'image au Maghreb: Audiovisuel et création cinématographique*. Tunis: Institut de Recherche sur le Maroc Contemporain (IRMC), 261–77.

Caillé, Patricia (2016), 'Au liban, le cinéma du monde, les classiques, les films d'art et d'essai sont presque totalement absents: entretien de Patricia Caillé avec Zeina Sfeir', in *La Circulation des films: Afrique du Nord et Moyen-Orient*, eds Abdelfettah Benchenna, Patricia Caillé, Nolwenn Mingant. Paris: L'Harmattan, *Africultures*, Nos 101–2: 178–85.

Caillé, Patricia and Claude Forest, eds (2017), *Regarder des films en Afriques*. Villeneuveuce d'Ascq: Presses Universitaires du Septentrion.

Caillé, Patricia and Florence Martin, eds (2012), *Les Cinémas du Maghreb et leurs publics*. Paris: L'Harmattan, *Africultures*, Nos 89–90.

Campaiola, Jim (2014), 'The Moroccan media field: an analysis of elite hybridity in television and film institutions', *Communication, Culture & Critique*, Vol. 7, No. 4, 487–505.

Carter, Sandra Gayle (2000), 'Farida Benlyazid's Moroccan women', *Quarterly Review of Film and Video*, Vol. 17, No. 4, 343–69.

Carter, Sandra Gayle (2008), 'Constructing an independent Moroccan nation and national identity through cinema and institutions', *Journal of North African Studies*, Vol. 13, No. 4, December: 531–59.

Carter, Sandra Gayle (2009), *What Moroccan Cinema? A Historical and Critical Study 1956–2006*. Lanham: Rowman & Littlefield.

Chahir, Aziz (2014), 'Women in Moroccan cinema: between tradition and modernity', in Foluke Ogunleye, ed. *African Film: Looking Back and Looking Forward*. Newcastle, Cambridge Scholars Publishing, 95–107.

Chemlal, Said (2018), 'Screening femininity and Amazighness in Narjiss Nejjar's *Dry Eyes*', *Journal of North African Studies*, Vol. 23, Nos 1–2, 1–20.

Chériaa, Tahar (1978), *Écrans d'abondance ou cinéma de libération, en Afrique?* Tunis: SATPEC and el Khayala.

Chreiteh, Alexandra (2018), 'Haunting the future: narratives of Jewish return in Israeli and Moroccan cinema', *Journal of North African Studies*. Vol. 23, Nos 1–2, 259–77.

Chtatou, Mohamed (2017), "The present and future of the Maghreb Arab Union', in George Joffé, ed., *North Africa: Nation, State and Region*. London: Routledge, 266–87.

Corriou, Morgan, ed. (2012), *Publics et spectacles cinématographiques en situation coloniale*. Tunis: CERES.

Crétois, Jules (2017), 'Cinéma marocain: le CCM tire la sonnette d'alarme et annonce la création d'un fond dédié à la création panafricaine', *Jeune Afrique*, 21 March: <http://www.jeuneafrique.com/419403/culture/cinema-marocain-ccm-tire-sonnette-dalarme-annonce-creation-dun-fonds-dedie-a-creation-panafricaine/> (accessed 20 May 2018).

Cunningham, Stuart and Jon Silver (2013), *Screen Distribution and the New King Kongs of the Online World*. London/New York, Palgrave.

Dale, Martin (2015), 'Nabil Ayouch preps social drama *Razzia*', *Variety*, 6 December: <https://variety.com/2015/film/global/morocco-nabil-ayouch-razzia-1201654998/> (accessed 13 August 2017).

Denson, Shane and Julia Leyda, eds (2016), *Post-Cinema: Theorizing 21st-Century Film*. Falmer: Reframe Books.

Desrues, Thierry (2006), 'De la Monarchie exécutive ou les apories de la gestion de la rente géostratégique', *L'Année du Maghreb*, 1, 243–71.

De Valck, Marijke (2007), *Film Festivals: From European Geopolitics to Global Cinephilia*. Amsterdam: Amsterdam University Press.

Devaux Yahi, Frédérique (2016), *De la naissance du cinéma kabyle au cinéma amazigh*. Paris: L'Harmattan.

Diawara, Manthia (2010), *African Film: New Forms of Aesthetics and Politics*. Munich: Prestel.

Dovey, Lindiwe (2015), *Curating Africa in the Age of Film Festivals*. New York: Palgrave Macmillan.

Durmelat, Sylvie (1998), 'Petite histoire du mot beur: ou comment prendre la parole quand on vous la prête', *French Cultural Studies*, 9, No. 26.

Ďurovičová, Nataša and Kathleen Newman, eds (2009), *World Cinemas, Transnational Perspectives*, New York: Routledge.

Dwyer, Kevin (2004), *Beyond Casablanca: Mohamed Abderrahman Tazi and the Adventure of Moroccan Cinema*. Bloomington and Indianapolis: Indiana University Press.

Dwyer, Kevin (2007), 'Moroccan cinema and the promotion of culture', *Journal of North African Studies*, Vol. 12, No. 3, September, 277–86.

Edwards, Brian T. (2007), '*Marock* in Morocco: reading Moroccan Films in the age of circulation', *Journal of North African Studies*, Vol. 12, No. 3, 287–307.

Edwards, Brian T. (2015), *After the American Century: The Ends of US Culture in the Middle East*. New York: Columbia University Press.

Elena, Alberto (2014), 'Towards a New Cartography of Arab Film Festivals', Dina Iordanova, Dina and Stefanie Van de Peer, eds. *Film Festival Yearbook 6: Film Festivals and the Middle East*. St Andrews, St Andrews Film Studies, 2014.

Elsaesser, Thomas (2010), *European Cinema Face to Face with Hollywood*. Amsterdam: Amsterdam University Press.

Enwezor, Okwui (2007), 'Coalition building: black audio film collective and transnational post-colonialism', in Kodwo Eshun and Anjalika Sagar (eds), *The Ghosts of Songs: the film art of the Black Audio Film Collective*. Liverpool: Liverpool University Press, 106–29.

Estrada, Javier H. (2014), 'A Festival of Resistance and Evolution: Interview with Mohamed Mediouni, Director of the JCC', Dina Iordanova and Stefanie Van de Peer, eds. *Film Festival Yearbook 6: Film Festivals and the Middle East*. St Andrews, St Andrews Film Studies, 2014: 320.

Ezra, Elizabeth and Terry Rowden, eds (2006), *Transnational Cinema: The Film Reader*, London: Routledge.

Falicov, Tamara (2010), 'Migrating from south to north: the role of film festivals in funding and shaping Global South film and video', in Greg Elmer, Charles H. Davis, Janice Marchessault and John McCollough, eds, *Locating Migrating Media*, Lexington Books, 3–22.

Falicov, Tamara L. (2016), 'The "festival film": film festival funds as cultural intermediaries', in Marijke de Valck, Brendan Kredell and Skadi Loist, eds, *Film Festivals: History, Theory, Method, Practice*, London: Routledge.

Fassi Fihri, Sarim (2016), 'La lutte contre le piratage n'est pas une priorité du gouvernement', Medias24– Site d'information. 3 June: <https://www.medias24.com/MAROC/CULTURE/164369-Sarim-Fassi Fihri-La-lutte-contre-le-piratage-n-est-pas-une-priorite-du-gouvernement.html> (accessed 2 January 2019).

Finney, Angus (2014), *The International Film Business: A Market Guide beyond Hollywood* (2nd edition). London: Routledge.

Forsdick, Charles and David Murphy (2009), *Postcolonial Thought in the French-speaking World*. Liverpool: Liverpool University Press.

Gaines, Jane M. (2006), 'Early cinema's heyday of copying: the too many copies of "L'arroseur arrosé" (The Waterer Watered)', *Cultural Studies*, Vol. 20, Nos 2–3, 227–44.

Galt, Rosalind (2016), 'Transnational cinema and critical roundtable' edited by Fisher and Smith, *Frames Cinema Journal*, <https://framescinemajournal.com/article/transnational-cinemas-a-critical-roundtable/#rgalt> (accessed 27 January 2020).

Gates, Henry Louis Jr (1988), *The Signifying Monkey: A Theory of African-American Literary Criticism*. Oxford: Oxford University Press.

Gershovich, Moshe (2000), *French Military Rule in Morocco: Colonialism and Its Consequences*. London and Portland, OR: Frank Cass.

Graiouid, Said and Taieb Belghazi (2013), 'Cultural production and cultural patronage in Morocco: the state, the Islamists, and the field of culture', *Journal of African Cultural Studies*, Vol. 25, No. 3: 261–74.

Grassmuck, Volker (2014), 'On the Benefits of Piracy', in Lars Eckstein and Anja Schwarz, eds, *Postcolonial Piracy: Media Distribution and Cultural Production in the Global South*. London: Bloomsbury Academic, 79–98.

Gregson, Fiona (2012), *Film Co-Production Agreements Review*, report prepared on behalf of the New Zealand Ministry for Culture and Heritage, May: <https://mch.govt.nz/sites/default/files/Film%20Co-production%20Agreements%20%28D-0493703%29.PDF> (accessed 17 February 2020).

Gugler, Josef, ed. (2011), *Film in the Middle East and North Africa: Creative Dissidence*. Austin: University of Texas Press.

Hagener, Malte (2016), 'Cinephilia and film culture in the age of digital networks', in Malte Hagener, Vinzenze Hediger and Alena Strohmeier, eds. *The State of Post-Cinema: Tracing the Moving Image in the Age of Digital Dissemination*. New York: Palgrave Macmillan, 181–94.

Hagener, Malte, Vinzenz Hediger and Alena Strohmaier, eds (2016), *The State of Post-Cinema: Tracing the Moving Image in the Age of Digital Dissemination*. New York: Palgrave Macmillan.

Hidass, Ahmed (2007), 'La régulation des médias audio-visuels au Maroc', *L'Année du Maghreb 2005–2006*, No. 2, CNRS, 539–47.

Higbee, Will (2007), 'Beyond the (trans)national: towards a cinema of transvergence in postcolonial and diasporic francophone cinema(s)', *Studies in French Cinema*, 7, No. 2.

Higbee, William (2013), *Post-beur Cinema: North African émigré and Maghrebi–French filmmaking in France since 2000*, Edinburgh: Edinburgh University Press.

Higbee, William (2018), 'Cinéma-monde and the transnational', in Michael Gott and Thibaut Schilt, eds, *Cinéma-monde: Decentred Perspectives on Global Filmmaking in French*, Edinburgh: Edinburgh University Press.

Higbee, William and Song Hwee Lim (2010), 'Concepts of transnational cinema: towards a critical transnationalism in film studies', *Transnational Cinemas*, Vol. 1, No. 1, 7–21.

Higson, Andrew (2000), 'The limiting imagination of national cinema', in Mette Hjort and Scott MacKenzie (eds), *Cinema and Nation*. London: Routledge, 63–74.

Hillauer, Rebecca (2005), *Encyclopedia of Arab Women Filmmakers*. Cairo: American University in Cairo Press.

Hirchi, Mohammed (2011), 'The ethics and politics of Laila Marrakchi's *Marock*', *South Central Review*, Vol. 28, No. 1, 90–108.

Hjort, Mette (2003), 'Dogma 95: A small nation's response to globalisation', *Purity and Provocation: Dogma 95* (2003): 31–47.

Hjort, Mette (2009), 'On the plurality of cinematic transnationalism', in Nataša Ďurovičová and Kathleen Newman, eds. *World Cinemas, Transnational Perspectives*, New York: Routledge, 12–33.

Hjort, Mette (2018), 'Film training and transnational talent development: the case of the Danish Film Institute and the Palestine Film Lab', unpublished paper delivered at the Film Education Journal Conference, Edinburgh, 19 June.

Hjort, Mette and Duncan Petrie, eds (2007), *The Cinema of Small Nations*. Edinburgh: Edinburgh University Press.

Hoffmann, Anja (2013), 'Morocco between decentralization and recentralization: encountering the state in the "Useless Morocco"', in Malika Bouziane, Cilja Harders and Anja Hoffmann, eds (2013), *Local Politics and Contemporary Transformations in the Arab World: Governance Beyond the Center*. London: Palgrave Macmillan.

Iddins, Anne-Marie (2017a), *No Concessions: Independent Media and the Reshaping of the American Public*, PhD Thesis, University of Michigan.

Iddins, Anne-Marie (2017b), 'Producing public intellectuals: shifting scales and social critique in Moroccan cinema', *Communication, Culture & Critique*, Vol. 10, No. 3, 499–517.

Idtnaine, Omar (2008), 'Le cinéma amazigh au Maroc: éléments d'une naissance artistique'. Paris: L'Harmattan, *Africultures*, 19 October: <http://africultures.com/le-cinema-amazigh-au-maroc-8117/> (accessed 22 July 2018).

Institut Français (2016), *Tanger Ville Symbole*: Du fantasme au réel. Tangier.

Iordanova, Dina (2016), 'Foreword: The film festival and film culture's transnational essence', in Marijke de Valck, Brendan Kredell and Skadi Loist, eds, *Film Festivals: History, Theory, Method, Practice*. London: Routledge.

Iordanova, Dina and Stuart D. Cunningham, eds (2012), *Digital Disruption: Cinema Moves Online*. St Andrews: St Andrews Film Studies.

Iordanova, Dina and Stefanie Van de Peer, eds (2014), *Film Festival Yearbook 6: Film Festivals and the Middle East*. St Andrews: St Andrews Film Studies.

Jaïdi, Moulay Driss (1994), *Vision(s) de la société marocaine à travers le court métrage*. Rabat: Al Majal.

Jaïdi, Moulay Driss (2010), *Cinéma et société*. Rabat: Al Majal.

Jaïdi, Moulay Driss (2012), 'Une étude de cas: le Maroc. Situation paradoxale d'une cinématographie en devenir', Patricia Caillé and Florence Martin, ed., *Les Cinémas du Maghreb*. Paris: L'Harmattan, *Africultures*, Nos 89–90: 208–218.

Jameson, Fredric (1986), 'Third-world literature in the era of multinational capitalism', *Social Text*, No. 15, 65–88.

Jensen, Jon and Alex Court (2015), 'Moroccan backdrop for Game of Thrones and Gladiator – CNN', 5 March: <https://edition.cnn.com/2015/03/05/business/morocco-filmmaking-ouarzazate/index.html> (accessed 10 July 2018).

Jones, Huw David (2016a), 'UK/European co-productions: the case of Ken Loach', *Journal of British Cinema and Television*, Vol. 13, No. 3: 368–92

Jones, Huw David (2016b), 'The cultural and economic implications of UK/European co-production', *Transnational Cinemas*, Vol. 7, No. 1: 1–20.

Jones, Michael (2007), 'Rising film festival stress: glut of events creates high-stakes rivalries', *Variety*, 7 December.

Kandiyoti, Deniz (2004), 'Identity and its discontents: women and the nation', *Women Living Under Muslim Law, Dossier 26: Identity Politics*: <http://www.wluml.org/node/482. (first published in *Millennium: Journal of International Studies*, London: London School of Economics, 1991, Vol. 20, No.3: 429–43).

Kellou, Dorothée Myriam (2018), 'Entretien avec Hicham Falah: la création documentaire au Maroc et en Afrique a totalement explosé', *Le Monde*, 26 June: <https://www.lemonde.fr/afrique/article/2018/06/26/la-creation-documentaire-au-maroc-et-en-afrique-a-totalement-explose_5321541_3212.html> (accessed 7 February 2019).

Khannous, Touria (2013), *African Pasts, Presents and Futures: Generational Shifts in African Women's Literature, Film, and Internet Discourse*. Lanham, MD: Lexington Books.

Laili, Kaoutar (2018), 'Le FIFM lance un programme d'aide au développement de talents émergents issus d'Afrique et du Moyen-Orient', *Huffpostmaghreb*, 12 November 2018: <https://www.huffpostmaghreb.com/entry/le-fifm-lance-un-programme-daide-au-developpement-de-talents-dafrique-et-du-moyen-orient_mg_5be95342e4b0769d24cf2e6e (accessed 10 August 2019).

Lamchaouat, Mohammed (2014), 'Aperçu sur l'informalité au Maroc', *Revue Économie & Kapital*, No. 6, 2–23.

Lange, André (2013), *Project of Statistical Data Collection on Film and Audiovisual Markets in 9 Mediterranean Countries. 2. Morocco*. Euromed Audiovisual.

Laredo, Samuel (2017), 'Samuel Laredo', in Elena Prentice, ed. *Quatre enfances à Tanger: Buckingham, Cherif d'Ouezzane, Laredo, Bouziane*. Tanger: Khbar Bladna, 76–7.

Lawrenson, Edwards (2009), 'Sands of time', *Sight and Sound*, Vol. 19, No. 3, 8–9.

Lebbady, Hasna (2012), 'Women in Northern Morocco: Between the documentary and the imaginary', Cairo, *Alif: Journal of Comparative Poetics*, No. 32, 127–50.

Lefebvre, Henri (1968), *Le droit à la ville*. Vol. 3. Paris: Anthropos: <https://core.ac.uk/download/pdf/33294827.pdf> (accessed 2 January 2019].

Le Morvan, Agnès (2017), 'Faouzi Bensaïdi, cinéaste entre le Maroc et la France', Ouest France, 10 February: <https://www.ouest-france.fr/bretagne/rennes-35000/rennes-fouad-bensaidi-cineaste-entre-le-maroc-et-la-france-4793630> (accessed 27 March 2019).

Lequeret, Elisabeth (2001), 'Partout sauf en Afrique: des films condamnés à être exportés pour être vus', *Cahiers du cinéma*, No. 557, May, 82–3.

Levine, Sidney (2016), 'Doha Film Institute announces Fall 2015 grant recipients', *Indiewire*, 5 January: <http://www.indiewire.com/2016/01/doha-film-institute-announces-fall-2015-grant-recipients-30-projects-from-19-countries-to-receive-funding-168296/> (accessed 15 May 2018).

Limbrick, Peter (2012), 'Moumen Smihi's Tanjawi/Tangérois/Tangerian cinema', *Third text*, Vol. 26, No. 4, 443–54.

Limbrick, Peter (2015), 'Vernacular modernism, film culture and Moroccan short film and documentary', *Framework: The Journal of Cinema and Media*, Vol. 56, No. 2, 388–413: <https://escholarship.org/uc/item/8vg5z0c2> (accessed 2 January 2019).

Lionnet, Francoise and Shu-mei Shih (2005), 'Thinking through the minor, transnationally', in Françoise Lionnet and Shumei Shi, eds. *Minor Transnationalism*. Durham, NC: Duke University Press.

Lobato, Ramon (2012), *Shadow Economies of Cinema: Mapping Informal Film Distribution*. London: Bloomsbury Publishing.

Loist, Skadi (2016), 'The film festival circuit: networks, hierarchies and circulation', in Marijke de Valck, Brendan Kredell and Skadi Loist, eds, *Film Festivals: History, Theory, Method, Practice*, Routledge.

MacNab, Geoffrey (2017), 'How the revised European co-pro treaty can benefit producers', *Screen Daily*, <https://www.screendaily.com/features/how-the-revised-european-co-pro-treaty-can-benefit-producers/5114776.article> (accessed 24 February 2018).

Maddy-Weitzman, Bruce (2012), 'Arabization and its discontents: the rise of the Amazigh movement in North Africa', *Journal of the Middle East and Africa*, Vol. 3, No. 2.

Marks, Laura (2000), *The Skin of the Film: Intercultural Cinema, Embodiment, and the Senses*. Durham and London: Duke University Press.

Martin, Florence (2011a), *Screens and Veils: Maghrebi Women's Cinema*. Bloomington: Indiana University Press.

Martin, Florence (2011b), 'Cinema and State in Tunisia', in Josef Gugler, ed. *Film in the Middle East and North Africa: Creative Dissidence*. Austin, University of Texas Press, 271–83.

Martin, Florence (2014), 'Farida Benlyazid and Juanita Narboni: two women from Tangier', *Black Camera*, Vol. 6, No. 1, 124–38.

Martin, Florence (2016), 'Cinéma-monde: De-orbiting Maghrebi cinema', *Contemporary French Civilization*, Vol. 41, Nos 3–4, 461–76.

Martin, Florence (2018), 'Sexes, masques et vérités sur les écrans des Maghrébines,' IEMed, Barcelona: AFKAR/IDEAS, Spring, 71–3.

Martin, Florence and Patricia Caillé (2011), 'Les "Cinémas du Maghreb": de la construction plurielle d'un label régional', *Akfar/Ideas* No. 29, *Le Réveil Arabe* (special issue), 87–90.

Martin, Florence and Patricia Caillé (2017), 'Reel bad Maghrebi women', in Nadia Yaqub and Rula Quawas, eds. *Bad Girls of the Arab World*. Austin, University of Texas Press, 167–84.

Marzouki, Ahmed (2000), *Tasmamart: Cellule 10*. Casablanca: Tarik Editions.

Merolla, Daniela (2005), 'De la parole aux vidéos: oralité, écriture et oralité médiatique dans la production culturelle amazigh (berbère)', *Afrika Focus*, Vol. 18, Nos 1–2.

Meyer, Birgit and Annelies Moor, eds (2005), *Religion, Media, and the Public Sphere*. Bloomington and Indianapolis: Indiana University Press.

Miller, Catherine (2017), 'Adapter et produire marocain: l'évolution des programmes de séries et films télévisés de la télévision marocaine entre 2003 et 2012' (Chapter 12), in Dominique Marchetti, ed. *Productions et circulations transnationales des biens médiatiques dans les mondes arabes et musulmans*. Rabat and Istanbul:

Centre Jacques-Berque, Institut Français d'Études Anatoliennes. Open edition ebook: <https://books.openedition.org/cjb/1201> (accessed 2 January 2019).

Musser, Charles (1991), *Before the Nickelodeon: Edwin S. Porter and the Edison Manufacturing Company*. Berkeley: University of California Press.

Naficy, Hamid (2001), *An Accented Cinema: Exile and Diasporic Filmmaking*. Princeton: Princeton University Press.

Nestingen, Andrew and Trevor G. Elkington (eds) (2005), *Transnational Cinema in a Global North: Nordic Cinema in Transition*. Detroit: Wayne State University Press.

Neumann, Per and Charlotte Appelgren (2007), *The Fine Art of Co-producing* (2nd edition). Copenhagen: Media Business School.

Nichols, Bill (1994), 'Global Image Consumption in the Age of Late Capitalism', *East–West Film Journal*, Vol. 8, No. 1, 68–85.

Nora, Pierre (1997), *Les Lieux de mémoire*. Paris: Gallimard.

Orlando, Valerie K. (2011), *Screening Morocco: Contemporary Depictions in Film of a Changing Society*. Athens, OH: Ohio University Press.

Orlando, Valerie K. (2013), 'Women, religion, and sexuality in contemporary Moroccan film: unveiling the veil in *Hijab al-hob* (*Veils of Love*, 2009)', *Palimpsest: A Journal of Women, Gender and the Black International*, Vol. 2, No. 1, 106–23.

Orlando, Valerie K. (2015), 'Revealing the past, conceptualizing the future on-screen: the social, political, and economic challenges of contemporary filmmaking in Morocco', In Frieda Ekotto and Kenneth W. Harrow, eds, *Rethinking African Cultural Production*. Indianapolis: Indiana University Press.

Oudrhiri, Kaouthar interviewing Bruno Barde (2016), *Tel Quel*, 8 December: <https://telquel.ma/2016/12/08/bruno-barde-nai-pas-envie-voir-jury-condescendant-face-film-marocain_1526665> (accessed 2 January 2019).

Peranson, Mark (2009), 'First you get the power, then you get the money: two models of film festivals', Chapter 3 in Richard Porton, ed. *Dekalog 3: On Film Festivals*, 23–37 (29–32). London: Wallflower.

Pham, Annika (2017), 'Interview with Bobby Allen: "At MUBI we build loyalty and invest in the long term"', Nordisk Film and TV Fond, 11 May: <http://www.nordiskfilmogtvfond.com/news/interview/bobby-allen-at-mubi-we-build-loyalty-and-invest-in-the-long-term> (accessed 4 February 2020).

Pisters, Patricia (2007), 'Refusal of reproduction: paradoxes of becoming-woman in transnational Moroccan filmmaking', in Katarzyna Marciniak, Anikó Imre and Áine O'Healy, eds. *Transnational Feminism in Film and Media*. New York: Palgrave Macmillan, 71–92.

Pisters, Patricia (2010), 'Filming the times of Tangier: Nostalgia, postcolonial agency, and preposterous history', in Dina Iordanova, David Martin-Jones and Belén Vidal, eds. *Cinema at the Periphery*. Detroit, Wayne State University Press, 175–89.

Ponte, Lucille M. (2008), 'Coming attractions: opportunities and challenges in thwarting global movie piracy', *American Business Law Journal*, Vol. 45, No. 2, 331–69.

Porton, Richard (2009), *Dekalog 3: On Film Festivals*. London: Wallflower.

Radner, Hilary (2015), 'The Historical Film and Contemporary French Cinema: Representing the Past in the Present', in Alistair Fox, Michael Marie, Raphaelle Moine and

Hilary Radner, eds, *The Wiley Guide to Contemporary French Cinema*, Hoboken, NJ: Wiley/Blackwell, 289–313.

Rastegar, Kamran (2017), 'Arab cinema through a narrow frame: a conversation with Tala Hadid', *Senses of Cinema*, Issue 82, March: <http://sensesofcinema.com/2017/movements-filmmaker-interviews/a-conversation-with-tala-hadid/> (accessed 9 February 2018).

Roger, Benjamin (2013), 'Le passage au numérique fait mal aux salles de cinéma marocaines', *Jeune Afrique*, 30 July: <http://www.jeuneafrique.com/18042/economie/le-passage-au-num-rique-fait-mal-aux-salles-de-cin-ma-marocaines/> (accessed 22 July 2018).

Roudaby, Youssef (2014), 'Box office: le cinéma marocain a toujours la cote', *Tel Quel*, 9 October: <https://telquel.ma/2014/10/09/box-office-cinema-marocain-toujours-cote_1418797> (accessed 23 July 2018).

Rutherford, Tristan (2017), 'Morocco's cinema city', *Aramco World*, September/October: <http://www.aramcoworld.com/pt-BR/Articles/September-2017/Morocco-s-Cinema-City> (accessed 2 January 2019).

Saadia, Dina and Kenza Oumlil (2016), 'Women in contemporary Moroccan cinema', *Journal of Middle East Media*, Vol. 12, 40–59.

Saeys, Arne (2017), *Imag(in)ed Diversity in a Small Nation:Constructing Ethnic Minorities in Dutch Cinema*, unpublished PhD thesis, University of Southampton.

Saïl, Noureddine (2009), 'Cinéma: "Ceux Qui se sont enrichis": entretien avec Noureddine Saïl, directeur du Centre Cinématographique Marocain', *L'Economiste*, 17 September: <https://www.leconomiste.com/article/cinema-ceux-qui-se-sont-enrichis-brientretien-avec-noureddine-sail-directeur-du-centre-cinem> (accessed 14 July 2018).

Saïl, Noureddine (2017), 'Vive le foot!', in Patricia Caillé and Claude Forest, *Regarder des Films en Afriques*. Villeneveuce d'Ascq: Presses Universitaires du Septentrion.

Saïl, Noureddine and Saad Eddine Lamzouwaq (2017), 'Isolation undermines Ouarzazate film industry', *Morocco World News*, 12 November: <https://www.moroccoworldnews.com/2017/11/233575/noureddine-sail-ouarzazate-film-industry/> (accessed 5 January 2019).

Sammarco, Maria Teresa (2014), 'FESTIVAL DI ROMA 2014 – Incontro con Tala Hadid e il cast di The Narrow Frame of Midnight', 17 October: <https://www.sentieriselvaggi.it/festival-di-roma-2014-incontro-con-tala-hadid-e-il-cast-di-the-narrow-frame-of-midnight/ (English translation available at: <http://www.thenarrowframeofmidnight.com/press; both accessed 28 January 2020).

Savage, Thomas (2017), 'Pourquoi Ciné Atlas investit-t-il des dizaines de millions de dirhams dans les salles du Maroc?' *Tel Quel*, 7 June: <https://telquel.ma/2017/06/07/pourquoi-cine-atlas-investit-il-des-dizaines-de-millions-de-dirhams-dans-les-salles-au-maroc_1549804> (accessed 22 July 2018).

Schneider, Simona (2008), 'Tanger fait son cinéma: portrait de la ville en images', *La Pensée de midi*, Vol. 1, No. 23, 80–9.

Schwarz, Anja and Lars Eckstein, eds (2014), *Postcolonial Piracy: Media Distribution and Cultural Production in the Global South*. London: Bloomsbury Publishing.

Sekler, Joan (2008), 'Middle East International Film Festival: Abu Dhabi and the Dubai International Film Festival', *IDA Documentary Magazine*, Spring: <http://www

.documentary.org/magazine/middle-east-international-film-festival-abu-dhabi-and-dubai-internaitonal-film-festival> (accessed 20 May 2018).

Serceau, Michel (2017), 'L'offre de films dans les salles du Maroc, de 2006 à 2015, et leur reception', in Patricia Caillé, and Claude Forest, eds, *Regarder des films en Afriques*. Villeneveuce d'Ascq: Presses Universitaires du Septentrion, 225–42.

Shafto, Sally (2011a), 'Moroccan cinema alive: the 12th Festival National du Film, Tangier', *Senses of Cinema*, Issue 58, March: <http://sensesofcinema.com/2011/festival-reports/moroccan-cinema-alive-the-12th-festival-national-du-film-tangier/> (accessed 2 January 2019).

Shafto, Sally (2011b), 'The Arab Spring and Maghrébin cinema: the 6th Panorama des Cinémas du Maghreb, Saint Denis', *Senses of Cinema*, Issue 59, June: <http://sensesofcinema.com/2011/festival-reports/the-arab-spring-and-maghrebin-cinema-the-6th-panorama-des-cinemas-du-maghreb-saint-denis/> (accessed 30 July 2018).

Shaviro, Steven (2010), 'Post-cinematic affect: on Grace Jones, boarding gate and southland tales', *Film-Philosophy*, Vol. 14, No. 1, 1–102.

Shaw, Deborah (2016), *The Three Amigos: The Transnational Filmmaking of Guillermo del Toro, Alejandro González Iñárritu, and Alfonso Cuarón*, Manchester: Manchester University Press.

Shirk, Allison (2014), 'Guerrilla filmmakers celebrate anniversary of Morocco's "Arab Uprising"', *Public Radio International*, PRI, 14 February: <http://www.pri.org/stories/2014–02–24/guerrilla-filmmakers-celebrate-anniversary-moroccos-arab-uprising> (accessed 5 January 2019).

Shohat, Ella (2006), *Taboo Memories, Diasporic Voices*. Durham and London: Duke University Press.

Skalli, Loubna H. (2006), 'Communicating gender in the public sphere: women and information technologies in the MENA', *Journal of Middle East Women's Studies*, Vol. 2, No. 1, Spring, 35–59.

Slyomovics, Susan (2005), *The Performance of Human Rights in Morocco*. Philadelphia, PA: University of Pennsylvania Press.

Smolin, Jonathan, (2015), 'Nabil Ayouch: transgression, identity, and difference (Morocco)', in Josef Gugler, ed., *Ten Arab Filmmakers: Political Dissent and Social Critique*. Bloomington, IN: Indiana University Press, 214–40.

Spivak, Gayatri Chakravorty and Sarah Harasym, eds (1990), *The Post-colonial Critic: Interviews, Strategies, Dialogues*. New York and London: Routledge.

Steele, Jamie (2016), 'Towards a "transnational regional" cinema: the francophone Belgian case study', *Transnational Cinemas*, 7, No. 1, 50–66.

Sundaram, Ravi (2010), *Pirate Modernity: Delhi's Media Urbanism*. London: Routledge.

Tartaglione, Nancy (2015), 'Morocco clears "Exodus: Gods and Kings" for release, with audio tweaks', *Deadline Hollywood*, 7 January: <http://deadline.com/2015/01/morocco-exodus-release-approved-changes-1201342929/> (accessed 5 January 2019).

Terrab, Sonia (2012), *Shamablanca*. Biarritz: Atlantico, 2011/Casablanca: La Croisée des Chemins, 2012.

Terrab, Sonia (2015), *La Révolution n'a pas eu lieu*. Casablanca: La Croisée des Chemins.

Tutt, Louise (2018), 'Industry reacts to sparse showing for UK films at Cannes', *Screen Daily*, 26 April: <https://www.screendaily.com/features/industry-reacts-to-sparse-showing-for-uk-films-at-cannes/5128468.article> (accessed 2 January 2019).

Vairel, Frédéric (2004), 'Le Maroc des années de plomb: équité et reconciliation?' *Politique Africaine*, No. 96, December, 181–95.

Van de Peer, Stefanie (2014), 'Homecoming through film: a Moroccan journey in *Adios Carmen*', in Dina Iordanova and Stefanie Van de Peer, eds, *Film Festival Yearbook 6: Film Festivals and the Middle East*. St Andrews, St Andreas Film Studies.

Van de Peer, Stefanie (2016), 'The north in African cinemas', *Journal of African Cinemas*, Vol. 8, No. 1, 3–128.

Vivarelli, Nick (2014), 'Doha Film Institute unveils new "Qumra" event', *Variety*, 6 December: <http://variety.com/2014/film/news/doha-film-institute-unveils-format-for-new-qumra-event-1201372978/> (accessed 2 January 2019).

Vivarelli, Nick (2015a), 'Productive learning curve: DFI uses a savvy mix of local talent and ambitious strategic initiatives to flourish on a global stage', *Variety*, 31 March.

Vivarelli, Nick (2015b), 'Dubai Film Festival: co-productions allow Gulf Fest to thrive', *Variety*, 4 December: <http://variety.com/2015/film/festivals/co-productions-enable-dubai-film-festival-to-thrive-1201651994/> (accessed 5 May 2018).

Vivarelli, Nick (2018a), 'Cannes: Arab filmmakers thrive despite regional upheavals', *Variety*, 10 May: <http://variety.com/2018/film/spotlight/cannes-arab-filmmakers-thrive-despite-regional-upheavals-1202801753/> (accessed 2 January 2019).

Vivarelli, Nick (2018b), 'Former Berlinale section director to head revived Marrakech Film Festival', *Variety*, 25 June: <https://variety.com/2018/film/news/christoph-terhechte-berlin-forum-marrakech-film-festival-1202856456/> (accessed 20 July 2018).

Wiseman, Andreas (2015), '"45 years" becomes first £1m day-and-date film in UK', *Screen International*, 9 September: <https://www.screendaily.com/distribution/45-years-becomes-first-1m-day-and-date-film-in-uk/5092741.article> (accessed 7 June 2018).

Wong, Cindy Hing-Yuk (2011), *Film Festivals: Culture, People, and Power on the Global Screen*. New Brunswick: Rutgers University Press.

Xavier, Ismail (1997), *Allegories of Underdevelopment: Aesthetics and Politics in Modern Brazilian Cinema*. Minneapolis: University of Minnesota Press.

Yamani, Myriame el, Gérard Grugeau and Thierry Horguelin (1991), 'Table ronde: l'Afrique à l'heure des grands choix', *24 images*, Nos 56–7, Fall, 75–81.

Yunis, Alia (2014), 'Film as nation building: the UAE goes into the movie business', *CINEJ Cinema Journal*, Vol. 3. No. 2, 50–75.

Zabunyan, Elvan (2009), 'Bouchra Khalili, Morocco/France 1975', *Tarjama Translationi*. Trans. Salima Semmar, New York: ArteEast.

Zaireg, Reda (2016), 'Quand les studios Souissi faisaient leur cinéma', *Le Desk*, 1 January: <https://ledesk.ma/grandangle/quand-les-studios-souissi-faisaient-leur-cinema/> (accessed 2 January 2019).

Zunes, Stephen and Jacob Mundy (2010), *Western Sahara: War, Nationalism, and Conflict Irresolution*. Syracuse University Press.

SELECT FILMOGRAPHY

24 h Marrakesh, Munir Abbar, Daniel Gräbner, Morocco/Germany: Rif Film, 2010.

#300kmSouth – Imider has a Speech, Nadir Bouhmouch. Morocco: Movement on Road '96, 2016.

44, or Tales of the Night (44, 'usturat a-llayl / 44, ou les récits de la nuit), Moumen Smihi. Morocco/France: Imago Filmodie, 1982.

475, When Marriage Becomes Punishment (475 aw 'indima yusbihu al-zawaj 'uquba / 475 Quand le mariage devient châtiment), Nadir Bouhmouch. Morocco: Guerilla Cinema, 2013.

475: Break the Silence (475: Trêve de Silence), Hind Bensari. Morocco/World: Independent Fundraisers, 2013.

Adios Carmen, Mohamed Amin Benamraoui. Morocco/Belgium/UAE: Enjaaz, Taziri Productions, Thank You & Good Night Productions, 2013.

Aïcha Bonheur, Hakim Belabbes. Qatar/Morocco: LTF Productions, 2012.

Ali Zaoua: Prince of the Streets (Ali Zawa / Ali Zaoua, prince de la rue), Nabil Ayouch. Morocco/Tunisia/France/Belgium/USA: 2M, Alexis Films, Ali n' Productions, Canal+, Gimages 3, Playtime Productions, 2000.

Ali, Rabia, and Others (Ali, Rabia wa al-akharun / Ali, Rabia et les autres), Ahmed Boulane. Morocco: Boulane & O'byrne Films, 1999.

American in Tangier, An (Un Américain à Tanger), Mohamed Ulad-Mohand, France/Morocco: Azilah Productions, 1993.

American Sniper, Clint Eastwood. USA: Warner Bros., Village Roadshow Pictures, RatPac-Dune Entertainment, Mad Chance, Joint Effort, Malpaso Productions, 2014.

Amussu, Nadir Bouhmouch. Morocco/Qatar: Movement on Road 96, 2019.

Ashiqat a-Rif (*L'amante du Rif* / *The Rif Lover*), Narjiss Nejjar. Morocco/France/ Belgium: Jbila Méditerranée Productions, Tarantula, La Prod, Mollywood, Urban Factory, 2011.

Auf der anderen Seite (*The Edge of Heaven*), Fatih Akin. Germany/Turkey/Italy: Anka Film, Corazón International, Do. Morocco/Qatar: rje Film, Norddeutscher Rundfunk, 2007.

Babel, Alejandro González Iñárritu. France/USA/Mexico: Paramount Pictures, Paramount Vantage, Anonymous Content, Zeta Film, Central Films, Media Rights Capital, 2006.

Bag of Flour, The (*Le Sac de farine*), Kadija Leclere. Belgium/Morocco: Centre du Cinéma et de l'Audiovisuel de la Fédération Wallonie-Bruxelles, La Compagnie Cinématographique, Sahara Productions, 2012.

Barons, The (*Les Barons*), Nabil Ben Yadir. Belgium/France: Entre Chien et Loup, Liaison Cinématographique, Prime Time, RTBF, 2009.

Basta: The Film That Was Never Made (*Basta*), Hamza Mahfoudi and Younes Belghazi. Morocco: Guerilla Cinema, 2013.

Baya's Mountain (*Adrar n Baya* / *La montagne de Baya*), Azzedine Baya. Algeria/ France: Caro-Line Production, ENPA, ENTV, Imago Films International.

Beyond Here (*Au-delà de Gibraltar*), Taylan Braman and Mourad Boucif. Belgium: Saga Film, 2001.

Bissara Overdose, web series, Hicham Lasri. Morocco: Hicham Lasri and Philippe Perrot, 2016.

Black Girl (*La noire de . . .*), Ousmane Sembène. Senegal/France: Filmi Domirev/ Les Actualités Françaises, 1966.

Black, Adil el Arbi and Bilall Fallah. Belgium: A Team Productions, Caviar Antwerp NV, Centre du Cinéma et de l'Audiovisuel de la Fédération Wallonie-Bruxelles, 2015.

Blessed, The (*Les Bienheureux*), Sofia Djama. Algeria/Belgium/France: Angoa, Artémis Productions, CNC, Ciné+, Cofinova Développement, Indéfilms 5, Le Tax Shelter du Gouvernement Fédéral de Belgique, Les Films de la Source, Liaison Cinématographique, Tax Shelter ING Invest de Tax Shelter Productions, Doha Film Institute, 2017.

Blindmen's Orchestra, The (*Juq al-'amyanin* / *L'orchestre des aveugles*), Mohamed Mouftakir. France/Morocco: Avalanche Productions/Chama Films, 2014.

Blood Wedding (*Urs dam* / *Noces de sang*), Souheil Ben-Barka. France/Morocco: Euro Maghreb Film/CCM, 1977.

Born Without Skis (*Uten ski på beina* / *Né sans ski aux pieds*), Nour-Eddine Lakhmari. Norway: Anders Tangen, 1996.

Borom Saret, Ousmane Sembène. Senegal/France: Filmi Domirev/ Les Actualités Françaises, 1963.

Boujad: A Nest in the Heat (*Boujad: 'Ush fi al-qayd* / *Un nid dans la chaleur*), Hakim Belabbes. Morocco: Hakim Belabbes, 1992.

Bourne Ultimatum, The, Paul Greengrass. USA/Germany/France/Spain: Universal Pictures, Motion Picture BETA Produktionsgesellschaft, The Kennedy/Marshall Company, Ludlum Entertainment, Bourne Again, KanZaman Services, Peninsula Films, Studio Babelsberg, 2007.

Breach in the Wall, A (Jurha fi al-hait / Une brèche dans le mur), Jillali Ferhati. Morocco: Heracles Production, 1978.

Brothers (Broeders), Adil el Arbi and Bilall Fallah. Belgium: Hogeschool Sint-Lukas Brussel, 2011.

Burned Hearts, The (Al-qoloub al-mohtariqa / Les Coeurs brûlés), Ahmed el Maanouni. Morocco: Rabii Films Productions, 2007.

Burnout, Nour-Eddine Lakhmari. Morocco/Norway: Nel Films, Icflixhuset AS, Umedia, 2017.

Caca-Mind, web series, Hicham Lasri. Morocco: Hicham Lasri and Philippe Perrot, 2016.

Call of the Desert, The (El Llamado del Desierto / L'Appel du Désert), Pablo César. Argentina/Morocco: César Producciones, Agora Films, 2019.

Camera/Woman, Karima Zoubir. Morocco: Les Films de Demain: 2012

Casanegra, Nour-Eddine Lakhmari. Morocco: Sigma Technologies, Soread-2M, 2008.

Catch the Wind (Prendre le large), Gaël Morel. France: TS Productions: 2017.

Catharsys, or the Afina Tales of the Lost World, Yassine Marco Marrocu. Morocco: NS Cine, Cinnamon Films, Amarcord Studio, 2018.

Changing Times (Les Temps qui changent), André Téchiné. France: Gemini Films, France 2 Cinéma, 2004.

Chergui or the Violent Silence (El Chergui / Chergui ou le silence violent), Moumen Smihi. Morocco: Aliph Film/CCM, 1975.

Comedy, The (La Comédie), Saïd Khallaf. Morocco: Oma Productions, 2017.

Crew, The (Braqueurs), Julien Leclercq. France: Labyrinthe Films, SND Films, Maje Productions, Emotions Films France, Cinéfrance Plus, Movie Pictures, Umedia, 2015.

Crossing the 7th Gate (En Quête de la 7e porte), Ali Essafi. Morocco: Cinemaat Productions, 2017.

Cry No More (Aln zwanin / Les yeux secs), Narjiss Nejjar. Morocco/France: AIF-CIREF, ADC Sud, CNC, Fonds Sud Cinéma, Jbila Méditerranée Productions, Soread-2M, Terre Sud Films, 2003.

Cursed Son, The (Al Ibn al-'aq / Le Fils maudit), Mohamed Ousfour, Morocco: 1956–1958. *Damascus Cover*, Daniel Zelik Berk. UK: Cover Films, H Films, 2017.

Dallas, Ali El Majboud. Morocco: Image Factory, 2016.

Damned of the Sea, The (Les Damnés de la mer), Jawad Rhalib. Belgium/Morocco/France: 2M, Arte, Clap d'Ort Films, Irène Production, Latcho Drom Production, RTBF, 2008.

Dark Room, The (Derb Moulay Cherif/La Chambre noire), Hassan Benjelloun. Morocco: Bentaquerla Films, 2004.

Days of Glory (Indigènes), Rachid Bouchareb. Algeria/France/Morocco/Belgium: Tessalit Productions, Kiss Films, France 2 Cinéma, France 3 Cinéma, StudioCanal, Taza Productions, Tassili Films, Versus Production, SCOPE Invest, 2006.

Dda Hmad Boutfounast and the 40 Thieves (Dda Hmad Boutfounast D 40 Oumkhar / Dda Hmad Boutfounaste et le 40 voleurs), Archach Agourram. Morocco: Warda Vision, 1993.

Death for Sale (Mawt li al-bay'i / Mort à vendre), Faouzi Bensaïdi. Belgium, France, Morocco, Germany, UAE: Entre Chien et Loup, Liaison Cinématographique, Agora Films, CCM, SANAD, World Cinema Fund, Visions Sud Est, 2011.

Desert Fish (*Les Poissons du desert*), Alaa Eddine Aljem. Morocco: Le Moindre Geste, Néon Rouge, 2014.

Divine (*Divines*), Houda Benyamina. France/Qatar: Easy Tiger, 2016.

Divorcee, The (*Al-motallaqa / La divorcée*), Rachid Larossi. Morocco: ECCF Prod, 2018.

Door to the Sky, A (*Bab al-sama maftuh / Une porte sur le ciel*), Farida Benlyazid. Maroc/Tunisia/France: France-Média, SATPEC, Interfilm, 1989.

Dunya & Desie, Dana Nechushtan. Netherlands/Belgium: Lemming Film Nederlandse Programma Stichting (NPS), A Private View, uFilm, Le Tax Shelter du Gouvernement Fédéral de Belgique, Umedia, 2009.

Eid (*Eid a-lahm*), Laila Ataalah. Morocco: Sahara Lab Productions, 2017.

El Ejido: The Law of Profit (*El Ejido, la loi du profit*), Jawad Rhalib. Morocco/Belgium/France: Arte, Latcho Drom Production, RTBF, 2007.

Ember, The (*Al-jamra / La Braise*), Farida Bourquia. Morocco: Mohamed Ismaïl, Farida Bourquia, 1982.

End, The (*A-nihaya*), Hicham Lasri. Morocco: La Prod, 2011.

Espionage in Tangier, Greg Tallas. Spain/Italy: Atlántida Films, Dorica Film, 1964.

Exodus: Gods and Kings, Ridley Scott. USA/Spain/UK: Chernin Entertainment, Scott Free Productions, Babieka, Volcano Films, 2014.

Eyes Without a Face (*Les Yeux sans visage*), Georges Franju. France/Italy: 1960–1975.

Fadma, Ahmed el Maanouni. Morocco/France: Amalif Productions, 2016.

Family Secrets (*Asrar al-'ila / Secrets de famille*), Farida Benlyazid. Morocco: 2M, 2009.

Far (*Loin*), André Téchiné. France/Spain: Union Générale Cinématographique (UGC), Ciné B, Vértigo Films, 2001.

Fevers (*Fièvres*), Hicham Ayouch. Morocco/France: La Vingt-Cinquième Heure, Président Production, Commune Image Média, Invest Image, 2013.

Fifth String, The (*Al-watar al-khamis / La 5ème Corde*), Selma Bargach. Morocco: Janaprod, 2011.

Forgotten Hill, The (*Tawrirt itwattun / La colline oubliée*), Abderrahmane Bouguermouh. Algeria: CAAIC, I. M. Films, 1996.

French Girl (*Française*), Souad el Bouhati. France/Morocco: 2M, France 2 Cinéma, Irène Productions, Jem Productions, 2008.

Gangsta (*Patser*), Adil el Arbi and Bilall Fallah. Belgium: A Team Productions, Column Film, 2018.

Gaze, The (*Le Regard*), Nour-Eddine Lakhmari. Morocco/Norway: Filmhuset AS, 2005.

Gladiator, Ridley Scott. USA/UK: DreamWorks, Universal Pictures, Scott Free Productions, Mill Film, C&L, Dawliz, 2000.

Golden Woman, The (*Tamghart n Wurgh / La femme en or*), Lahoucine Bizguaren. Morocco/France/Belgium: Boussivision, 1989.

Goodbye Morocco, Nadir Moknèche, France/Belgium: Blue Monday Productions, France 2 Cinéma, Rhône-Alpes Cinéma, Need Productions, Agora Films, 2012.

Hammu Unamir, Fatima Boubekdi. Morocco: Warda Vision, 2003.

Hassan's Way (*El Rayo*), Fran Araújo and Ernesto de Nova. Portugal/Spain/Morocco: Altube Filmeak, Malas Compañías, Ukbar Filmes, Dosdecatorce Producciones, 2013.

Headbang Lullaby (*Derba f rras*), Hicham Lasri. Morocco/France: Les Films de L'Heure Bleue, Pan production Company, 2017.

Healer, The (*M'barka* / *La Guérisseuse*), Mohamed Zineddine. Morocco/Italy/Qatar: Ouarzazate Films, Janaprod, Imago orbis, Doha Film Institute, 2018.

Homeland (*Né quelque part*), Mohamed Hamidi. France/Morocco/Belgium: Quad Productions, Kiss Films, France 3 Cinéma, Mars Films, Jouror Productions, Agora Films, Frakas Productions, Ten Films, 2013.

Homu al-kilab (*C'est eux les chiens*/*They Are the Dogs*), Hicham Lasri. Morocco: Ali n' Productions, 2013.

Hope (*Anaruz* / *Espoir*), Abdellah el Abdaoui. Morocco: Zaza Films, 2008.

Hope, Boris Lojkine. France: Zadig Films, 2014.

Horses of God (*Khayl Allah* / *Les chevaux de Dieu*), Nabil Ayouch. France/Belgium/Tunisia/Morocco: Ali n' Productions, Les Films du Nouveau Monde, Stone Angels, YC Alligator Film, Artémis Productions, 2012.

House in the Fields (*Tigmmi n Yigran*), Tala Hadid. Morocco/Qatar: Kairos Film, 2017.

Hyménée (*Bakara*), Violaine Bellet. France: A2L Production Films, 2016.

I Have Something to Tell You (*Ghuri maydak tinikh* / *Je voudrais vous raconter*), Dalila Ennadre. Morocco/France: Playfilm, NMO & Images Plus, 2005.

I Loved So Much (*J'ai tant aimé*), Dalila Ennadre. Morocco/France: Aya Films, 2008.

Image, Adil el Arbi and Bilall Fallah. Belgium: A Team Productions, Eyeworks Film & TV Drama, 2014.

In Casablanca, Angels Don't Fly (*Al malaika la tuhaliq fi al-dar albayda* / *A Casablanca, les anges ne volent pas*), Mohamed Asli. Morocco/Italy: Dagham Film, Gam Films, 2004.

In My Father's House (*In het huis van mijn vader*), Fatima Jebli Ouazzani. Netherlands: MM Produkties, Nederlandse Programma Stichting (NPS), 1997.

In Pieces (*Ashlaa* / *En fragments*), Hakim Belabbes. Morocco: LTF Productions, 2009.

In/Out, Olivier Guerpillon. Sweden: DFM, 2015.

Iron Bone, The (*Azm al-hadid* / *L'os de fer*), Hicham Lasri. Morocco: Ali n' Productions, SNRT, 2007.

Island, The (*Layla* / *La Isla*), Ahmed Boulane. Morocco/Spain: Boulane O'Byrne Production, Canal Sur Televisión, Maestranza Films, 2016.

Itto, the Morning Star (*Itto Titrit* / *Itto, l'étoile du matin*), Mohamed Abbazi. Morocco: Thagmat Films, 2008.

Jahiliya, Hicham Lasri. Morocco/France: La Prod, Moon & Deal Films, 2018.

Jawhara, the Jail Girl (*Jawhara bent el-hebs* / *Jawahara, fille de prison*), Saâd Chraibi. Morocco: Cinautre, 2003.

Khadija's Journey (*El Viaje de Khadija* / *Le voyage de Khadija*), Tarik el Idrissi. Netherlands/Morocco: Farfira Films, 2017.

Killer Elite, Gary McKendry. UK/Australia: Omnilab Media, Ambience Entertainment, Current Entertainment, Sighvatsson Films Victoria, Wales Creative IP Fund, Agora Films, International Traders, Mascot Pictures Wales, 2011.

Kundun, Martin Scorsese. USA/Monaco: De Fina-Cappa, Dune Films Refuge Productions, Touchstone Pictures (presents), 1997.

Laaziza, Mohcine Besri. Morocco: FPP Prod, 2018

Lancer ce poids (*We Could Be Heroes*), Hind Bensari. Denmark/Tunisia/Morocco/Qatar: Bullitt Film, DR, 2M, Cinetelefilms, Doha Film Institute, 2018.

Last Temptation of Christ, The, Martin Scorsese. Canada/USA: Universal Pictures, Cineplex Odeon Films, 1988.

Lawrence of Arabia, David Lean. UK: Horizon Pictures, 1962.

Legionnaire, Peter MacDonald. USA: Edward R. Pressman Film Corporation, Long Road Productions, Quadra Entertainment, 1998.

Life is a Fight (Al-hayat kifah / Vaincre pour vivre), Ahmed Mesnaoui and Mohamed Abderrahman Tazi. Morocco: CCM, 1968.

Little Rosiñol, The (El Pequeño Rosiñol), Antonio del Amo. Spain: Argos, 1958.

Living Daylights, The, John Glen. UK: Eon Productions, 1987.

Lola Pater, Nadir Moknèche. France/Belgium: Blue Monday Productions, Versus Production, Proximus, 2017.

Looking for My Wife's Husband (Al-baht 'an zawj imra'ati / A la recherche du mari de ma femme), Mohamed Abderrahman Tazi. Morocco/France: Arts Techniques Audiovisuels, 1993.

Love Affair in Casablanca, A (Hub fi dar al-beida / Un amour à Casablanca/), Abdelkader Lagtaâ. Morocco: Cinéstar, 1991.

Love is What We Need (Par instinct), Nathalie Marchak. France/Luxembourg: Les Films d'Ici, Nida Films, AJR Participations, Lovensial, L'Amour Qu'il Nous Faut, Shanti Financial Holdings, Canal+, Ciné+, 2017.

Make-Believe Horses (Khuyul al-haz / Chevaux de fortune), Jillali Ferhati. Morocco: Héracles Production, 1995.

Man Who Would Be King, The, John Huston. UK/USA: Columbia Pictures Corporation, Devon/Persky-Bright, 1975.

March, The (La Marche), Nabil Ben Yadir. France/Belgium: Chi-Fou-Mi Productions, EuropaCorp, France 3 Cinéma, Entre Chien et Loup, L'Antilope Joyeuse, 2013.

Marock, Laïla Marrakchi. France/Morocco: Lazennec & Associés, France 3 Cinéma, Canal+, CNC, 2005.

Mektoub, Nabil Ayouch. France/Morocco: Playtime Productions, Shem's, 1997.

Memory in Detention (Dakira mu'ataqala / Mémoire en detention), Jillali Ferhati. Morocco/France: Héraclès Production/MPS-Cinéma, 2004.

Message, The, Moustapha Akkad. Lebanon/Libya/Kuwait/Morocco/UK: Filmco International Productions, 1976.

Mile in My Shoes, A (Massafat mil bi-hidai), Saïd Khallaf. Morocco: OMA Prod, 2015.

Mimosas, Oliver Laxe. Spain/Morocco/France/Romania/Qatar: Zeitun Films, La Prod, Rouge International, Studio Indie Productions, 2015.

Mirage, The (As-sarab / Mirage), Ahmed Bouanani. Morocco: Basma Production, CCM, 1979.

Miscreants, The (Les mécreants/ Al-maghdub 'alyahim), Mohcine Besri. Switzerland/Morocco: Akka Films, Fusion Films, Tamawayt Productions, 2011.

Mission in Tangier (Mission à Tanger), André Hunebelle. France: P. A. C., 1949.

Moker, Larbi Altit. Morocco: Warda Vision, 1996.

Mona Saber, Abdelhaï Laraki. Morocco: Casablanca Films, A2L Production Films, 2002.

Moroccan Goatherd, The (Le Chevrier marocain), Louis Lumière. France: Frères Lumière, 1896.

Morocco: Body and soul (Maroc, corps et âme), Izza Génini. France: OHRA: 1987–1992.

Much Loved (*Zine li fik*), Nabil Ayouch. France/Morocco: Les Films du Nouveau Monde, New District, Barney Production, Ali n' Productions, 2015.

Muslim Childhood, A (*El Ayel / Le gosse de Tanger*), Moumen Smihi. Morocco: Imago Films International, 2005.

My Land, Nabil Ayouch. Morocco/France: Ali n' Productions, French Connection Films, Les Films du Nouveau Monde, 2011.

My Makhzen and Me (*Ana wa makhzani*), Nadir Bouhmouch. Morocco: SeaUrchin Productions, 2012.

Narrow Frame of Midnight, The (*Itar al-layl*), Tala Hadid. Morocco/USA/Qatar/France/UK: Autonomous, Louverture Films, K Films, Asap Films, 2014.

Night Boats (*Tighruba n Djit*), Mustapha Chaâbi. Morocco: 1997.

Niño, El, Daniel Monzon. Spain/France: Telecinco Cinema, Ikiru Films, 2014.

Nizar's Spectrum (*Tayf nizar / Le Spectre de Nizar*), Kamal Kamal. Morocco: Sonya Disc Awatif, 2001.

No Vaseline Fatwa, web series, Hicham Lasri. Morocco: Hicham Lasri, 2016.

Nomads (*Nomades*), Olivier Coussemacq. France/Morocco: Local Films, À Perte De Vue, 2019.

Number One, Zakia Tahiri. Morocco: Made In Morocco Film, SNRT, Soread-2M, 2008.

Oedipus Rex (*Edipo Re*), Pier Paolo Pasolini. Italy: Arco Film, Somafis, 1966.

Of Walls and Men (*Des murs et des hommes*), Dalila Ennadre. Morocco/UAE/Algeria/France/Qatar: Enjaaz, 2013.

Oh, the Days (*Alyam, alyam! O les jours*), Ahmed el Maanouni. Morocco: Rabii Film/CCM, 1978.

On the Edge (*Sur la planche*), Leïla Kilani. Germany/Morocco/France: Aurora Films, Socco Chico Films, INA, DKB Productions, Vandertastic Films, Fonds Sud Cinéma, Fonds Francophone de Production Audiovisuelle du Sud, World Cinema Fund, 2010.

Once Upon a Time (*Machaho / Il était une fois*), Belkacem Hadjadj. France/Algeria: Les Films Sur La Place, 1996.

One Man and His Cow (*La Vache*), Mohamed Hamidi. France: Quad Productions, Kiss Films, Pathé, France 3 Cinéma, Agora Films, 14eme Art Productions, Ten Films, 2016.

Only Lovers Left Alive, Jim Jarmusch. Germany/UK/France/Greece/USA/Cyprus: Recorded Picture Company, Pandora Filmproduktion, Snow Wolf Produktion, ARD Degeto Film, Lago Film, Neue Road Movies, 2013.

Ouarzazate Movie, Ali Essafi. Morocco/France: France 3, Quark Productions, 2001.

Our Forbidden Places (*Nos lieux interdits*), Leïla Kilani. France/Morocco: Catherine Dussart Productions, 2008.

Paradises of the Earth (*Jannat al-ard*), web documentary series, Nadir Bouhmouch. UK/Morocco/Tunisia: War on Want, 2017

Paris by the Sea (*Paris sur mer*), Munir Abbar. Morocco/Germany: Fiftyseven, 2007.

Passages (*Zad Moultaka*), Leila Kilani. France: La Huit Production, Mezzo & Zad EURL, 2003.

Pegasus (*Pégase*), Mohamed Mouftakir. Morocco: Dreamaker Productions, 2009.

Pillow Secrets (*Sarirou al-asrar*), Jillali Ferhati. Morocco/Qatar: Heracles Production, 2013.

Pirates of Sale (*Pirates de Salé*), Merieme Addou & Rosa Rogers. Morocco/UK/France/ UAE: Redbirds Prod, 2013.

Playground Chronicles (*Chroniques d'une cour de récré*), Brahim Fritah. France: Furutikon, 2012.

Razzia, Nabil Ayouch. France/Morocco/Belgium: Unité de Production Les Films du Nouveau Monde, Artémis Productions, Ali n' Productions, France 3 Cinéma, VOO, BE TV, RTBF, Shelter Prod, Soread-2M, 2017.

Rear Window, Alfred Hitchcock. USA: Patron, 1954.

Rebellious (*Insoumise*), Jawad Rhalib. Belgium/Morocco: Iota Films/F Films, 2015.

Return to Hansala (*Retorno a Hansala*), Chus Gutiérrez. Spain: Maestranza Films/Muac Films, 2008.

Rif 58/59: Breaking the Silence (*Rif 58/59: Iseggasn Ik'harn / Rif 58/59: Briser le Silence*), Tarik el Idrissi. Morocco/Netherlands: Farfira Films, Gumus Production, 2014.

Rif Blues (*Timnadin N Rif*), Nadir Bouhmouch. Morocco: Movement on Road 96, 2017.

Road to Kabul, The (*A-tariq ila Kabul*), Brahim Chkiri. Morocco: Image Factory, 2011.

Roads, Sebastian Schipper. Germany/France/UK: Missing Link Films/Arte/Komplizen Film/HanWay Films/Kazak Productions, 2019.

Rock the Casbah, Laïla Marrakchi. France/Morocco: Estrella Productions, Pathé, Agora Films, La Chauve Souris, 2013.

Rooster, The (*El Ferrouj / Le coq*), Abdellah Ferkous. Morocco: Chaoui Production, 2015.

Salvation Army (*L'Armée du salut*), Abdellah Taïa. France/Morocco/Switzerland: Les Films de Pierre, Les Films Pelléas (co-production) Rita Productions, Ali n' Productions, 2013.

Sasbo, Ali Ait Bouzide. Morocco: Disco Vision, 2004.

Sea is Behind, The (*Al-bahr min waraikoum*), Hicham Lasri. Morocco/France/UAE/ Lebanon: La Prod, Pan Production Company, 2014.

Sheltering Sky, The, Bernardo Bertolucci. UK/Italy: Recorded Picture Company, Warner Bros., Aldrich Group Trustees, Sahara Company, TAO Film, 1990.

Short Life (*Courte vie*), Adil Al Fadili. Morocco: Prodapart Drama, 2010.

Sidewalks of Dakar (*Dakar Trottoirs*), Hubert Laba Ndao. Senegal: Mediatik Communication, Mat Films, 2013.

The Sky Trembles and the Earth is Afraid and the Two Eyes Are Not Brothers, Ben Rivers. UK: Artangel, 2015.

Sleeping Child, The (*Al-ragued / L'enfant endormi*), Yasmine Kassari. Belgium/Morocco: Les Films de la Drève/Soread-2M, 2004.

Sofia, Meryem Benm'Barek. France/Qatar/Belgium: Curiosa Films, Versus Production, Doha Film Institute, 2018.

Sorrows of a Young Tangerian, The (*Tanjaoui / Tanjaoui: Peines de coeur et tourments du jeune Tanjaoui Larbi Salmi*), Moumen Smihi. Morocco: Imago Film International, 2013.

SOS Mediterranean (*Alerte en Méditerranée*), Léo Joannon. France: Société des Films Vega, 1938.

Sotto Voce, Kamal Kamal. Morocco/UAE: Enjaaz, 2013.

Source, The (*La Source des femmes*), Radu Mihâileanu, France/Belgium/Italy: Elzévir Films, Oï Oï Oï Productions, EuropaCorp, France 3 Cinéma, La Compagnie Cinématographique Européenne, Panache Productions, RTBF, BIM Distribuzione, Indigo Film, Agora Films, 2011.

Special Correspondants (*Envoyés très spéciaux*), Frédéric Auburtin. France: Les Films Manuel Munz, 2009.

Spectre, Sam Mendes. UK/USA: B24, Columbia Pictures Corporation, Danjaq, Eon Productions, Metro-Goldwyn-Mayer (MGM), Sony, 2015.

Spring Sun (*Shams al-rabii / Soleil de printemps*), Latif Lahlou. Morocco: CCM, 1969.

Starve Your Dog (*Jewa' kelbk*), Hicham Lasri. Morocco: Pan Production Company, Matrice Media Production, 2015.

Stateless (*Bila mawtin / Apatride*), Narjiss Nejjar. Morocco/France/Qatar: La Prod, Moon & Deal Films, 2018.

Suspended Wives (*Moalakat*), Merieme Addou, Morocco/Qatar: IrisProd, 2017.

Sweat Rain (*'arq štā / Pluie de sueur*), Hakim Belabbes. Morocco: Ali N' Productions, 2017.

Tangerine, Irene von Alberti. Germany/Morocco: Filmgalerie 451, Kasbah Films, ZDF, 2008.

Tangier, the Burners' Dream (*Tanger, le rêve des brûleurs*), Leïla Kilani. France: Vivement Lundi, INA, France 3, 2003.

Target, The (*Al-hadaf / La cible*), Munir Abbar. Morocco: Kasbah-Film Tanger, 2012.

Tawnza, Malika el Manoug. Morocco: Tufawt Production, 2014.

Tea or Electricity (*Le Thé ou l'électricité*), Jérôme le Maire. Belgium/Morocco/France: Iota Production, Perspective Films, HKS Productions, K Films, 2011.

Tears of Satan (Dumu' Iblis/*Larmes de Satan*), Hicham El Jebbari. Morocco: Ounssa Média Film, 2015.

Testament (*Tenja*), Hassan Legzouli. France/Morocco: Why Not Productions, Vidéorama, Soread-2M, 2004.

They Were Promised the Sea (*Pour une nouvelle Séville*), Kathy Wazana. Canada/USA/Morocco/Israel: Bicom Productions, 2013.

Thousand and One Hands, A (*Alf yad wa yad / Les Milles et une main*), Souheil Ben-Barka. Morocco/France: Euro Maghreb Film, 1973.

Thousand Months, A (*Alf shahr / Mille mois*), Faouzi Bensaïdi. France/Belgium/Morocco/Germany: Agora Films, Radio Télévision Belge Francophone (RTBF), Soread-2M, Zweites Deutsches Fernsehen (ZDF), 2003.

Tihia, Larbi Altit. Morocco: Warda Vision, 1994.

Tilila, Mohamed Mernich. Morocco: M'zouda Vision, 2007.

Timbuktu, Abderrahmane Sissoko. Mauritania/France: Les Films du Worso, Dune Vision, Arches Films, 2014.

Tinghir-Jerusalem: Echoes from the Mellah (*Tinghir-Jérusalem: Les échos du Mellah*), Kamal Hachkar. France/Morocco: Les Films d'un Jour, 2M, Berbère Télévision, 2012.

TiphinaR, Hicham Lasri. Morocco: Ali n' Productions, SNRT, 2006.

Traces (*Wechma / Traces*), Hamid Bennani. Morocco: Sigma 3, 1970.

Trances (*Al-hal / Transes*), Ahmed el Maanouni. Morocco/France: Interfilms, Ohra-Sogeav, 1981.

Tree, The (*A-shajara*), Cheikh Mohammed Horma. Morocco: Sahara Film Lab H.D:H., 2017.

Turtle's Song: A Moroccan Revolution (*Chant des tortues, une révolution Marocaine, Le*), Jawad Rhalib. Belgium: Iota Production, 2013.

Two Lives of Daniel Shore, The (Die zwei Leben des Daniel Shore), Michael Dreher. Germany: ARTE, Bayerische Rundkunft, Hessischer Rundfunk (HR), Kasbah Films, Starhaus Filmproduktion, Zum Goldenen Lamm Filmproduktion, 2009.

Ultimate Revolt (*Ultime révolte*), Jillali Ferhati. Morocco : Héraclès Productions, 2018.

Unknown Saint, The (*Le Miracle du Saint inconnu*), Alla Eddine Aljem, Morocco/France/Qatar : Le Moindre Geste, Altamar Films, 2019.

Upper Village, The (*Tamazirt Oufella / Village du haut*), Mohamed Mernich. Morocco: M'zouda Vision, 2008.

Urgent (*Une Urgence ordinaire*), Mohcine Besri. Morocco/Switzerland : La Prod/Louise Productions/Radio Télévision Suisse (RTS), 2018.

Volubilis (*Walili*), Faouzi Bensaïdi. Morocco/France/Qatar: Barney Production, Mont Fleuri Production, Shadi Films, 2017.

Waiting for Pasolini (*Fi intidar Pasolini / En attendant Pasolini*), Daoud Aoulad-Syad. France/Morocco: Films du Sud, Soread-2M, Vidéorama, 2007.

Wall, The (*Le Mur*), Faouzi Bensaïdi, Morocco / France, Gloria Films: Les Films du Worso, Dune Vision, 2000.

Water and Blood (*Ma wa dam / De l'Eau et du sang*), Abdelillah el Jaouhary. Morocco, 2013.

Weight of the Shadow (*Thiklou a-thil*), Hakim Belabbes. Morocco/UAE: Hak Films, 2015.

Whatever Lola Wants, Nabil Ayouch. Canada/France/Morocco: Ali n' Productions, BC Films, Pathé, The 7th Floor, 2007.

When Are Palm Dates Ripe? (*Indama Tanduju al-Timar / Quand mûrissent les dattes?*), Abdelaziz Ramdani and Larbi Bennani. Morocco: CCM, 1968.

When Men Cry (*Indama Yabki al-Rijal / Quand les hommes pleurent*), Yasmine Kassari. Belgium: Centre de l'Audiovisuel à Bruxelles (CBA), Les Films de la Drève, Unité Documentaire RTBF-Liège, 2001.

Where Are You Going, Moshe? (*Fin ghadi ya Moshé? / Ou vas-tu Moshé?*), Hassan Benjelloun. Morocco/Canada: Bentaqueria Productions, Productions Jeux d'Ombres, 2007.

Withered Greens (*Akhdar yabes*), Mohammed Hammad. Egypt: Film Clinic, 2016.

Women and Women (*Nissa wa nissa / Femmes et femmes*), Saâd Chraïbi. Morocco: Cinautre, 1999.

Women's Wiles (*Keïd Ensa / Ruses de femmes*), Farida Benlyazid. Morocco/France/Switzerland/Tunisia: Céphéide Productions, Tingitania Films, Touza Productions, Waka Films, 1999.

WWW: What a Wonderful World, Faouzi Bensaïdi. France/Morocco/Germany: Gloria Films, Agora Films, Heimatfilm, Soread-2M, ZDF, Das Kleinfernsehspiel, 2006.

You All Are Captains (*Todos vós sodes capitáns*), Oliver Laxe. Spain: Zeitun Films, 2010.

Your Dark Hair, Ihsan (*Tes cheveux noirs, Ihsan*), Tala Hadid. USA/Mexico: Kairo Films, 2005.

INDEX

#300km South – Imider has a Speech (2016), 117–19

2M, 16, 21, 33, 35–8, 84, 138, 139, 144, 146, 147, 153, 157, 168, 170, 171

475 (2013), 116–17

A Breach in the Wall (1977), 30, 178

A Thousand Months (2003), 21, 33, 34, 56, 189

Abbar, Munir, 25, 31–2, 39, 59, 194

Abdelmalek Essaâdi University (Tetouan), 97–9, 101, 105

Abou-Zeid, Peri (Movie Pigs), 228, 235, 236, 237

Adios, Carmen (2013), 76–7, 78, 127, 129, 216

Agora Films, 34, 38, 46, 47, 48–9, 139

Aïdouni, Hamid, 99, 121

Ali Zaoua, Prince of the Streets (2000), 21, 36, 68, 69, 204, 221, 222

Amazigh/Imazighen/Tamazight, 4, 8, 19, 21, 23, 26, 29, 30, 36, 38, 77, 113, 115, 117, 118, 119, 123–30, 134, 141, 144, 148, 150, 151, 152, 156, 165, 186, 208, 216, 226, 227, 240

Amussu (2019), 119–20

Arab Cinema Centre (ACC), 219

Armes, Roy, 59, 137, 139

Ayouch, Nabil, 1, 16, 21, 22, 34, 36–8, 39, 58, 59, 67, 68–9, 79, 80, 84, 88, 111, 138, 145, 147, 152, 153, 155, 165, 193, 194, 199, 202, 204, 205, 212, 215, 221–3, 228, 234, 240, 245

Barlet, Olivier, 4, 52, 58, 90, 124, 198, 216

Belabbes, Hakim, 66–7, 69, 73, 74, 77, 78, 79, 88, 103–7, 121, 122, 145, 154, 157, 165, 186, 199

Benamraoui, Mohamed Amin, 76–7, 78, 79, 89, 127–8

Benlyazid, Farida, 3, 25, 30, 36, 58, 83–4, 85, 137, 140, 151–2, 153, 154, 178, 188, 244

Bensaïdi, Faouzi, 1, 21, 33, 34, 48, 56, 59–62, 72, 74, 78, 84, 87, 154, 156, 157, 186, 189, 199, 200, 205, 212, 221, 240

Berlinale, 11, 31, 43, 49, 50, 51, 56, 60, 71, 86, 87, 88, 111, 131, 134, 167, 192, 193, 195, 196–201, 207, 211, 213, 218, 221, 230, 231, 233, 236, 237, 245

Bouhmouch, Nadir, 8, 9, 10, 93, 108, 113–19, 121, 226

Boujad, a Nest in the Heat (1992), 66–7

Bral, Tinne (Imagine Distribution), 222–5

Cannes, 20, 30, 49, 50, 53, 55, 58, 70, 71, 76, 82, 89, 90, 99, 167, 178, 183, 192, 193, 194, 195, 196–201, 210, 211, 218, 221, 222–3, 229, 230, 231, 245

Carter, Sandra Gayle, 1, 8, 17, 27, 37, 42, 86, 96, 178, 217, 220

Casablanca, 4, 9, 15, 16, 17, 20, 24, 31–8, 39, 44, 58, 67, 68, 73, 75, 104, 107, 109, 111, 112, 122, 126, 132, 138, 146, 147, 150, 151, 152, 155, 157, 165, 172, 179, 184, 186, 188, 227

Casanegra (2008), 68, 79, 143, 175

Centre Cinématographique Marocain (CCM), 1, 4, 5, 8, 9, 10, 11, 15, 16–23, 27, 29, 30, 33, 34, 35, 38, 41, 42, 43, 44, 45, 47–50, 53–4, 55, 57–8, 60, 63, 65, 67–70, 76, 80–4, 93, 95–7, 100–102 105–7, 110–12, 116, 117, 121, 123, 124, 128, 130, 131, 137, 138, 139, 142, 144, 145, 146, 147, 149, 150, 151, 153, 154, 156, 163, 165, 166, 168, 170, 171, 172–6, 177–81, 183, 185, 191–3, 198–200, 204, 210, 217, 219, 220, 222, 227, 231, 234, 239, 240–2, 243

Centre National Cinématographique (CNC) (France), 1, 56, 82, 85, 100, 142, 146, 197, 213

César, Pablo, 46, 50, 85, 218, 233

Chergui, The Eastern Wind (1975), 20, 29

Cheriaa, Tahar, 161, 203, 206, 211, 212, 216, 233

Chraibi, Lamia (La Prod/Moon & Deal), 35, 48–50, 52, 54, 56, 59, 60, 83, 85, 86, 139, 154, 167, 197, 200–1, 211, 221, 230, 245

Cinéaste de passage, 5, 9, 59–63, 66, 100, 145, 200–1, 205, 221–2, 229, 240

colonialism/neocolonialism, 3, 4, 6, 15, 16, 17, 18, 28, 33, 42, 45, 52, 67, 70, 103, 126, 132, 135, 156, 178, 182, 198, 204, 212, 225, 243

de-orbiting, 4, 45, 80, 241
diaspora/diasporic, 9, 21, 34, 37,
    41, 47, 45, 48–52, 57–9, 63–9,
    73, 86, 87, 100, 108, 125, 126,
    128–36, 144, 153, 154, 165,
    186, 200, 201, 206, 208–10,
    217, 221, 227, 228, 232, 235,
    236, 240, 241, 243, 244
digital disruption, 2, 3, 6, 8, 10,
    162, 175, 215–33
DISCOP, 199, 206–7, 213, 216, 233
distribution, 2, 3, 5, 6, 7, 8, 9–10,
    17, 40, 43, 48, 50, 55, 56, 57,
    60, 65, 70, 71, 75, 82, 85, 108,
    112, 116, 117, 124, 152, 161–2,
    163, 164, 166, 167, 168, 169,
    170, 171
  international distribution online,
    225–32, 233, 234, 235, 236,
    2404
  in Morocco, 172–81, 186, 188,
    189, 191, 194–5, 196, 200–1,
    202, 203, 204, 206–7, 209, 210,
    212, 213
  outside Morocco, 215–22, 223–5
documentary/documentaries, 3, 4,
    5, 11, 17, 18, 19, 24, 30, 31,
    32, 38, 42, 45, 49, 66, 68, 71,
    72, 73, 74, 75, 78, 79, 81, 86,
    88, 89, 93, 96, 98, 99–106,
    112, 115–20, 121, 127, 131–7,
    138, 139, 140, 142–4, 146–50,
    151, 152, 154, 156, 157, 165,
    168, 169, 171, 182, 185, 193,
    205, 206, 210, 213, 219,
    230, 244
Doha (Film Institute), 4, 5, 44,
    53–4, 56, 60, 70, 73–4, 80, 83,
    89, 131, 201–2

Dubai International Film Festival,
    31, 70, 75–7, 78, 79, 80, 89,
    153, 198, 199, 201–2, 218,
    221
Dwyer, Kevin, 8, 18, 164, 172, 178,
    180, 239

Ennadre, Dalila, 73, 74, 75, 78, 137,
    139, 146, 150, 153, 157
ESAV (Marrakesh), 73, 96–8, 102,
    138, 187
European Audio-visual Observatory
    (EAO), 53, 85, 86, 87, 221,
    224, 233, 234
European Film Market (EFM),
    Berlin, 49, 86, 196, 197,
    198
exhibition, 2, 6, 7–9, 10, 17, 28,
    70–1, 98, 129, 149, 153, 161,
    163, 166, 172, 177–8, 180–2,
    184, 191, 194–5, 200, 202,
    204–5, 215–16, 218, 223, 225,
    226, 231, 240, 242, 244;
    see also film theatres
Exodus, Gods and Kings (2014),
    22, 38

Fassi Fihri, Sarim, 10, 21, 22–3, 82,
    172, 176, 198, 222, 234
feminism/feminist, 11, 140, 148,
    152, 257
Ferhati, Jillali, 3, 20, 25, 30, 36,
    39, 58, 73, 74, 79, 84, 85, 86,
    97, 121, 140, 142, 155, 167,
    178, 222
FESPACO/Pan-African Film
    and Television Festival,
    Ouagadougou, 19, 80, 166,
    192, 194, 199, 201, 203–8

Festival National du Film (FNF)/
Moroccan National Film
Festival, 58, 67, 83, 87, 88, 101,
121, 127, 128–9, 134, 164–70,
185, 205, 208
FIDADOC/Agadir International
Documentary Film Festival, 101,
102, 105, 120, 121, 185
FIDEC/international film school
festival, Tetouan, 99, 169,
181
film festivals, 1, 8, 10, 19, 20, 22,
30, 35, 43, 50, 56, 60, 70–3,
81–2, 96, 98, 101, 102, 111,
129, 136
European A-list, 195–201
international festivals beyond
Europe, 201–7
link to sales and distribution,
216–26; 231, 232, 240,
241, 248
in Morocco, 163–72
niche festivals in Europe and
North America, 208–10
transnational film festival
network, 191–5
see also individual film festivals by
name
film theatres, 26, 27, 51, 60, 75,
146, 161, 170, 172, 175–83,
209, 223, 224, 225, 226
French Girl (2008), 63–4, 67, 131,
132, 135–6, 144

global/globalisation, 2–8, 16, 19,
20, 21, 23, 28, 41, 44, 54, 60,
66, 69–73, 75, 76, 77, 80, 83,
84, 88, 97, 98, 108, 114, 117,
118, 120, 121, 123, 125, 130,

134–46, 141, 143, 144, 145,
152, 153, 154, 155, 168, 171,
172, 173, 174–7, 191, 193, 197,
198, 201, 202, 203, 206, 219,
225–8, 244

Hadid, Tala, 9, 66, 69, 74, 79, 87,
130–4, 135, 136–8, 148, 153,
154, 167, 199, 229
Hirchi, Mohamed, 148
Hjort, Mette, 2, 11, 43, 71, 76, 100,
101, 108
Horses of God (2012), 68, 193–4,
210, 221
House in the Fields, 74, 131, 133–4,
148, 229

I Loved So Much (2008), 150
I Wanna Tell You (2005), 146
IcFlix, 176, 227
Iddins, Anne-Marie, 37, 140, 143
IFFR (Rotterdam), 198, 199, 221,
223, 231, 237
In Pieces (2009), 66–7, 79
ISMAC, 96–8, 101, 102, 103, 107

Jahilya (2018), 35, 110, 113, 228
JCC (Carthage International Film
Festival, Tunis), 80, 161, 192,
199, 201, 203–8

Kassari, Yasmine, 21, 74, 78, 128,
137, 143–4, 148, 154, 186
Khourigba African Film Festival, 4,
5, 11, 22, 81, 90, 169–71, 185,
213
Kilani, Leïla, 1, 35, 31, 33, 56, 59,
60, 72, 74, 78, 137, 142–5, 146,
154, 198, 199, 200

Lage, Felipe (Zeitun Films), 53–4, 56
Lasri, Hicham, 8, 9, 35, 37, 38, 51,
    57, 69, 72, 74, 78, 79, 86, 88,
    93, 95, 108–13, 122, 129, 149,
    154, 165, 170, 186, 193, 194,
    195, 198, 199, 200, 202, 205,
    212, 226, 228, 245
Laxe, Oliver, 25, 31, 32, 50, 53–6,
    74, 86, 183, 189, 230

MAD SOLUTIONS, 196, 218–19
Malmo Arab Film Festival, 193,
    194, 197, 198, 218, 219
Marché International du Film
    (Cannes), 49, 196, 198
Marock (2005), 60, 146, 147, 165,
    186, 234
Marrakchi, Leila, 34, 79, 137, 139,
    146, 147–8, 157, 165, 186, 199,
    209, 233, 234
Marrakech International Film
    Festival (FIFM), 164, 166–8,
    170, 180, 185, 186, 195
Meditalents, 98, 100–1
Mimosas (2015), 32, 35, 50, 53–6,
    74, 183, 194, 200, 219,
    229–31
MUBI, 56, 60, 229–32, 242
Much Loved (2015), 22, 68, 69,
    145, 150, 221, 222–5, 228
Mudawana, 138, 140, 145–8
My Makhzen and Me (2012),
    115–16, 119

Nejjar, Narjiss, 1, 21, 34, 35,
    50, 59, 60–1, 62, 74, 77, 78,
    137, 139, 144, 148 149, 154,
    157, 186, 199, 200, 221,
    236, 240

Netflix, 7, 168, 176, 218, 225,
    227, 228, 229, 230, 232, 233,
    235
Number One (2008), 146, 147

On the Edge (2011), 31, 33, 39, 56,
    60, 72, 144–5, 146, 154, 198,
    228
Orlando, Valerie, 1, 140, 154, 156
Ouarzazate, 9, 15, 16, 22, 23–35,
    38, 44, 59, 96, 97, 100, 107,
    113, 114, 127, 129, 131, 163,
    213
Ouarzazate Movie (2001), 24
Our Forbidden Places (2008), 31,
    39, 142–3, 144, 154

Paris by the Sea (2007), 31
pioneer/pioneering, 3, 8, 25, 33,
    137, 151, 167, 243
piracy, 8, 130, 172–7, 226, 240
Pisters, Patricia, 28, 140, 141
post-cinema, 2, 3, 7–8, 242, 244, 245
postcolonial, 2–6, 11, 15, 16, 18,
    19, 20, 25, 28, 29, 30, 31, 33,
    57, 61, 67, 75, 77, 82, 83, 123,
    126, 130, 173, 177, 182, 185,
    201, 202, 203, 212, 241–4

Qumra, 70, 73, 103

Reed Dolls (1981), 30, 140
Rhalib, Jawad, 9, 66, 130, 135–7

Sahara Lab, 9, 66, 102–8
Saïl, Noureddine, 21–3, 27, 42, 45,
    53, 88, 100, 161, 166, 172, 174,
    176, 178, 179, 187, 188, 206,
    213, 239

Salé Women's Film Festival, 138, 169–70, 174, 179, 185, 187
sales agents, 57, 162, 168, 196, 119, 218–21, 225, 228, 231, 232, 240
Shakespeare in Casablanca (2016), 152, 157
Shohat, Ella, 6
Sidewalks of Dakar (2013), 82
small nation cinema, 2, 3, 57, 242
Smihi, Moumen, 3, 20, 25, 29, 39, 85
Société Anonyme Tunisienne de Production et d'Expansion Cinématographique (SATPEC) (Tunisia), 30, 80, 84
Spivak, Gayatri, 6, 243, 245
Starve Your Dog (2015), 79, 109–10
Stateless (2018), 35, 50, 60–1, 74, 77, 78, 200, 221

Tahiri, Zakia, 39, 127, 139, 146, 147, 157
Tamghart wurgh/The Golden Woman (1992), 125–6, 129, 130
Tangier, 9, 11, 15, 16, 19, 21, 25–33, 38, 39, 40, 41, 53, 5, 58, 60, 67, 68, 83, 85, 86, 88, 89, 90, 99, 100, 121, 134, 140, 142, 143, 144, 151, 153, 154, 156, 161, 163, 164, 165, 169, 178, 179, 181, 182–4, 185, 188, 189, 194, 210, 212, 219, 230
Tangier Cinémathèque, 27, 99, 151, 154, 161, 181–5, 188, 189
Tazi, Mohamed, Abderrahman, 18, 19, 34, 36, 154, 185, 193

Terrab, Sonia, 37, 137, 139, 152–3, 157
Testament (2004), 28, 51, 56, 63, 64, 67
Tetouan, 27, 60, 99, 101, 151, 169, 171, 179, 181, 184, 185
The Call of the Desert (2018), 46–8, 50, 88, 218
The Damned of the Sea (2008), 135–6
The March (2013), 65
The Mirage (1979):18, 20, 193
The Narrow Frame of Midnight (2014), 79, 131–4
The Sea is Behind (2014), 35, 78, 110
The Sleeping Child (2004), 21, 128, 143, 148, 154, 186, 216
The Target (2012), 31–2, 194
The Turtles Song, a Moroccan Revolution (2013), 135
They are the Dogs (2013), 50, 79, 110, 112, 193, 194, 195, 202, 212
third cinema, 116, 203
Timnadin N Rif (2017), 117–19
Tinghir-Jerusalem, Echoes of the Mellah (2012), 129, 156, 165, 186
Toronto International Film Festival (TIFF), 199, 221
transnational (cinema), 1–6, 15, 16, 19, 25, 33, 41–3, 46, 48, 52, 57–69, 71, 75, 76, 83, 84, 95, 98, 125, 130, 132, 133, 134, 136, 141, 149, 150, 153, 164, 173, 181–5, 184–5, 191–5, 198, 201, 207, 219, 232

Venice International Film Festival, 10, 87, 119, 120, 133, 192, 195, 196, 199, 201 video on demand (VOD), 225–32, 235–7, 242

Volubilis (2017), 60–2, 74, 87, 156, 186, 212

World Cinema Fund (WCF), 31, 33, 43, 56, 83, 197–200

Years of Lead, 4, 19, 20, 47, 67, 115, 124, 140, 141–3, 155, 230

You Are All Captains (2010), 32, 53, 183, 230

Zardi, Hédi (Luxbox), 194, 219, 220, 228